Does anyone remember off the top of their head where this scene is from? I guess I was in a rush when I drew it, given how awkward it turned out. But when I reviewed it while making revisions for the graphic novel, there was just something about it that charmed me, so I left it as is. Trying to copy this pose in real life is kind of fun.

HARUICHI FURUDATE began his manga career when he was 25 years old with the one-shot Ousama Kid (King Kid), which won an honorable mention for the 14th Jump Treasure Newcomer Manga Prize. His first series, Kiben Gakuha, Yotsuya Sensei no Kaidan (Philosophy School, Yotsuya Sensei's Ghost Stories), was serialized in Weekly Shonen Jump in 2010. In 2012, he began serializing Haikyu!! in Weekly Shonen Jump, where it became his most popular work to date.

HAIKYU!!
VOLUME 14
SHONEN JUMP Manga Edition

Story and Art by
HARUICHI FURUDATE

Translation **1** ADRIENNE BECK
Touch-Up Art & Lettering **2** ERIKA TERRIQUEZ
Design **3** YUKIKO WHITLEY
Editor **4** MARLENE FIRST

HAIKYU!! © 2012 by Haruichi Furudate
All rights reserved.
First published in Japan in 2012 by SHUEISHA Inc., Tokyo.
English translation rights arranged by SHUEISHA Inc.

The stories, characters and incidents mentioned
in this publication are entirely fictional.

Printed in the U.S.A.

Published by VIZ Media, LLC
P.O. Box 77010
San Francisco, CA 94107

10 9 8 7 6 5 4 3 2 1
First printing, August 2017

www.shonenjump.com   www.viz.com

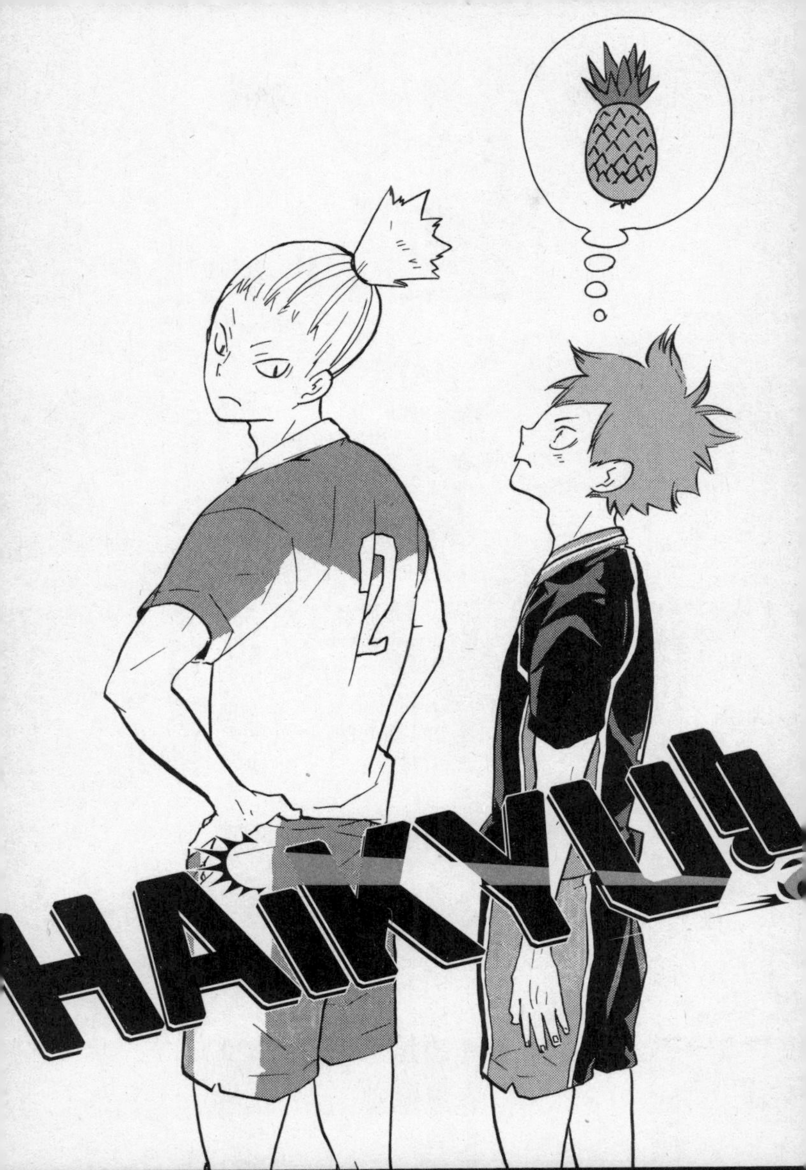
HAIKYU!!

HARUICHI
FURUDATE

QUITTER'S BATTLE

14

Karasuno High School Volleyball Club

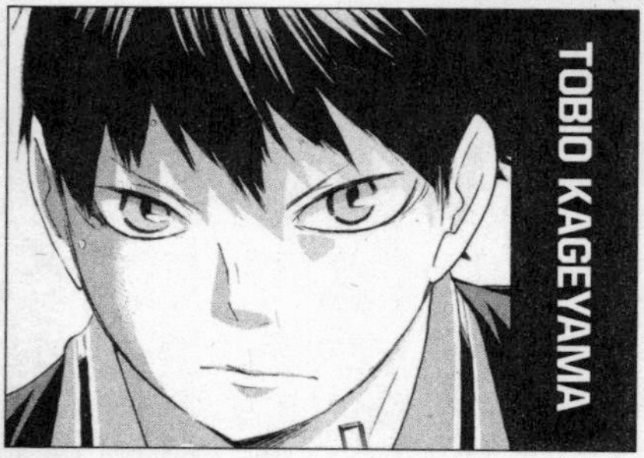

TOBIO KAGEYAMA

1ST YEAR / SETTER

His instincts and athletic talent are so good that he's like a "king" who rules the court. Demanding and egocentric.

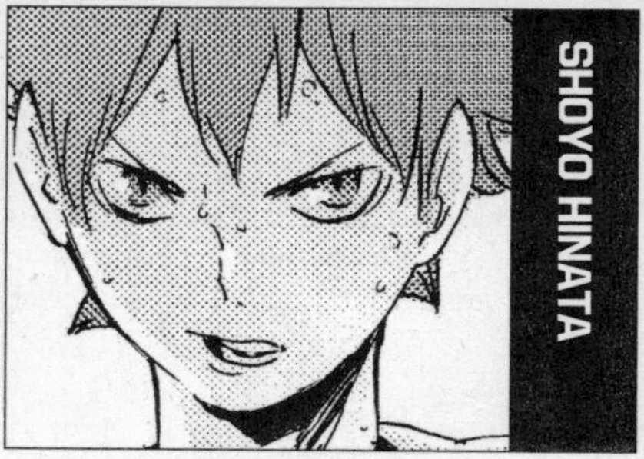

SHOYO HINATA

1ST YEAR / MIDDLE BLOCKER

Even though he doesn't have the best body type for volleyball, he is super athletic. Gets nervous easily.

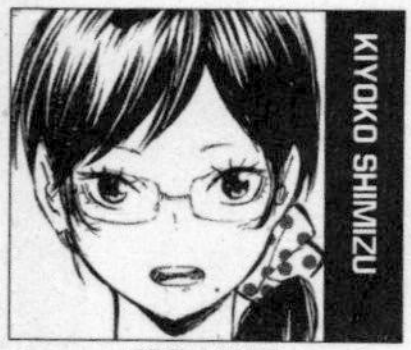

KIYOKO SHIMIZU

3RD YEAR
MANAGER

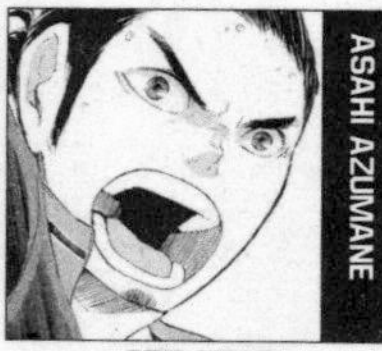

ASAHI AZUMANE

3RD YEAR
WING SPIKER

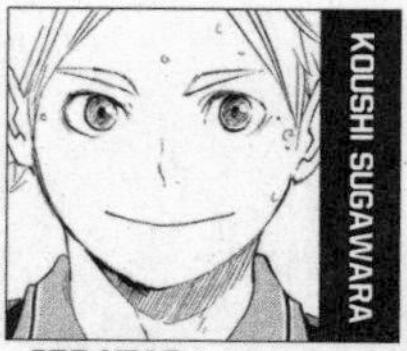

KOUSHI SUGAWARA

3RD YEAR (VICE CAPTAIN)
SETTER

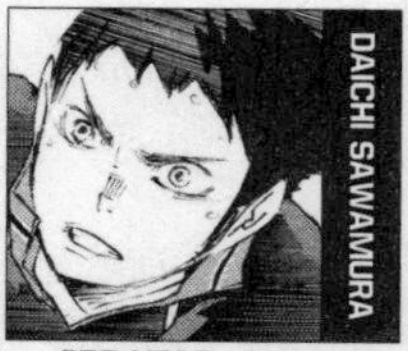

DAICHI SAWAMURA

3RD YEAR (CAPTAIN)
WING SPIKER

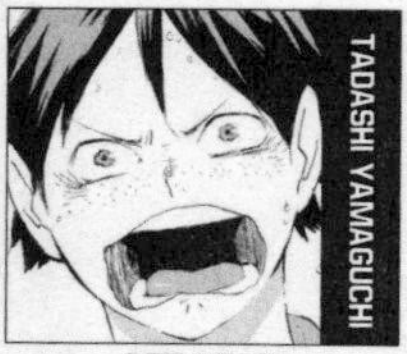

TADASHI YAMAGUCHI

1ST YEAR
MIDDLE BLOCKER

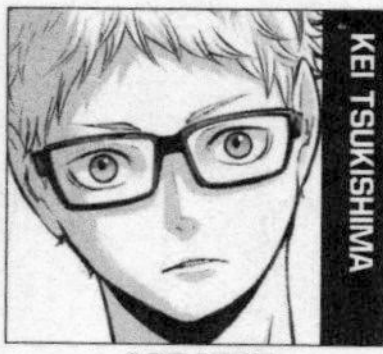

KEI TSUKISHIMA

1ST YEAR
MIDDLE BLOCKER

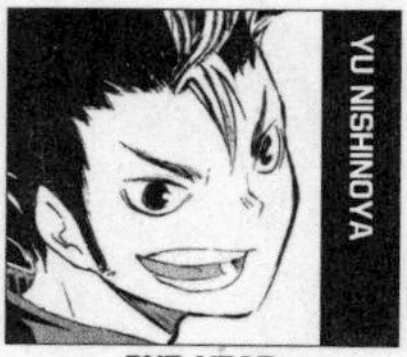

YU NISHINOYA

2ND YEAR
LIBERO

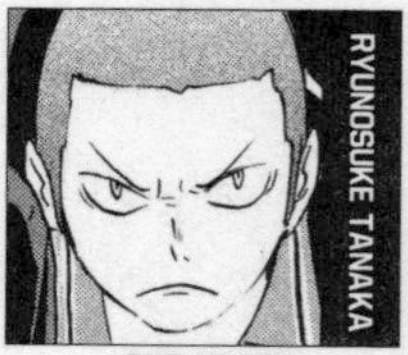

RYUNOSUKE TANAKA

2ND YEAR
WING SPIKER

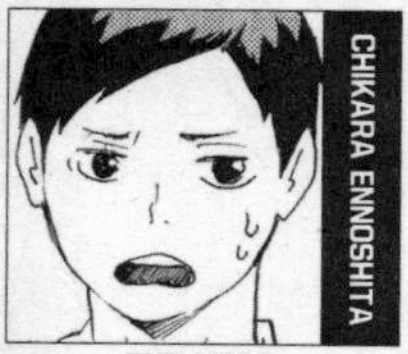

CHIKARA ENNOSHITA

2ND YEAR
WING SPIKER

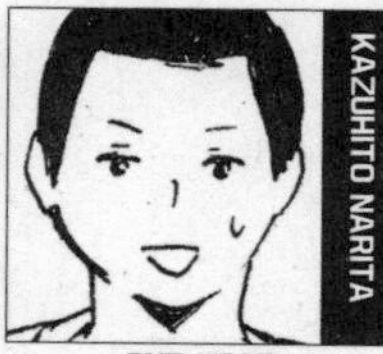

KAZUHITO NARITA

2ND YEAR
MIDDLE BLOCKER

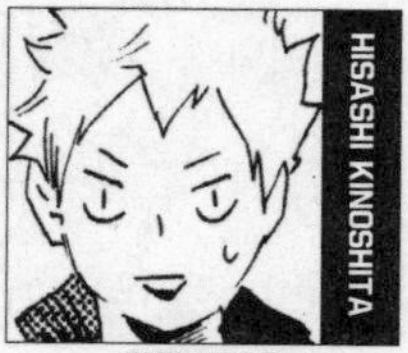

HISASHI KINOSHITA

2ND YEAR
WING SPIKER

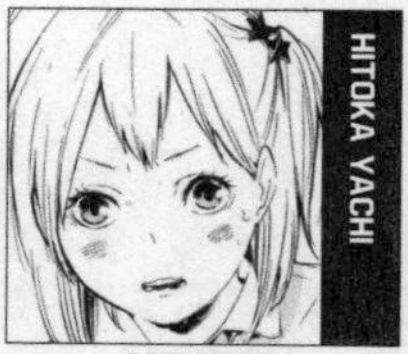

HITOKA YACHI

1ST YEAR
MANAGER

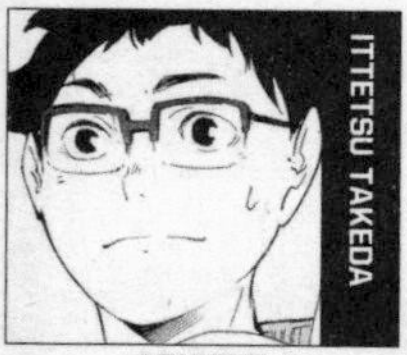

ITTETSU TAKEDA

ADVISER

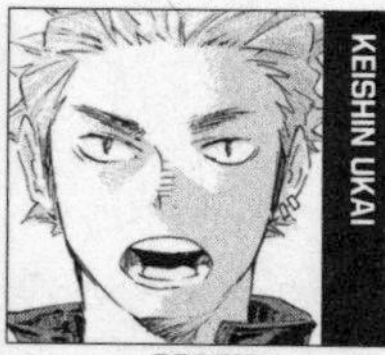

KEISHIN UKAI

COACH

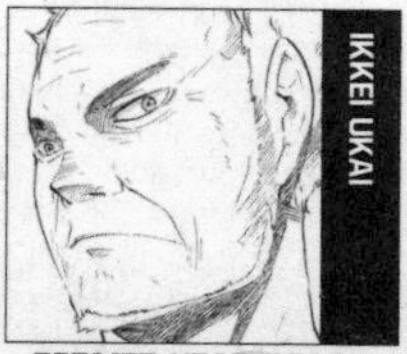

IKKEI UKAI

FORMER HEAD COACH

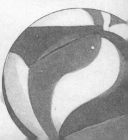

CHARACTERS

MIYAGI PREFECTURE SPRING TOURNAMENT QUALIFIER TOURNAMENT ARC

SHIRATORIZAWA

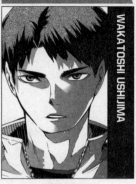

WAKATOSHI USHIJIMA

3RD YEAR
WING SPIKER

WAKUTANI MINAMI

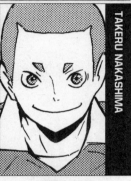

TAKERU NAKASHIMA

3RD YEAR
WING SPIKER

AOBA JOHSAI

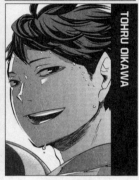

TOHRU OIKAWA

3RD YEAR
SETTER

KARASUNO'S MAJOR RIVALS

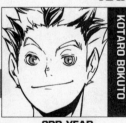

FUKURODANI (Tokyo)

KOTARO BOKUTO

3RD YEAR
WING SPIKER

NEKOMA (Tokyo)

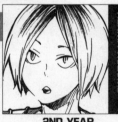

KENMA KOZUME

2ND YEAR
SETTER

Ever since he saw the legendary player known as "the Little Giant" compete at the national volleyball finals, Shoyo Hinata has been aiming to be the best volleyball player ever! He decides to join the volleyball club at his middle school and gets to play in an official tournament during his third year. His team is crushed by a team led by volleyball prodigy Tobio Kageyama, also known as "the King of the Court." Swearing revenge on Kageyama, Hinata graduates middle school and enters Karasuno High School, the school where the Little Giant played. However, upon joining the club, he finds out that Kageyama is there too! The two of them bicker constantly, but they bring out the best in each other's talents and become a powerful combo! Eliminated from the Inter-High Qualifiers, the Karasuno team sets their sights on the Spring Tournament. They travel to Tokyo for a weeklong training camp with Nekoma and a bunch of other Tokyo powerhouse teams. Later, armed with an arsenal of new weapons, Karasuno heads to the Spring Tournament! Advancing through the prelims and into the quarterfinal round of the qualifiers, Karasuno runs into a team lead by an ace whose play style is like the Little Giant's—Takeru Nakashima of Wakutani Minami! Facing a skilled and stable team with a bevy of clever combination attacks, Karasuno just barely holds off their opponent. But then disaster strikes and Sawamura goes down...!

HAIKYU!!

14 QUITTER'S BATTLE

CHAPTER 118:
Substitute Foundation — 007

CHAPTER 119:
Quitter's Battle — 027

CHAPTER 120:
Quitter's Battle: Part 2 — 047

CHAPTER 121:
Battle with the Little Giant Resumed — 067

CHAPTER 122:
Challenger — 087

CHAPTER 123:
Another Idol — 107

CHAPTER 124:
Battle's End — 129

CHAPTER 125:
Those Who Lost — 149

BONUS STORY
Nisekyu!! — 169

BONUS STORY
V-ball Cards! The Road to Greatness! — 185

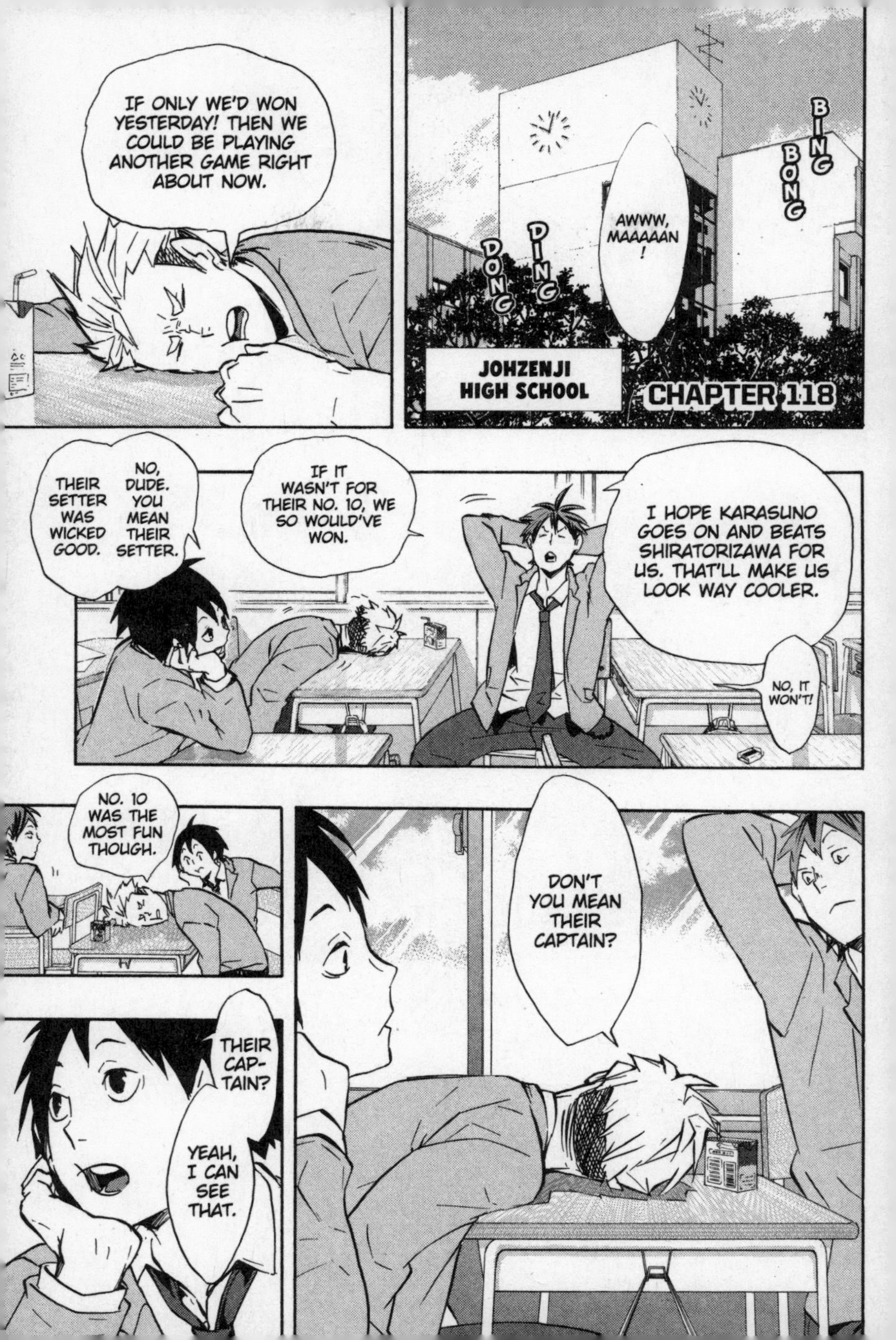
BING BONG
DING DONG
AWWW, MAAAAAN!
JOHZENJI HIGH SCHOOL
CHAPTER 118
IF ONLY WE'D WON YESTERDAY! THEN WE COULD BE PLAYING ANOTHER GAME RIGHT ABOUT NOW.
I HOPE KARASUNO GOES ON AND BEATS SHIRATORIZAWA FOR US. THAT'LL MAKE US LOOK WAY COOLER.
NO, IT WON'T!
IF IT WASN'T FOR THEIR NO. 10, WE SO WOULD'VE WON.
NO, DUDE. YOU MEAN THEIR SETTER.
THEIR SETTER WAS WICKED GOOD.
DON'T YOU MEAN THEIR CAPTAIN?
NO. 10 WAS THE MOST FUN THOUGH.
THEIR CAP-TAIN?
YEAH, I CAN SEE THAT.

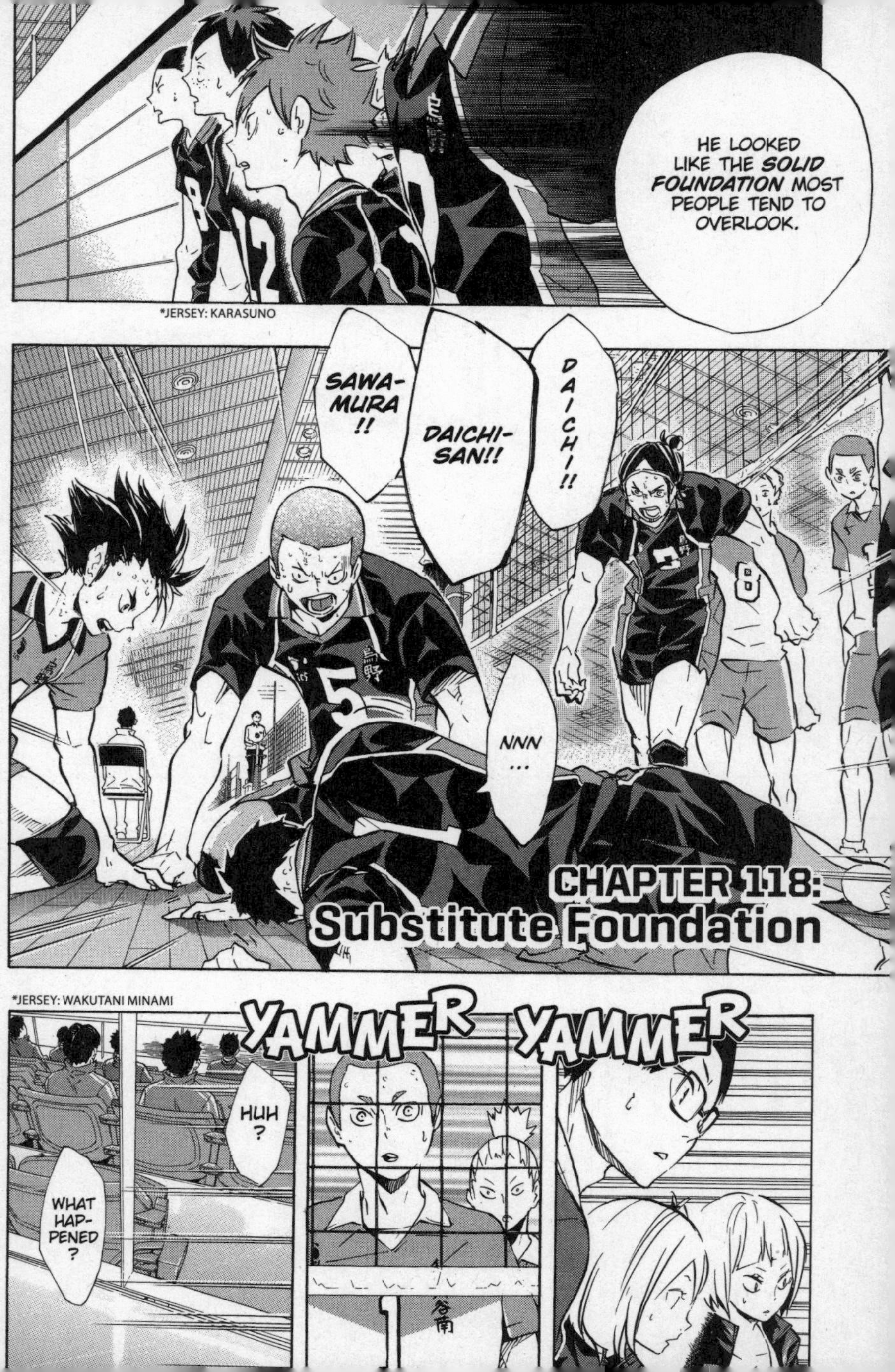
HE LOOKED LIKE THE SOLID FOUNDATION MOST PEOPLE TEND TO OVERLOOK.
*JERSEY: KARASUNO
DAICHI!!
DAICHI-SAN!!
SAWAMURA!!
NNN...
CHAPTER 118: Substitute Foundation
*JERSEY: WAKUTANI MINAMI
YAMMER YAMMER
HUH?
WHAT HAPPENED?

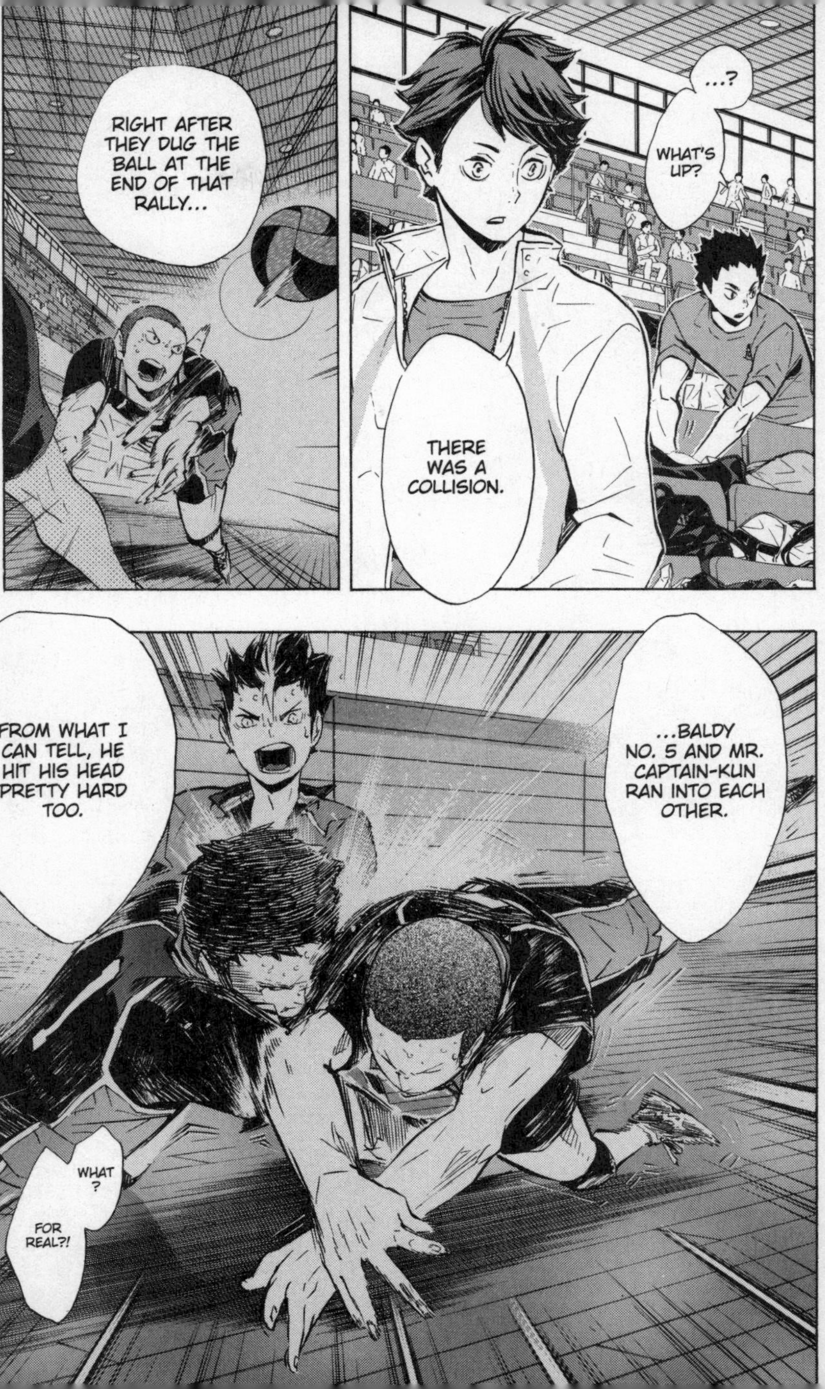

...?
WHAT'S UP?
THERE WAS A COLLISION.
RIGHT AFTER THEY DUG THE BALL AT THE END OF THAT RALLY...
...BALDY NO. 5 AND MR. CAPTAIN-KUN RAN INTO EACH OTHER.
FROM WHAT I CAN TELL, HE HIT HIS HEAD PRETTY HARD TOO.
WHAT?
FOR REAL?!

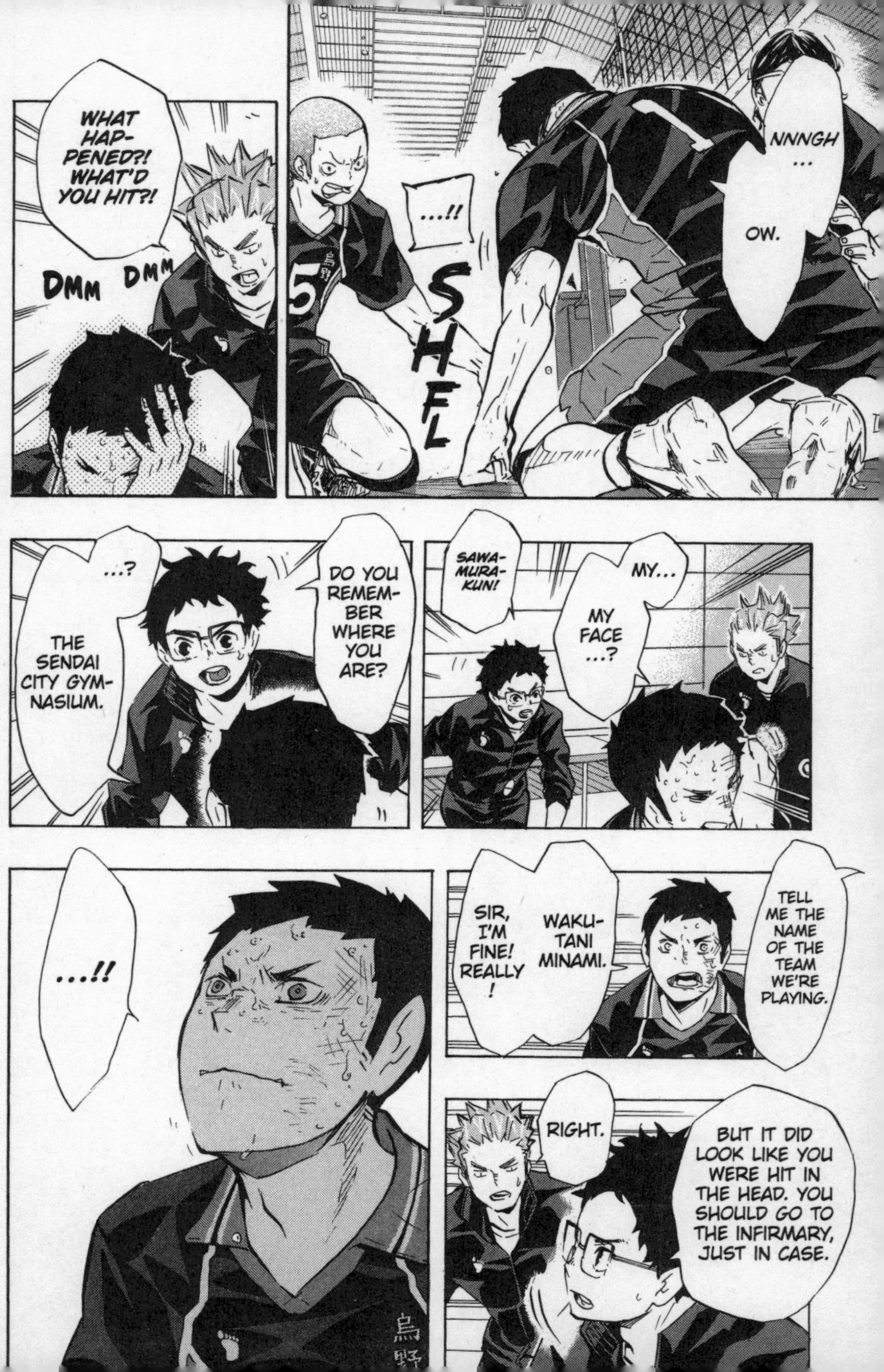
NNNGH ... OW.
...!!
SHFL
WHAT HAP-PENED?! WHAT'D YOU HIT?!
DMM DMM
MY...
SAWAMURA-KUN!
MY FACE ...?
DO YOU REMEMBER WHERE YOU ARE?
...?
THE SENDAI CITY GYM-NASIUM.
TELL ME THE NAME OF THE TEAM WE'RE PLAYING.
WAKU-TANI MINAMI.
SIR, I'M FINE! REALLY!
BUT IT DID LOOK LIKE YOU WERE HIT IN THE HEAD. YOU SHOULD GO TO THE INFIRMARY, JUST IN CASE.
RIGHT.
...!!

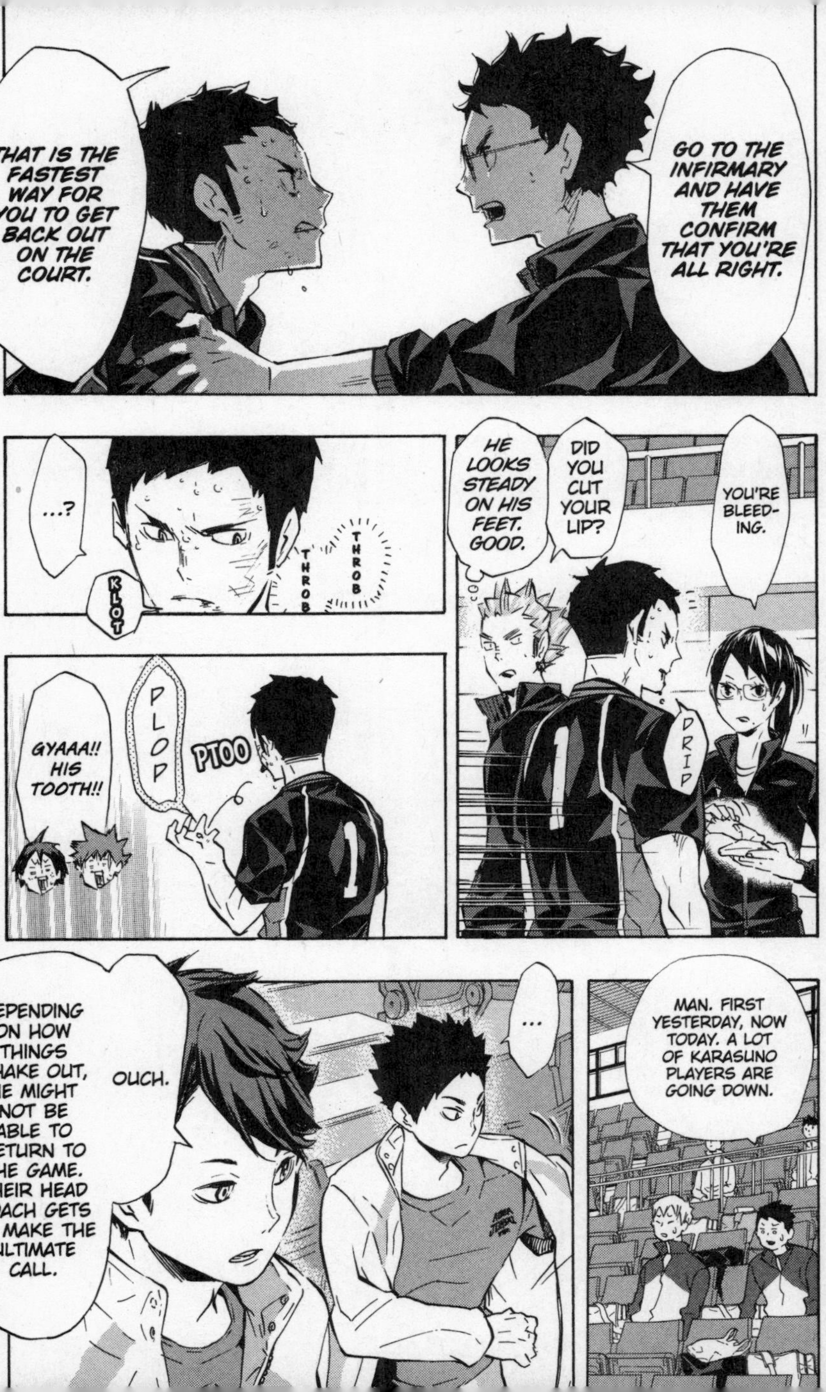
GO TO THE INFIRMARY AND HAVE THEM CONFIRM THAT YOU'RE ALL RIGHT.
THAT IS THE FASTEST WAY FOR YOU TO GET BACK OUT ON THE COURT.
YOU'RE BLEEDING.
DID YOU CUT YOUR LIP?
HE LOOKS STEADY ON HIS FEET. GOOD.
DRIP
...?
THROB
THROB
KLOT
PLOP
PTOO
GYAAA!! HIS TOOTH!!
MAN. FIRST YESTERDAY, NOW TODAY. A LOT OF KARASUNO PLAYERS ARE GOING DOWN.
...
OUCH.
DEPENDING ON HOW THINGS SHAKE OUT, HE MIGHT NOT BE ABLE TO RETURN TO THE GAME. THEIR HEAD COACH GETS TO MAKE THE ULTIMATE CALL.

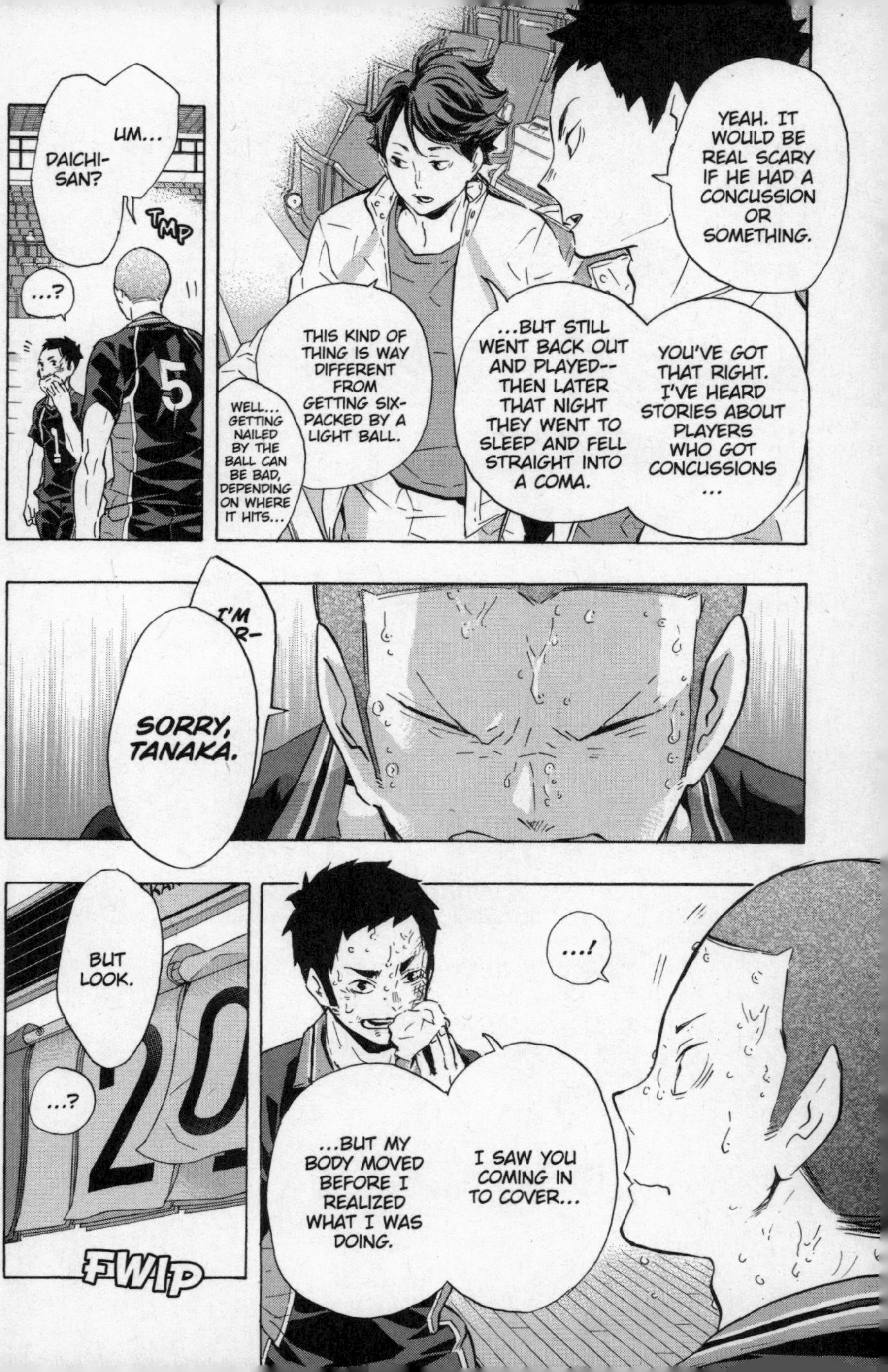

YEAH. IT WOULD BE REAL SCARY IF HE HAD A CONCUSSION OR SOMETHING.
YOU'VE GOT THAT RIGHT. I'VE HEARD STORIES ABOUT PLAYERS WHO GOT CONCUSSIONS ...
...BUT STILL WENT BACK OUT AND PLAYED-- THEN LATER THAT NIGHT THEY WENT TO SLEEP AND FELL STRAIGHT INTO A COMA.
THIS KIND OF THING IS WAY DIFFERENT FROM GETTING SIX-PACKED BY A LIGHT BALL.
WELL... GETTING NAILED BY THE BALL CAN BE BAD, DEPENDING ON WHERE IT HITS...
UM... DAICHI-SAN?
TMP
...?
I'M R-
SORRY, TANAKA.
...!
I SAW YOU COMING IN TO COVER...
...BUT MY BODY MOVED BEFORE I REALIZED WHAT I WAS DOING.
BUT LOOK.
...?
FWIP

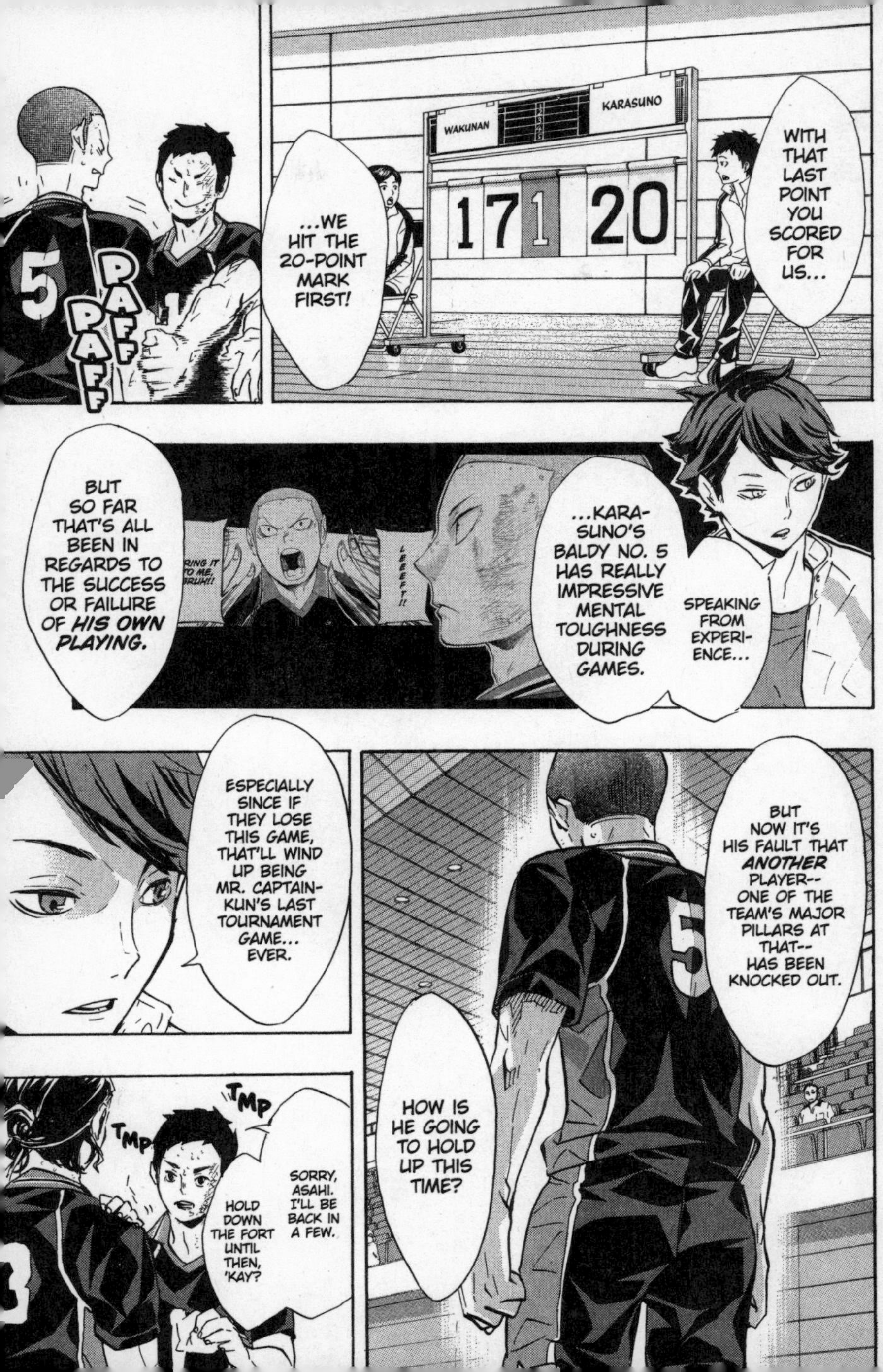
KARASUNO
WAKUNAN
17 1 20
WITH THAT LAST POINT YOU SCORED FOR US...
...WE HIT THE 20-POINT MARK FIRST!
PAFF PAFF
PAFF PAFF
SPEAKING FROM EXPERIENCE...
...KARASUNO'S BALDY NO. 5 HAS REALLY IMPRESSIVE MENTAL TOUGHNESS DURING GAMES.
LEEEFT!!
BUT SO FAR THAT'S ALL BEEN IN REGARDS TO THE SUCCESS OR FAILURE OF *HIS OWN PLAYING.*
BUT NOW IT'S HIS FAULT THAT *ANOTHER* PLAYER--ONE OF THE TEAM'S MAJOR PILLARS AT THAT--HAS BEEN KNOCKED OUT.
HOW IS HE GOING TO HOLD UP THIS TIME?
ESPECIALLY SINCE IF THEY LOSE THIS GAME, THAT'LL WIND UP BEING MR. CAPTAIN-KUN'S LAST TOURNAMENT GAME... EVER.
TMP
TMP
SORRY, ASAHI. I'LL BE BACK IN A FEW.
HOLD DOWN THE FORT UNTIL THEN, 'KAY?

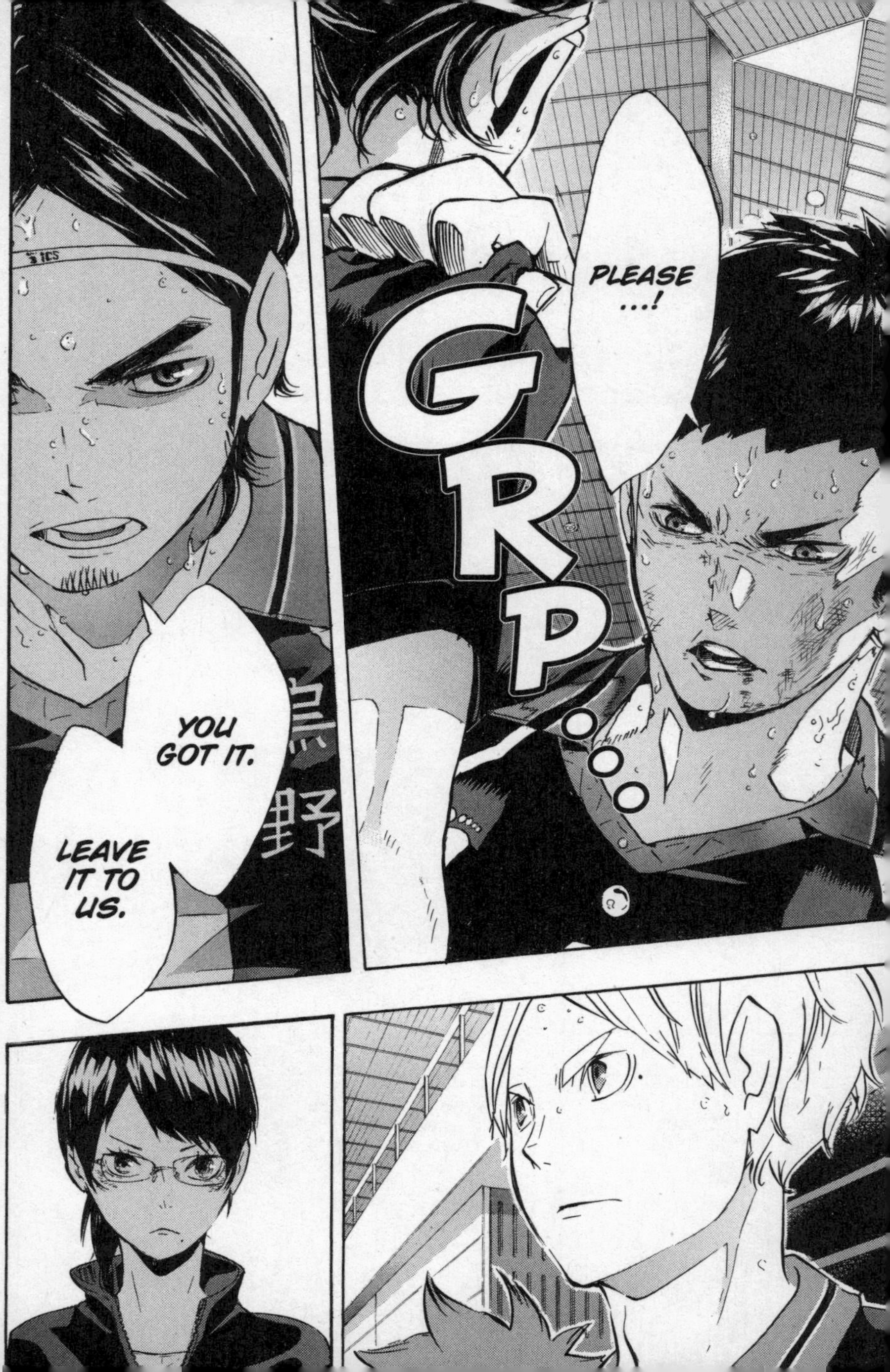
PLEASE ...!
GRP...
YOU GOT IT.
LEAVE IT TO US.

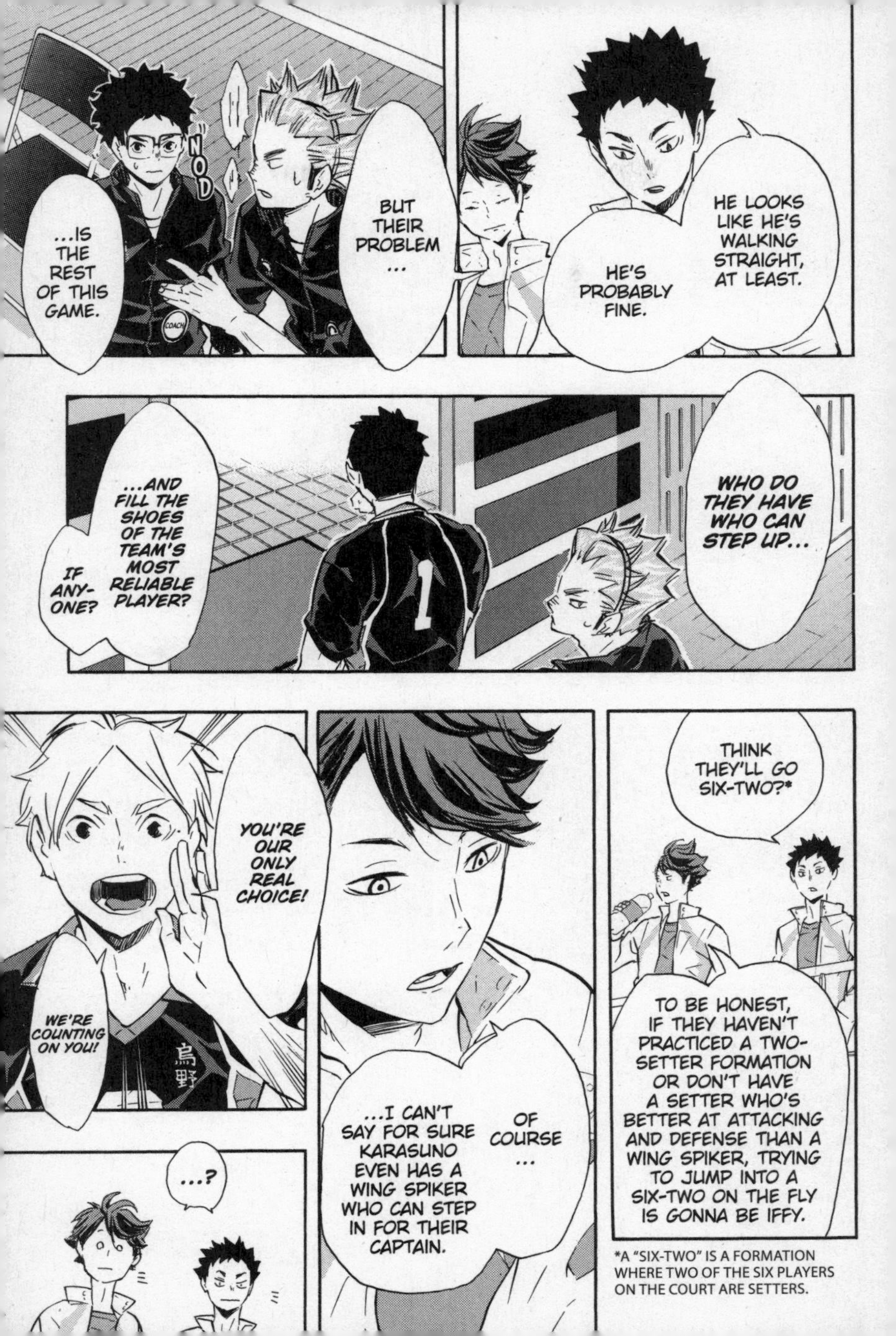
HE LOOKS LIKE HE'S WALKING STRAIGHT, AT LEAST.
HE'S PROBABLY FINE.
NOD
BUT THEIR PROBLEM ...
...IS THE REST OF THIS GAME.
COACH
WHO DO THEY HAVE WHO CAN STEP UP...
...AND FILL THE SHOES OF THE TEAM'S MOST RELIABLE PLAYER?
IF ANY-ONE?
THINK THEY'LL GO SIX-TWO?*
TO BE HONEST, IF THEY HAVEN'T PRACTICED A TWO-SETTER FORMATION OR DON'T HAVE A SETTER WHO'S BETTER AT ATTACKING AND DEFENSE THAN A WING SPIKER, TRYING TO JUMP INTO A SIX-TWO ON THE FLY IS GONNA BE IFFY.
OF COURSE ...
...I CAN'T SAY FOR SURE KARASUNO EVEN HAS A WING SPIKER WHO CAN STEP IN FOR THEIR CAPTAIN.
YOU'RE OUR ONLY REAL CHOICE!
WE'RE COUNTING ON YOU!
...?

*A "SIX-TWO" IS A FORMATION WHERE TWO OF THE SIX PLAYERS ON THE COURT ARE SETTERS.

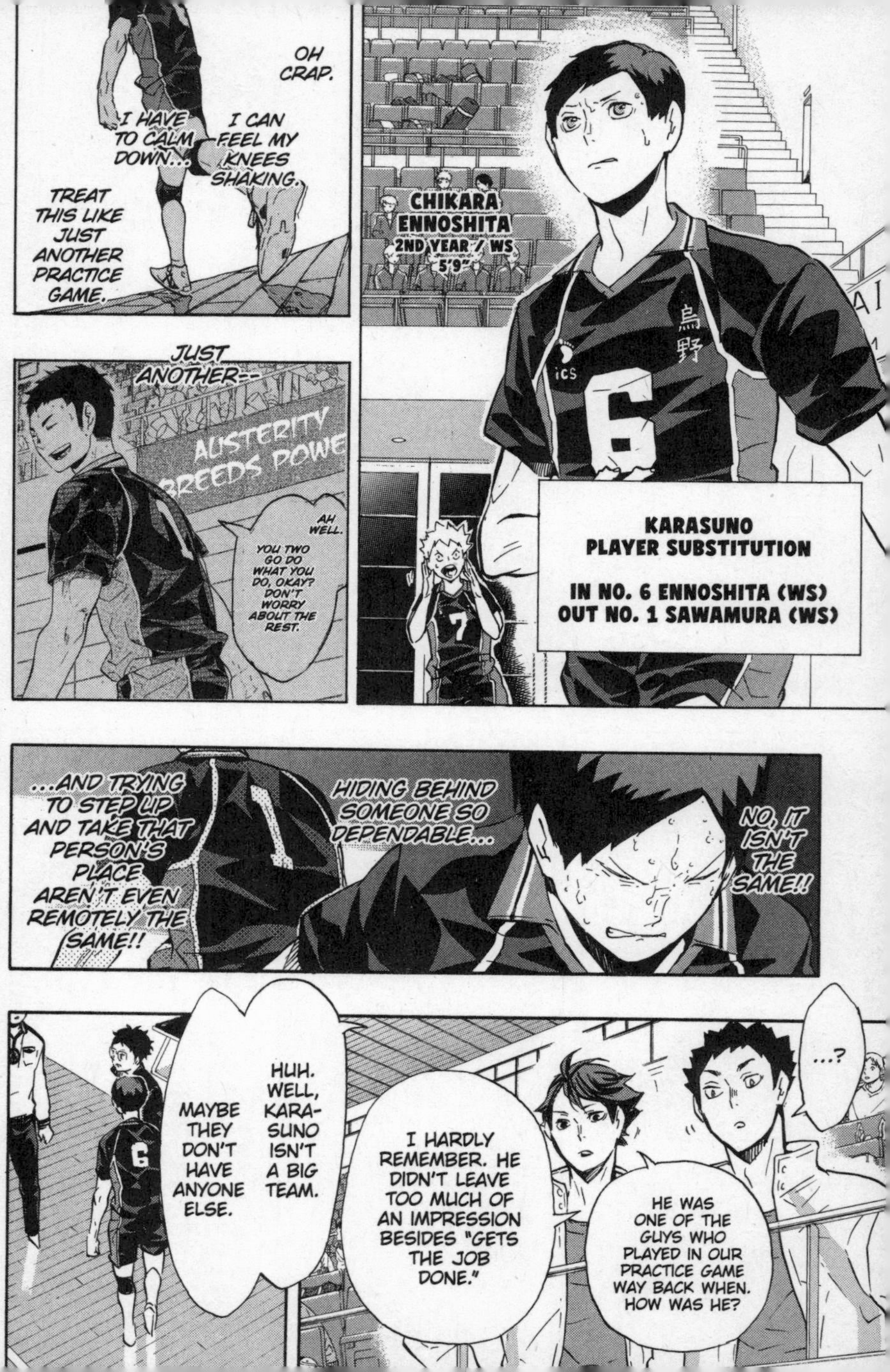
CHIKARA ENNOSHITA 2ND YEAR / WS 5'9"
KARASUNO PLAYER SUBSTITUTION
IN NO. 6 ENNOSHITA (WS) OUT NO. 1 SAWAMURA (WS)
OH CRAP.
I CAN FEEL MY KNEES SHAKING.
I HAVE TO CALM DOWN...
TREAT THIS LIKE JUST ANOTHER PRACTICE GAME.
JUST ANOTHER--
AUSTERITY BREEDS POWE
AH WELL.
YOU TWO GO DO WHAT YOU DO, OKAY? DON'T WORRY ABOUT THE REST.
NO, IT ISN'T THE SAME!!
HIDING BEHIND SOMEONE SO DEPENDABLE...
...AND TRYING TO STEP UP AND TAKE THAT PERSON'S PLACE AREN'T EVEN REMOTELY THE SAME!!
...?
HE WAS ONE OF THE GUYS WHO PLAYED IN OUR PRACTICE GAME WAY BACK WHEN. HOW WAS HE?
I HARDLY REMEMBER. HE DIDN'T LEAVE TOO MUCH OF AN IMPRESSION BESIDES "GETS THE JOB DONE."
HUH. WELL, KARASUNO ISN'T A BIG TEAM.
MAYBE THEY DON'T HAVE ANYONE ELSE.

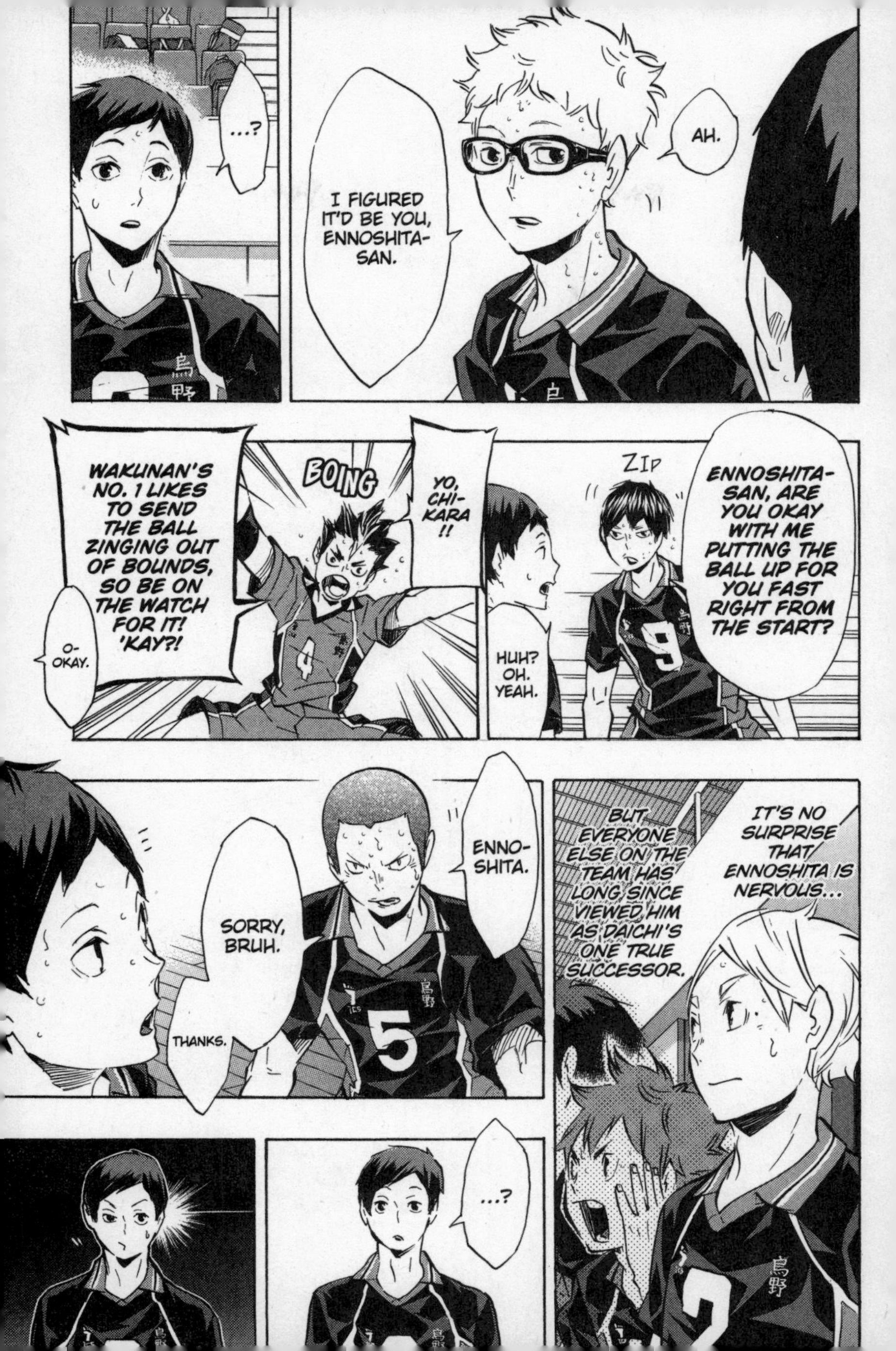
AH.
I FIGURED IT'D BE YOU, ENNOSHITA-SAN.
...?
ZIP
ENNOSHITA-SAN, ARE YOU OKAY WITH ME PUTTING THE BALL UP FOR YOU FAST RIGHT FROM THE START?
HUH? OH. YEAH.
YO, CHI-KARA!!
BOING
WAKUNAN'S NO. 1 LIKES TO SEND THE BALL ZINGING OUT OF BOUNDS, SO BE ON THE WATCH FOR IT! 'KAY?!
O-OKAY.
IT'S NO SURPRISE THAT ENNOSHITA IS NERVOUS...
BUT EVERYONE ELSE ON THE TEAM HAS LONG SINCE VIEWED HIM AS DAICHI'S ONE TRUE SUCCESSOR.
ENNO-SHITA.
SORRY, BRUH.
THANKS.
...?

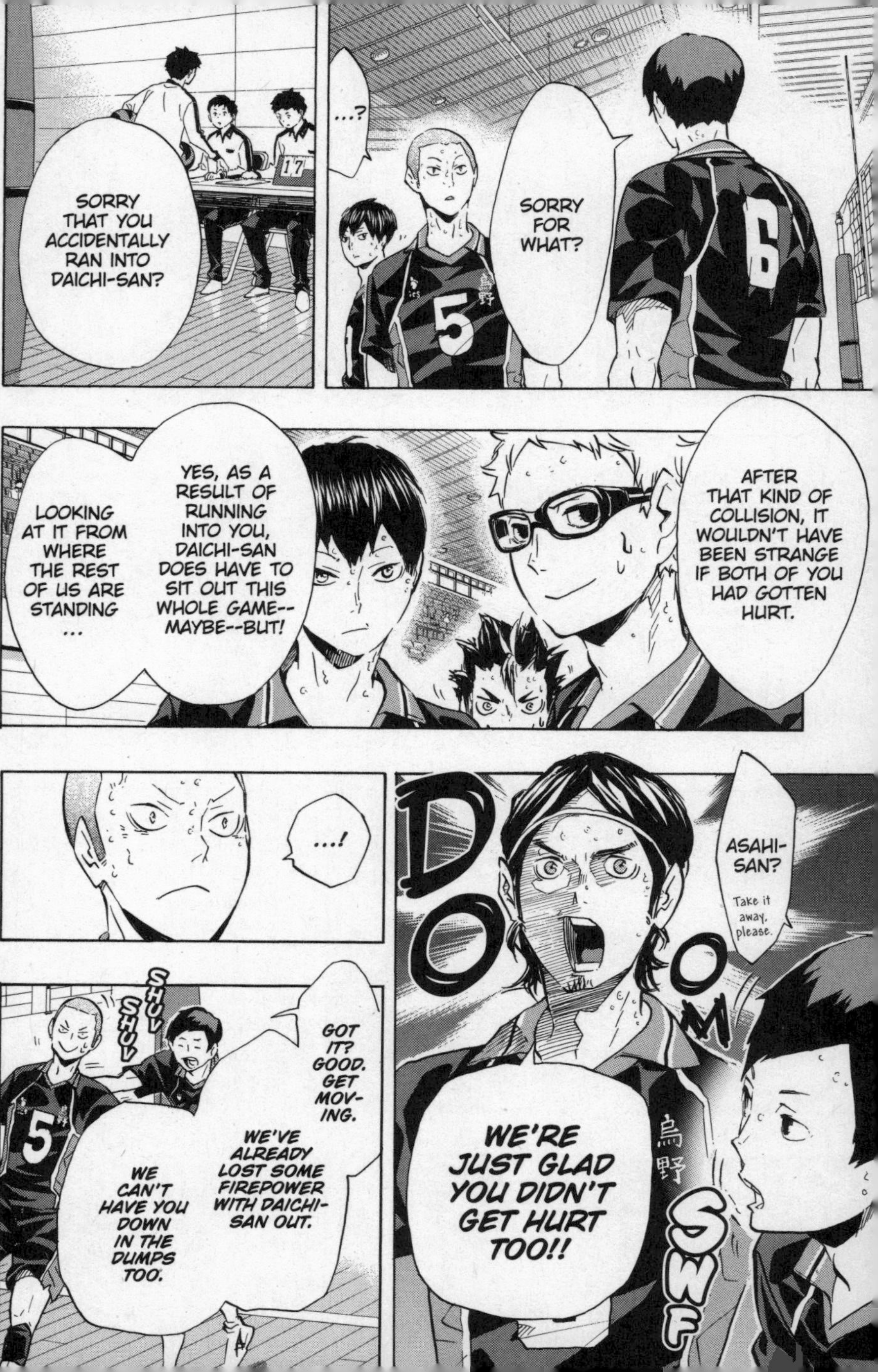
...?
SORRY FOR WHAT?
SORRY THAT YOU ACCIDENTALLY RAN INTO DAICHI-SAN?
17
AFTER THAT KIND OF COLLISION, IT WOULDN'T HAVE BEEN STRANGE IF BOTH OF YOU HAD GOTTEN HURT.
YES, AS A RESULT OF RUNNING INTO YOU, DAICHI-SAN DOES HAVE TO SIT OUT THIS WHOLE GAME--MAYBE--BUT!
LOOKING AT IT FROM WHERE THE REST OF US ARE STANDING ...
ASAHI-SAN?
Take it away, please.
DOOOM
WE'RE JUST GLAD YOU DIDN'T GET HURT TOO!!
SWF
...!
SHUV SHUV
GOT IT? GOOD. GET MOV-ING.
WE'VE ALREADY LOST SOME FIREPOWER WITH DAICHI-SAN OUT.
WE CAN'T HAVE YOU DOWN IN THE DUMPS TOO.

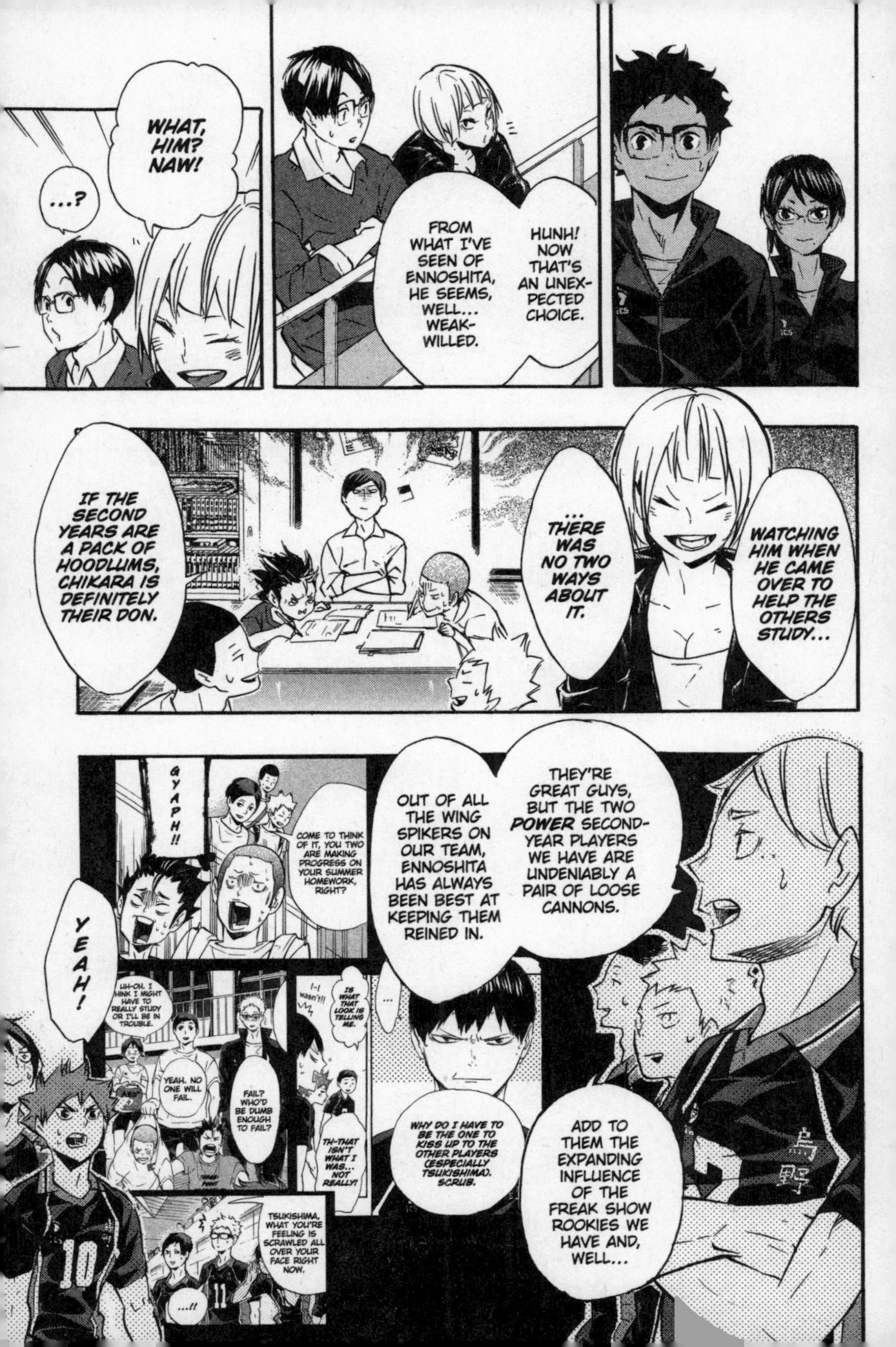
HUNH! NOW THAT'S AN UNEXPECTED CHOICE.
FROM WHAT I'VE SEEN OF ENNOSHITA, HE SEEMS, WELL... WEAK-WILLED.
WHAT, HIM? NAW!
...?
WATCHING HIM WHEN HE CAME OVER TO HELP THE OTHERS STUDY...
...THERE WAS NO TWO WAYS ABOUT IT.
IF THE SECOND YEARS ARE A PACK OF HOODLUMS, CHIKARA IS DEFINITELY THEIR DON.
THEY'RE GREAT GUYS, BUT THE TWO POWER SECOND-YEAR PLAYERS WE HAVE ARE UNDENIABLY A PAIR OF LOOSE CANNONS.
OUT OF ALL THE WING SPIKERS ON OUR TEAM, ENNOSHITA HAS ALWAYS BEEN BEST AT KEEPING THEM REINED IN.
ADD TO THEM THE EXPANDING INFLUENCE OF THE FREAK SHOW ROOKIES WE HAVE AND, WELL...
WHY DO I HAVE TO BE THE ONE TO KISS UP TO THE OTHER PLAYERS (ESPECIALLY TSUKISHIMA). SCRUB.
...
IS WHAT THAT LOOK IS TELLING ME.
I-I wasn't!!
TH-THAT ISN'T WHAT I WAS... NOT REALLY!
COME TO THINK OF IT, YOU TWO ARE MAKING PROGRESS ON YOUR SUMMER HOMEWORK, RIGHT?
GYAPH!!
YEAH!
FAIL? WHO'D BE DUMB ENOUGH TO FAIL?
YEAH. NO ONE WILL FAIL.
UH-OH. I HINK I MIGHT HAVE TO REALLY STUDY OR I'LL BE IN TROUBLE.
TSUKISHIMA, WHAT YOU'RE FEELING IS SCRAWLED ALL OVER YOUR FACE RIGHT NOW.
...!!

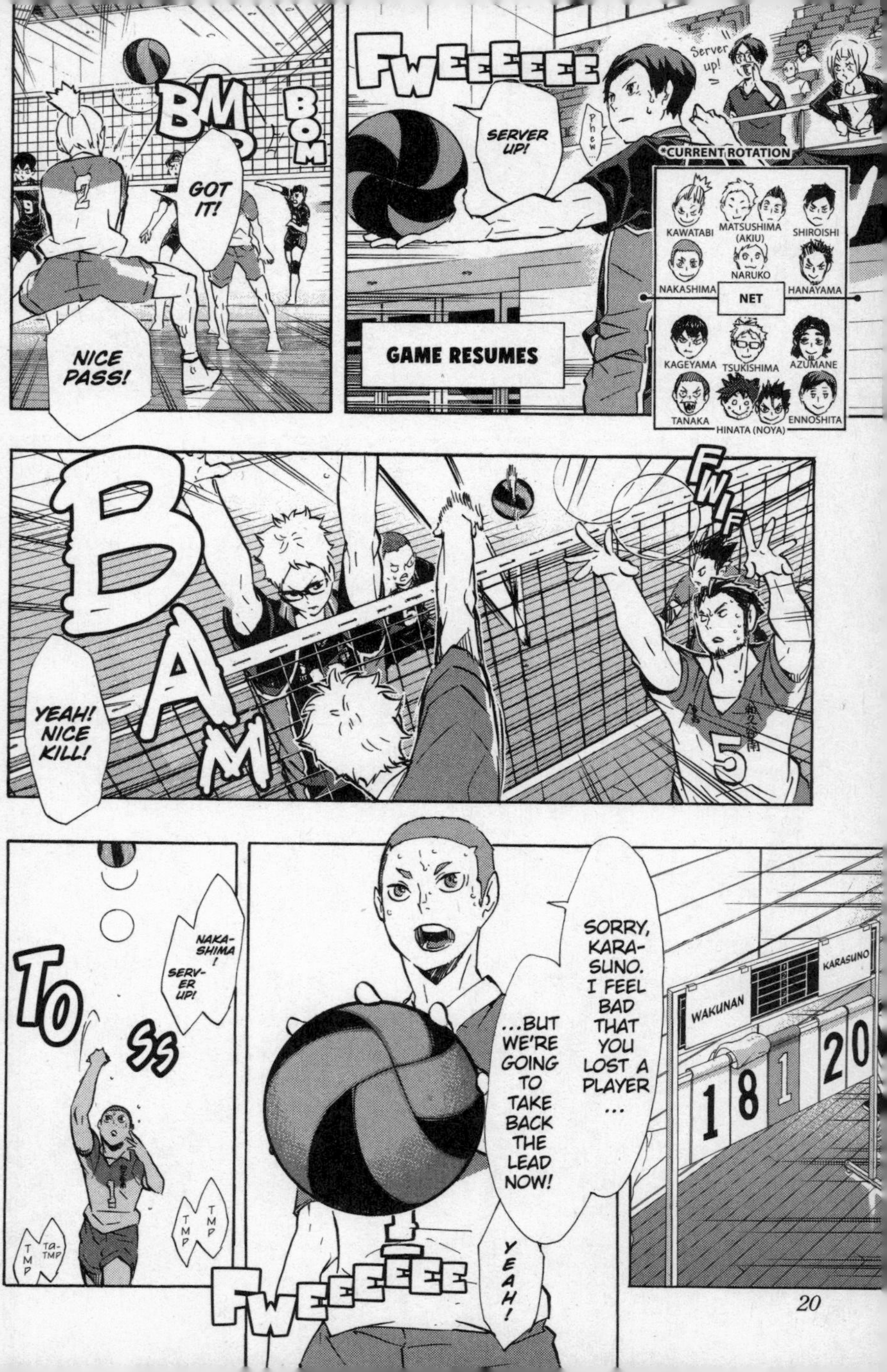
FWEEEEEE
Server up!
Phew...
SERVER UP!
*CURRENT ROTATION
KAWATABI
MATSUSHIMA (AKIU)
SHIROISHI
NAKASHIMA
NARUKO
HANAYAMA
NET
KAGEYAMA
TSUKISHIMA
AZUMANE
TANAKA
HINATA (NOYA)
ENNOSHITA
GAME RESUMES
BOM
BM
GOT IT!
NICE PASS!
FWIF
BAM
YEAH! NICE KILL!
KARASUNO
WAKUNAN
18
1
20
SORRY, KARASUNO. I FEEL BAD THAT YOU LOST A PLAYER...
...BUT WE'RE GOING TO TAKE BACK THE LEAD NOW!
YEAH!
FWEEEEEE
NAKASHIMA! SERVER UP!
TOSS
TMP TMP
TMP TA-TMP

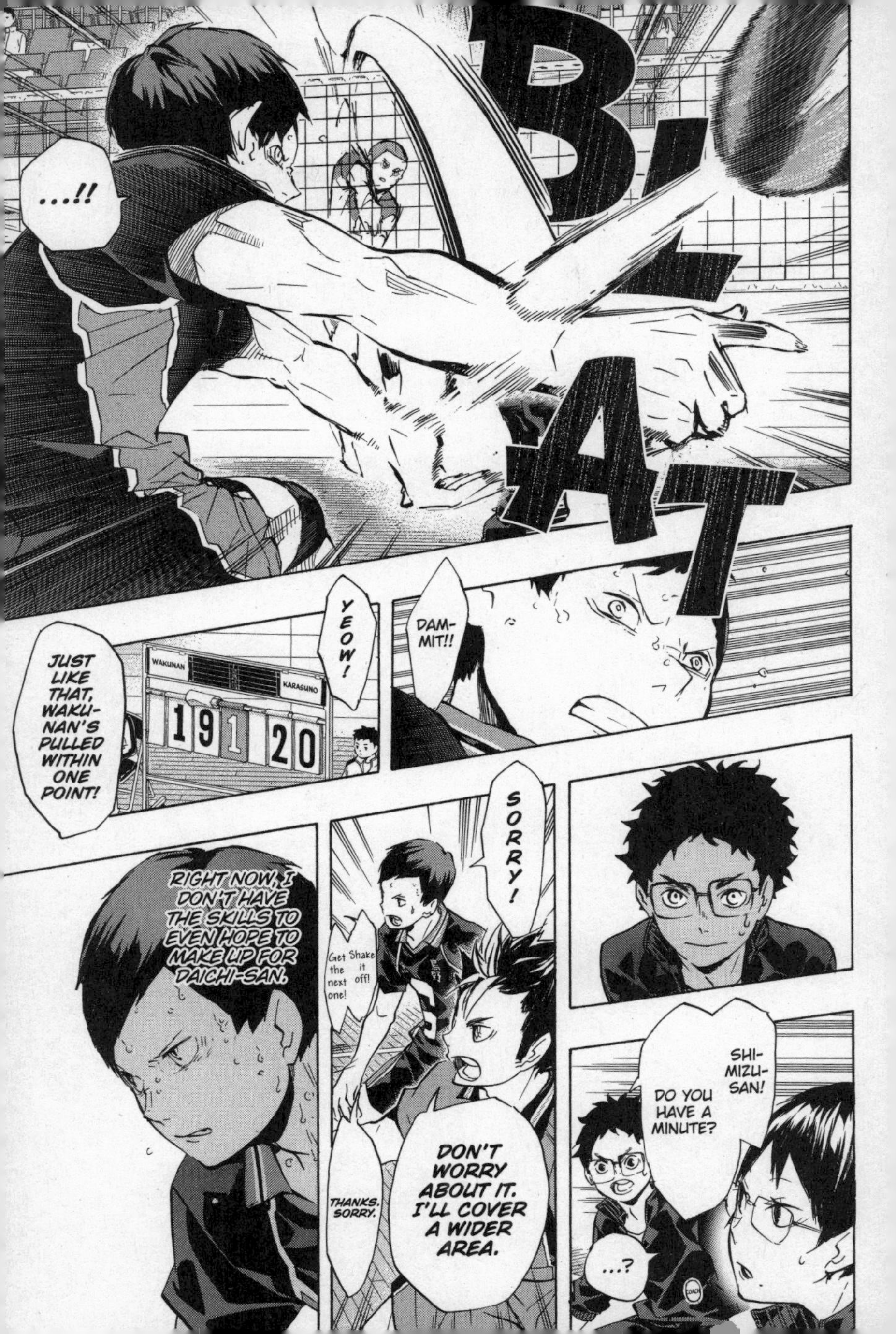
BLAT
...!!
DAM-MIT!!
YEOW!
JUST LIKE THAT, WAKU-NAN'S PULLED WITHIN ONE POINT!
WAKUNAN
KARASUNO
19
20
SHI-MIZU-SAN!
DO YOU HAVE A MINUTE?
...?
SORRY!
Shake it off!
Get the next one!
DON'T WORRY ABOUT IT. I'LL COVER A WIDER AREA.
THANKS. SORRY.
RIGHT NOW, I DON'T HAVE THE SKILLS TO EVEN HOPE TO MAKE UP FOR DAICHI-SAN.

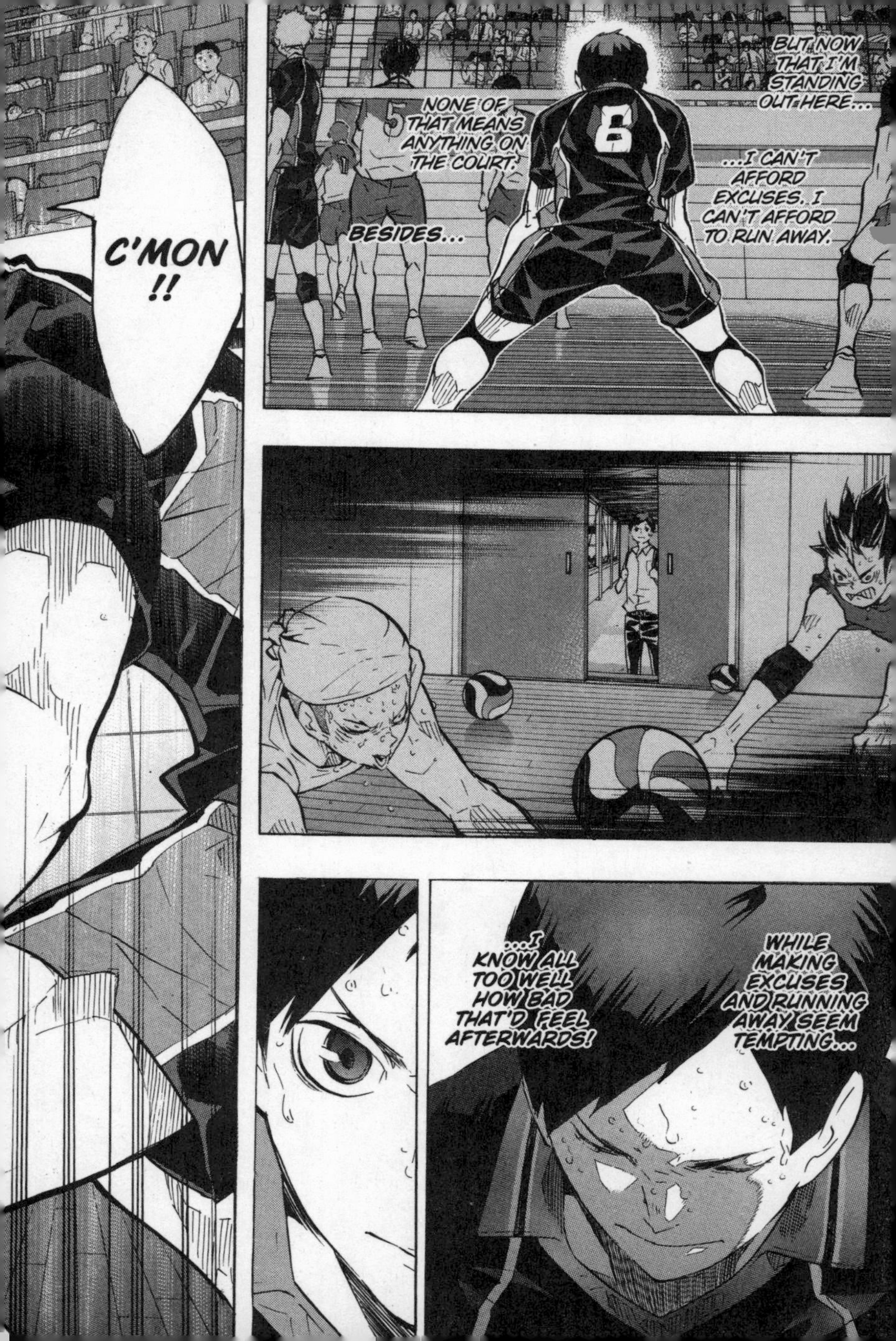
BUT NOW THAT I'M STANDING OUT HERE...
...I CAN'T AFFORD EXCUSES. I CAN'T AFFORD TO RUN AWAY.
NONE OF THAT MEANS ANYTHING ON THE COURT.
BESIDES...
WHILE MAKING EXCUSES AND RUNNING AWAY SEEM TEMPTING...
...I KNOW ALL TOO WELL HOW BAD THAT'D FEEL AFTERWARDS!
C'MON !!

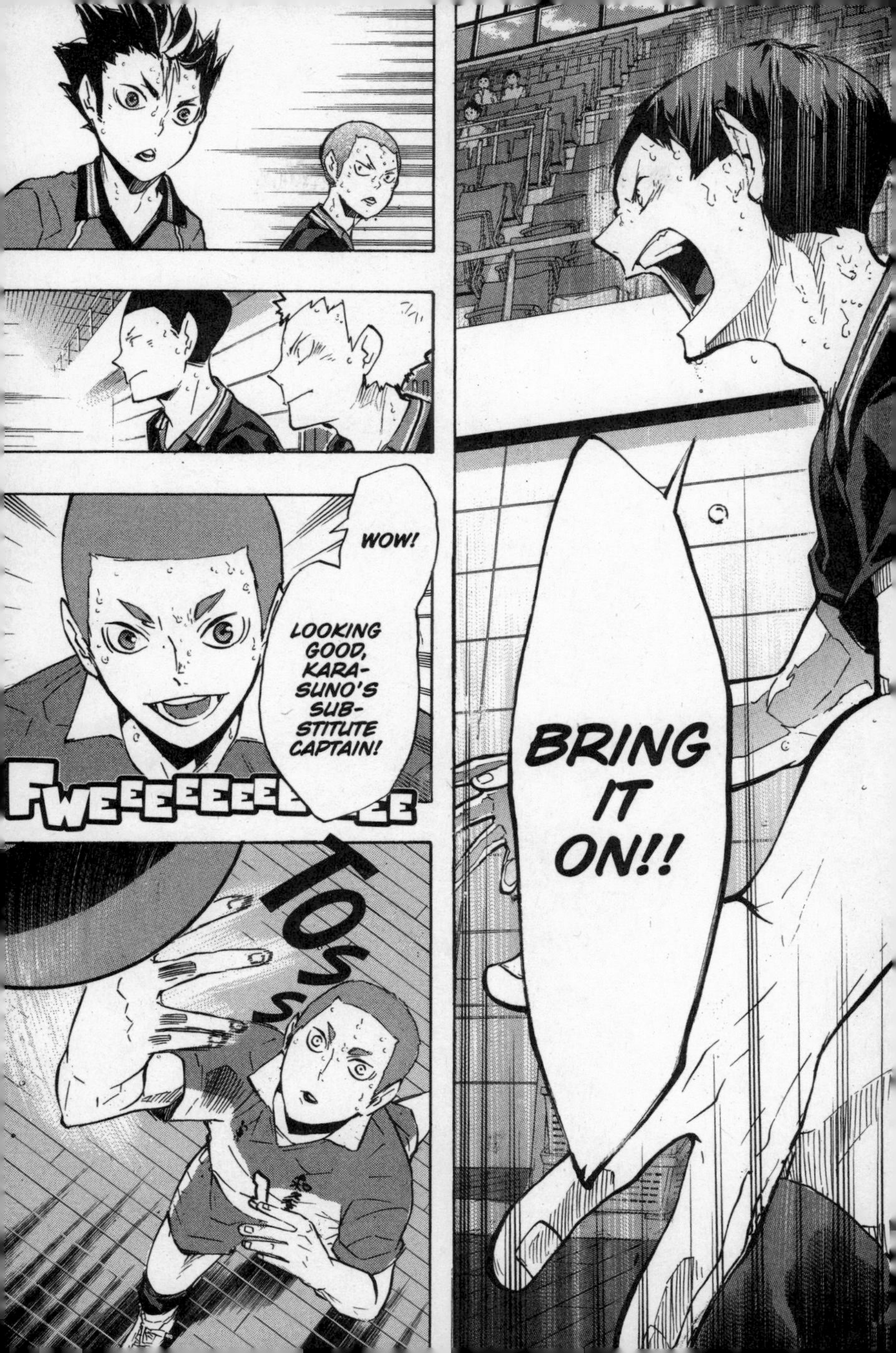
BRING IT ON!!
WOW!
LOOKING GOOD, KARA-SUNO'S SUB-STITUTE CAPTAIN!
FWEEEEEEEEEEEE
TOSS

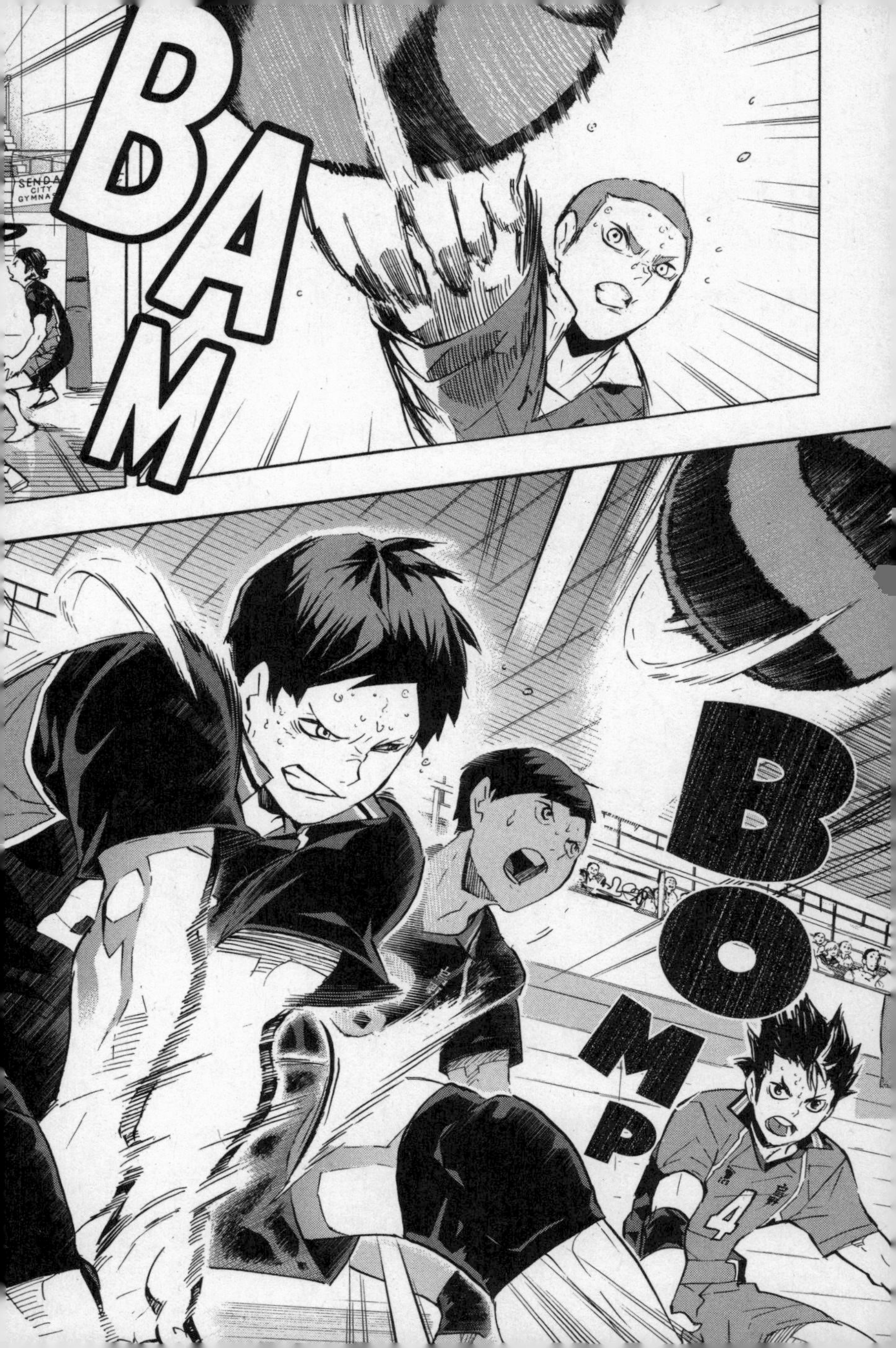
BAM
BOMP

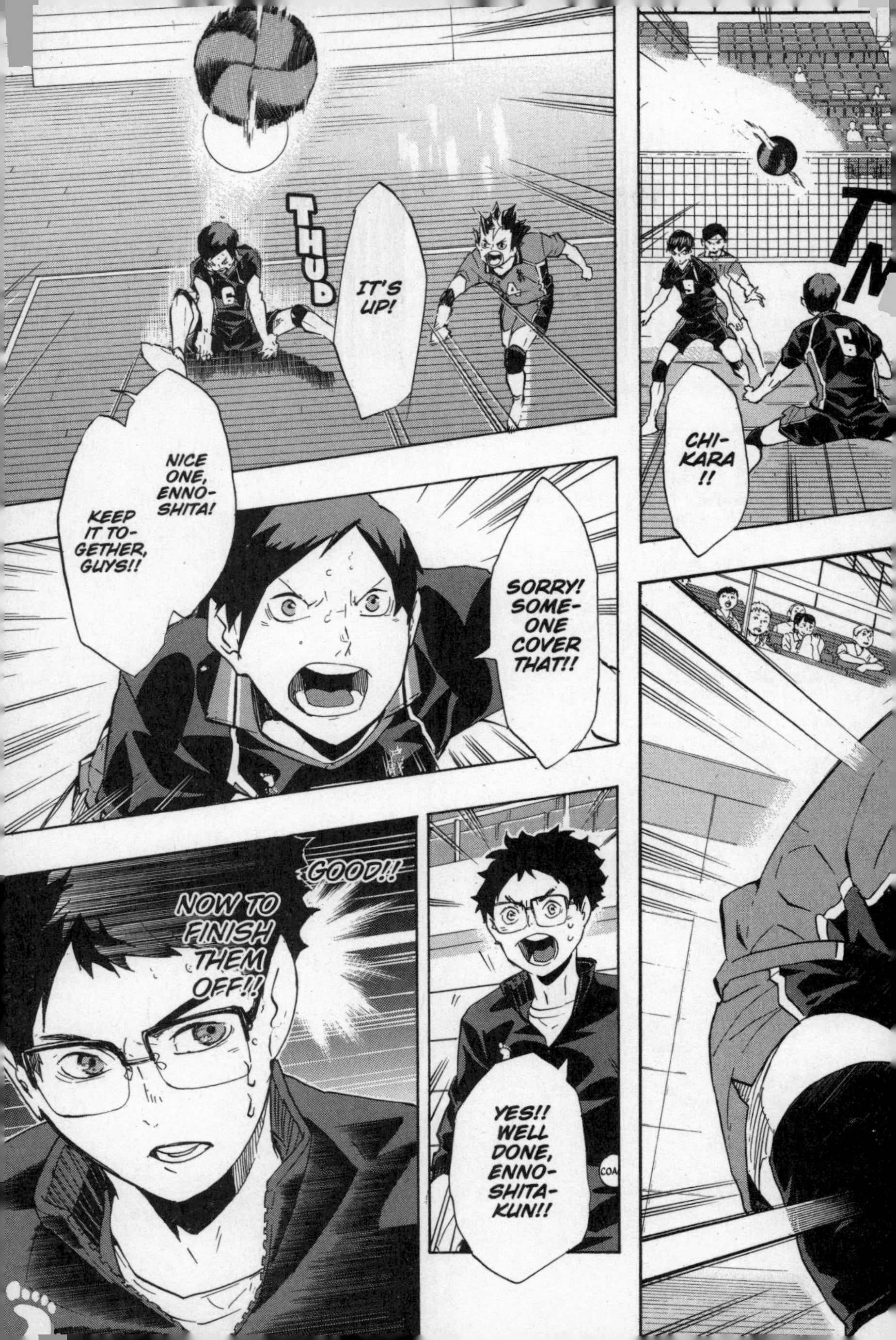
CHI-KARA!!
THUD
IT'S UP!
NICE ONE, ENNO-SHITA!
KEEP IT TO-GETHER, GUYS!!
SORRY! SOME-ONE COVER THAT!!
YES!! WELL DONE, ENNO-SHITA-KUN!!
GOOD!!
NOW TO FINISH THEM OFF!!

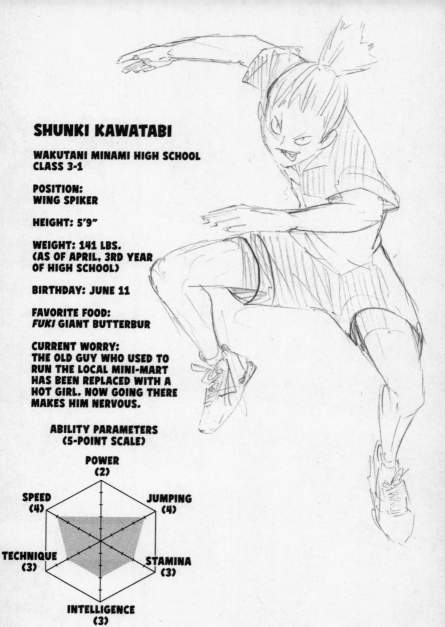

SHUNKI KAWATABI

WAKUTANI MINAMI HIGH SCHOOL
CLASS 3-1

POSITION:
WING SPIKER

HEIGHT: 5'9"

WEIGHT: 141 LBS.
(AS OF APRIL, 3RD YEAR OF HIGH SCHOOL)

BIRTHDAY: JUNE 11

FAVORITE FOOD:
***FUKI* GIANT BUTTERBUR**

CURRENT WORRY:
THE OLD GUY WHO USED TO RUN THE LOCAL MINI-MART HAS BEEN REPLACED WITH A HOT GIRL. NOW GOING THERE MAKES HIM NERVOUS.

ABILITY PARAMETERS
(5-POINT SCALE)

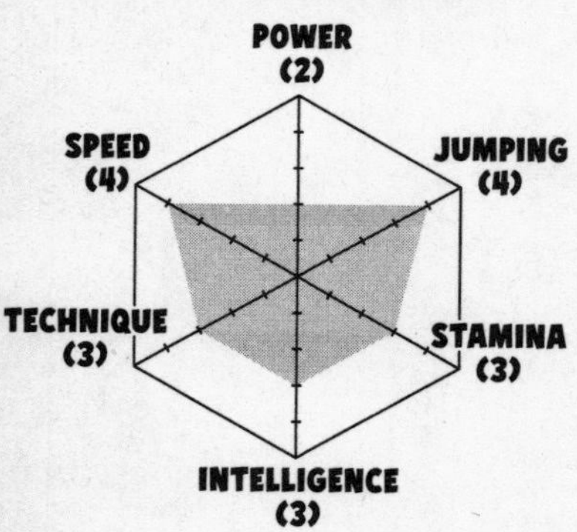
POWER
(2)
JUMPING
(4)
STAMINA
(3)
INTELLIGENCE
(3)
TECHNIQUE
(3)
SPEED
(4)

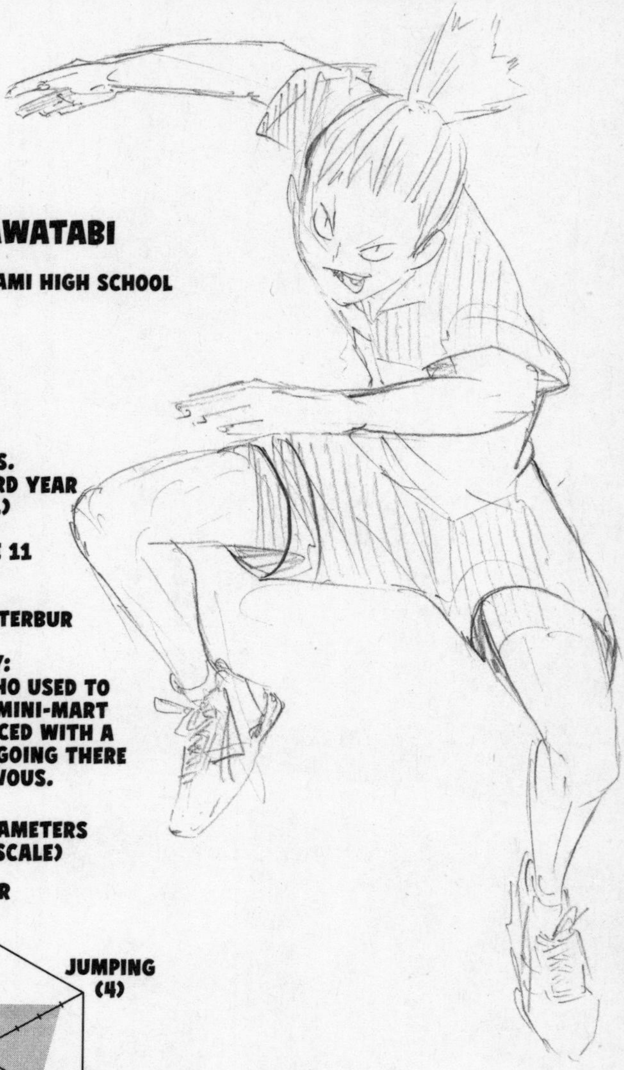

CHAPTER 119: Quitter's Battle

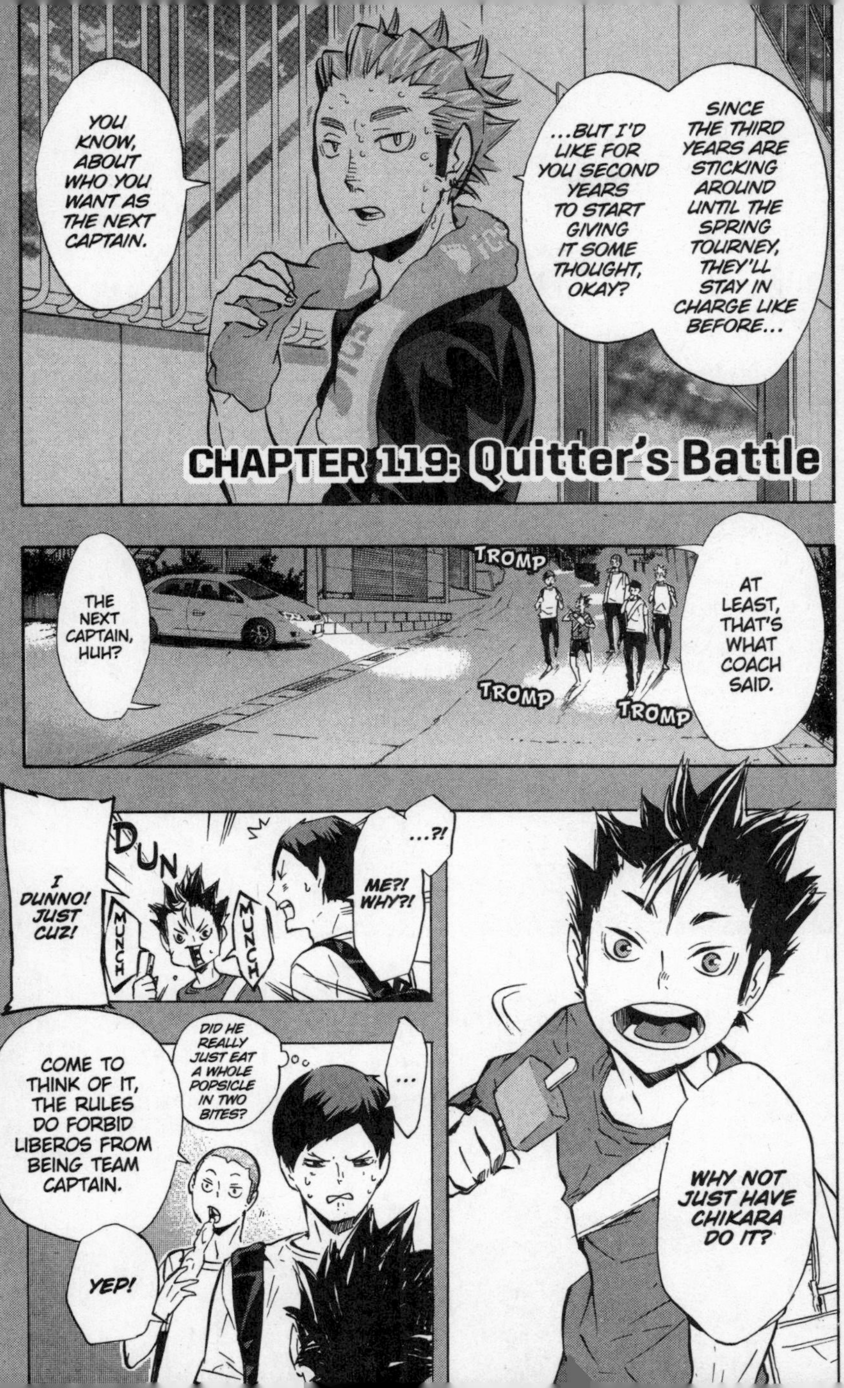
SINCE THE THIRD YEARS ARE STICKING AROUND UNTIL THE SPRING TOURNEY, THEY'LL STAY IN CHARGE LIKE BEFORE...
...BUT I'D LIKE FOR YOU SECOND YEARS TO START GIVING IT SOME THOUGHT, OKAY?
YOU KNOW, ABOUT WHO YOU WANT AS THE NEXT CAPTAIN.
AT LEAST, THAT'S WHAT COACH SAID.
TROMP
TROMP
TROMP
THE NEXT CAPTAIN, HUH?
WHY NOT JUST HAVE CHIKARA DO IT?
...?!
ME?! WHY?!
MUNCH
MUNCH
DUN
I DUNNO! JUST CUZ!
...
DID HE REALLY JUST EAT A WHOLE POPSICLE IN TWO BITES?
COME TO THINK OF IT, THE RULES DO FORBID LIBEROS FROM BEING TEAM CAPTAIN.
YEP!

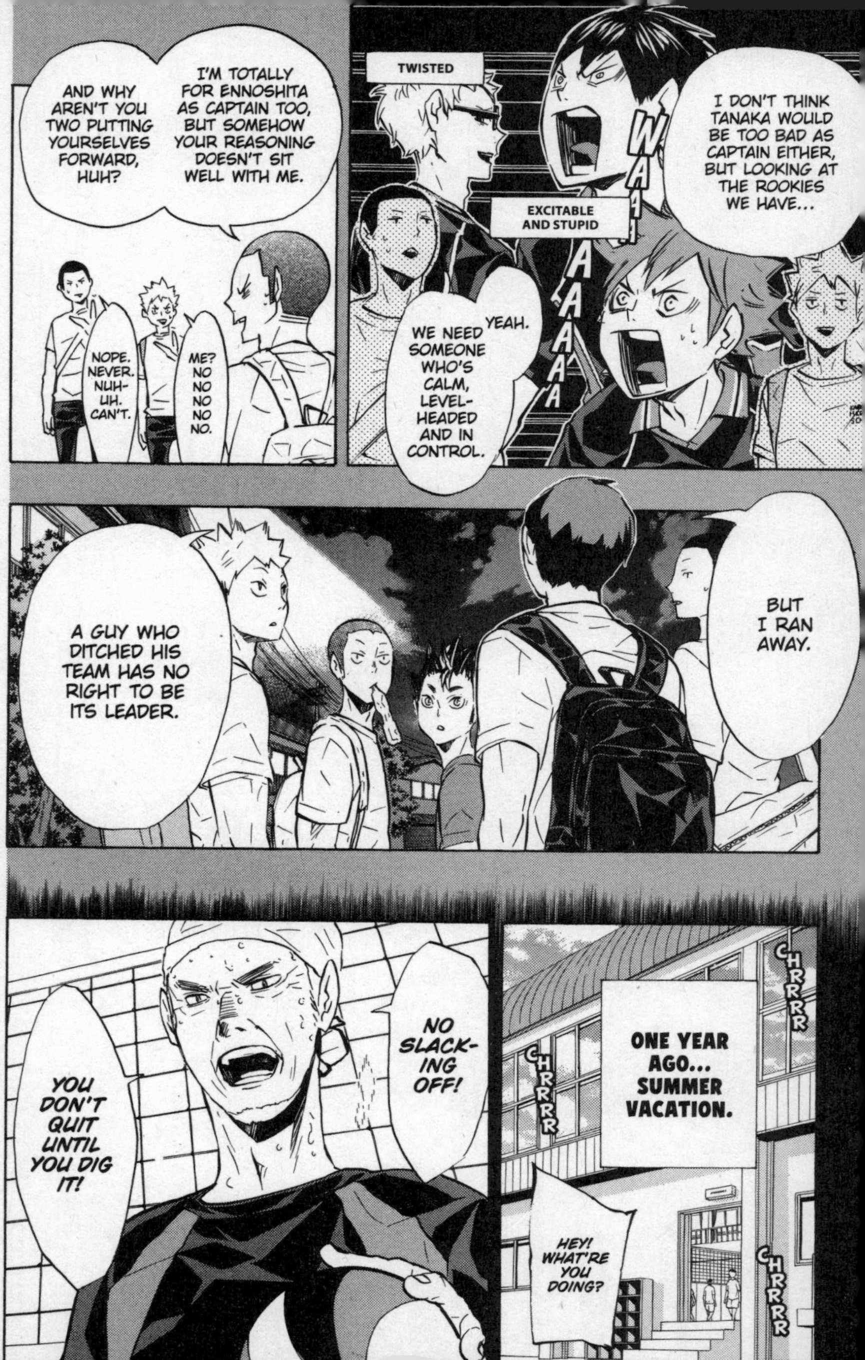
I DON'T THINK TANAKA WOULD BE TOO BAD AS CAPTAIN EITHER, BUT LOOKING AT THE ROOKIES WE HAVE...
TWISTED
EXCITABLE AND STUPID
WAAAAAAAAAA
YEAH.
WE NEED SOMEONE WHO'S CALM, LEVEL-HEADED AND IN CONTROL.
I'M TOTALLY FOR ENNOSHITA AS CAPTAIN TOO, BUT SOMEHOW YOUR REASONING DOESN'T SIT WELL WITH ME.
AND WHY AREN'T YOU TWO PUTTING YOURSELVES FORWARD, HUH?
ME? NO NO NO NO NO.
NOPE. NEVER. NUH-UH. CAN'T.
BUT I RAN AWAY.
A GUY WHO DITCHED HIS TEAM HAS NO RIGHT TO BE ITS LEADER.
CHRRRR
ONE YEAR AGO... SUMMER VACATION.
CHRRRR
HEY! WHAT'RE YOU DOING?
CHRRRR
NO SLACKING OFF!
YOU DON'T QUIT UNTIL YOU DIG IT!

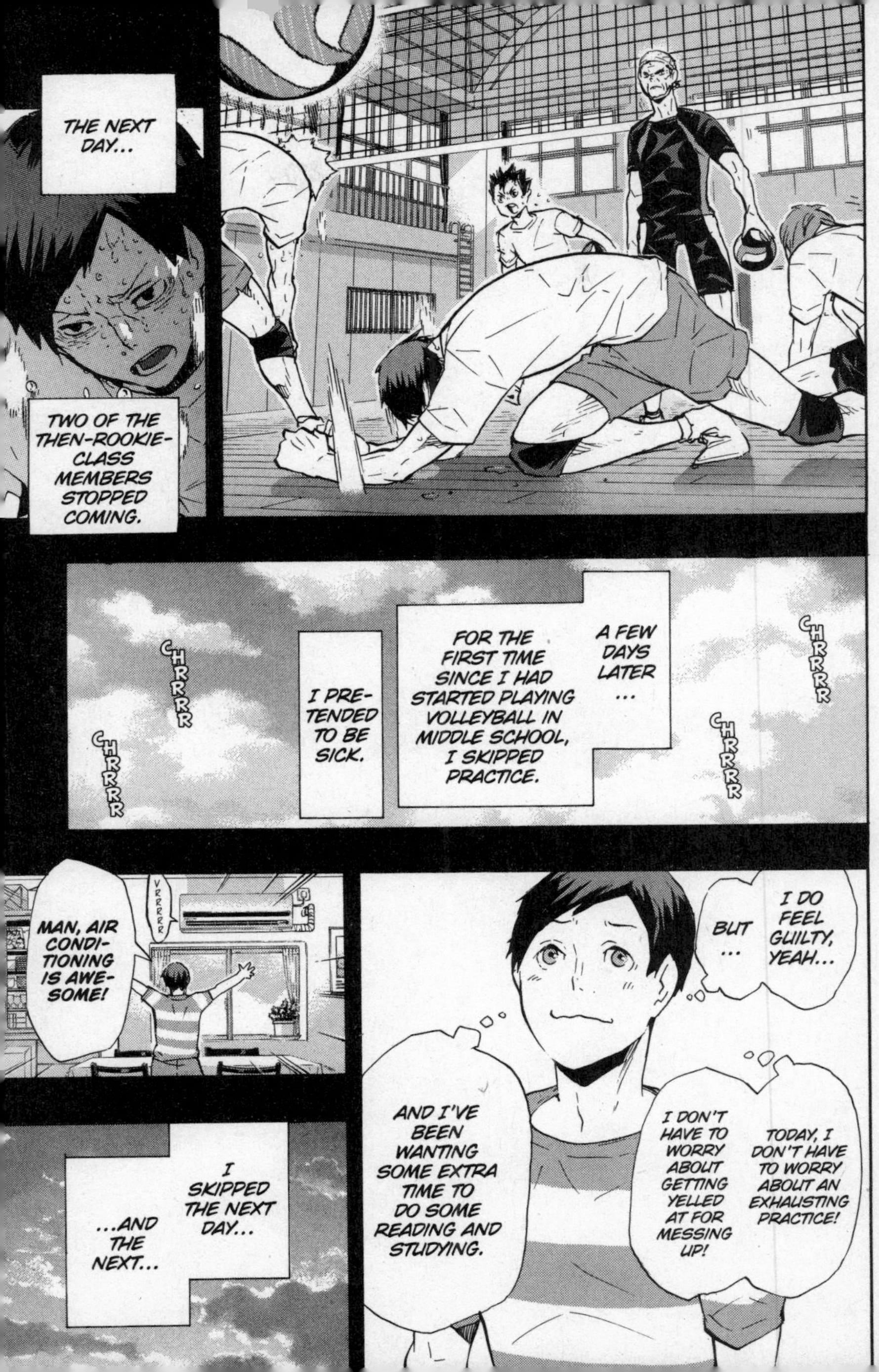
THE NEXT DAY...
TWO OF THE THEN-ROOKIE-CLASS MEMBERS STOPPED COMING.
CHRRRR
A FEW DAYS LATER ...
FOR THE FIRST TIME SINCE I HAD STARTED PLAYING VOLLEYBALL IN MIDDLE SCHOOL, I SKIPPED PRACTICE.
CHRRRR
I PRETENDED TO BE SICK.
CHRRRR
CHRRRR
I DO FEEL GUILTY, YEAH...
BUT ...
TODAY, I DON'T HAVE TO WORRY ABOUT AN EXHAUSTING PRACTICE!
I DON'T HAVE TO WORRY ABOUT GETTING YELLED AT FOR MESSING UP!
AND I'VE BEEN WANTING SOME EXTRA TIME TO DO SOME READING AND STUDYING.
VRRRRR
MAN, AIR CONDITIONING IS AWESOME!
I SKIPPED THE NEXT DAY...
...AND THE NEXT...

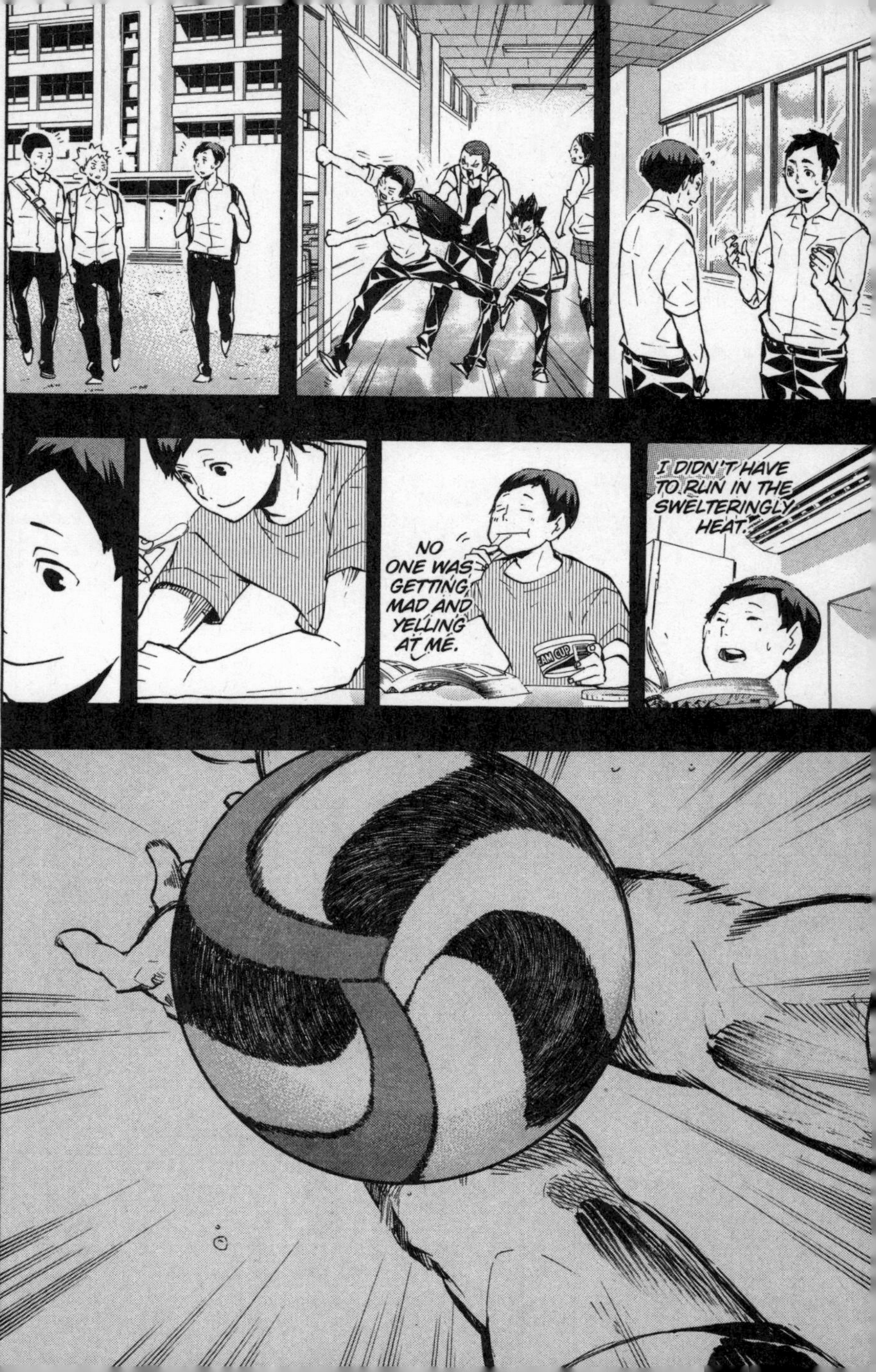
I DIDN'T HAVE TO RUN IN THE SWELTERINGLY HEAT.
NO ONE WAS GETTING MAD AND YELLING AT ME.

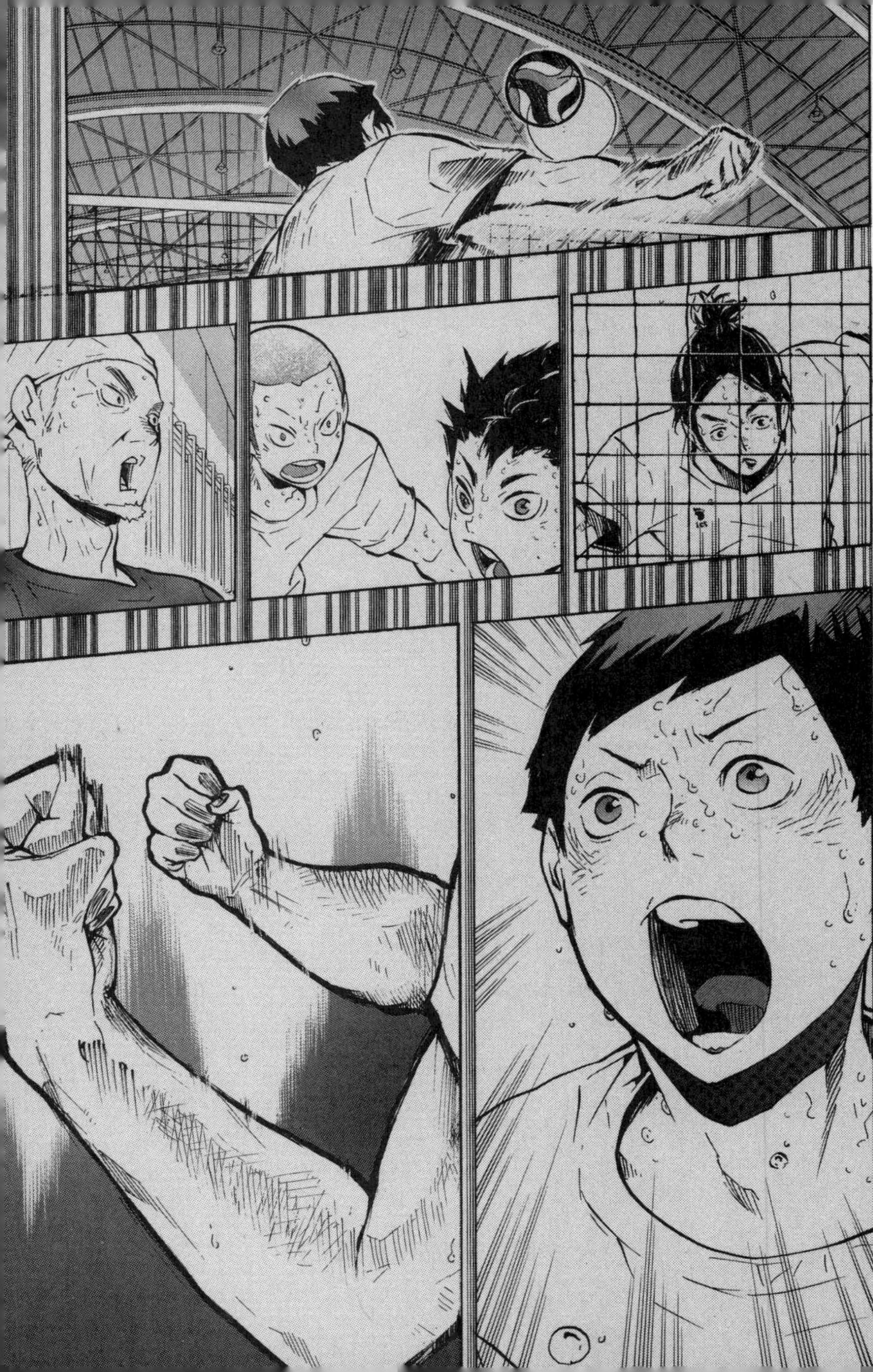

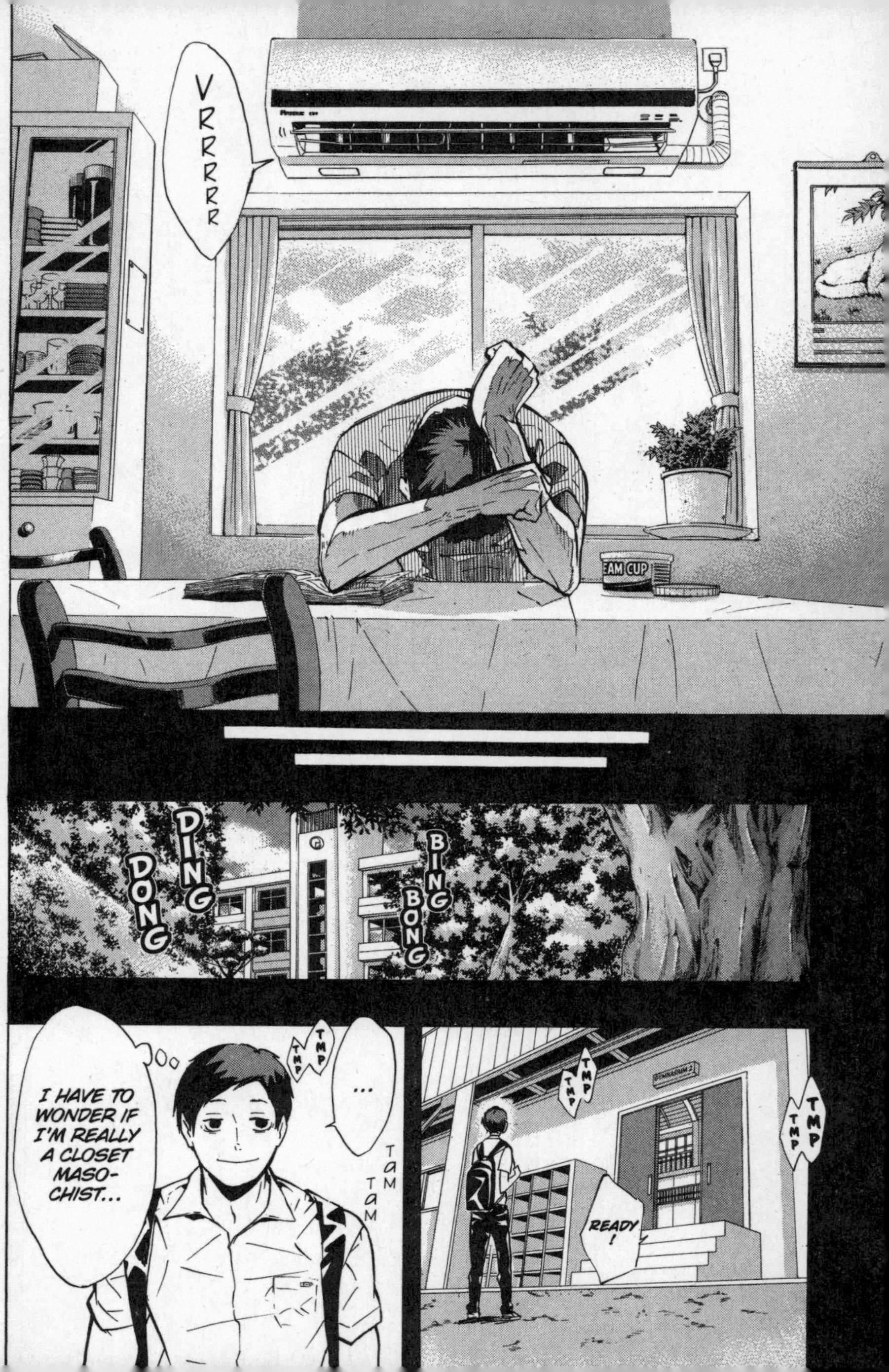
VRRRRRR
EAM CUP
BING BONG
DING DONG
TMP TMP
TMP TMP
READY!
TMP TMP
...
I HAVE TO WONDER IF I'M REALLY A CLOSET MASO-CHIST...
TAM TAM

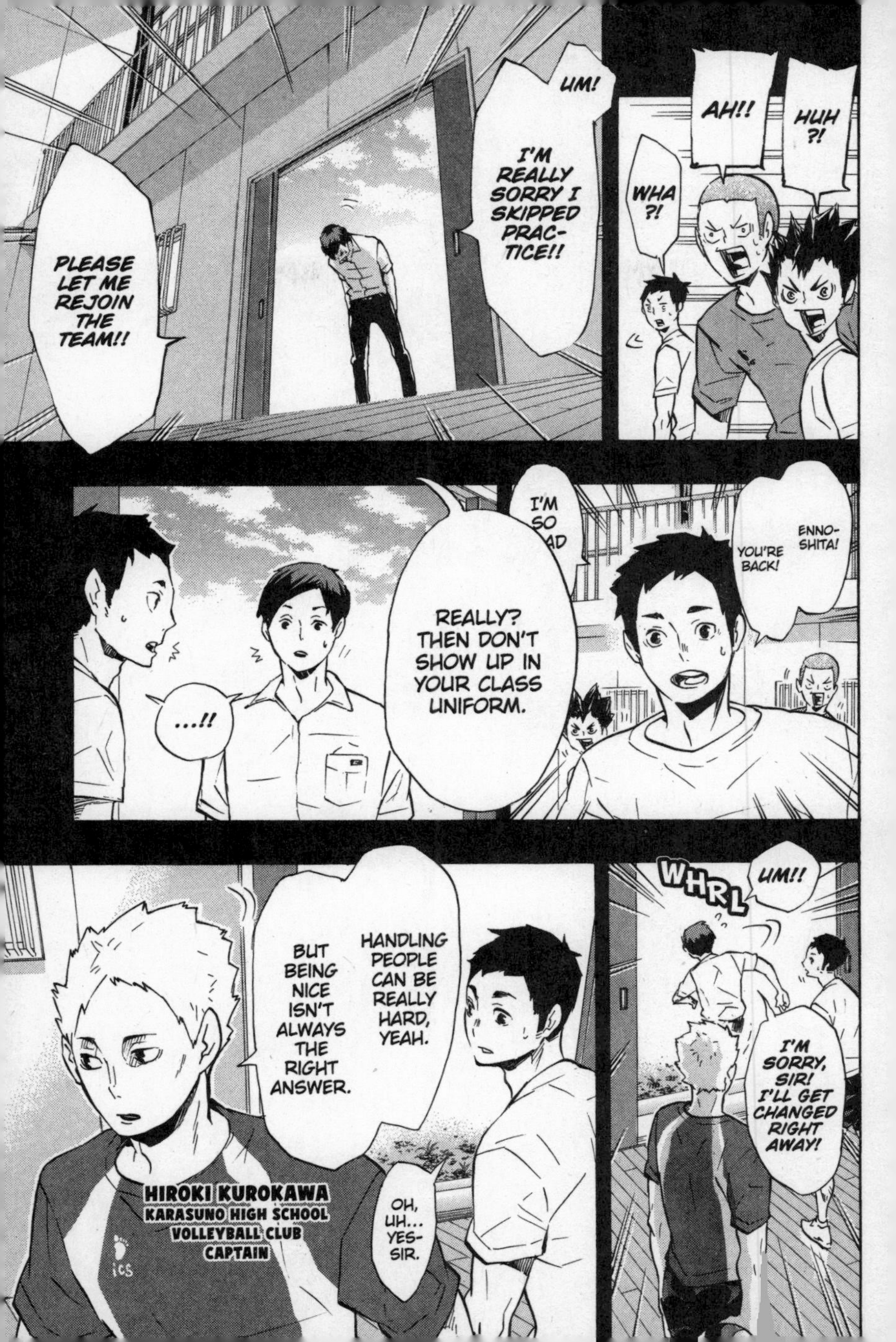
HUH ?!
AH!!
WHA ?!
UM!
I'M REALLY SORRY I SKIPPED PRAC- TICE!!
PLEASE LET ME REJOIN THE TEAM!!
ENNO- SHITA!
YOU'RE BACK!
I'M SO
REALLY? THEN DON'T SHOW UP IN YOUR CLASS UNIFORM.
...!!
UM!!
WHRL
I'M SORRY, SIR! I'LL GET CHANGED RIGHT AWAY!
HANDLING PEOPLE CAN BE REALLY HARD, YEAH.
BUT BEING NICE ISN'T ALWAYS THE RIGHT ANSWER.
HIROKI KUROKAWA
KARASUNO HIGH SCHOOL VOLLEYBALL CLUB CAPTAIN
OH, UH... YES- SIR.

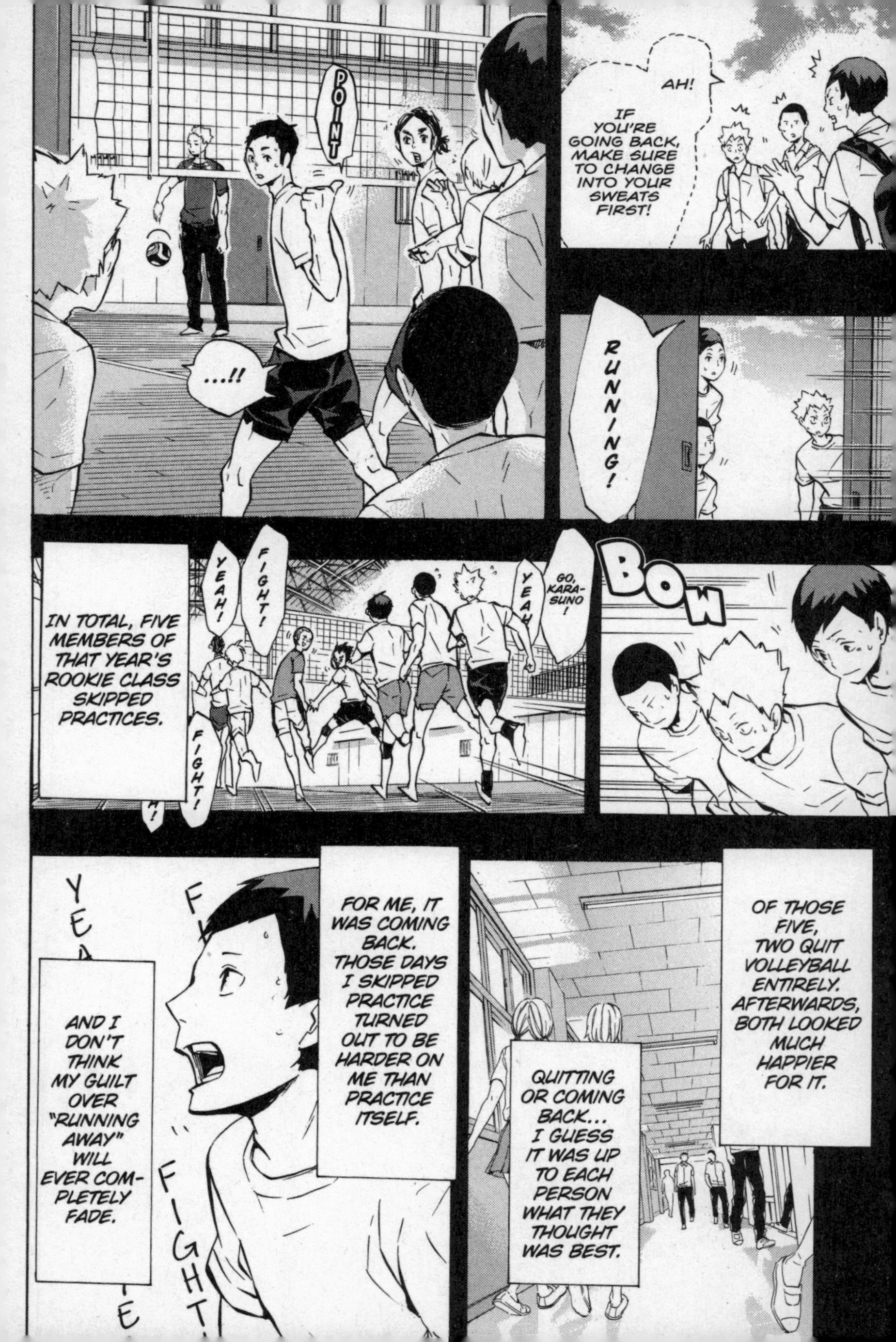
AH!
IF YOU'RE GOING BACK, MAKE SURE TO CHANGE INTO YOUR SWEATS FIRST!
RUNNING!
POINT
...!!
BOW
GO, KARASUNO!
YEAH
FIGHT!
YEAH!
IN TOTAL, FIVE MEMBERS OF THAT YEAR'S ROOKIE CLASS SKIPPED PRACTICES.
FIGHT!
OF THOSE FIVE, TWO QUIT VOLLEYBALL ENTIRELY. AFTERWARDS, BOTH LOOKED MUCH HAPPIER FOR IT.
QUITTING OR COMING BACK... I GUESS IT WAS UP TO EACH PERSON WHAT THEY THOUGHT WAS BEST.
FOR ME, IT WAS COMING BACK. THOSE DAYS I SKIPPED PRACTICE TURNED OUT TO BE HARDER ON ME THAN PRACTICE ITSELF.
AND I DON'T THINK MY GUILT OVER "RUNNING AWAY" WILL EVER COMPLETELY FADE.
FIGHT!

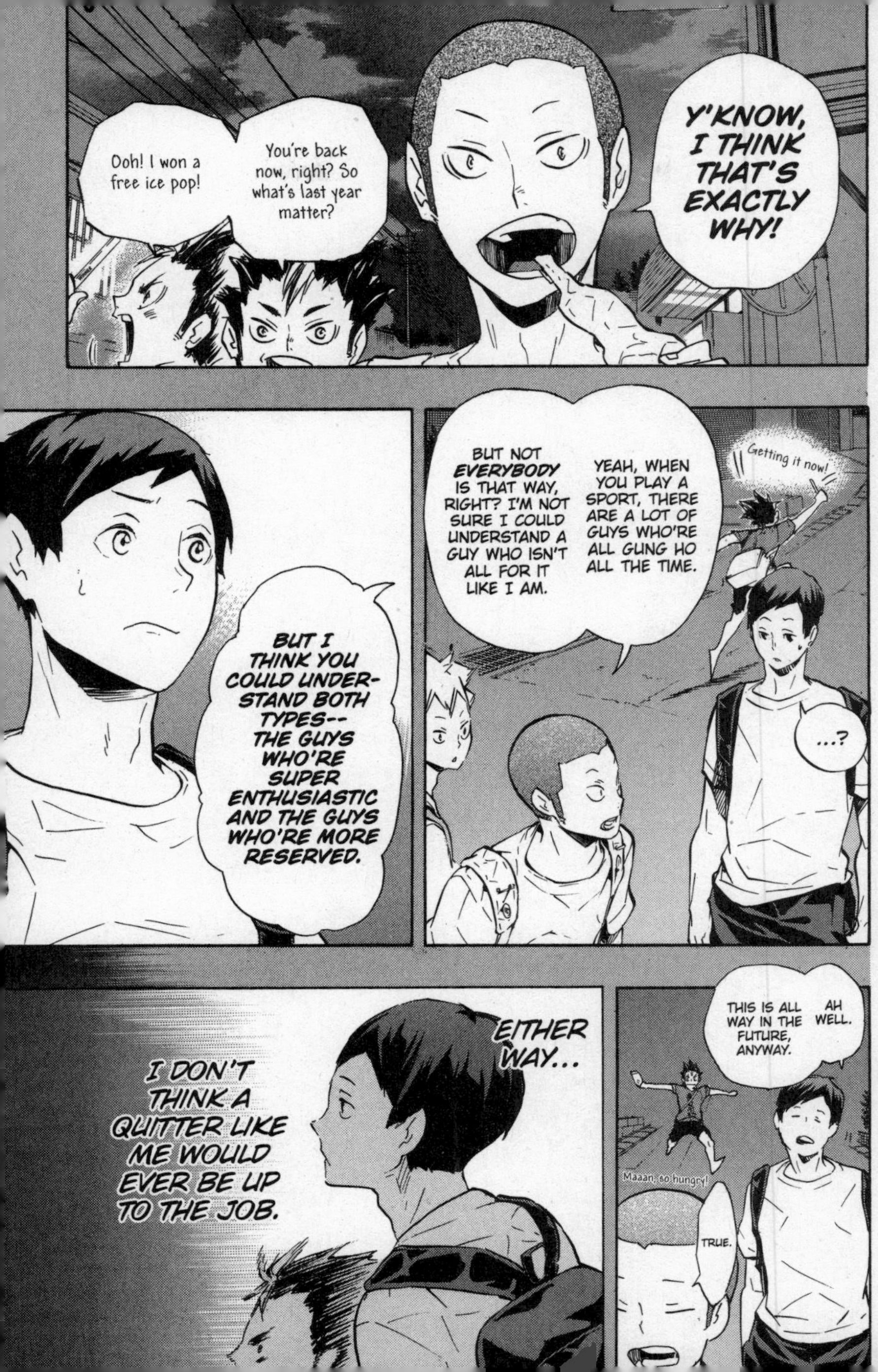

Y'KNOW, I THINK THAT'S EXACTLY WHY!
You're back now, right? So what's last year matter?
Ooh! I won a free ice pop!
Getting it now!
YEAH, WHEN YOU PLAY A SPORT, THERE ARE A LOT OF GUYS WHO'RE ALL GUNG HO ALL THE TIME.
BUT NOT EVERYBODY IS THAT WAY, RIGHT? I'M NOT SURE I COULD UNDERSTAND A GUY WHO ISN'T ALL FOR IT LIKE I AM.
...?
BUT I THINK YOU COULD UNDER-STAND BOTH TYPES-- THE GUYS WHO'RE SUPER ENTHUSIASTIC AND THE GUYS WHO'RE MORE RESERVED.
AH WELL.
THIS IS ALL WAY IN THE FUTURE, ANYWAY.
Maaan, so hungry!
TRUE.
EITHER WAY...
I DON'T THINK A QUITTER LIKE ME WOULD EVER BE UP TO THE JOB.

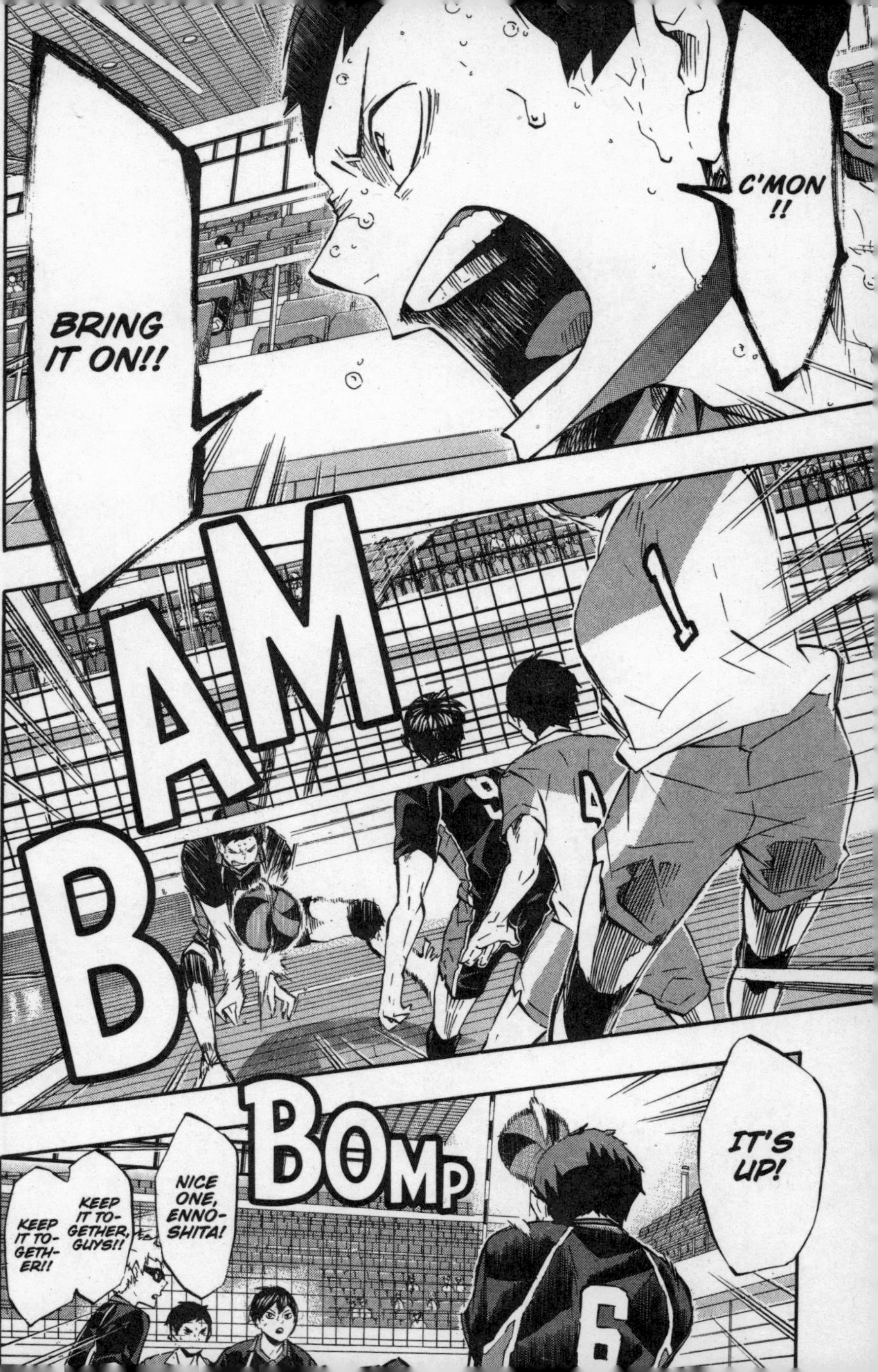
C'MON !!
BRING IT ON!!
BAM
IT'S UP!
BOMP
NICE ONE, ENNO-SHITA!
KEEP IT TO-GETHER, GUYS!!
KEEP IT TO-GETH-ER!!

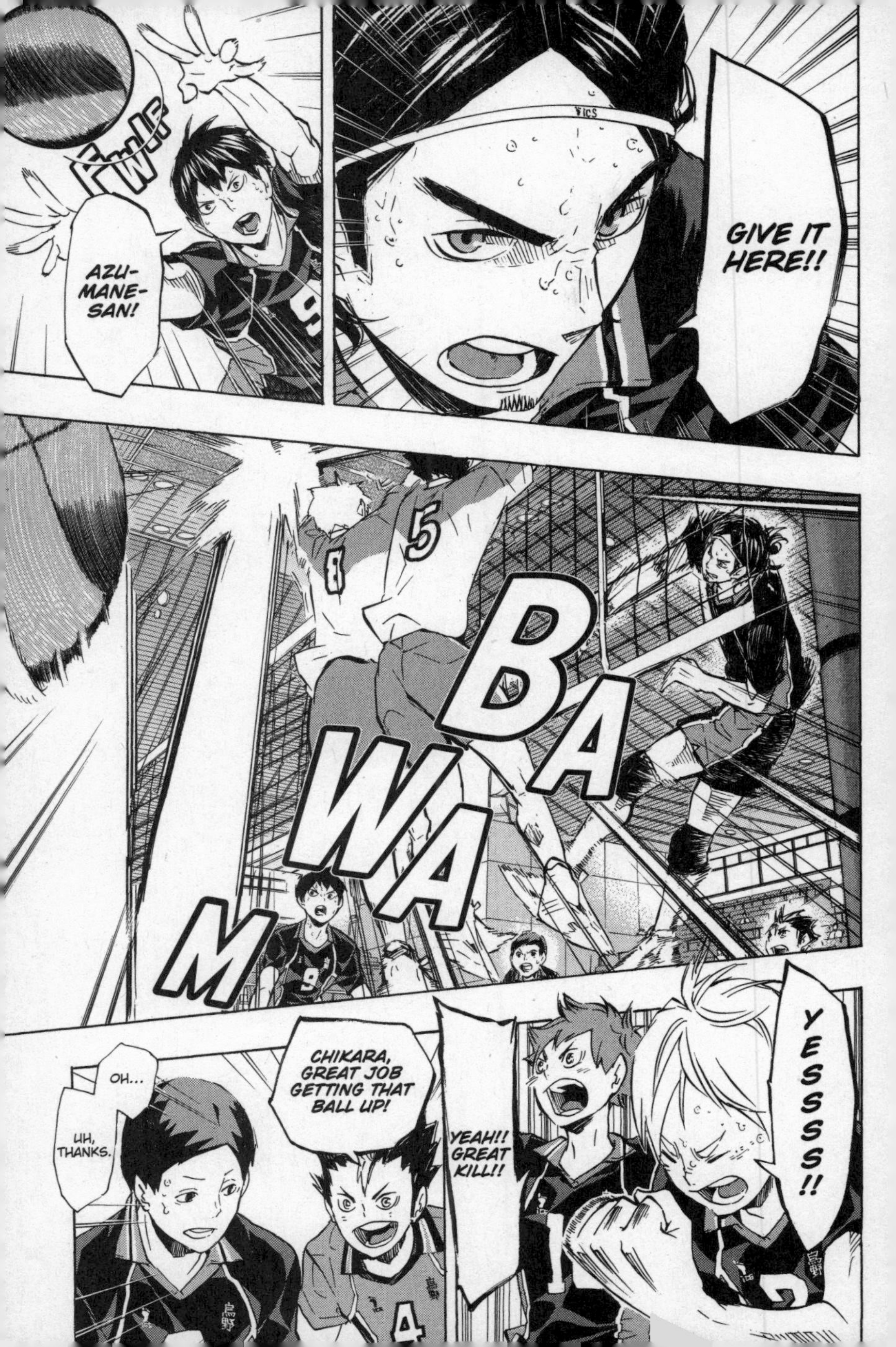
GIVE IT HERE!!
AZU-MANE-SAN!
BAWAM
YESSSS!!
YEAH!! GREAT KILL!!
CHIKARA, GREAT JOB GETTING THAT BALL UP!
OH...
UH, THANKS.

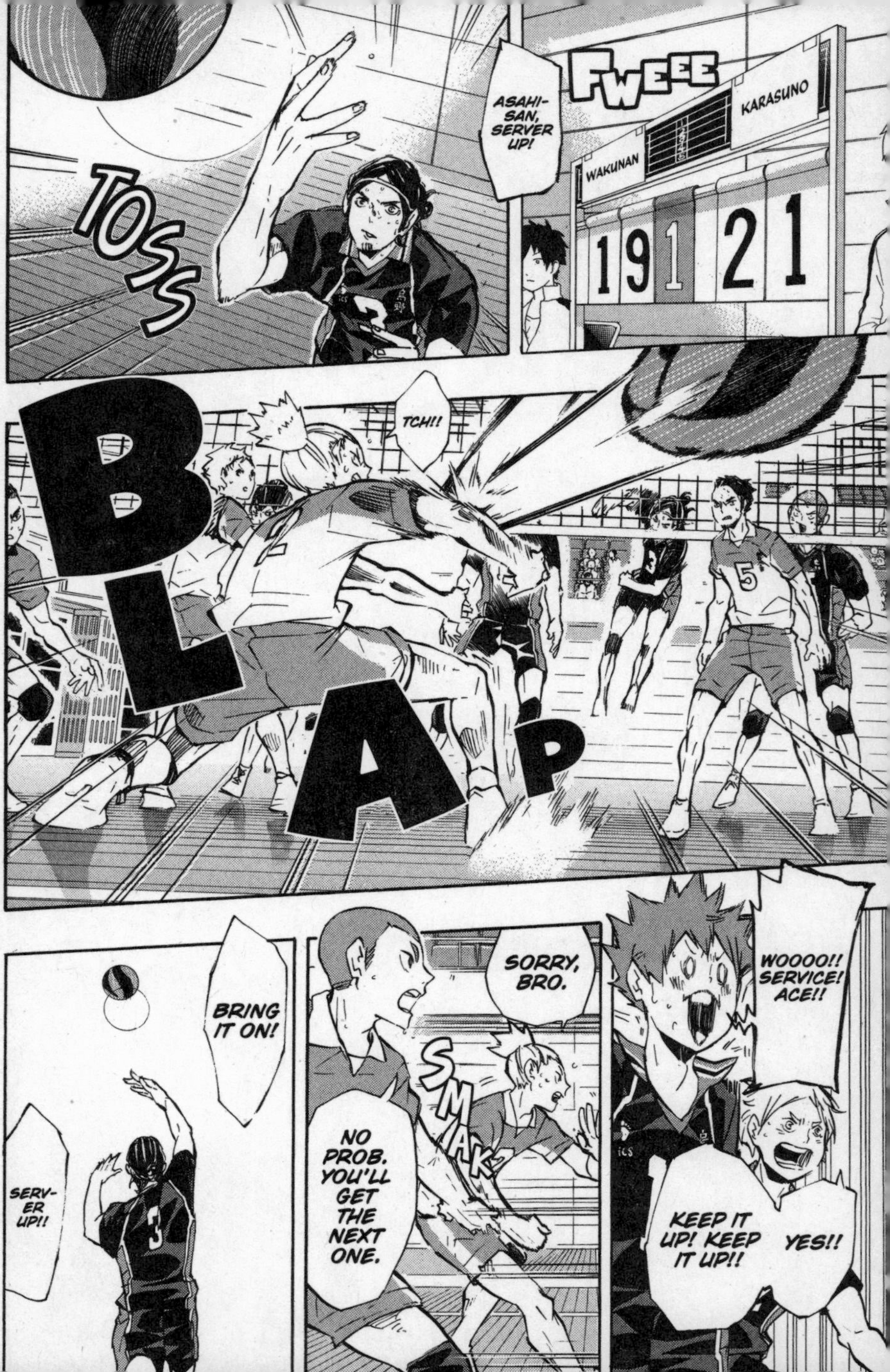
FWEEE
KARASUNO
WAKUNAN
19 1 21 1
ASAHI-SAN, SERVER UP!
TOSS
TCH!!
BLAP
WOOOO!! SERVICE! ACE!!
YES!!
KEEP IT UP! KEEP IT UP!!
SORRY, BRO.
SMAK
NO PROB. YOU'LL GET THE NEXT ONE.
BRING IT ON!
SERV-ER UP!!

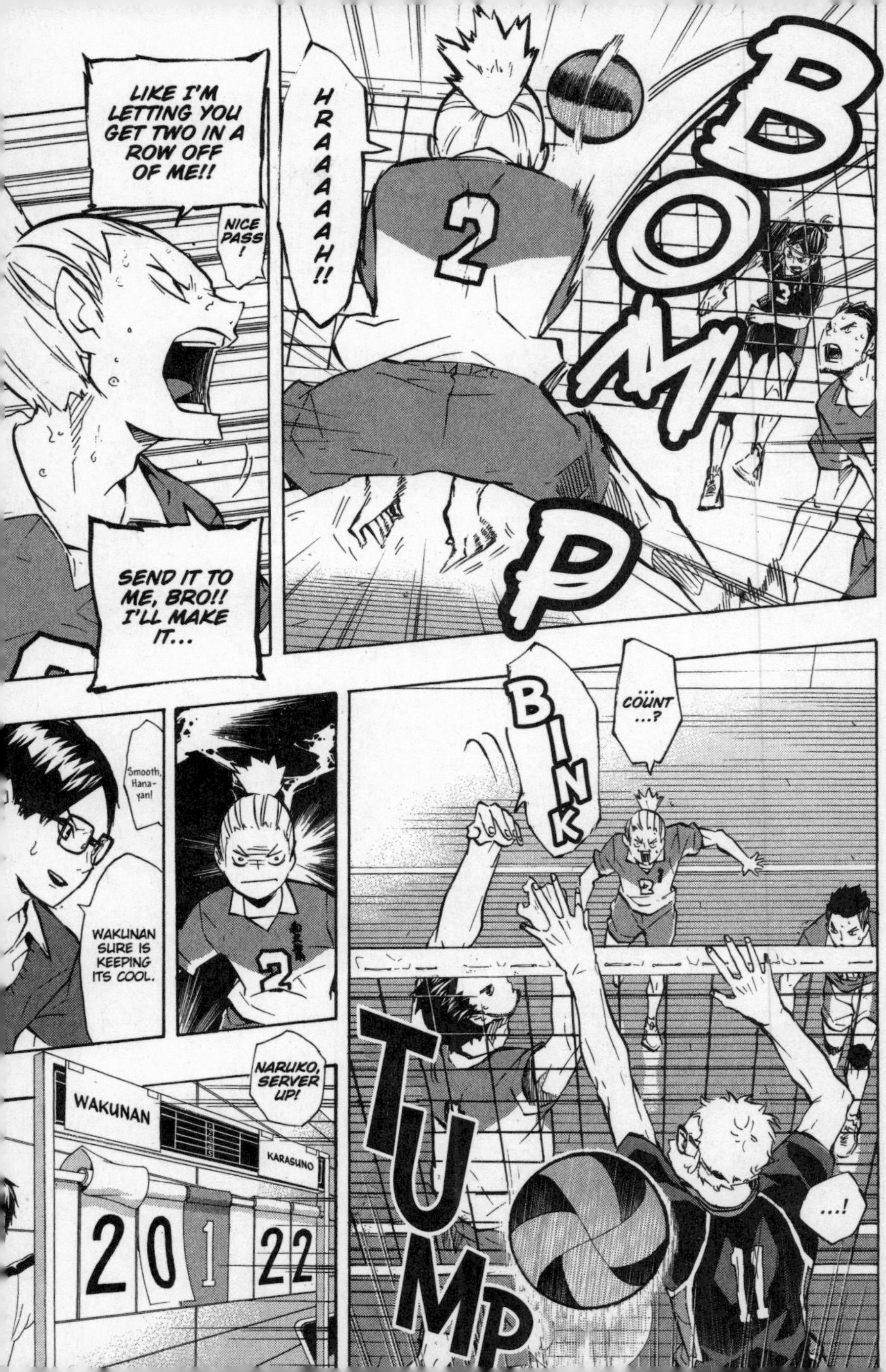

BOOMP
HRAAAAAAH!!
LIKE I'M LETTING YOU GET TWO IN A ROW OFF OF ME!!
NICE PASS!
SEND IT TO ME, BRO!! I'LL MAKE IT...
BINK
...COUNT...?
TUMP
...!
Smooth, Hana-yan!
WAKUNAN SURE IS KEEPING ITS COOL.
NARUKO, SERVER UP!
WAKUNAN
KARASUNO
20
1
22

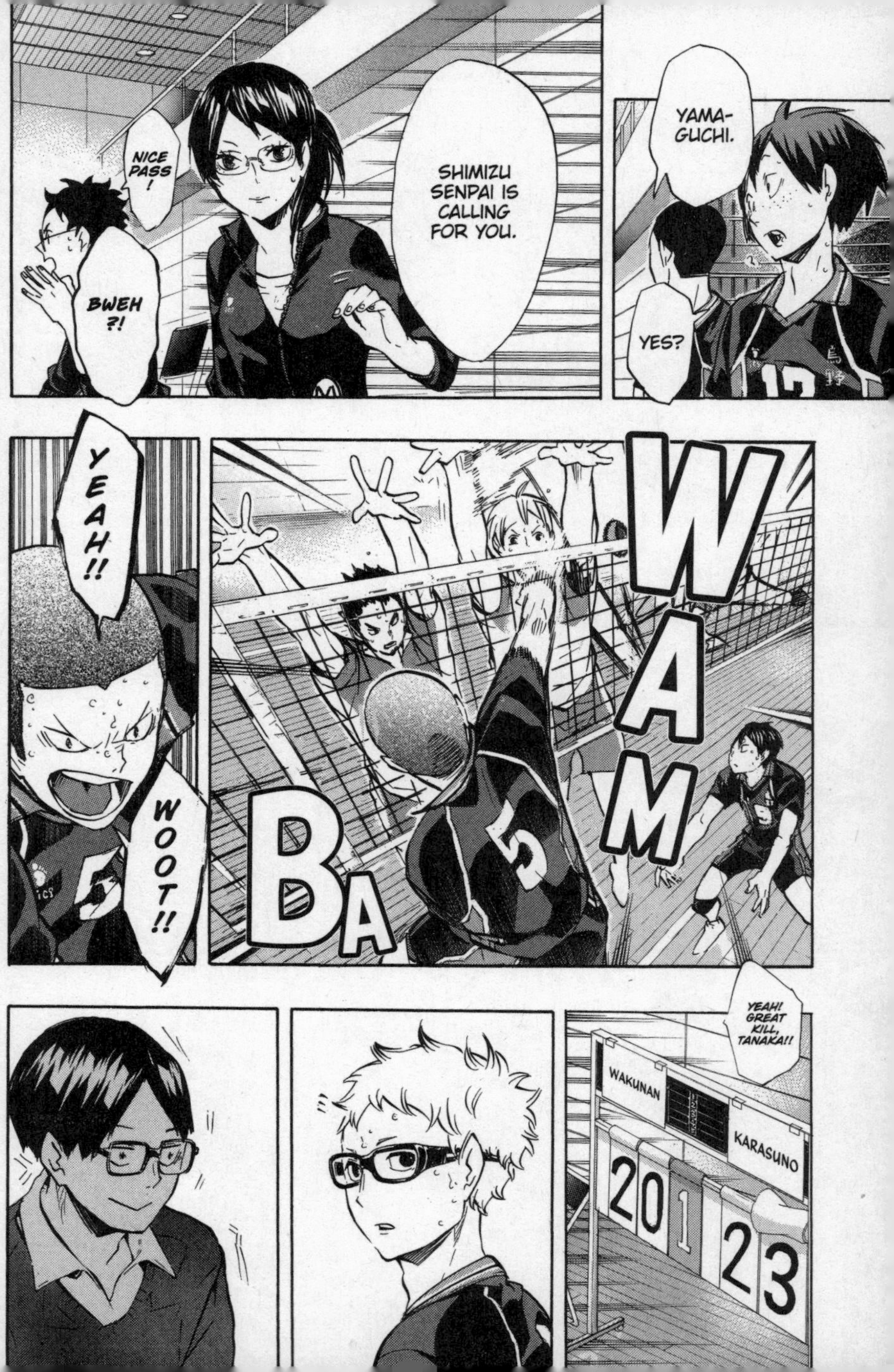
YAMA-GUCHI.
YES?
SHIMIZU SENPAI IS CALLING FOR YOU.
NICE PASS!
BWEH?!
WAM
BA
YEAH!!
WOOT!!
YEAH! GREAT KILL, TANAKA!!
WAKUNAN
KARASUNO
20
23

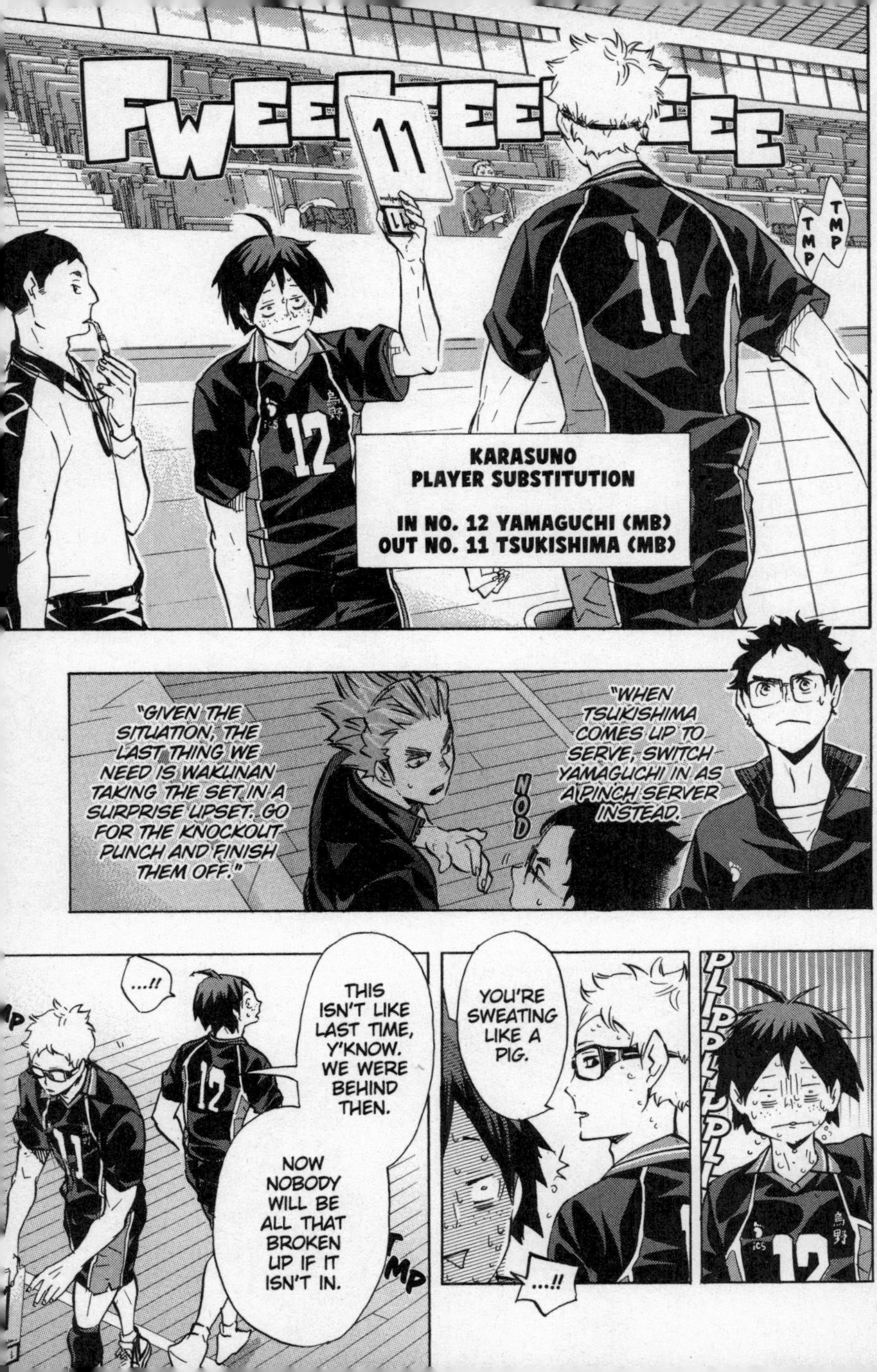
FWEEEEEEEEE
TMP TMP TMP TMP
KARASUNO PLAYER SUBSTITUTION
IN NO. 12 YAMAGUCHI (MB)
OUT NO. 11 TSUKISHIMA (MB)
"WHEN TSUKISHIMA COMES UP TO SERVE, SWITCH YAMAGUCHI IN AS A PINCH SERVER INSTEAD.
NOD
"GIVEN THE SITUATION, THE LAST THING WE NEED IS WAKUNAN TAKING THE SET IN A SURPRISE UPSET. GO FOR THE KNOCKOUT PUNCH AND FINISH THEM OFF."
PLIPPLIPPLI
YOU'RE SWEATING LIKE A PIG.
...!!
...!!
THIS ISN'T LIKE LAST TIME, Y'KNOW. WE WERE BEHIND THEN.
NOW NOBODY WILL BE ALL THAT BROKEN UP IF IT ISN'T IN.
TMP

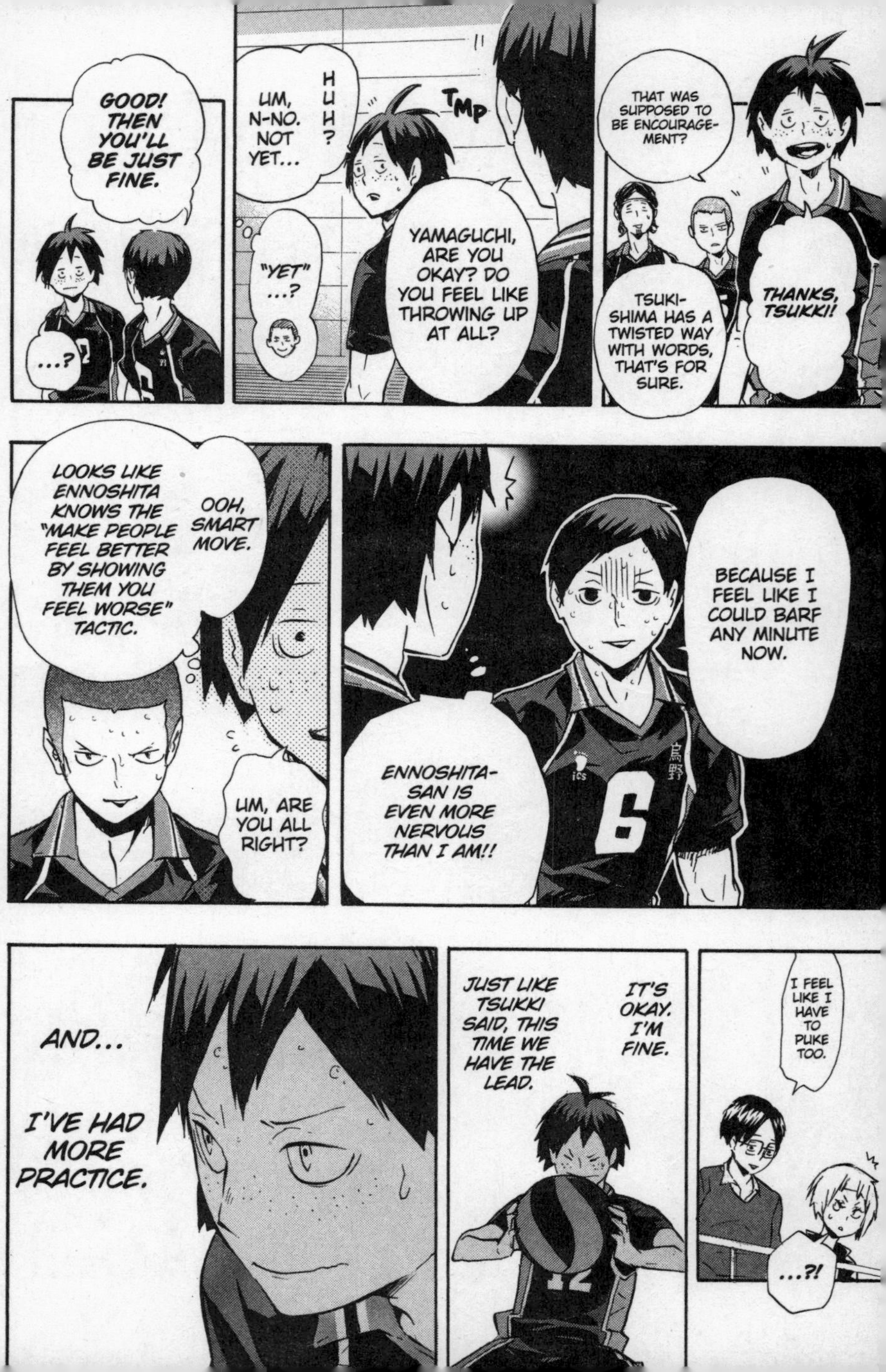
THANKS, TSUKKI!
THAT WAS SUPPOSED TO BE ENCOURAGE-MENT?
TSUKI-SHIMA HAS A TWISTED WAY WITH WORDS, THAT'S FOR SURE.
TMP
YAMAGUCHI, ARE YOU OKAY? DO YOU FEEL LIKE THROWING UP AT ALL?
HUH?
UM, N-NO. NOT YET...
"YET" ...?
GOOD! THEN YOU'LL BE JUST FINE.
...?
BECAUSE I FEEL LIKE I COULD BARF ANY MINUTE NOW.
ENNOSHITA-SAN IS EVEN MORE NERVOUS THAN I AM!!
OOH, SMART MOVE.
LOOKS LIKE ENNOSHITA KNOWS THE "MAKE PEOPLE FEEL BETTER BY SHOWING THEM YOU FEEL WORSE" TACTIC.
UM, ARE YOU ALL RIGHT?
I FEEL LIKE I HAVE TO PUKE TOO.
...?!
IT'S OKAY. I'M FINE.
JUST LIKE TSUKKI SAID, THIS TIME WE HAVE THE LEAD.
AND...
I'VE HAD MORE PRACTICE.

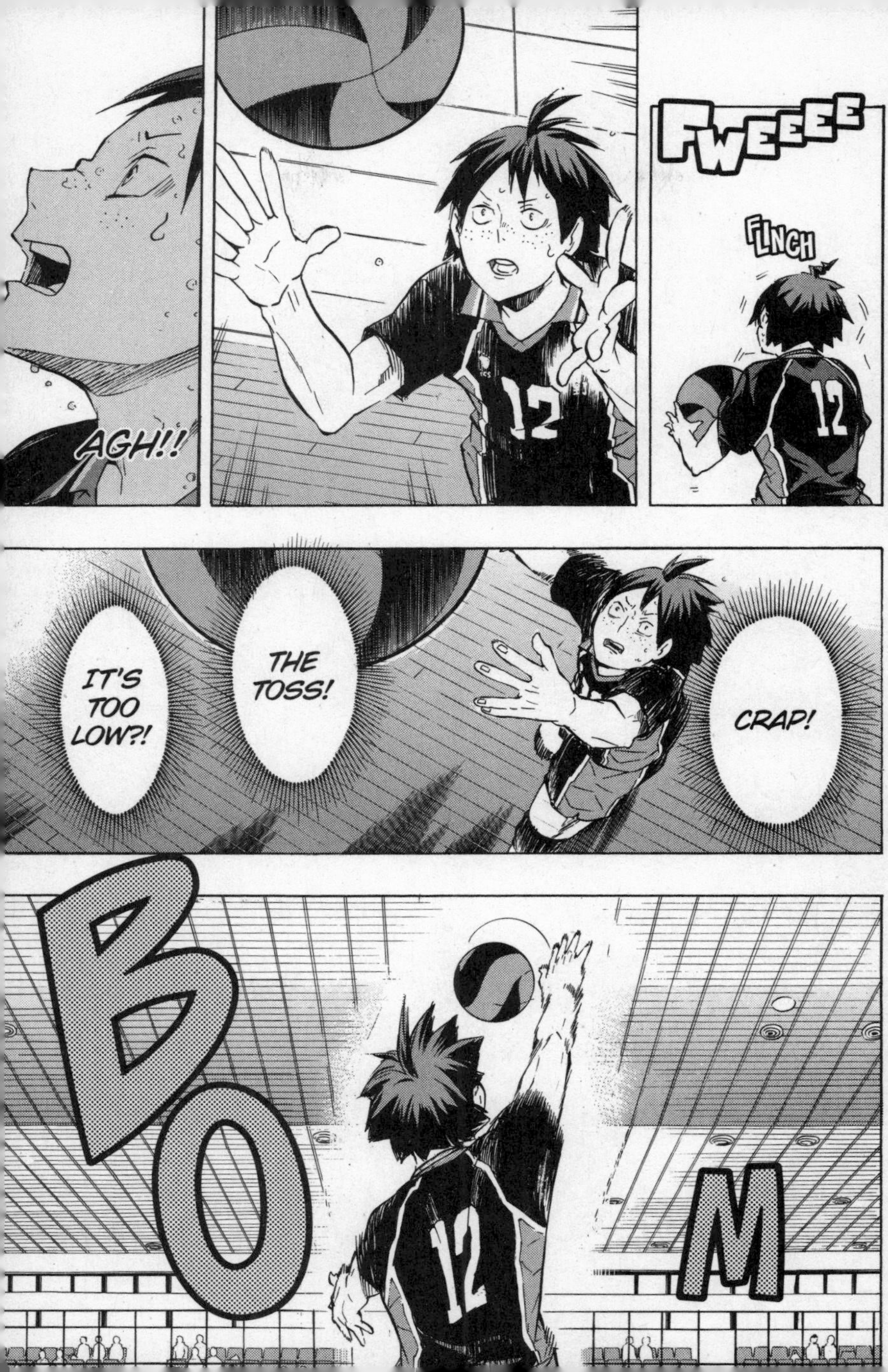
FWEEEE
FLINCH
AGH!!
CRAP!
THE TOSS!
IT'S TOO LOW?!
BOOM

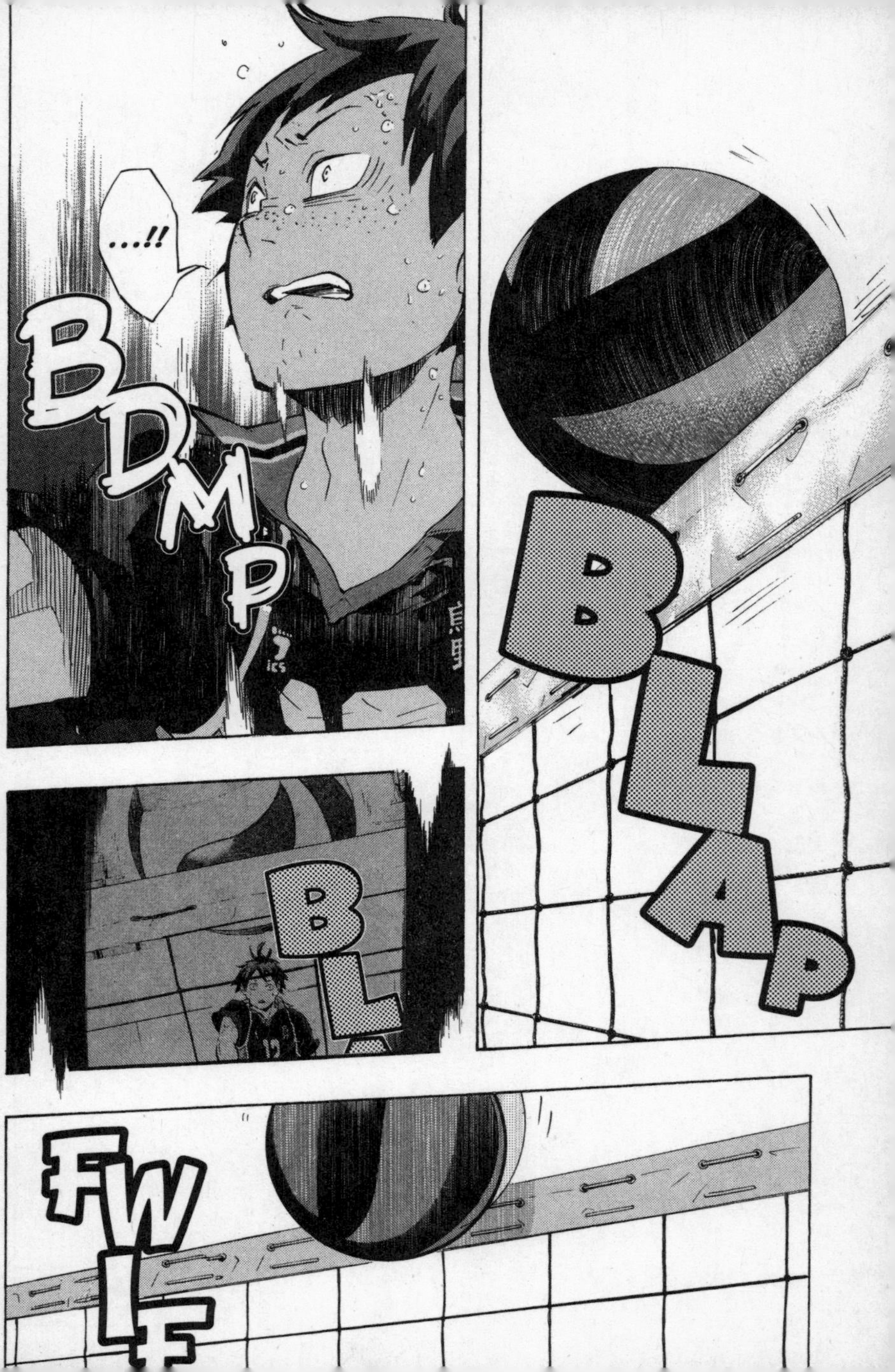
BLAP
...!!
BDMP
BLA
FWIF

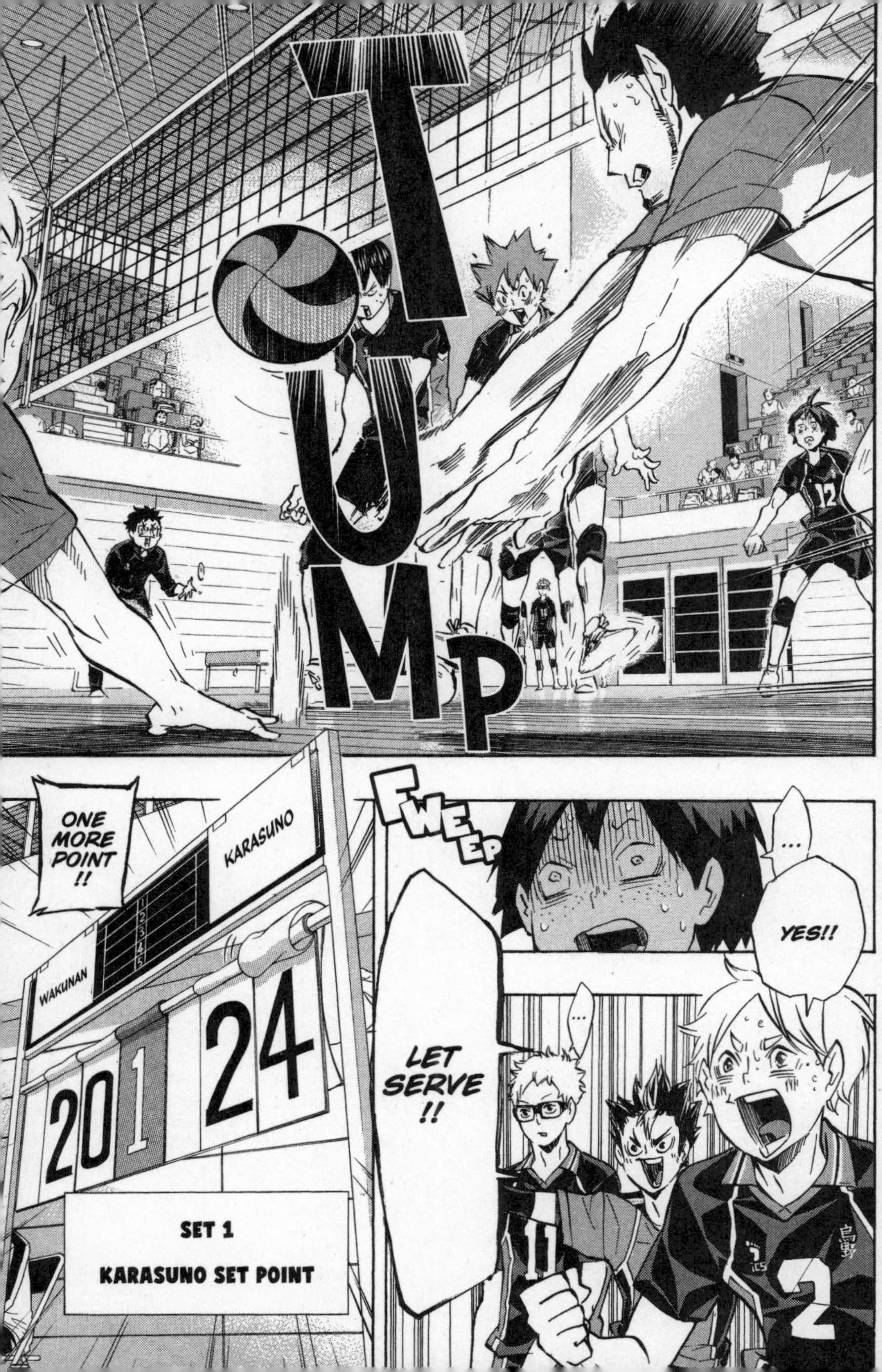
JUMP
FWEEP
...
YES!!
LET SERVE!!
...
ONE MORE POINT!!
KARASUNO
WAKUNAN
20
1
24
SET 1
KARASUNO SET POINT

DURING THE SUMMER OF MY
SECOND YEAR OF HIGH SCHOOL,
I SKIPPED VOLLEYBALL PRACTICE
ONCE. TO MY TEAM AND MY
COACH FROM THEN…I'M SORRY.

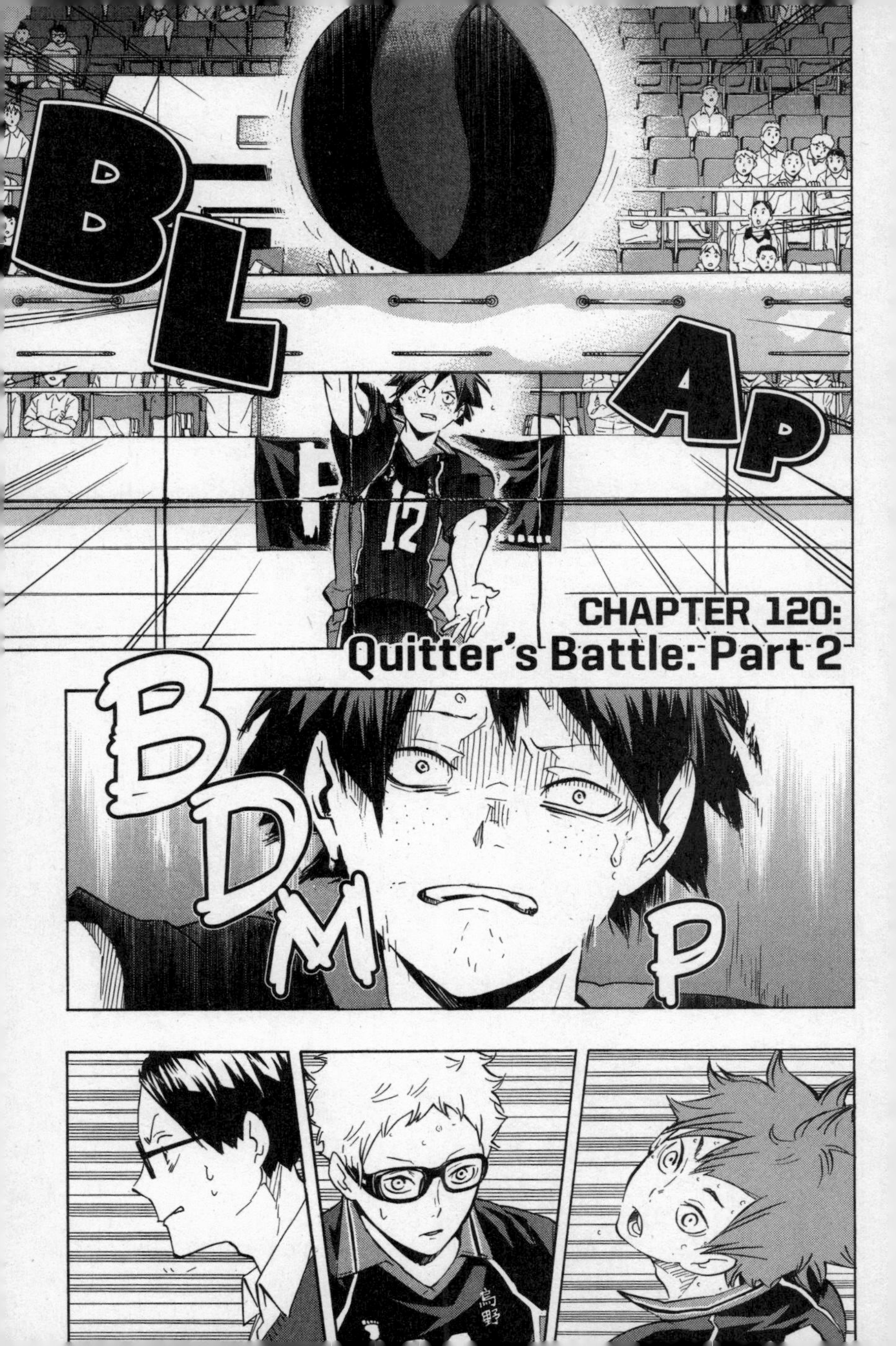

BLAP
CHAPTER 120:
Quitter's Battle: Part 2
BDMP

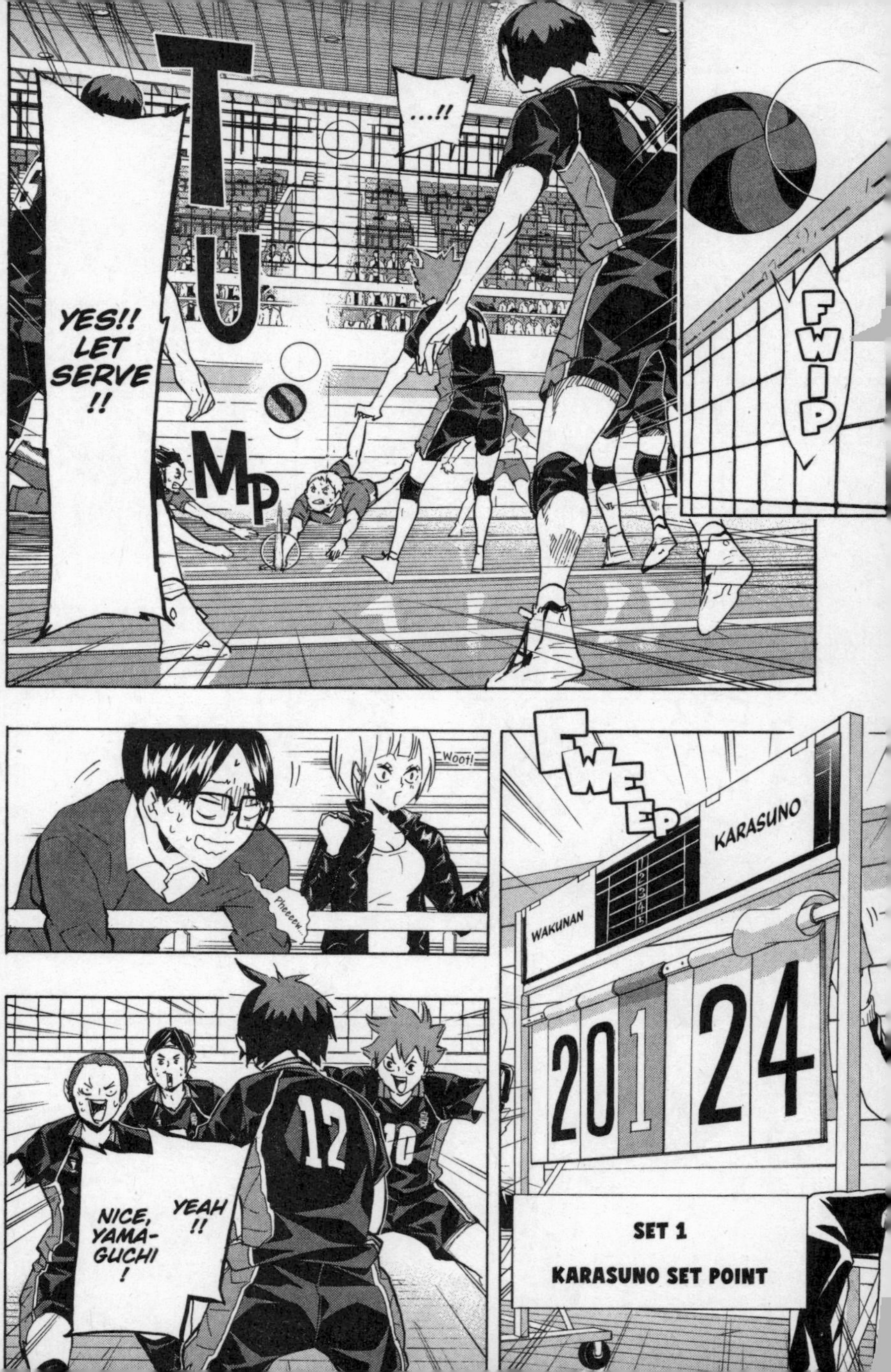
FWIP
...!!
TUMP
YES!! LET SERVE !!
FWEEP
KARASUNO
WAKUNAN
20 1 24
SET 1
KARASUNO SET POINT
Woot!
Pheeew...
YEAH !!
NICE, YAMA-GUCHI !

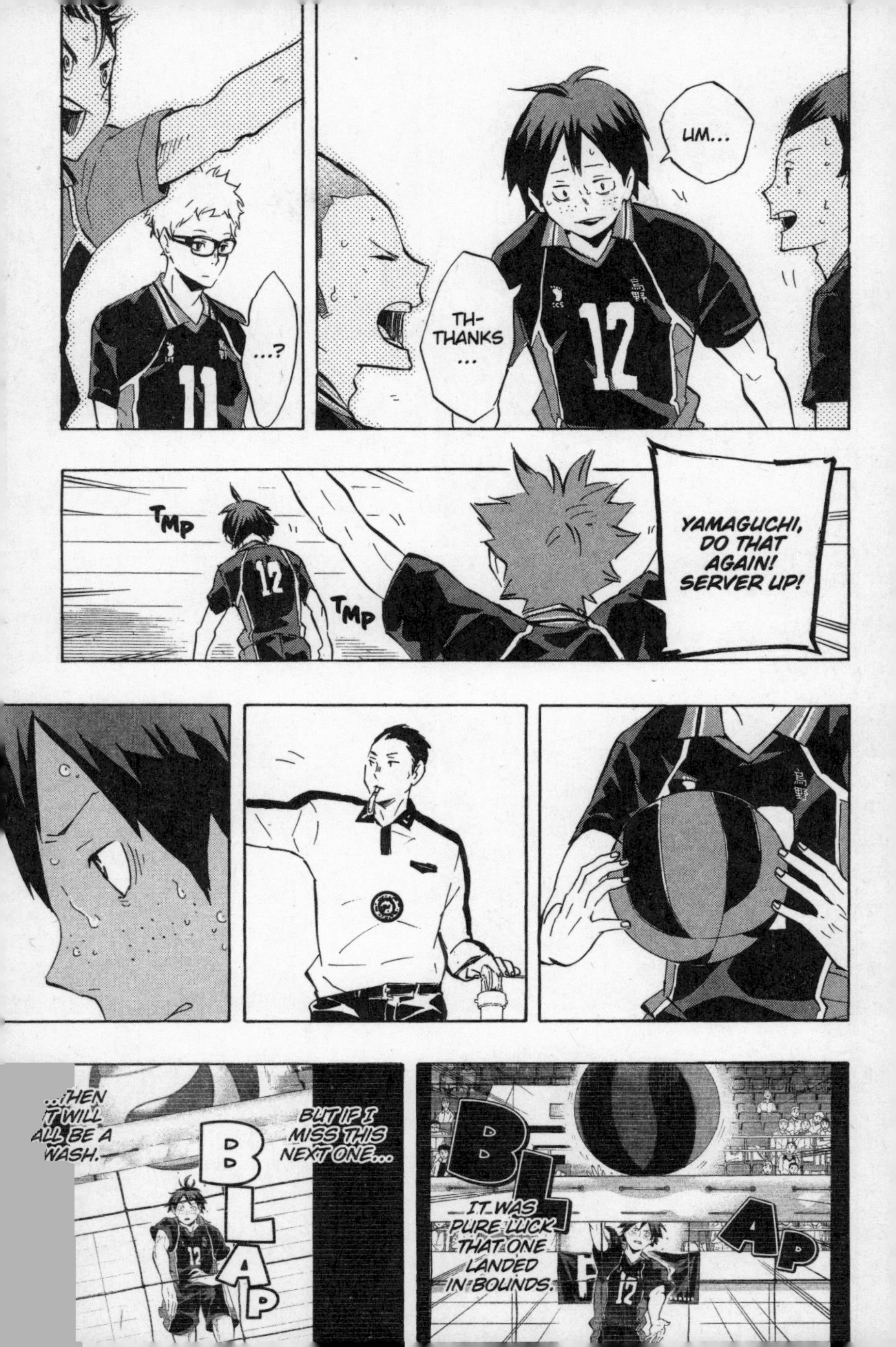
UM...
TH- THANKS ...
...?
YAMAGUCHI, DO THAT AGAIN! SERVER UP!
TMP
TMP
BLAP
IT WAS PURE LUCK THAT ONE LANDED IN BOUNDS.
BUT IF I MISS THIS NEXT ONE...
...THEN IT WILL ALL BE A WASH.
BLAP

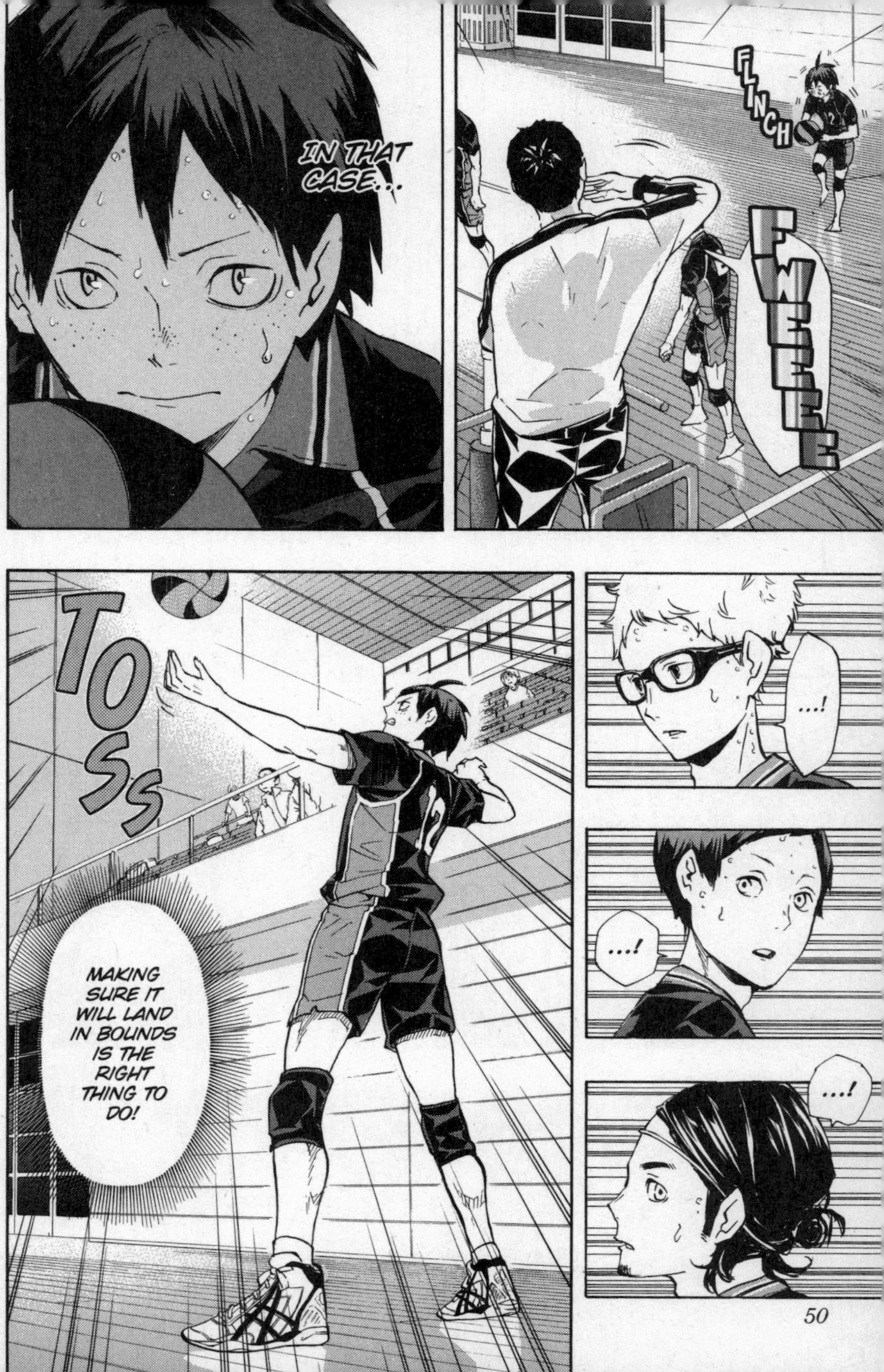
FLINCH
FWEEEE
IN THAT CASE...
...!
...!
...!
TOSS
MAKING SURE IT WILL LAND IN BOUNDS IS THE RIGHT THING TO DO!

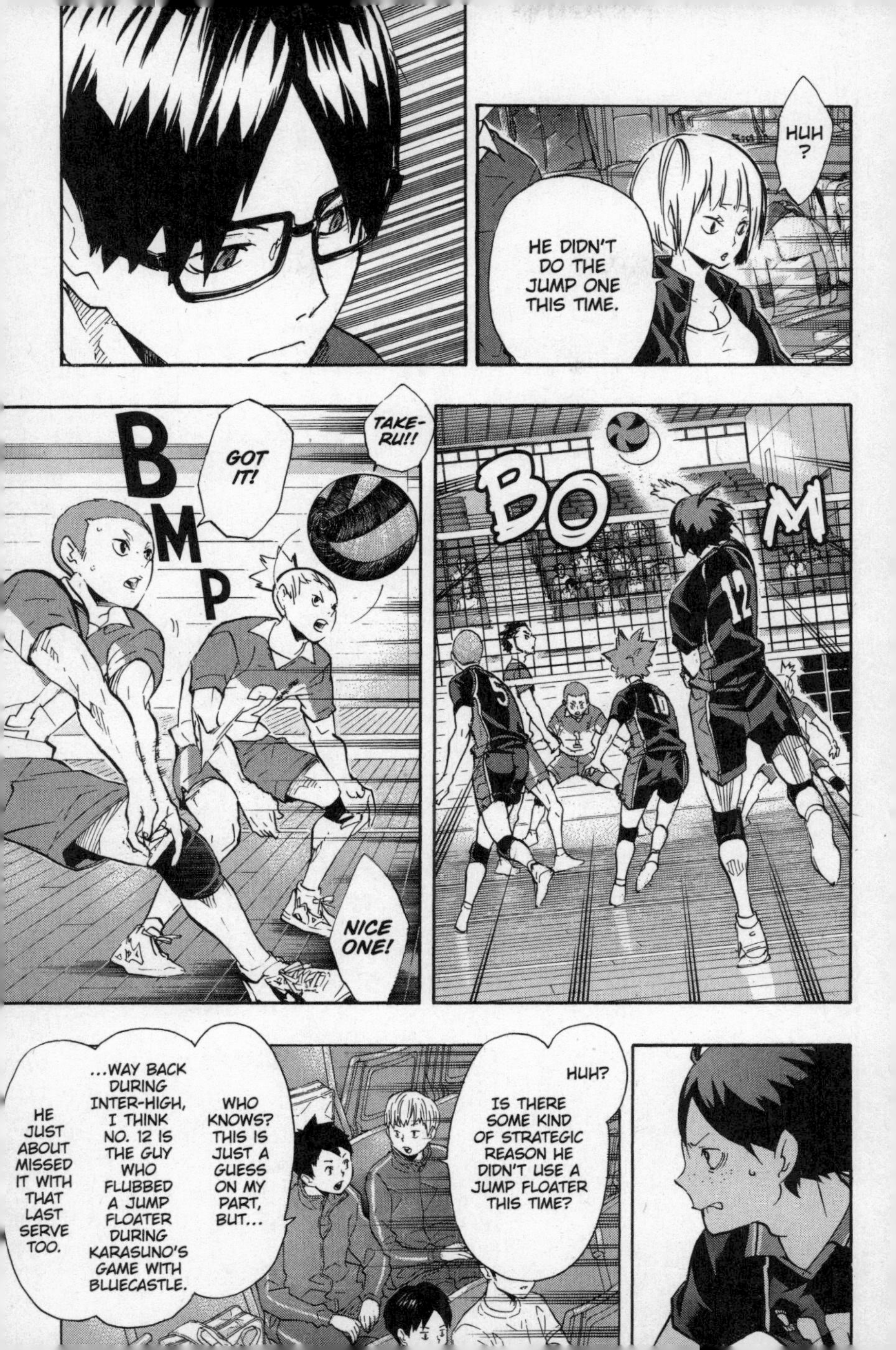
HUH?
HE DIDN'T DO THE JUMP ONE THIS TIME.
BOM
TAKE-RU!!
GOT IT!
BMP
NICE ONE!
HUH?
IS THERE SOME KIND OF STRATEGIC REASON HE DIDN'T USE A JUMP FLOATER THIS TIME?
WHO KNOWS? THIS IS JUST A GUESS ON MY PART, BUT...
...WAY BACK DURING INTER-HIGH, I THINK NO. 12 IS THE GUY WHO FLUBBED A JUMP FLOATER DURING KARASUNO'S GAME WITH BLUECASTLE.
HE JUST ABOUT MISSED IT WITH THAT LAST SERVE TOO.

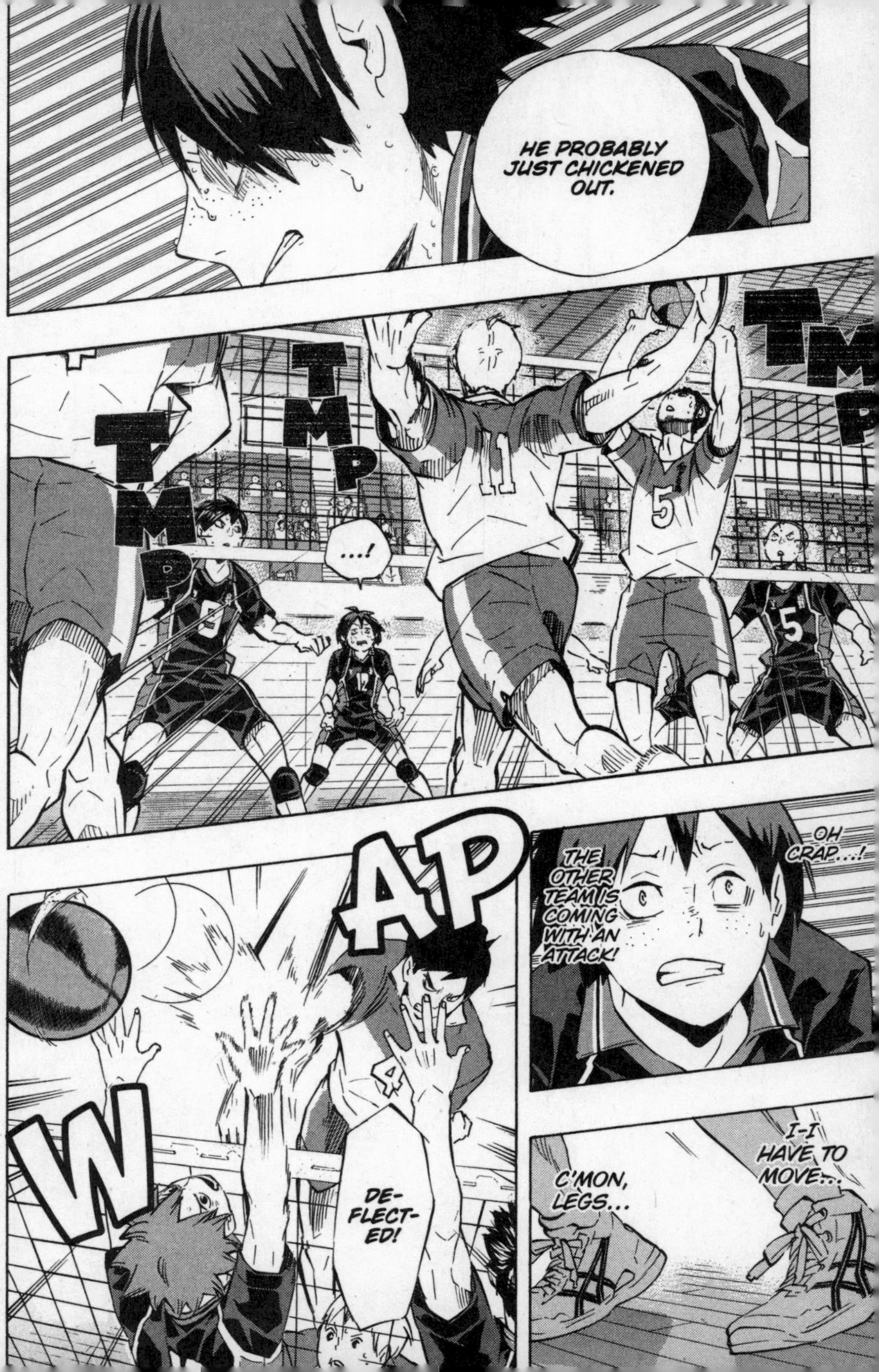
HE PROBABLY JUST CHICKENED OUT.
TMP
TMP
TMP
...!
OH CRAP...!
THE OTHER TEAM IS COMING WITH AN ATTACK!
I-I HAVE TO MOVE...
C'MON, LEGS...
WHAP
DE-FLECTED!

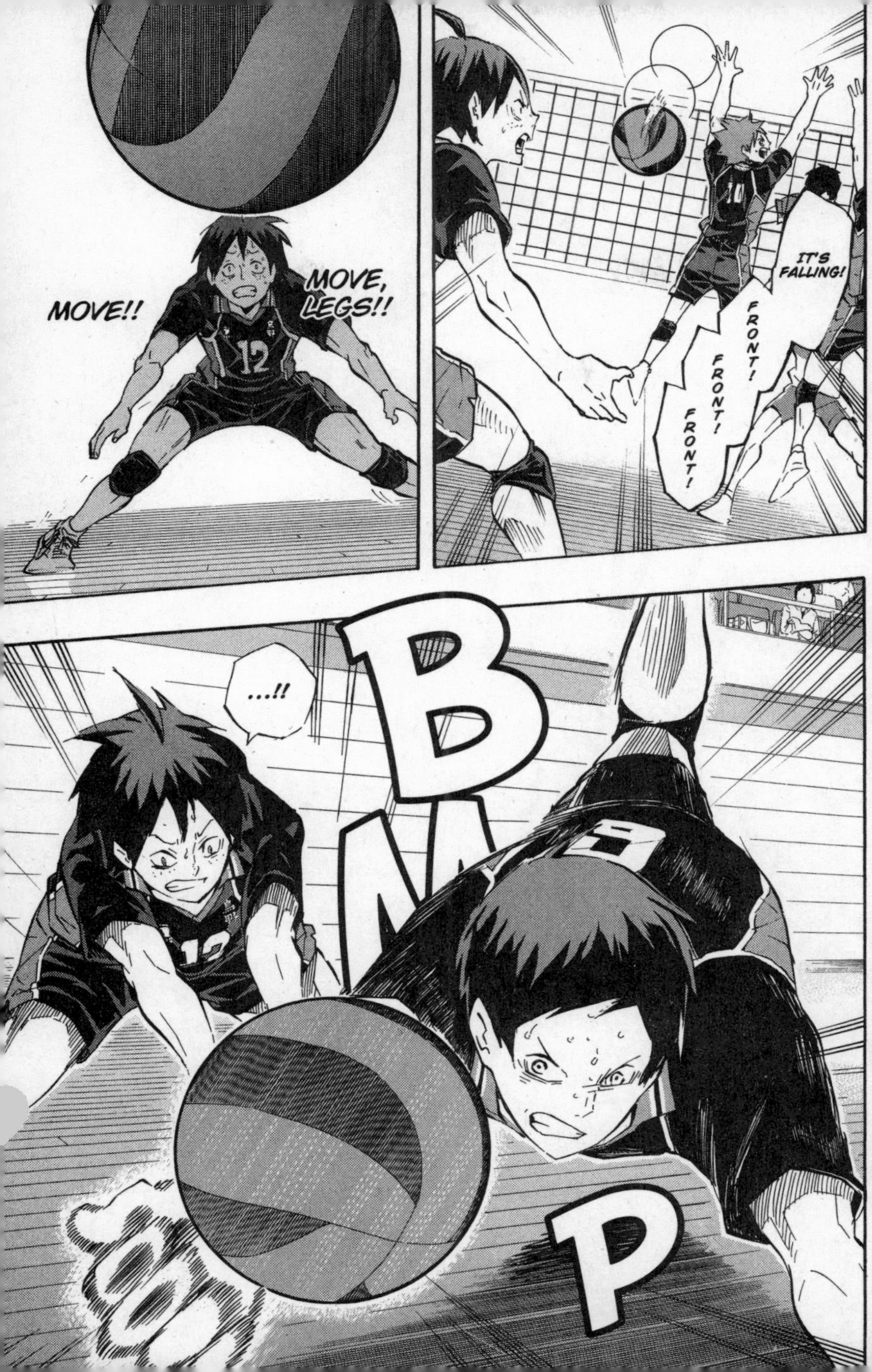
IT'S FALLING!
FRONT! FRONT! FRONT!
MOVE, LEGS!!
MOVE!!
BMP
...!!

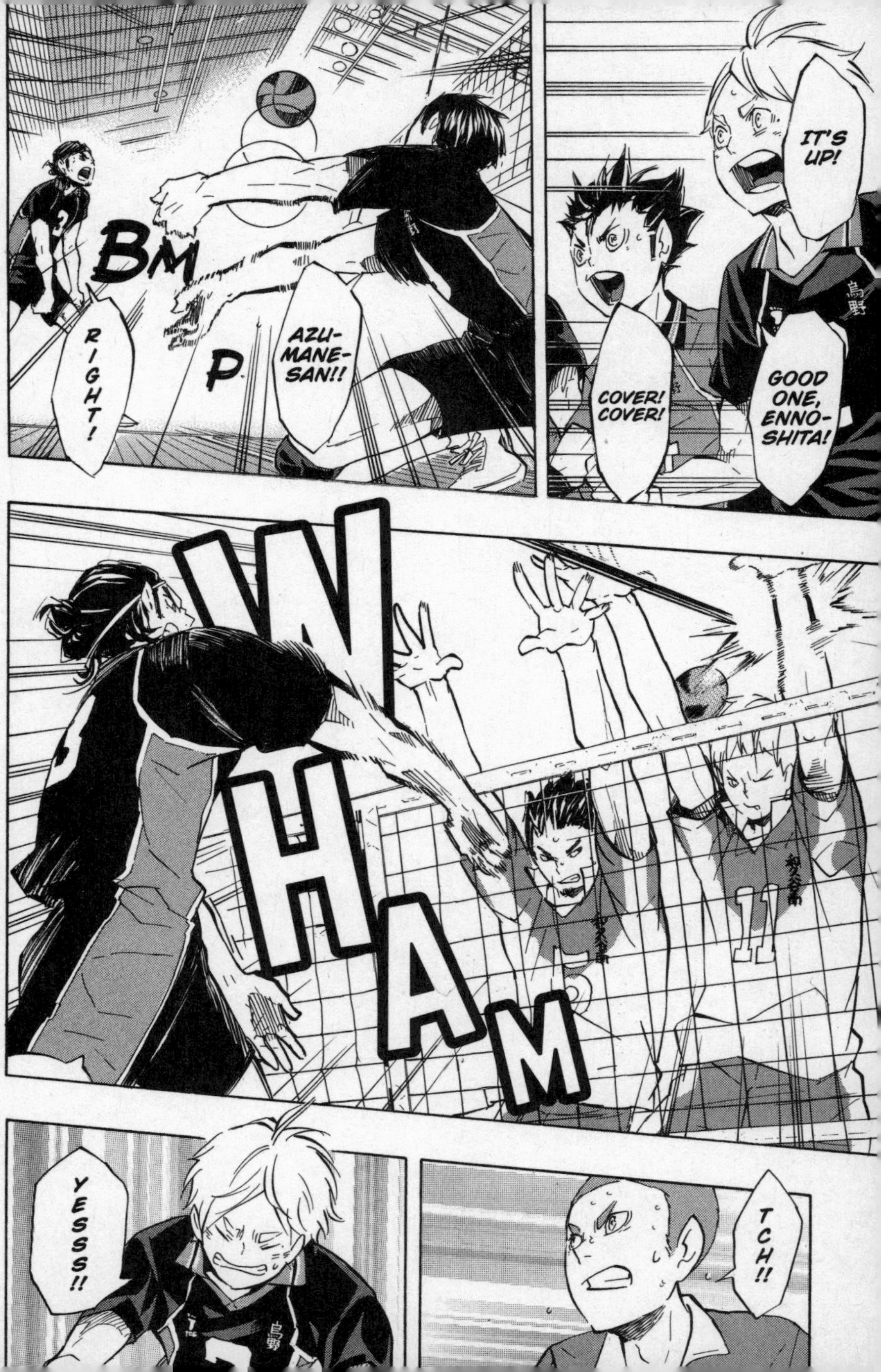
IT'S UP!
GOOD ONE, ENNOSHITA!
COVER! COVER!
AZUMANE-SAN!!
BMP
RIGHT!
WHAM
TCH!!
YESSS!!

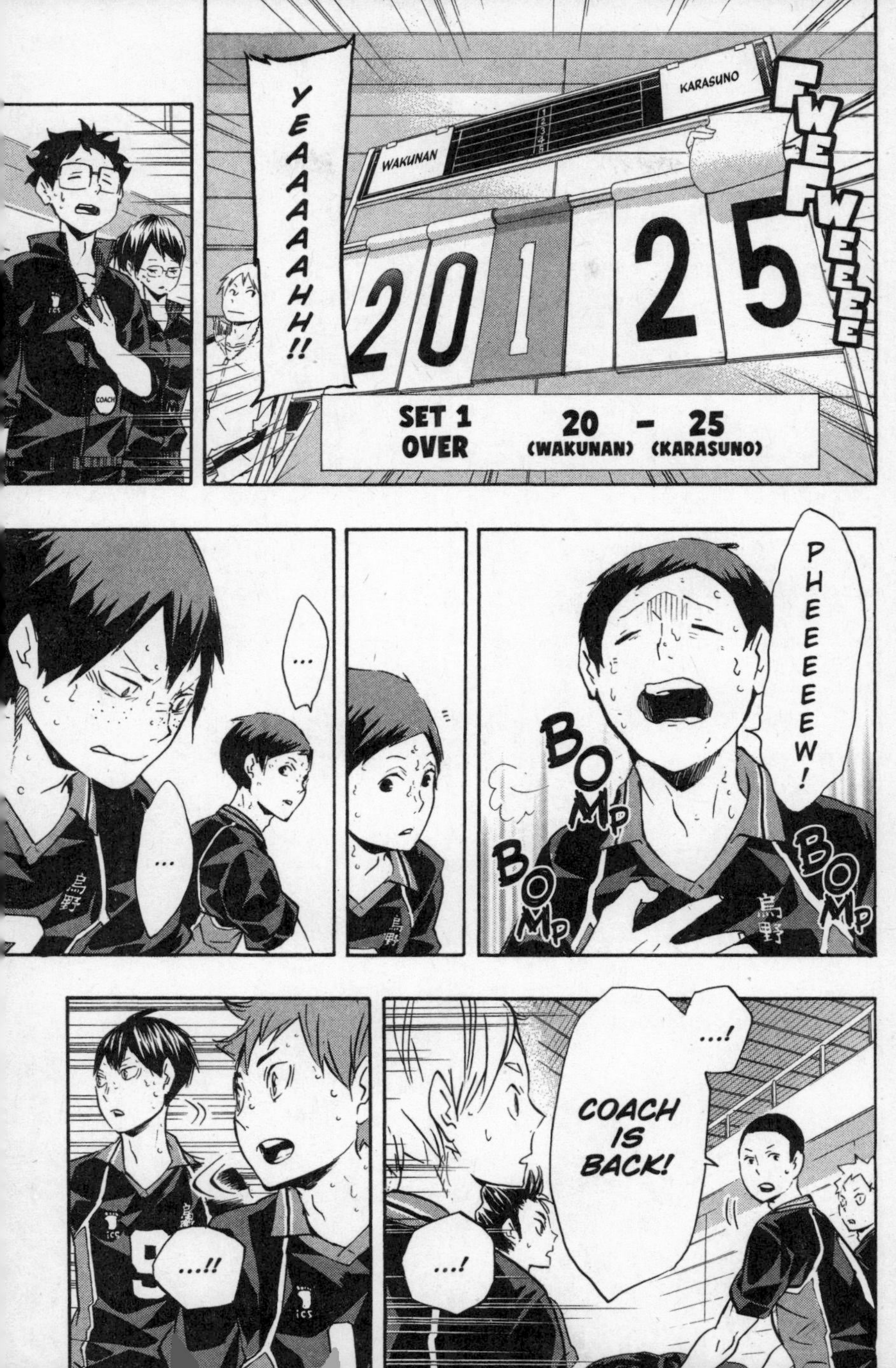

KARASUNO
WAKUNAN
1
2
3
4
5
20
1
25
FWE FWEEEE
YEAAAAAAHH!!
SET 1 OVER 20 - 25 (WAKUNAN) (KARASUNO)
COACH
PHEEEEEEW!
BOMP BOMP BOMP
...
...
...!
COACH IS BACK!
...!
...!!

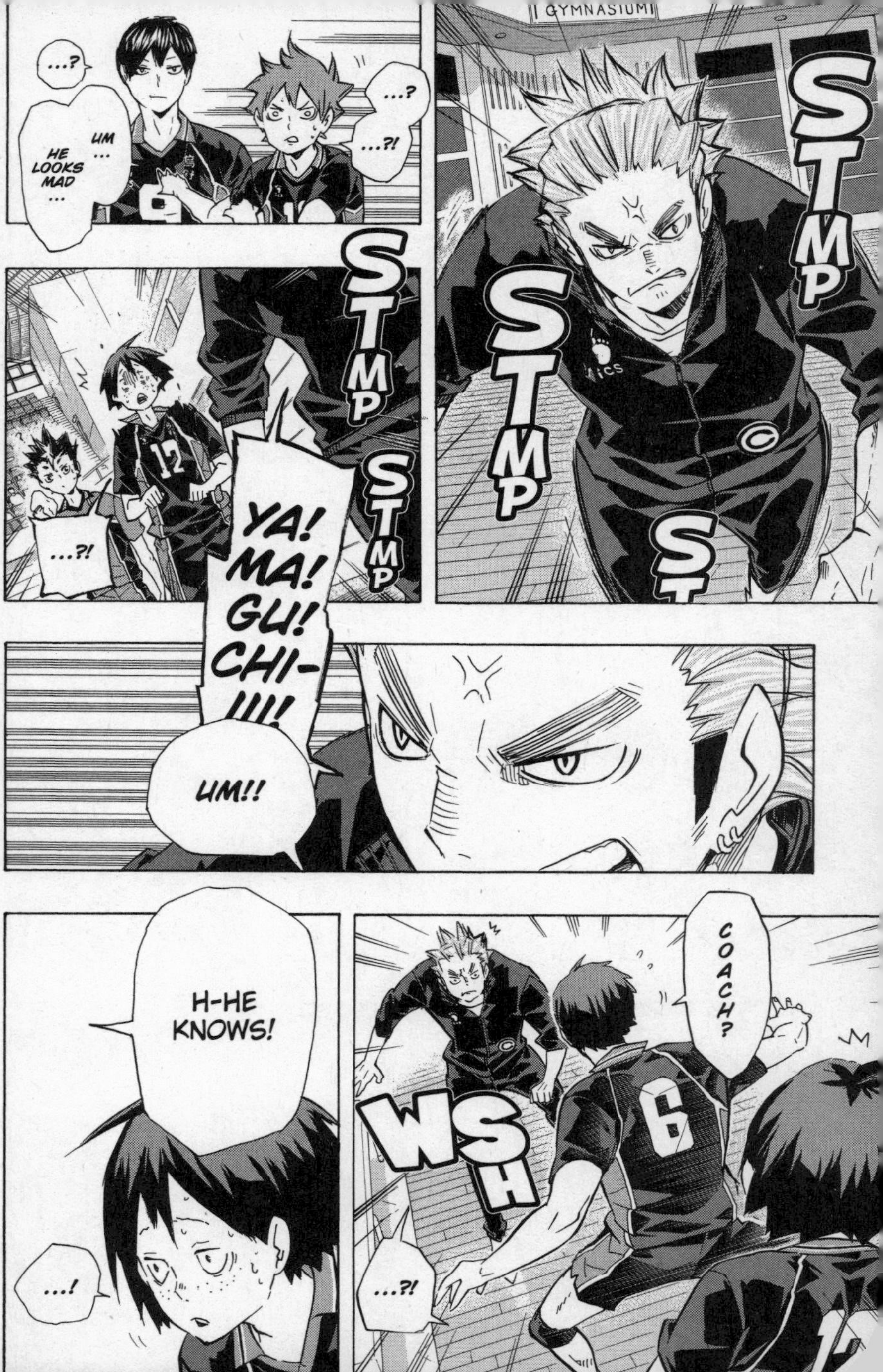
GYMNASIUM
STMP
STMP
ST
...?
...?!
...?
UM ... HE LOOKS MAD ...
STMP
STMP
YA! MA! GU! CHI-!!!!
...?!
UM!!
COACH?
WSH
...?!
H-HE KNOWS!
...!

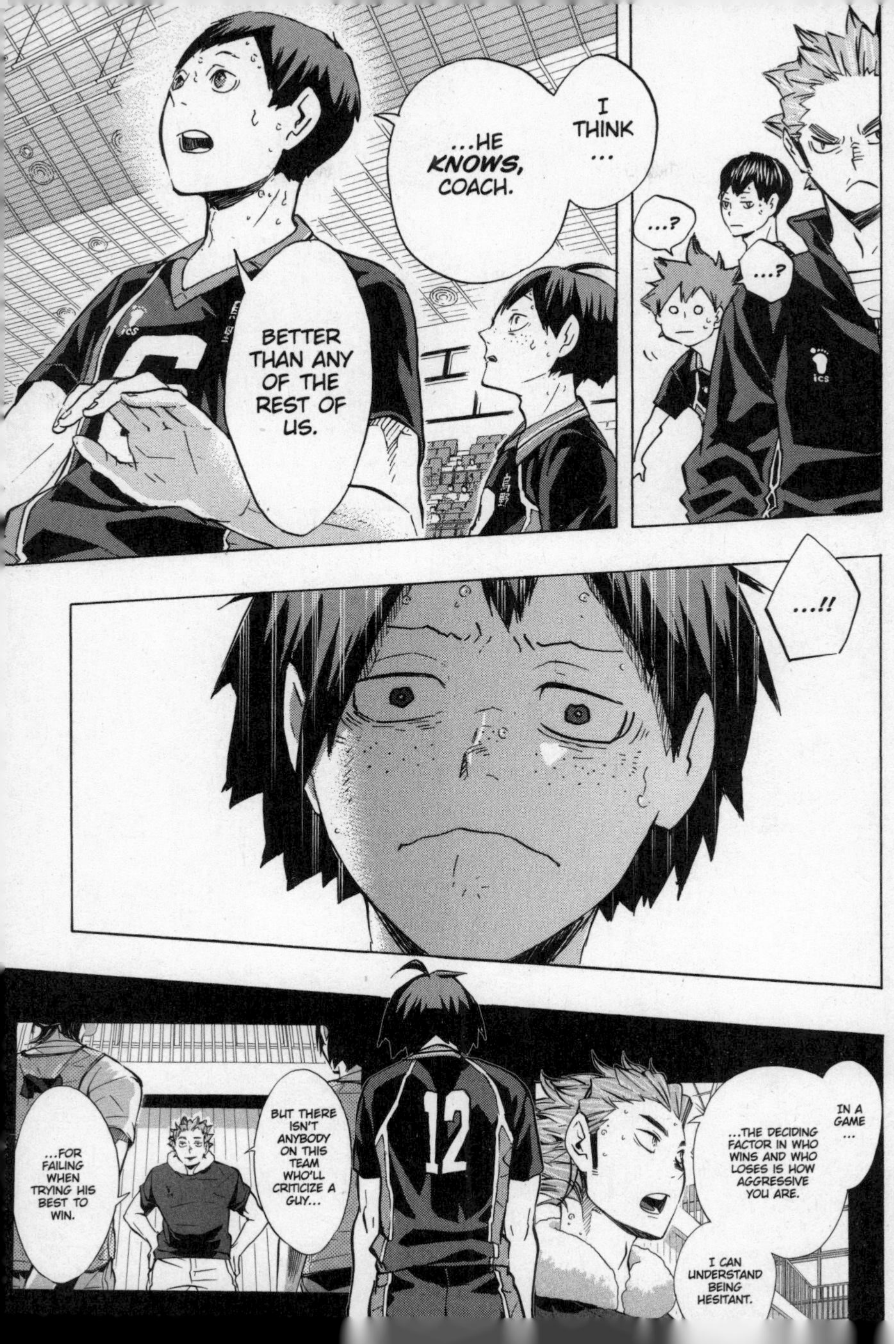
...?
...?
I THINK ...
...HE *KNOWS*, COACH.
BETTER THAN ANY OF THE REST OF US.
...!!
IN A GAME ...
...THE DECIDING FACTOR IN WHO WINS AND WHO LOSES IS HOW AGGRESSIVE YOU ARE.
I CAN UNDERSTAND BEING HESITANT.
BUT THERE ISN'T ANYBODY ON THIS TEAM WHO'LL CRITICIZE A GUY...
...FOR FAILING WHEN TRYING HIS BEST TO WIN.

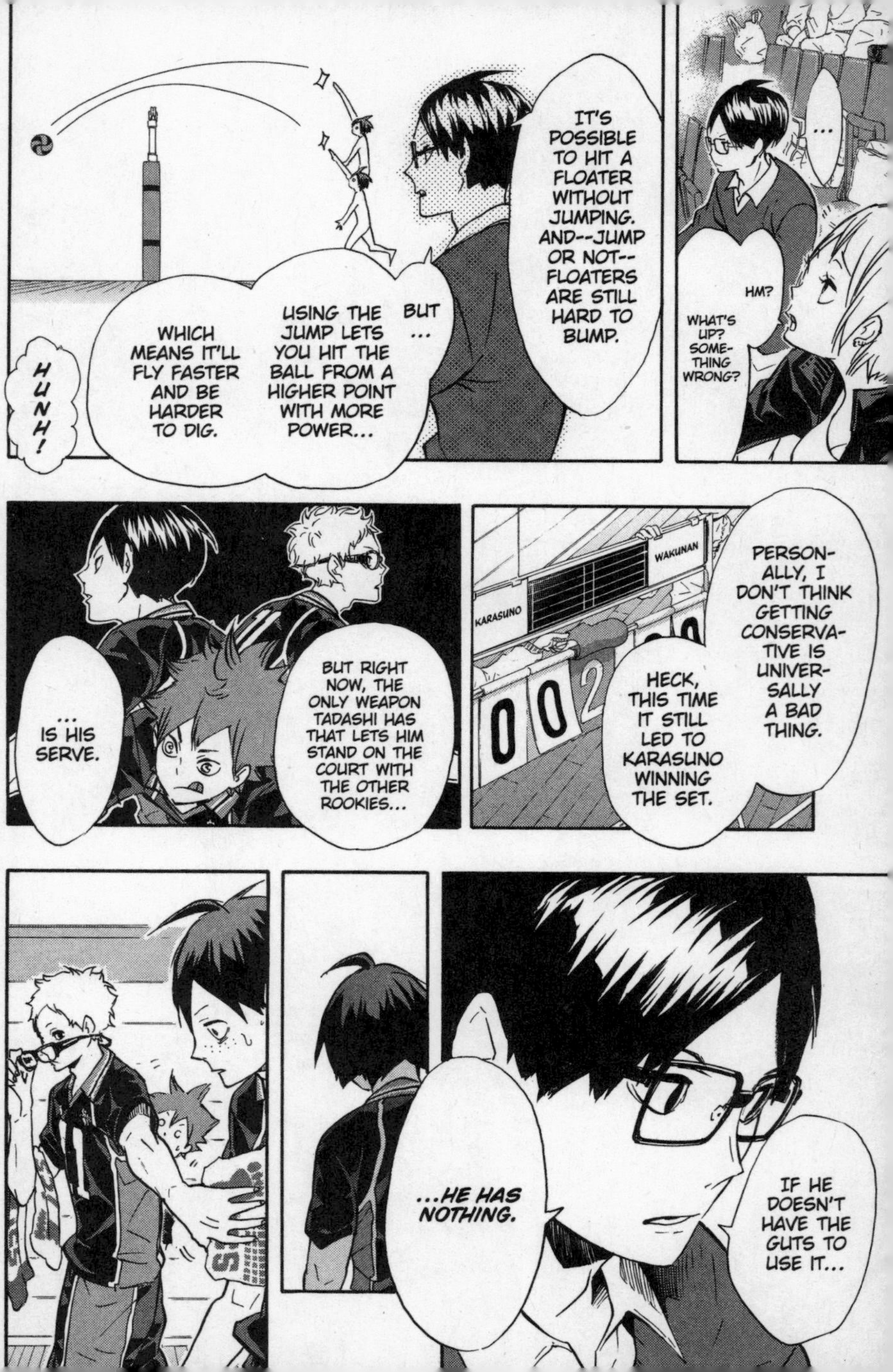

...
HM?
WHAT'S UP? SOMETHING WRONG?
IT'S POSSIBLE TO HIT A FLOATER WITHOUT JUMPING. AND--JUMP OR NOT--FLOATERS ARE STILL HARD TO BUMP.
BUT...
USING THE JUMP LETS YOU HIT THE BALL FROM A HIGHER POINT WITH MORE POWER...
WHICH MEANS IT'LL FLY FASTER AND BE HARDER TO DIG.
HUNH!
WAKUNAN
KARASUNO
PERSONALLY, I DON'T THINK GETTING CONSERVATIVE IS UNIVERSALLY A BAD THING.
HECK, THIS TIME IT STILL LED TO KARASUNO WINNING THE SET.
BUT RIGHT NOW, THE ONLY WEAPON TADASHI HAS THAT LETS HIM STAND ON THE COURT WITH THE OTHER ROOKIES...
... IS HIS SERVE.
IF HE DOESN'T HAVE THE GUTS TO USE IT...
...HE HAS NOTHING.

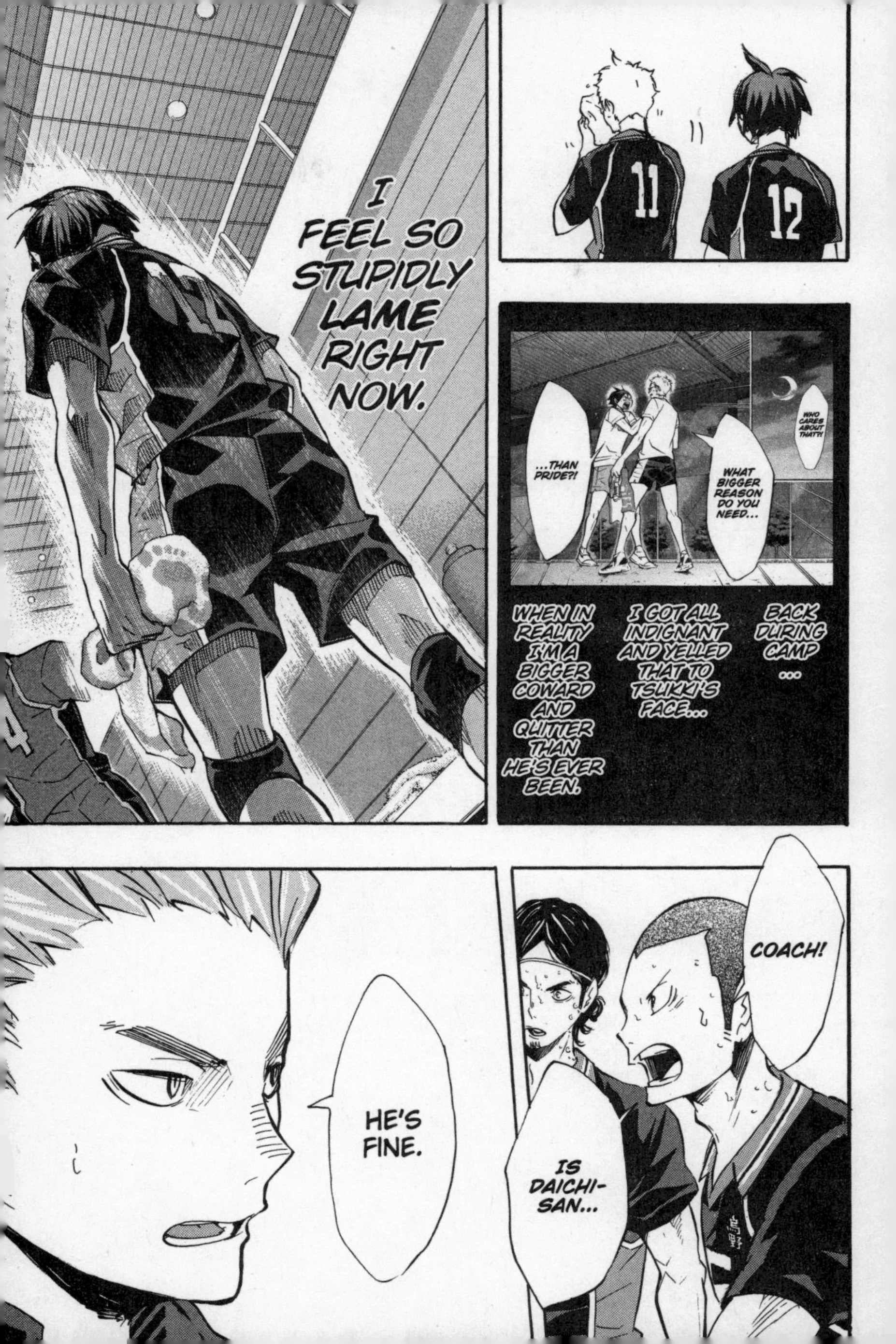
WHO CARES ABOUT THAT?!
WHAT BIGGER REASON DO YOU NEED...
...THAN PRIDE?!
BACK DURING CAMP...
I GOT ALL INDIGNANT AND YELLED THAT TO TSUKKI'S FACE...
WHEN IN REALITY I'M A BIGGER COWARD AND QUITTER THAN HE'S EVER BEEN.
I FEEL SO STUPIDLY LAME RIGHT NOW.
COACH!
IS DAICHI-SAN...
HE'S FINE.

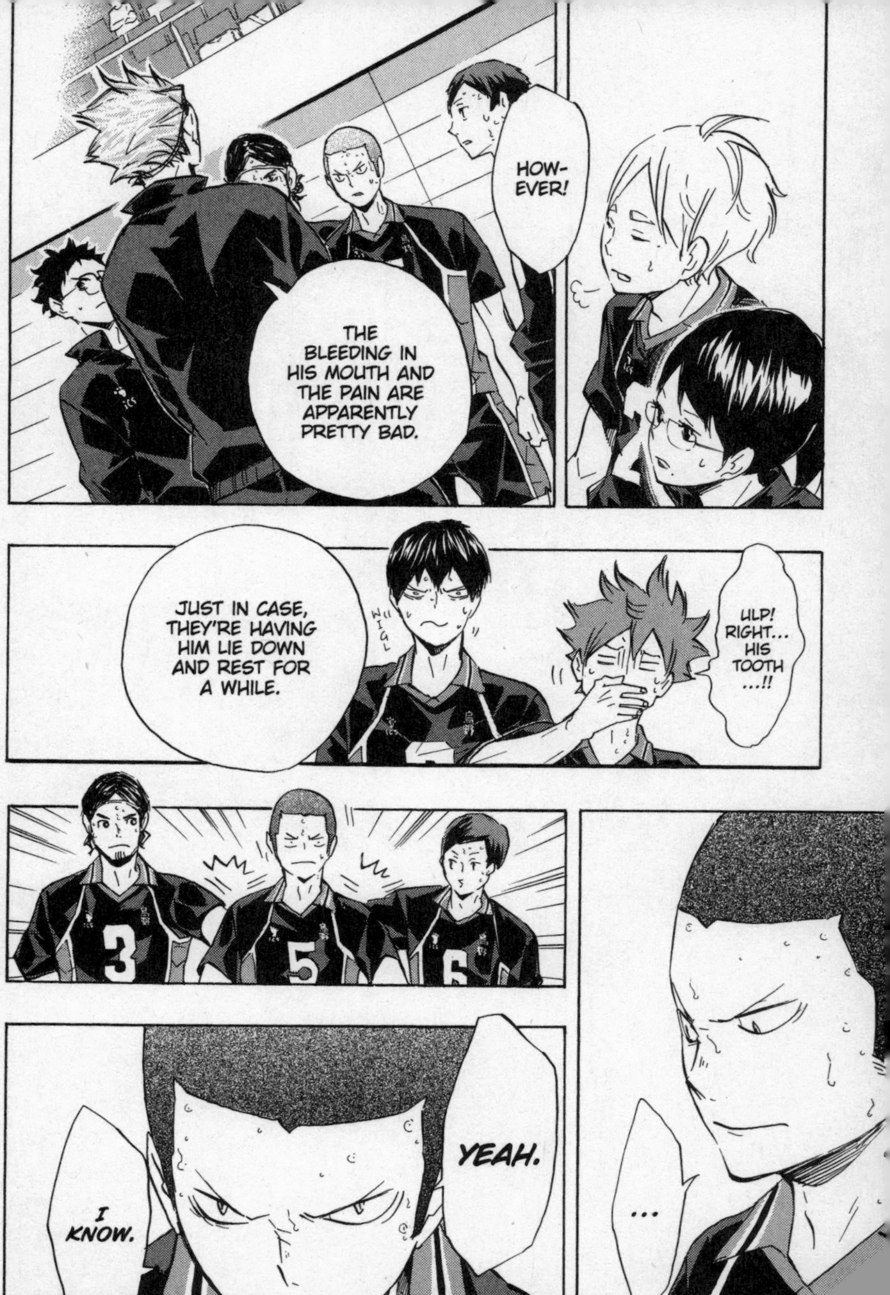
HOW-
EVER!
THE BLEEDING IN HIS MOUTH AND THE PAIN ARE APPARENTLY PRETTY BAD.
JUST IN CASE, THEY'RE HAVING HIM LIE DOWN AND REST FOR A WHILE.
WIGL
ULP! RIGHT... HIS TOOTH ...!!
...
YEAH.
I KNOW.

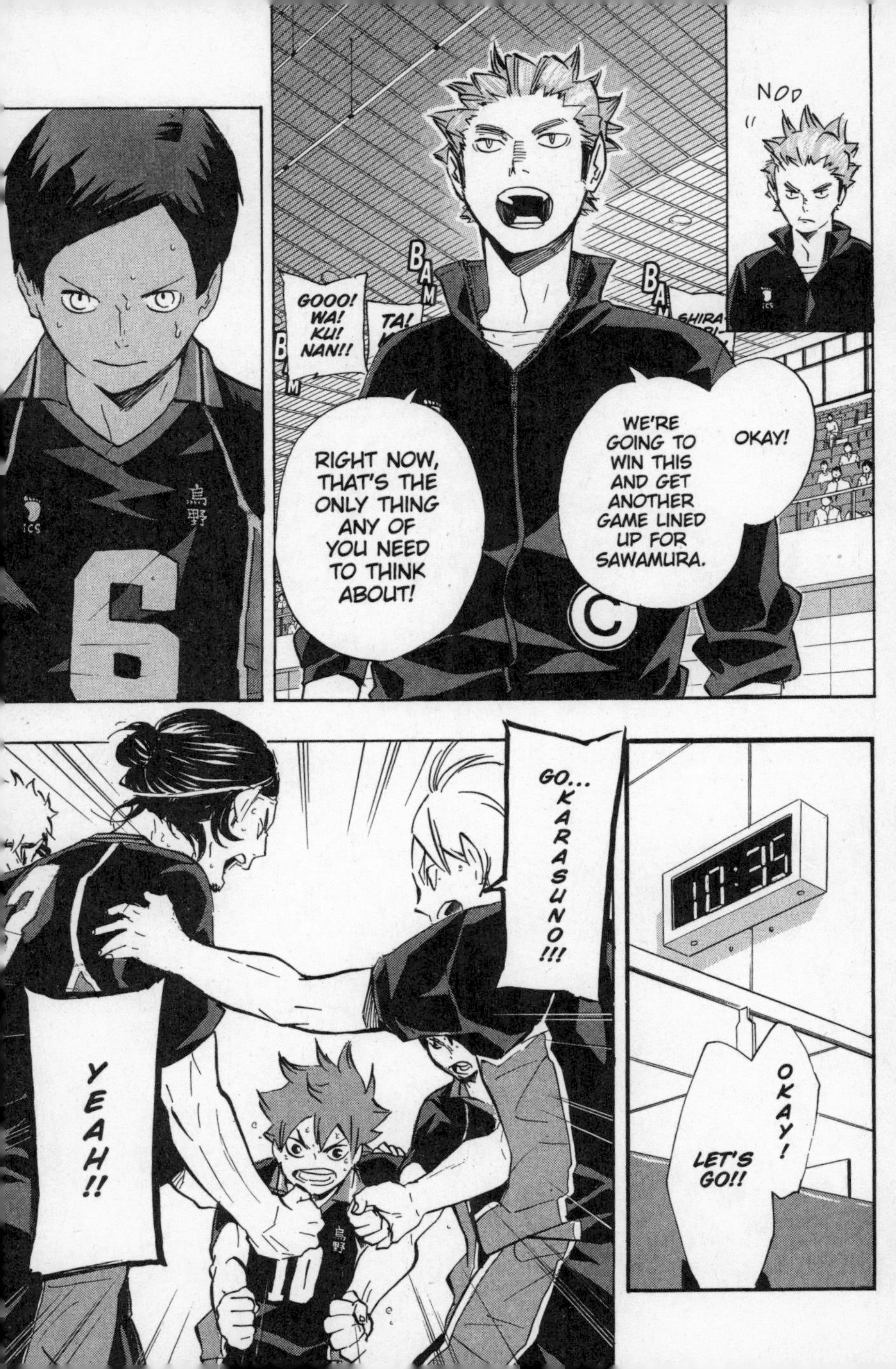
NOD
OKAY!
BAM
SHIRA
TA!
GOOO! WA! KU! NAN!!
BAM
WE'RE GOING TO WIN THIS AND GET ANOTHER GAME LINED UP FOR SAWAMURA.
RIGHT NOW, THAT'S THE ONLY THING ANY OF YOU NEED TO THINK ABOUT!
OKAY! LET'S GO!!
GO... KARASUNO!!!
YEAH!!

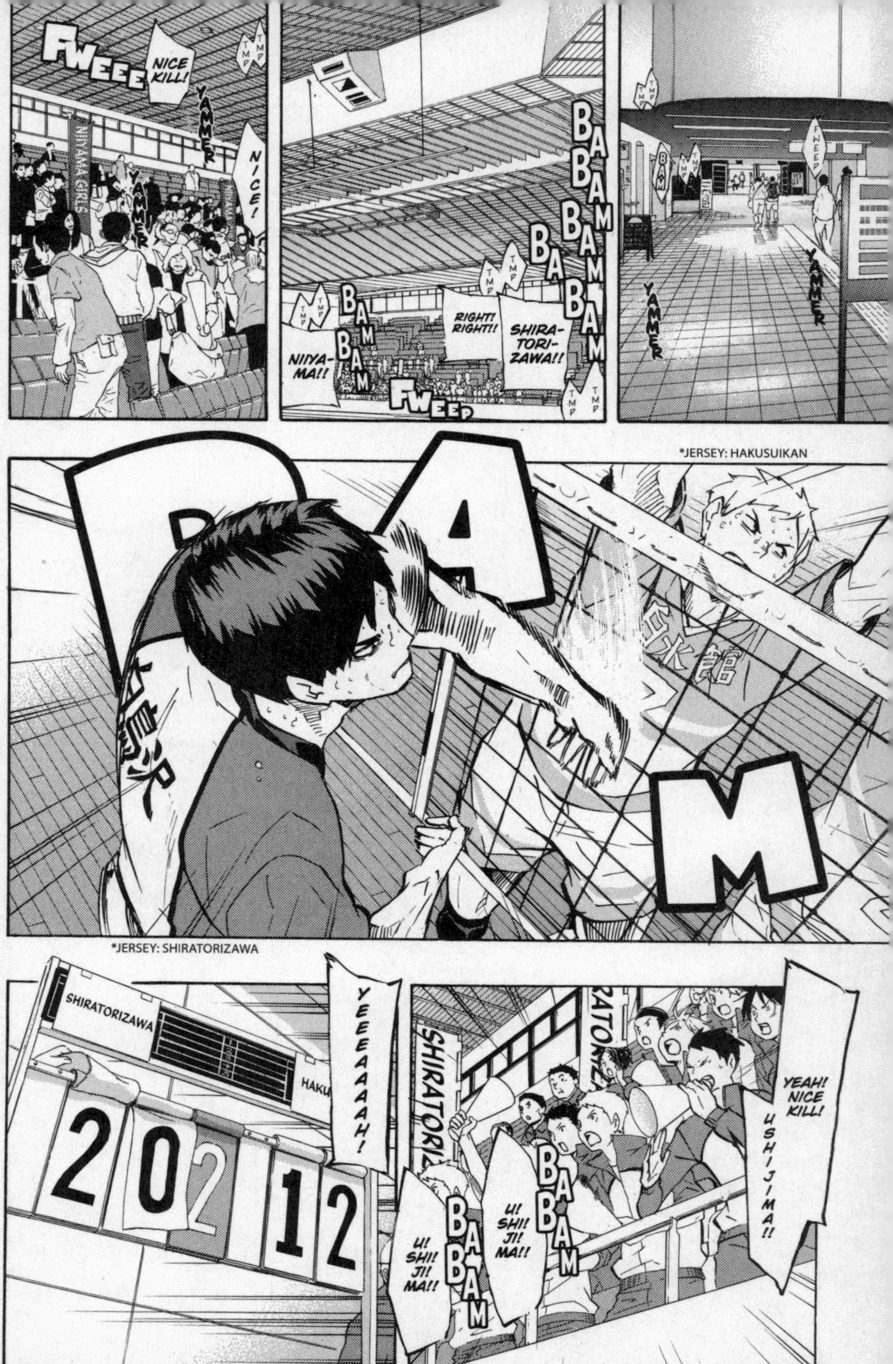
TMP TMP
BAM
TMP TMP
FWEEP
YAMMER
YAMMER
BABAM
BABAM
BABAM
TMP TMP
SHIRATORI-ZAWA!!
RIGHT! RIGHT!!
TMP TMP
TMP TMP
BABAM
NIIYAMA!!
FWEEP
TMP TMP
NICE KILL!
FWEEE
YAMMER
YAMMER
NICE!
NIIYAMA GIRLS
BAM
SHIRATORIZAWA
YEAH! NICE KILL!
USHIJIMA!!
BABAM
U! SHI! JI! MA!!
BABAM
U! SHI! JI! MA!!
YEEEAAAAAH!
SHIRATORIZAWA
HAKU
20
12

*JERSEY: HAKUSUIKAN

*JERSEY: SHIRATORIZAWA

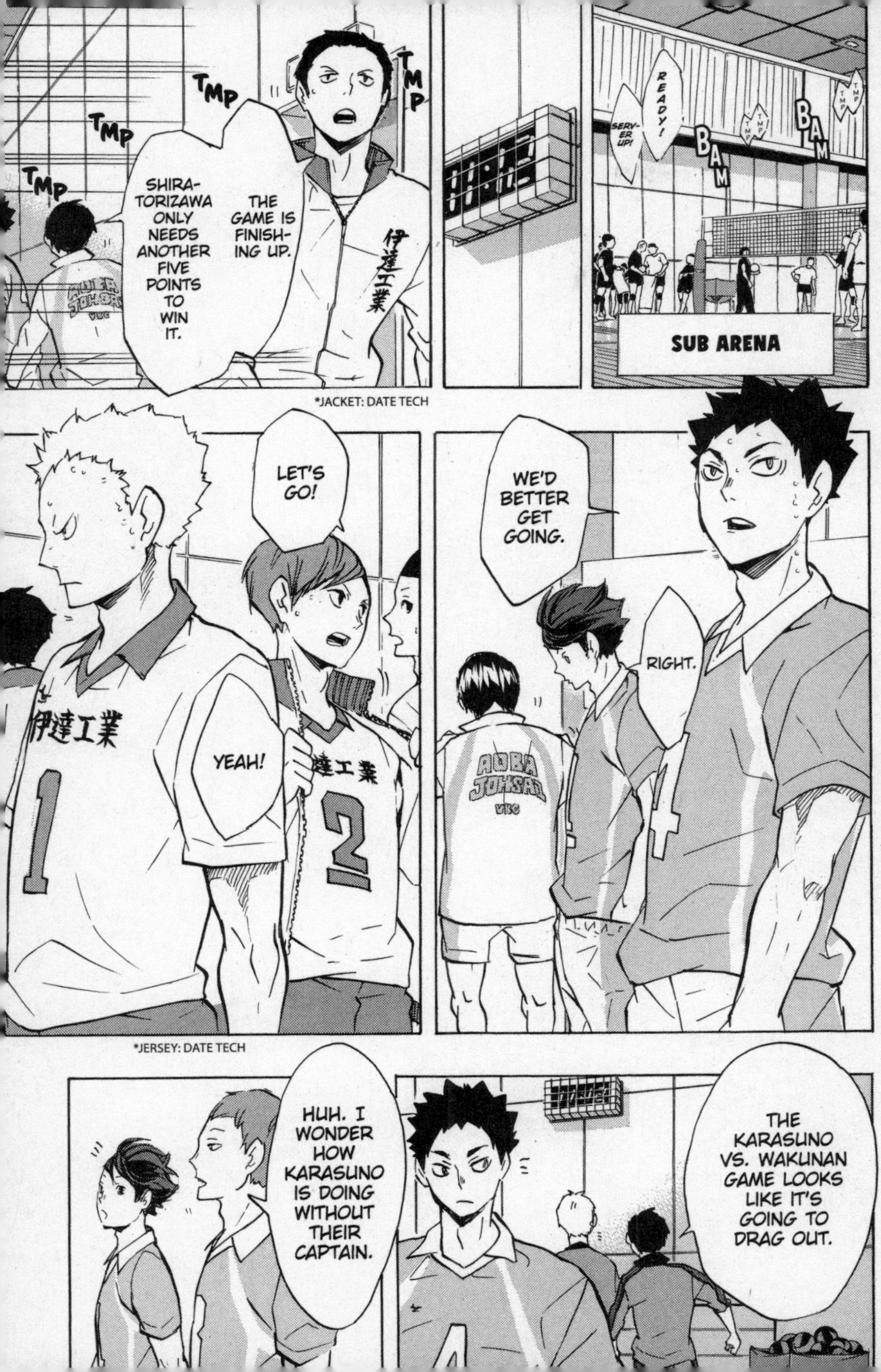
SUB ARENA
READY!
SERV-ER UP!
BAM
BAM
TMP TMP
TMP TMP
TMP
TMP
TMP
TMP
THE GAME IS FINISHING UP.
SHIRATORIZAWA ONLY NEEDS ANOTHER FIVE POINTS TO WIN IT.
*JACKET: DATE TECH
WE'D BETTER GET GOING.
RIGHT.
LET'S GO!
YEAH!
*JERSEY: DATE TECH
THE KARASUNO VS. WAKUNAN GAME LOOKS LIKE IT'S GOING TO DRAG OUT.
HUH. I WONDER HOW KARASUNO IS DOING WITHOUT THEIR CAPTAIN.

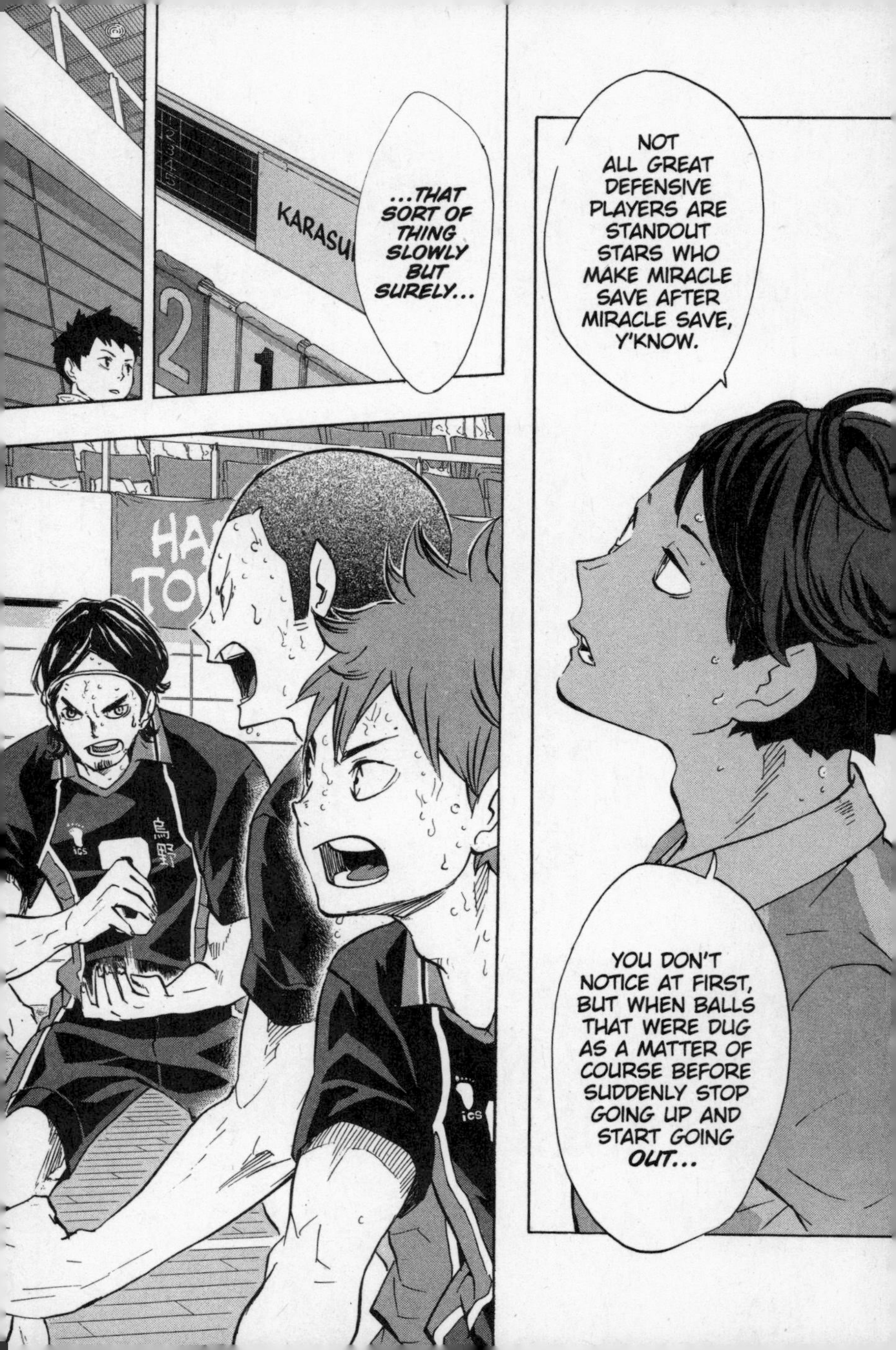
NOT ALL GREAT DEFENSIVE PLAYERS ARE STANDOUT STARS WHO MAKE MIRACLE SAVE AFTER MIRACLE SAVE, Y'KNOW.
YOU DON'T NOTICE AT FIRST, BUT WHEN BALLS THAT WERE DUG AS A MATTER OF COURSE BEFORE SUDDENLY STOP GOING UP AND START GOING *OUT*...
...THAT SORT OF THING SLOWLY BUT SURELY...

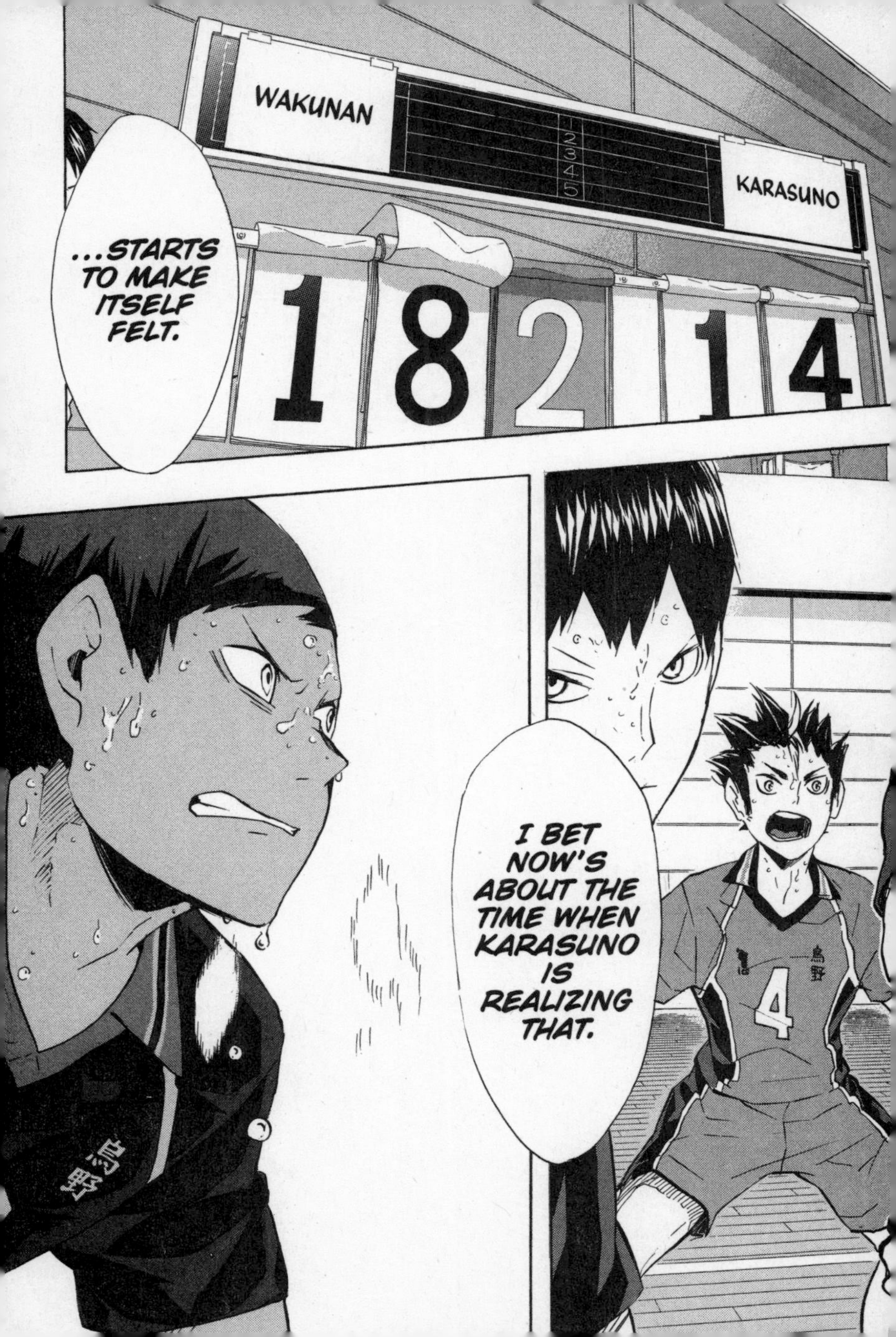
WAKUNAN
KARASUNO
1 2 3 4 5
18
2
14
...STARTS TO MAKE ITSELF FELT.
I BET NOW'S ABOUT THE TIME WHEN KARASUNO IS REALIZING THAT.

CHAPTER 121

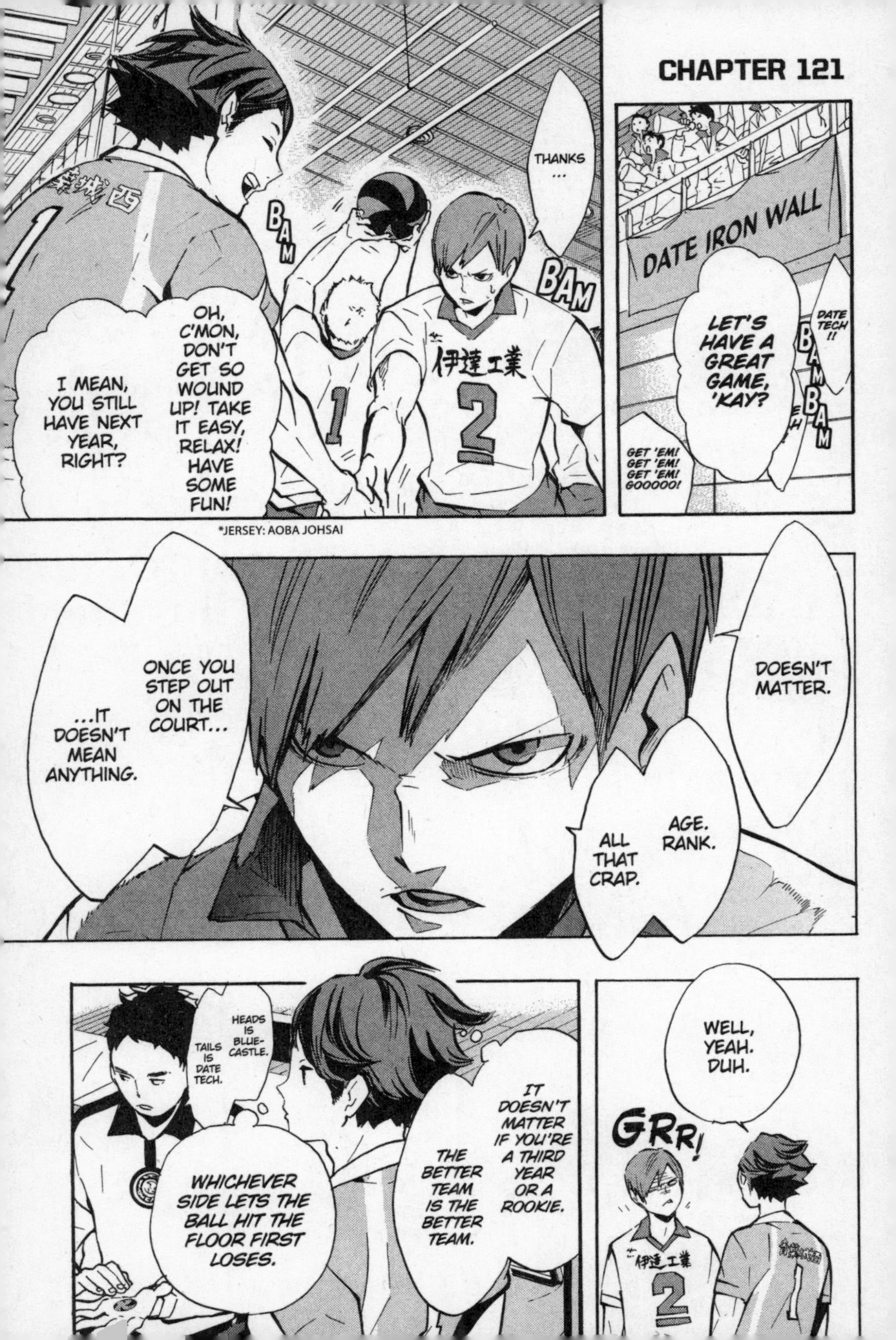
DATE IRON WALL
DATE TECH!!
BAM BAM
LET'S HAVE A GREAT GAME, 'KAY?
GET 'EM! GET 'EM! GET 'EM! GOOOOO!
THANKS...
BAM
BAM
OH, C'MON, DON'T GET SO WOUND UP! TAKE IT EASY, RELAX! HAVE SOME FUN!
I MEAN, YOU STILL HAVE NEXT YEAR, RIGHT?
*JERSEY: AOBA JOHSAI
DOESN'T MATTER.
AGE. RANK.
ALL THAT CRAP.
ONCE YOU STEP OUT ON THE COURT...
...IT DOESN'T MEAN ANYTHING.
WELL, YEAH. DUH.
GRR!
IT DOESN'T MATTER IF YOU'RE A THIRD YEAR OR A ROOKIE.
THE BETTER TEAM IS THE BETTER TEAM.
HEADS IS BLUE-CASTLE.
TAILS IS DATE TECH.
WHICHEVER SIDE LETS THE BALL HIT THE FLOOR FIRST LOSES.

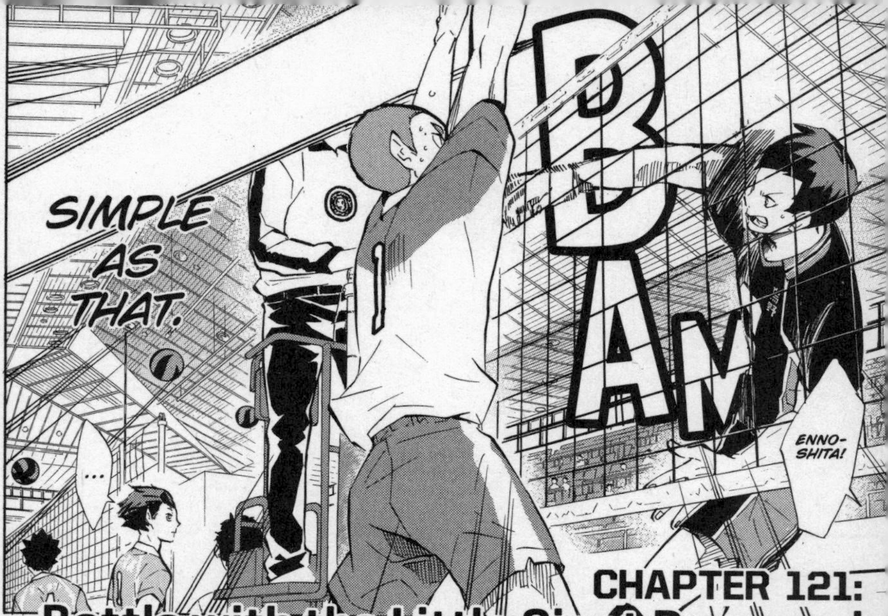
ENNO-SHITA!
DAM
...
SIMPLE AS THAT.

CHAPTER 121: Battle with the Little Giant Resumed

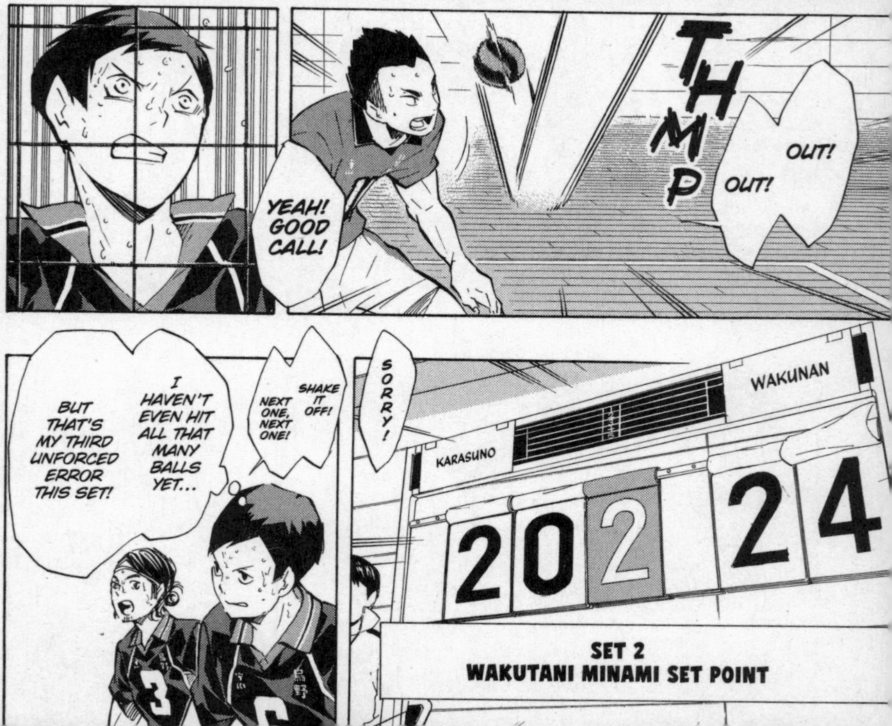
OUT!
OUT!
THMP
YEAH! GOOD CALL!
WAKUNAN
KARASUNO
20
2
24
SET 2
WAKUTANI MINAMI SET POINT
SORRY!
SHAKE IT OFF!
NEXT ONE, NEXT ONE!
I HAVEN'T EVEN HIT ALL THAT MANY BALLS YET...
BUT THAT'S MY THIRD UNFORCED ERROR THIS SET!

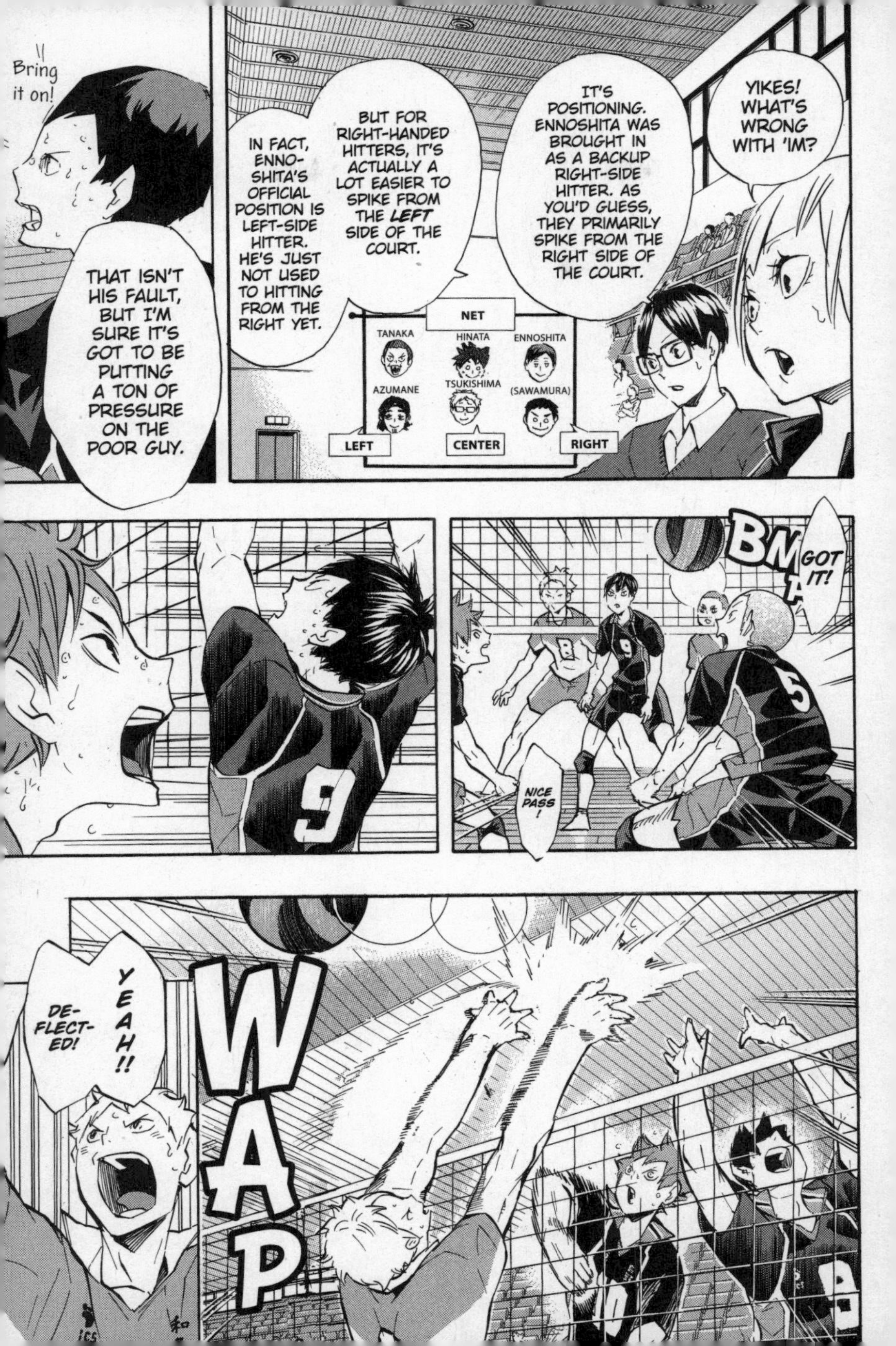

YIKES! WHAT'S WRONG WITH 'IM?
IT'S POSITIONING. ENNOSHITA WAS BROUGHT IN AS A BACKUP RIGHT-SIDE HITTER. AS YOU'D GUESS, THEY PRIMARILY SPIKE FROM THE RIGHT SIDE OF THE COURT.
BUT FOR RIGHT-HANDED HITTERS, IT'S ACTUALLY A LOT EASIER TO SPIKE FROM THE LEFT SIDE OF THE COURT.
IN FACT, ENNOSHITA'S OFFICIAL POSITION IS LEFT-SIDE HITTER. HE'S JUST NOT USED TO HITTING FROM THE RIGHT YET.
NET
ENNOSHITA
HINATA
TANAKA
(SAWAMURA)
TSUKISHIMA
AZUMANE
RIGHT
CENTER
LEFT
Bring it on!
THAT ISN'T HIS FAULT, BUT I'M SURE IT'S GOT TO BE PUTTING A TON OF PRESSURE ON THE POOR GUY.
GOT IT!
BM
NICE PASS!
YEAH!!
DE-FLECTED!
WAP

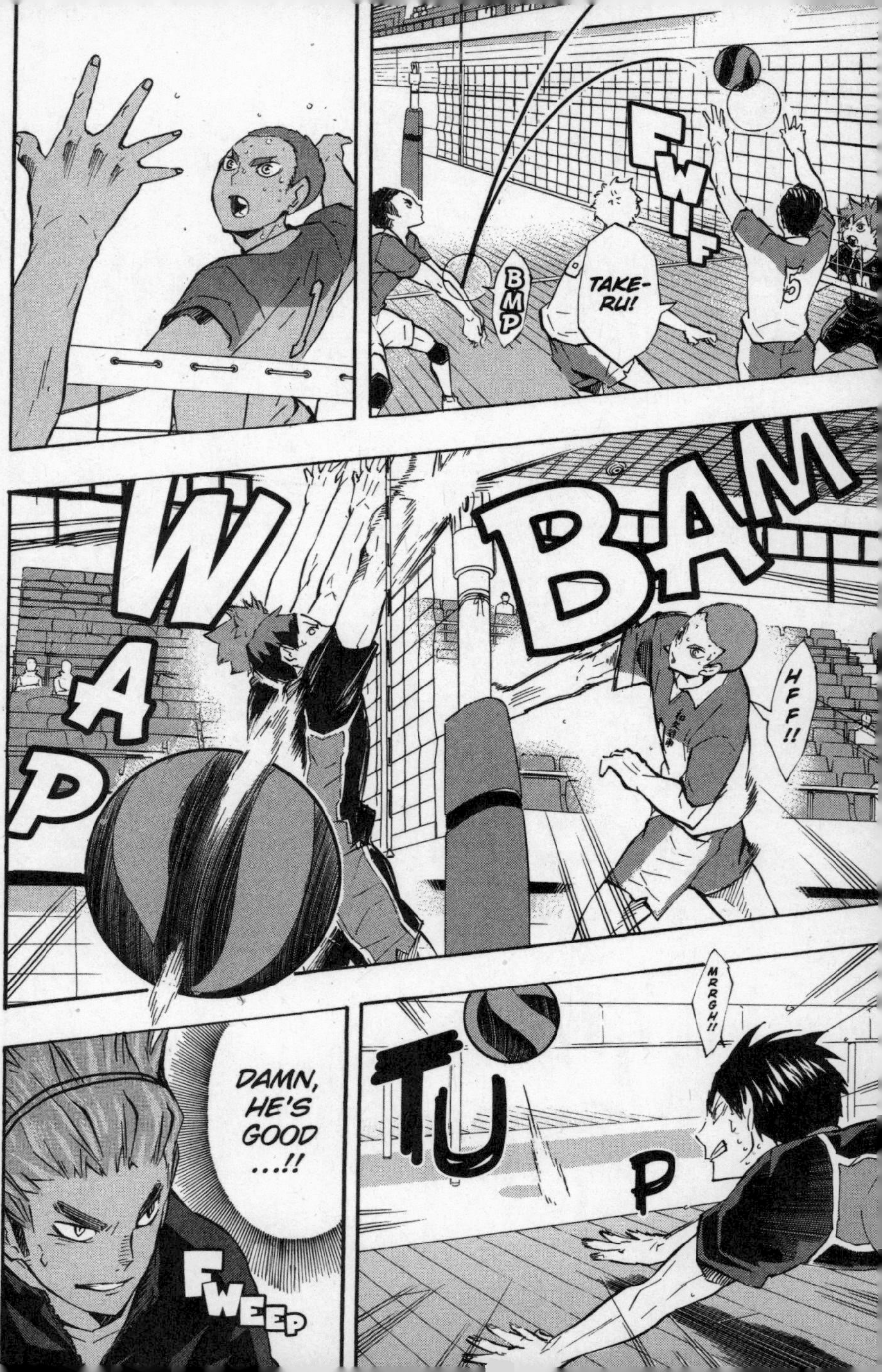
FWIF
TAKE-RU!
BMP
BAM
HFF!!
WAP
MRRGH!!
TUP
DAMN, HE'S GOOD ...!!
FWEEP

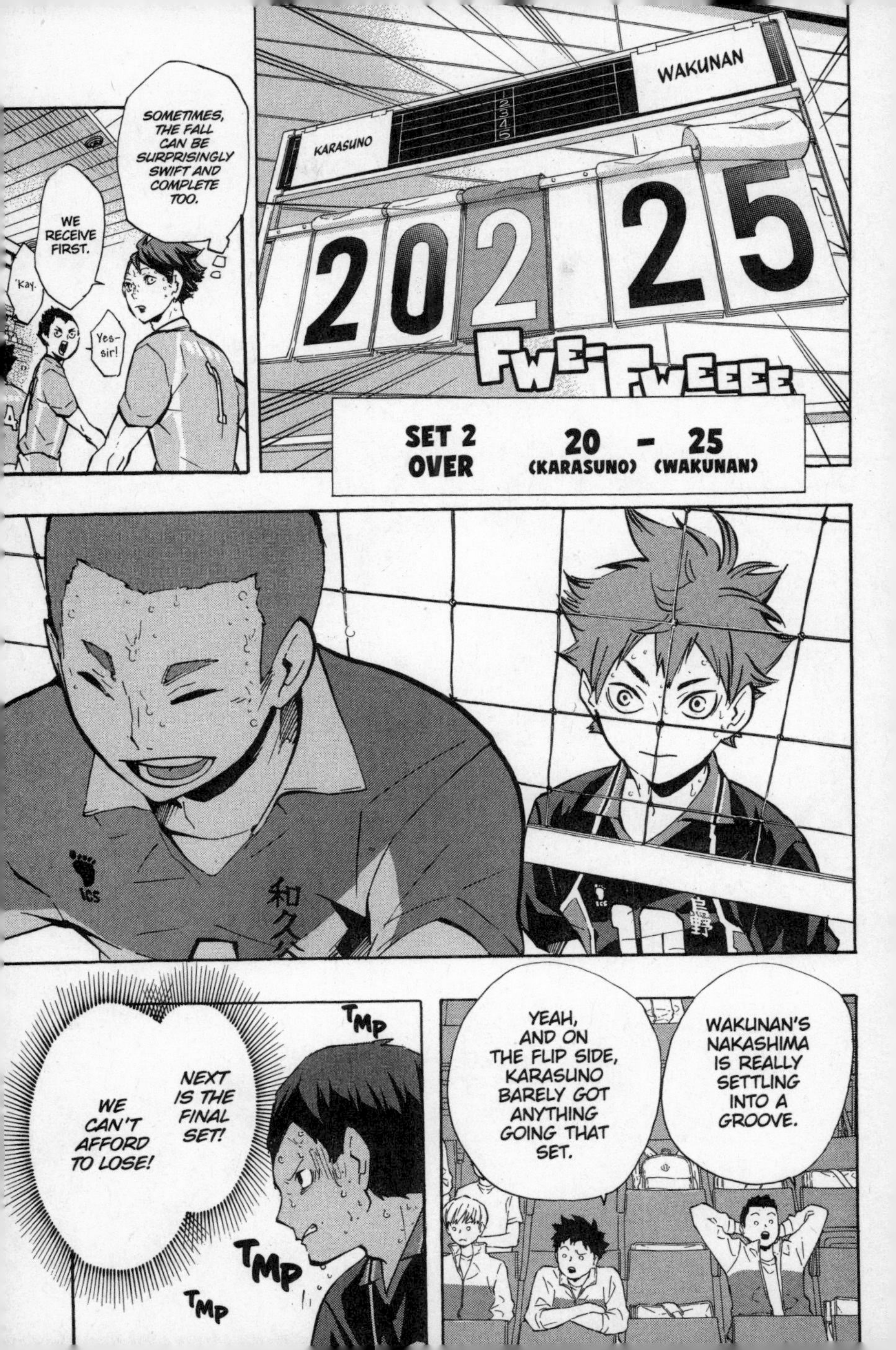
WAKUNAN
KARASUNO
20 25
FWE-FWEEEE
SET 2 OVER 20 - 25 (KARASUNO) (WAKUNAN)
SOMETIMES, THE FALL CAN BE SURPRISINGLY SWIFT AND COMPLETE TOO.
WE RECEIVE FIRST.
Yes-sir!
'Kay.
WAKUNAN'S NAKASHIMA IS REALLY SETTLING INTO A GROOVE.
YEAH, AND ON THE FLIP SIDE, KARASUNO BARELY GOT ANYTHING GOING THAT SET.
TMP
NEXT IS THE FINAL SET!
WE CAN'T AFFORD TO LOSE!
TMP
TMP

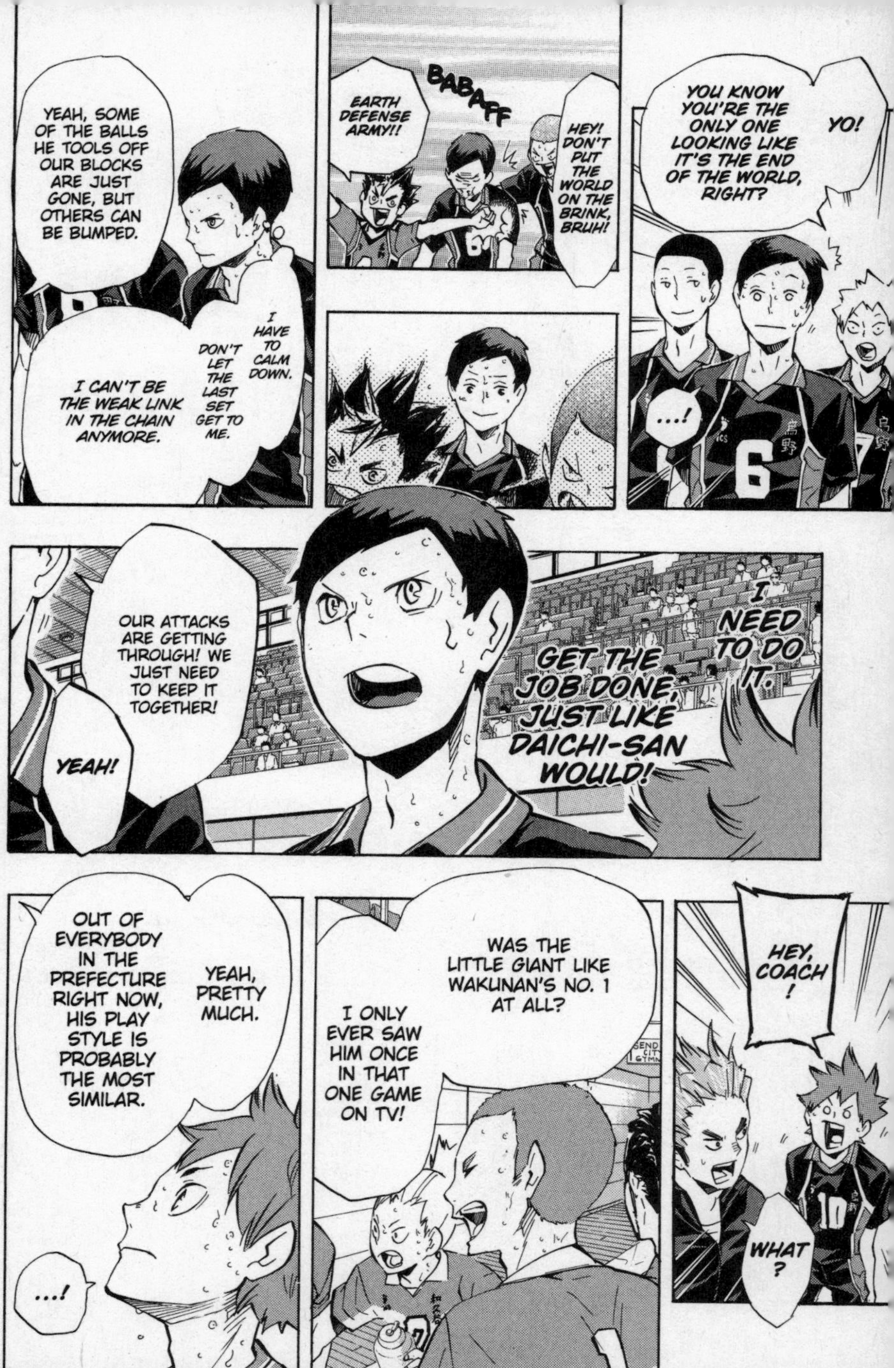
YO!
YOU KNOW YOU'RE THE ONLY ONE LOOKING LIKE IT'S THE END OF THE WORLD, RIGHT?
...!
BABAFF
EARTH DEFENSE ARMY!!
HEY! DON'T PUT THE WORLD ON THE BRINK, BRUH!
YEAH, SOME OF THE BALLS HE TOOLS OFF OUR BLOCKS ARE JUST GONE, BUT OTHERS CAN BE BUMPED.
I HAVE TO CALM DOWN.
DON'T LET THE LAST SET GET TO ME.
I CAN'T BE THE WEAK LINK IN THE CHAIN ANYMORE.
I NEED TO DO IT.
GET THE JOB DONE, JUST LIKE DAICHI-SAN WOULD!
OUR ATTACKS ARE GETTING THROUGH! WE JUST NEED TO KEEP IT TOGETHER!
YEAH!
HEY, COACH!
WHAT?
WAS THE LITTLE GIANT LIKE WAKUNAN'S NO. 1 AT ALL?
I ONLY EVER SAW HIM ONCE IN THAT ONE GAME ON TV!
OUT OF EVERYBODY IN THE PREFECTURE RIGHT NOW, HIS PLAY STYLE IS PROBABLY THE MOST SIMILAR.
YEAH, PRETTY MUCH.
...!

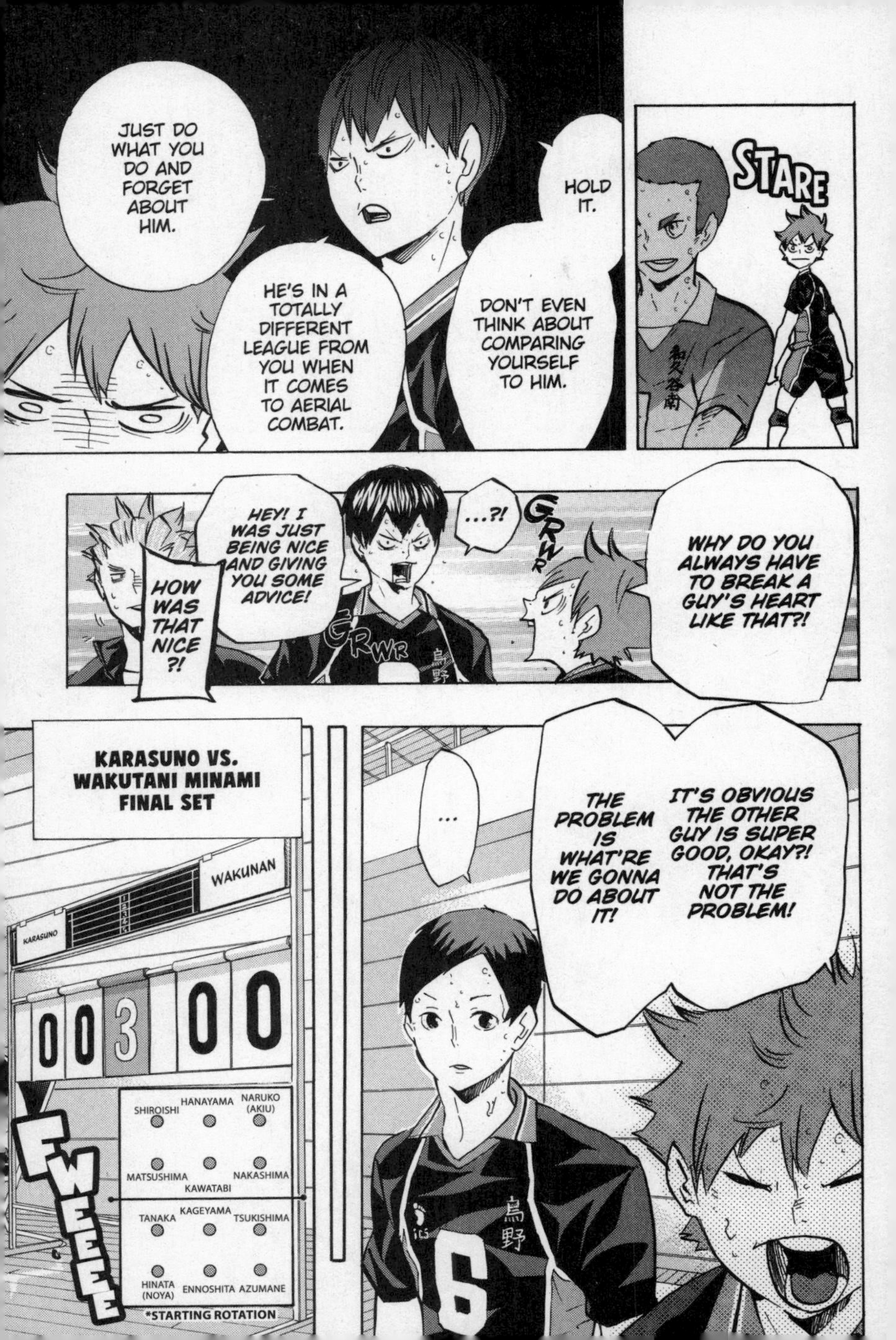
STARE
HOLD IT.
DON'T EVEN THINK ABOUT COMPARING YOURSELF TO HIM.
HE'S IN A TOTALLY DIFFERENT LEAGUE FROM YOU WHEN IT COMES TO AERIAL COMBAT.
JUST DO WHAT YOU DO AND FORGET ABOUT HIM.
WHY DO YOU ALWAYS HAVE TO BREAK A GUY'S HEART LIKE THAT?!
GRWR
...?!
HEY! I WAS JUST BEING NICE AND GIVING YOU SOME ADVICE!
GRWR
HOW WAS THAT NICE?!
IT'S OBVIOUS THE OTHER GUY IS SUPER GOOD, OKAY?! THAT'S NOT THE PROBLEM!
THE PROBLEM IS WHAT'RE WE GONNA DO ABOUT IT!
...
KARASUNO VS. WAKUTANI MINAMI FINAL SET
WAKUNAN
KARASUNO
0 0 3 0 0
SHIROISHI
HANAYAMA
NARUKO (AKIU)
MATSUSHIMA
KAWATABI
NAKASHIMA
TANAKA
KAGEYAMA
TSUKISHIMA
HINATA (NOYA)
ENNOSHITA
AZUMANE
FWEEEE
*STARTING ROTATION

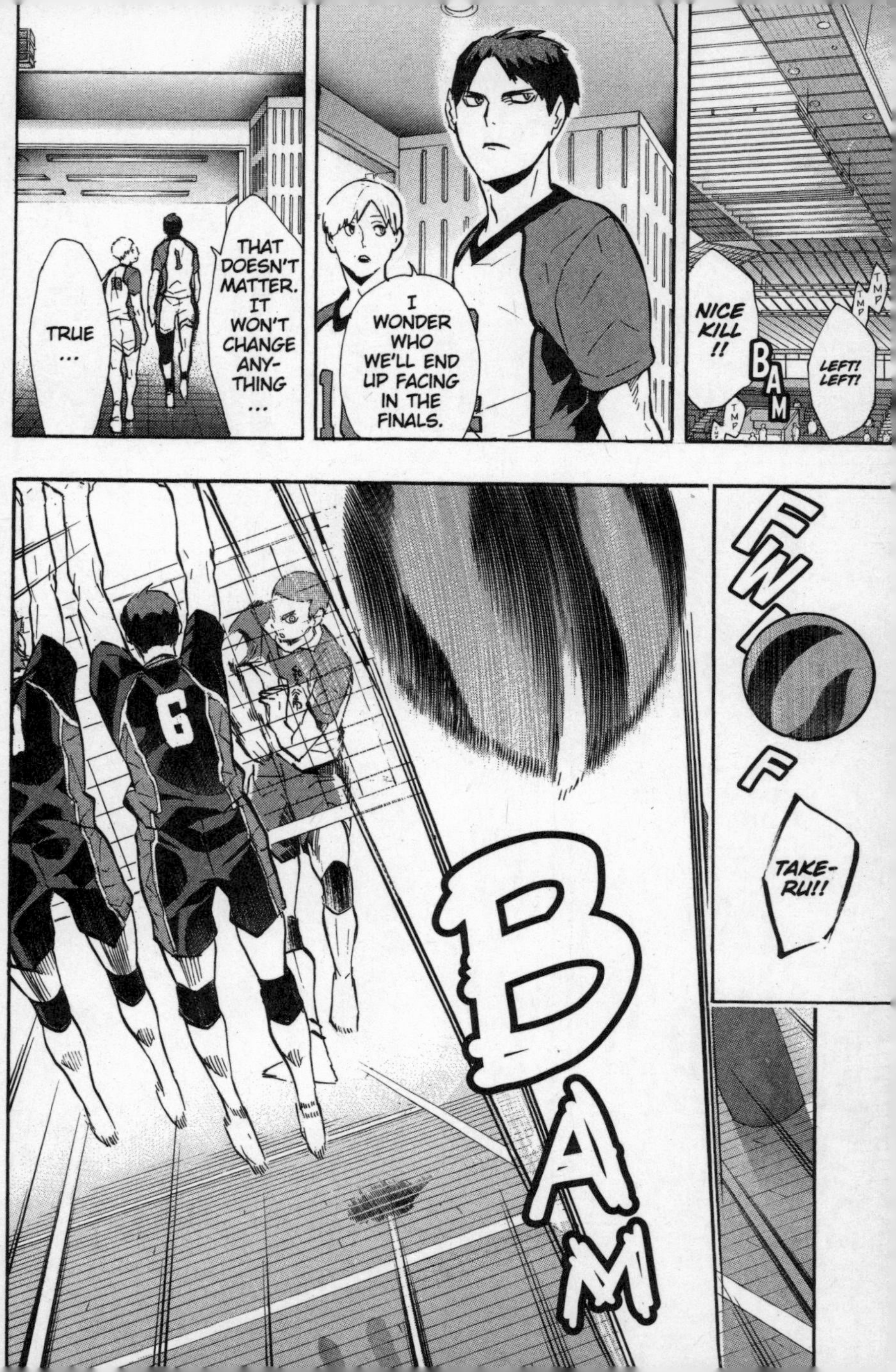
TMP TMP
LEFT! LEFT!
NICE KILL!!
BAM
TMP
I WONDER WHO WE'LL END UP FACING IN THE FINALS.
THAT DOESN'T MATTER. IT WON'T CHANGE ANY-THING...
TRUE...
FWIF
TAKE-RU!!
BAM

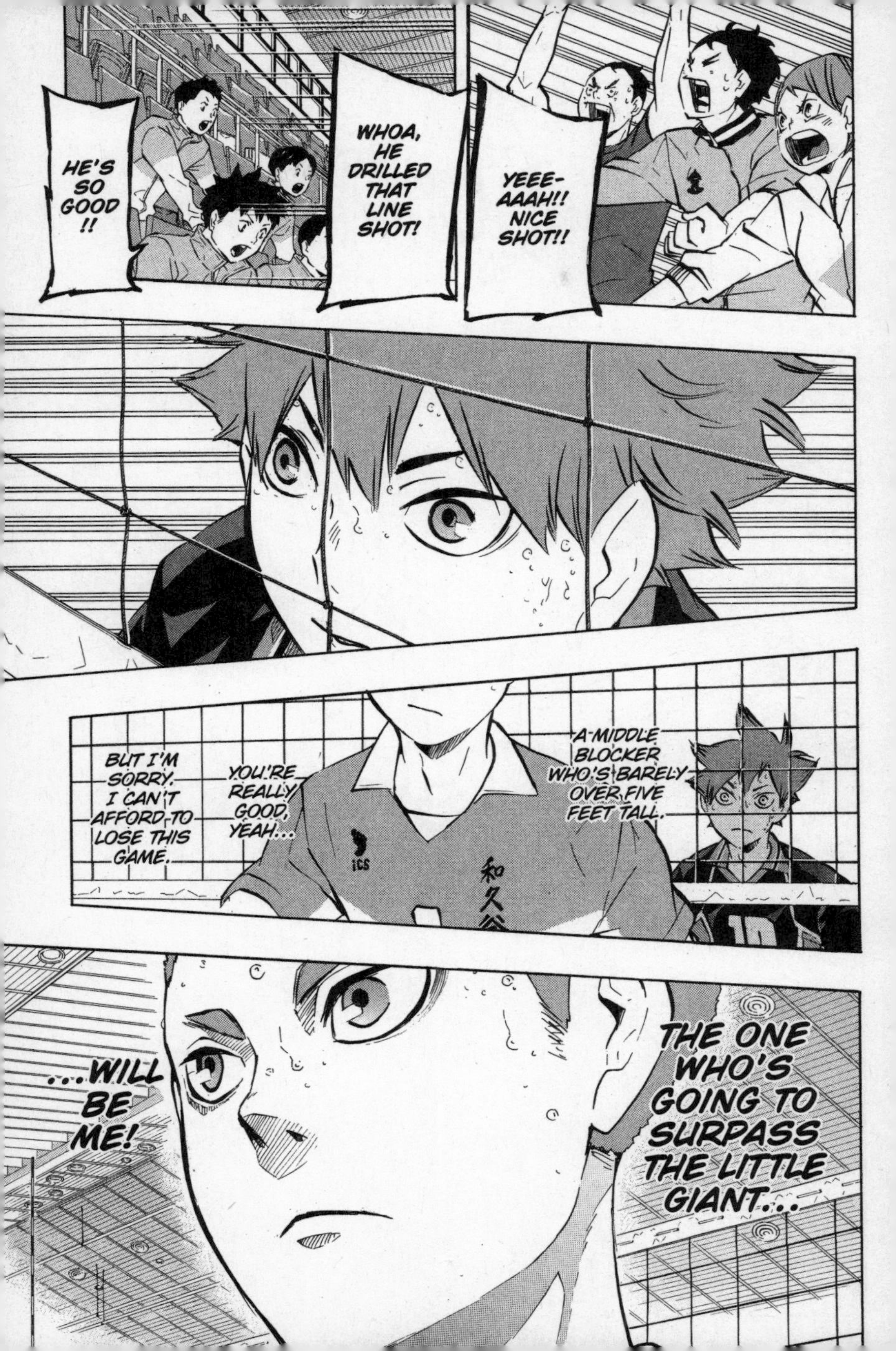
YEEE-AAAH!! NICE SHOT!!
WHOA, HE DRILLED THAT LINE SHOT!
HE'S SO GOOD!!
A MIDDLE BLOCKER WHO'S BARELY OVER FIVE FEET TALL.
YOU'RE REALLY GOOD, YEAH...
BUT I'M SORRY. I CAN'T AFFORD TO LOSE THIS GAME.
THE ONE WHO'S GOING TO SURPASS THE LITTLE GIANT...
...WILL BE ME!

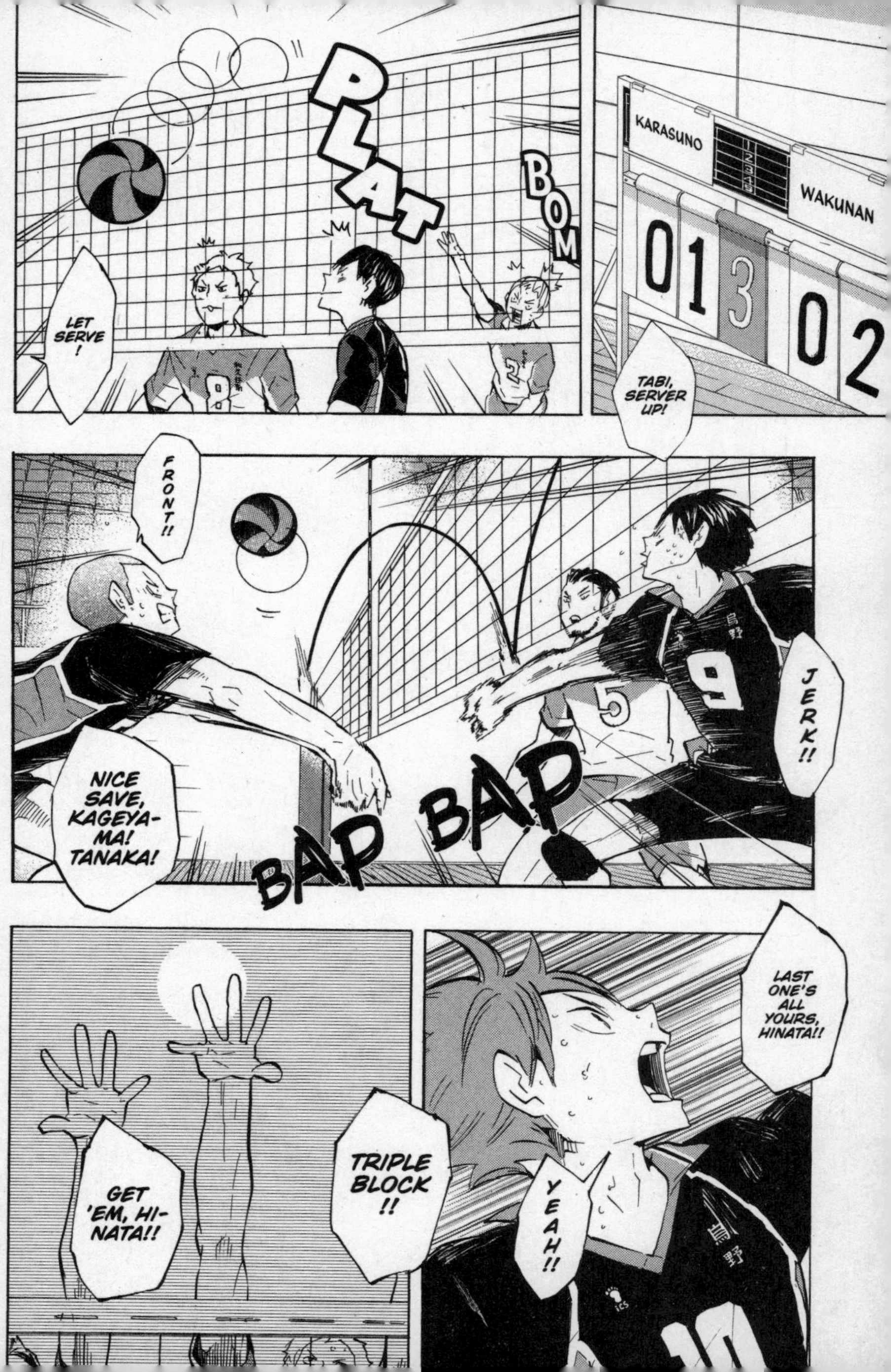
KARASUNO
WAKUNAN
01
3
02
TABI, SERVER UP!
PLAT
BOM
LET SERVE!
JERK!!
FRONT!!
NICE SAVE, KAGEYA-MA! TANAKA!
BAP BAP
LAST ONE'S ALL YOURS, HINATA!!
YEAH!!
TRIPLE BLOCK!!
GET 'EM, HI-NATA!!

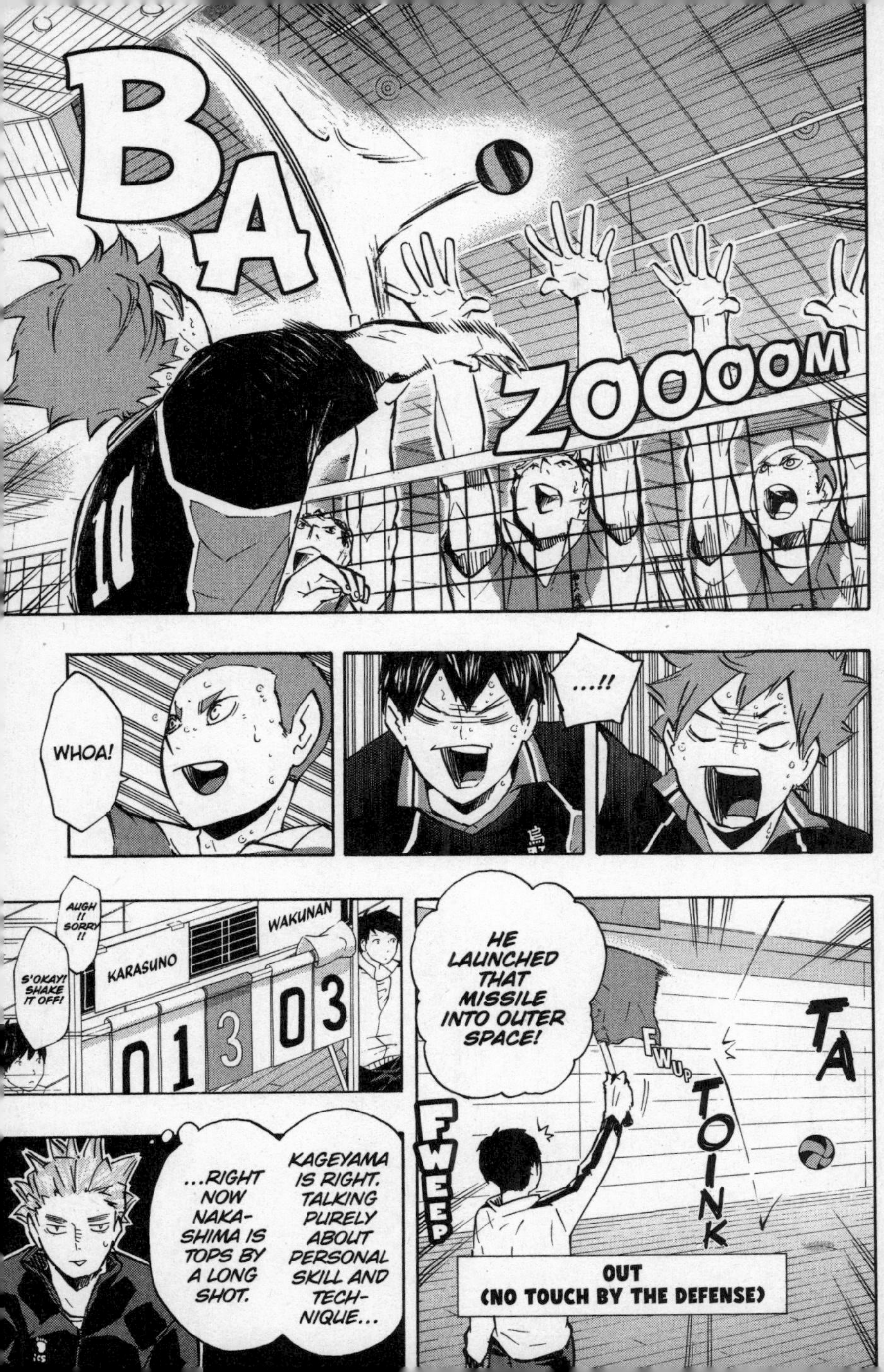
BA
ZOOOOOM
...!!
WHOA!
HE LAUNCHED THAT MISSILE INTO OUTER SPACE!
TA
FWUP
TOINK
FWEEP
OUT
(NO TOUCH BY THE DEFENSE)
AUGH!! SORRY!!
S'OKAY! SHAKE IT OFF!
WAKUNAN
KARASUNO
01 3 03
KAGEYAMA IS RIGHT. TALKING PURELY ABOUT PERSONAL SKILL AND TECH-NIQUE...
...RIGHT NOW NAKA-SHIMA IS TOPS BY A LONG SHOT.

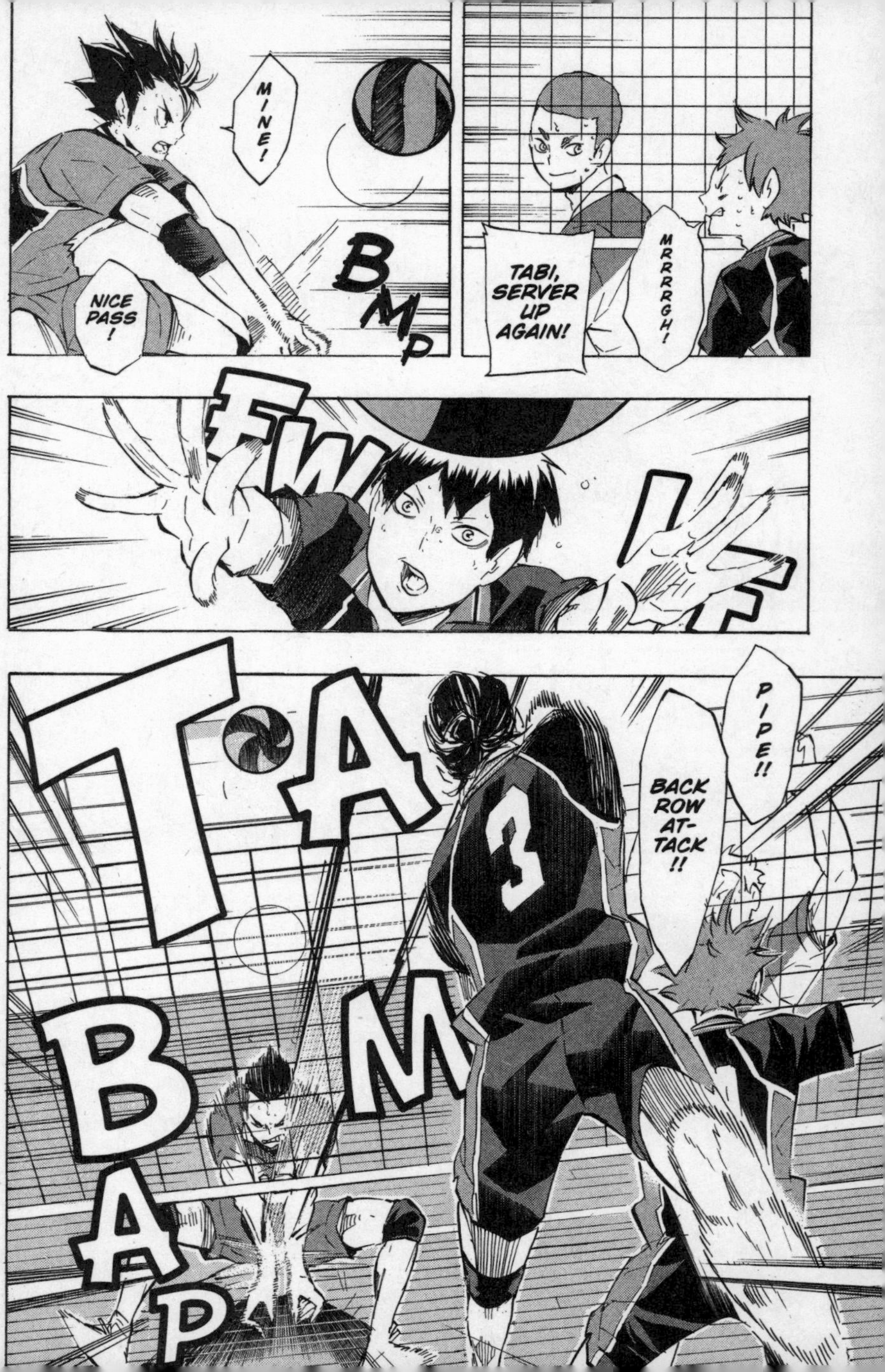
MRRRRGH!
TABI, SERVER UP AGAIN!
MINE!
BMP
NICE PASS!
PIPE!!
BACK ROW AT-TACK!!

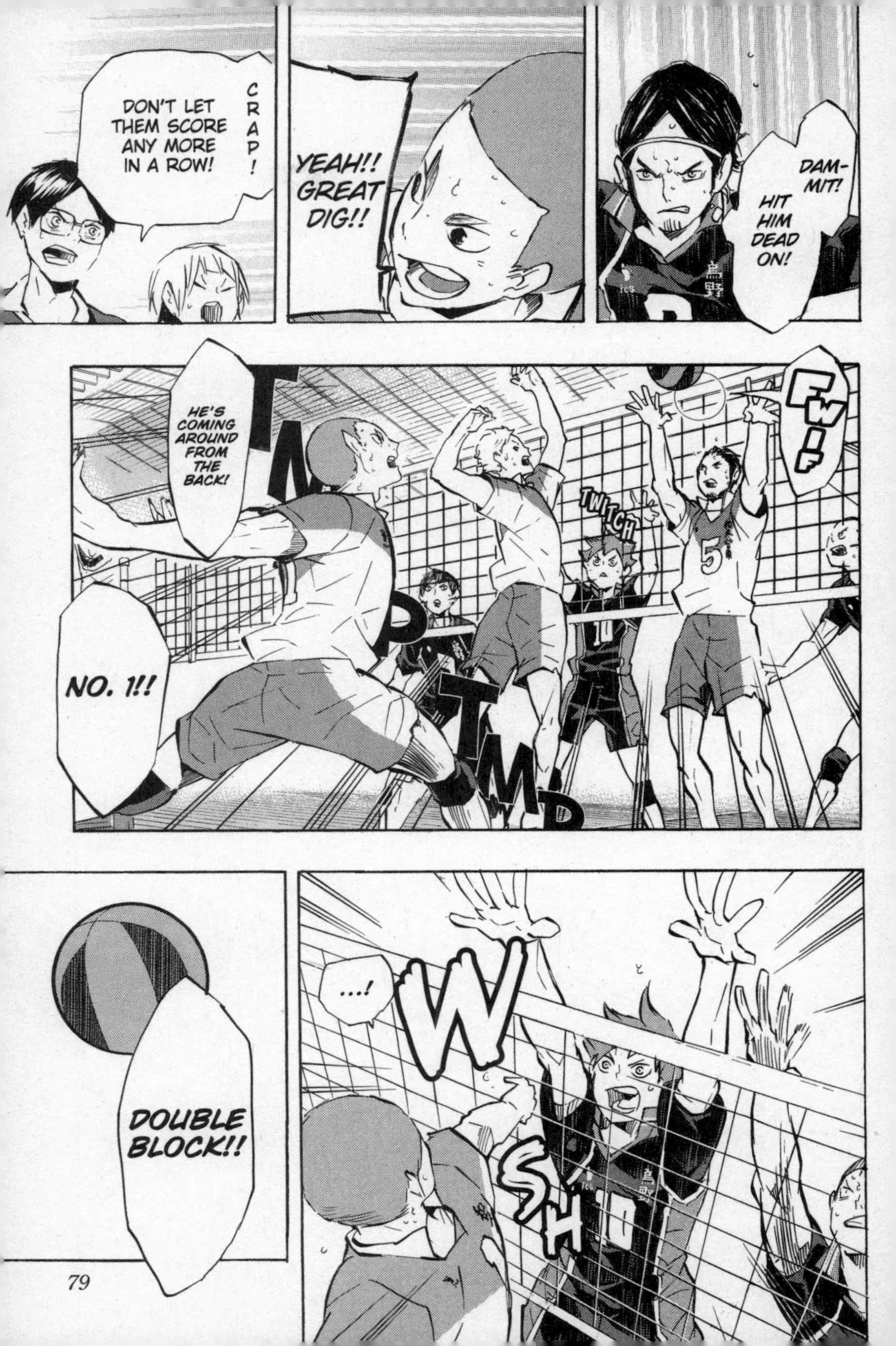
DAM-MIT!
HIT HIM DEAD ON!
YEAH!! GREAT DIG!!
CRAP!
DON'T LET THEM SCORE ANY MORE IN A ROW!
FWIF
TWITCH
HE'S COMING AROUND FROM THE BACK!
TMP
NO. 1!!
TMP
TMP
...!
W
SH
DOUBLE BLOCK!!

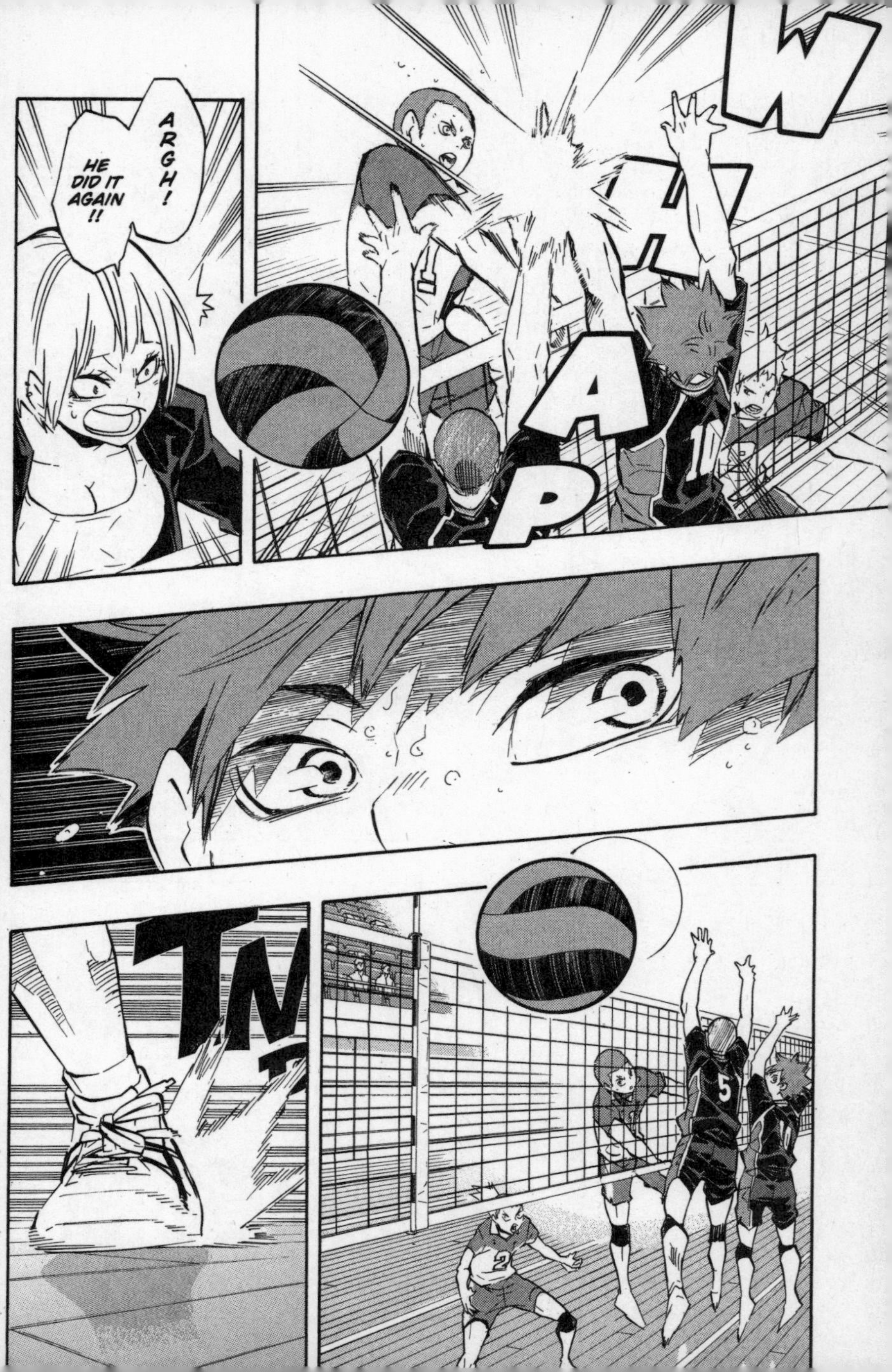
WHAP
ARGH! HE DID IT AGAIN !!
TMP

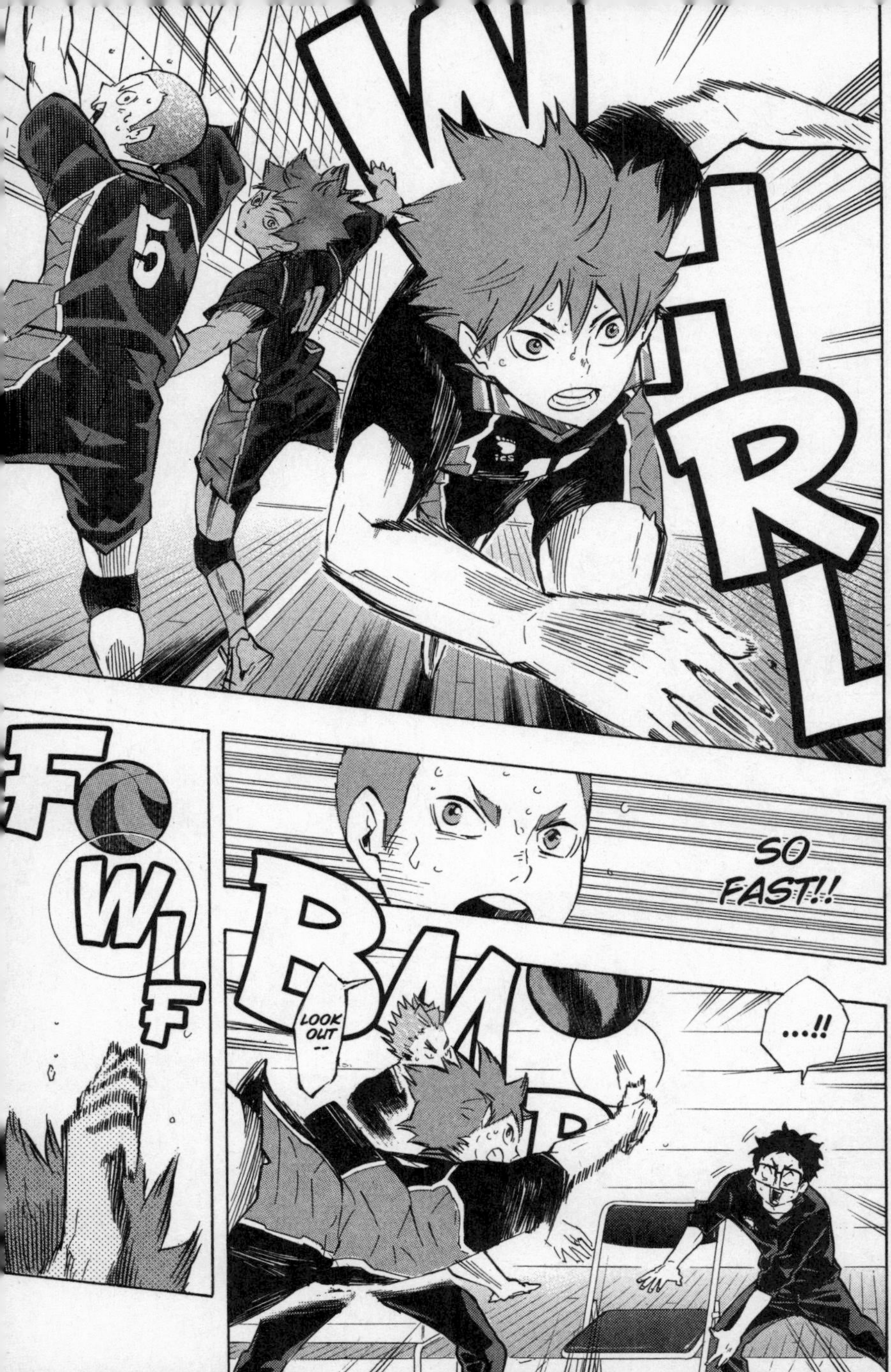
WHIRL
SO FAST!!
BAM
FWIF
...!!
LOOK OUT --

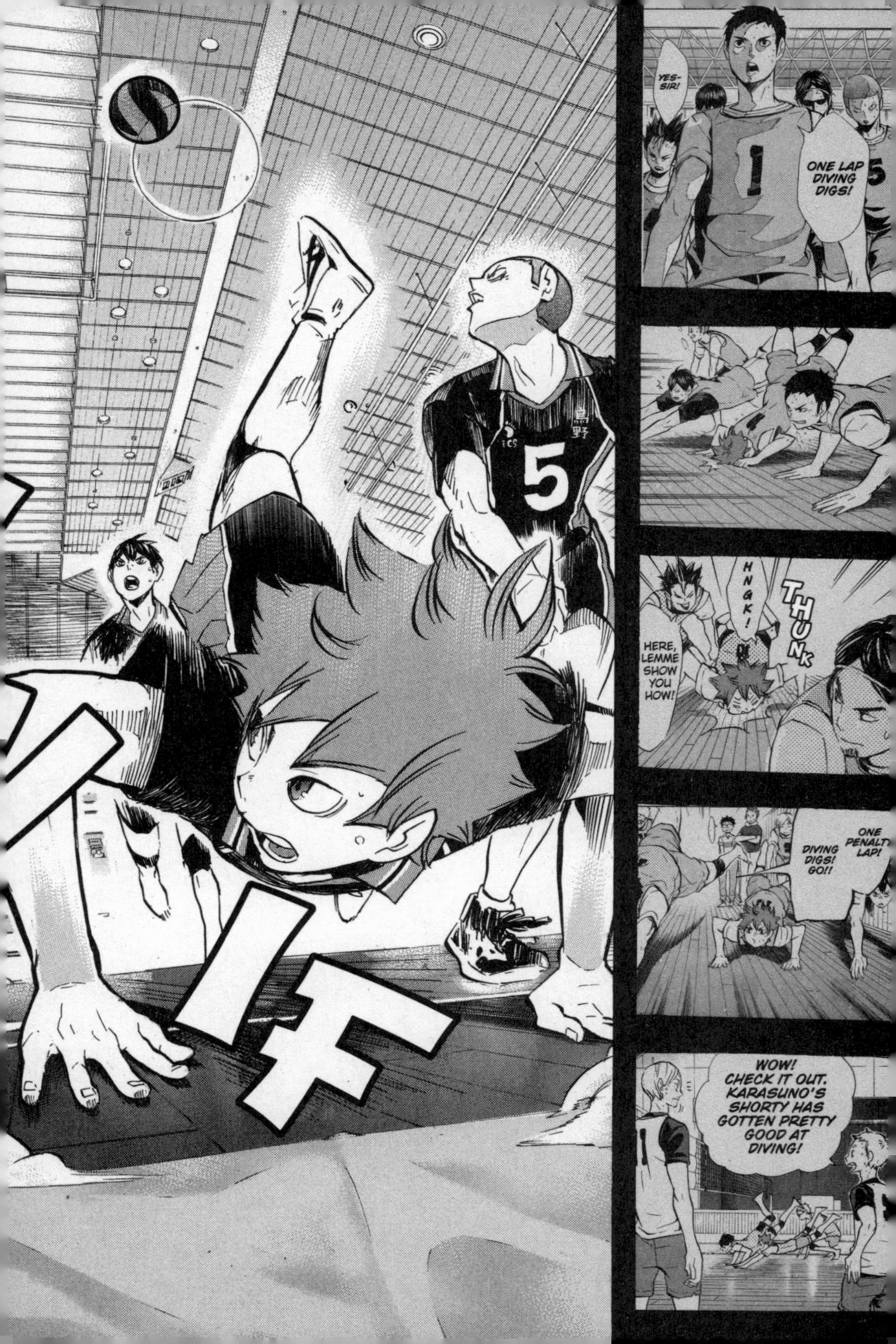
ONE LAP DIVING DIGS!
YES-SIR!
THUNK
HNGK!
HERE, LEMME SHOW YOU HOW!
ONE PENALTY LAP!
DIVING DIGS! GO!!
WOW! CHECK IT OUT. KARASUNO'S SHORTY HAS GOTTEN PRETTY GOOD AT DIVING!

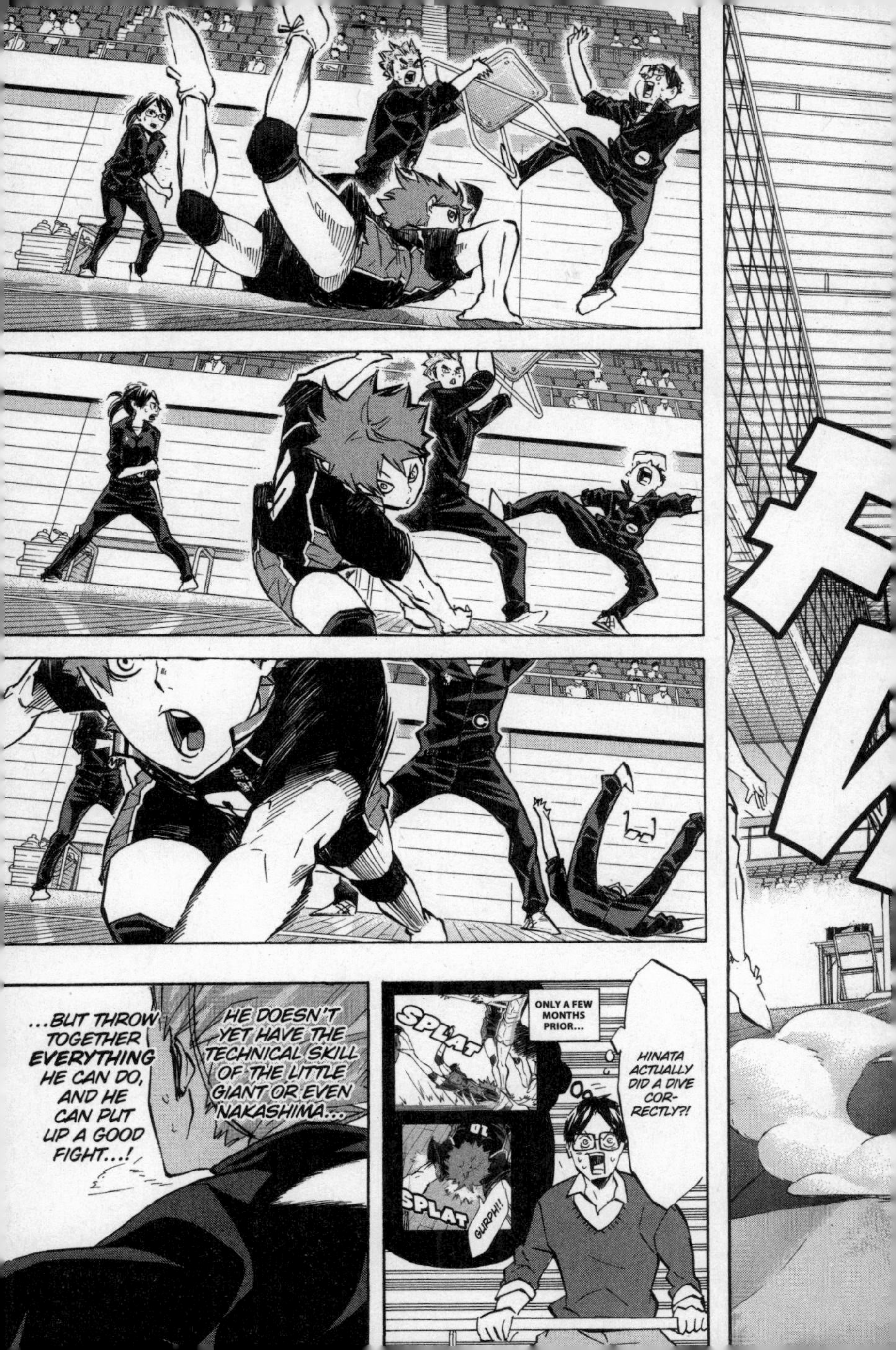
HINATA ACTUALLY DID A DIVE COR-RECTLY?!
ONLY A FEW MONTHS PRIOR...
SPLAT
SPLAT
GURPH!!
HE DOESN'T YET HAVE THE TECHNICAL SKILL OF THE LITTLE GIANT OR EVEN NAKASHIMA...
...BUT THROW TOGETHER EVERYTHING HE CAN DO, AND HE CAN PUT UP A GOOD FIGHT...!

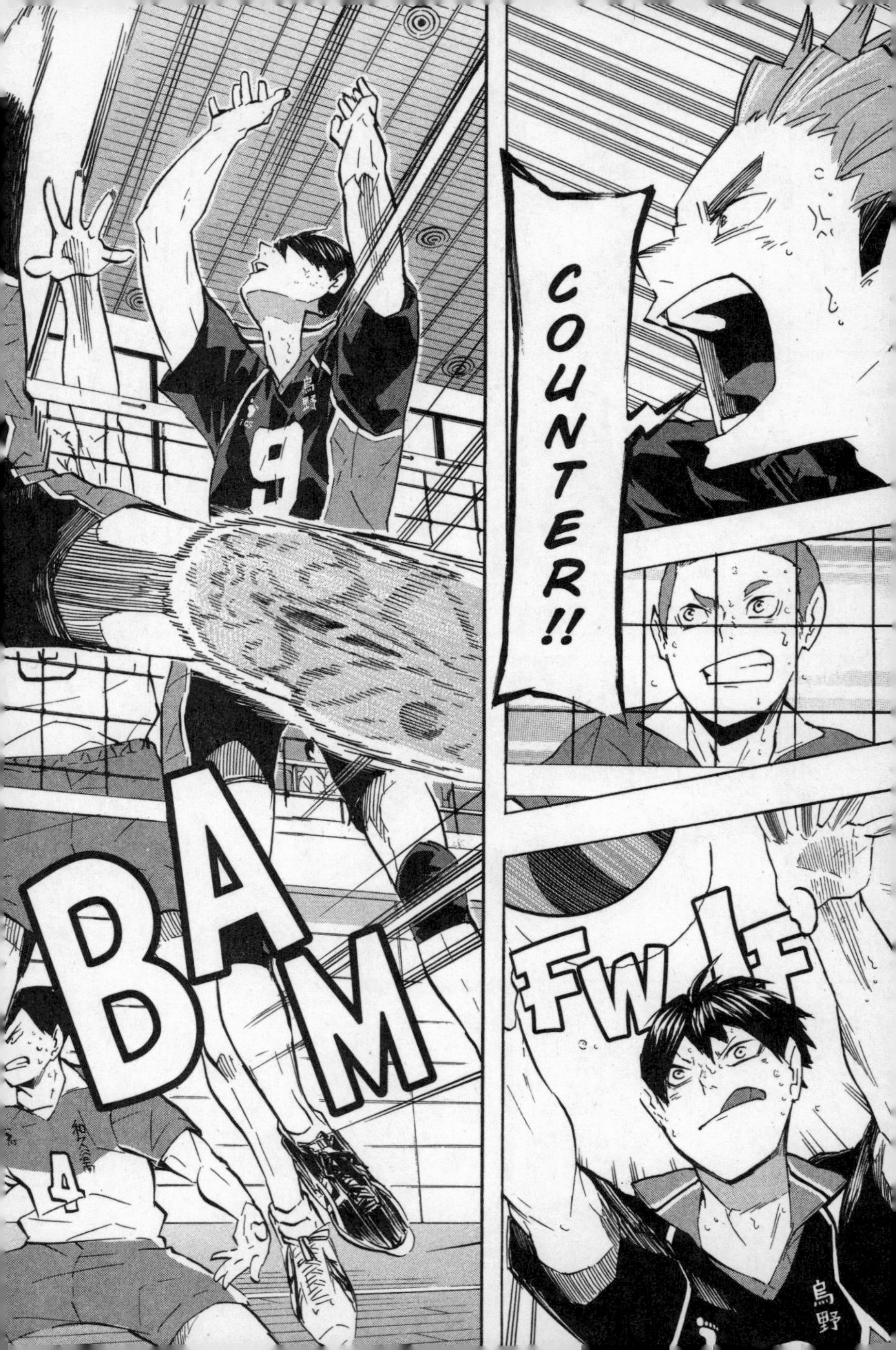
COUNTER!!
BAM

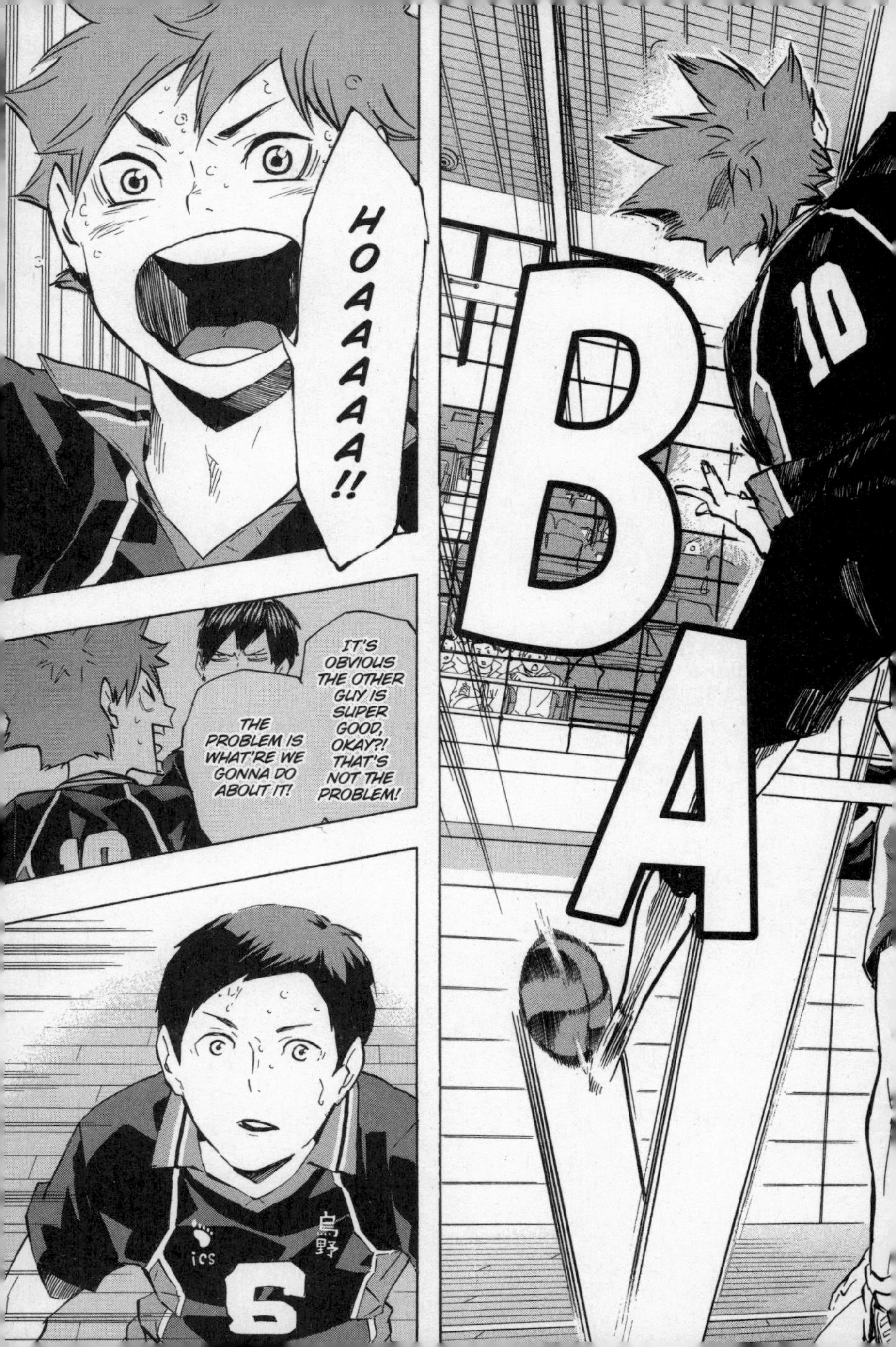
BA
HOAAAAA!!
IT'S OBVIOUS THE OTHER GUY IS SUPER GOOD, OKAY?! THAT'S NOT THE PROBLEM!
THE PROBLEM IS WHAT'RE WE GONNA DO ABOUT IT!

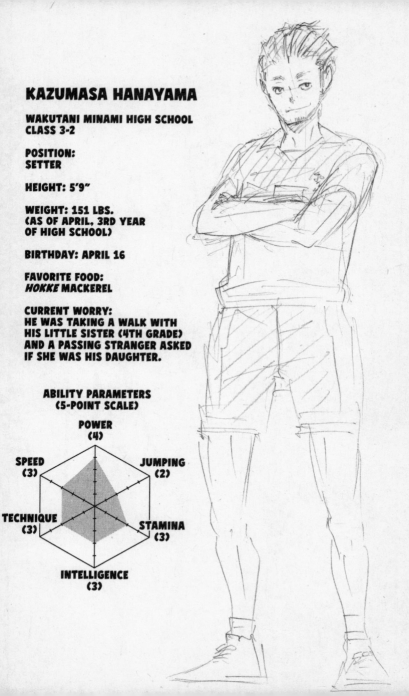

KAZUMASA HANAYAMA

WAKUTANI MINAMI HIGH SCHOOL
CLASS 3-2

POSITION:
SETTER

HEIGHT: 5'9"

WEIGHT: 151 LBS.
(AS OF APRIL, 3RD YEAR
OF HIGH SCHOOL)

BIRTHDAY: APRIL 16

FAVORITE FOOD:
***HOKKE* MACKEREL**

CURRENT WORRY:
HE WAS TAKING A WALK WITH
HIS LITTLE SISTER (4TH GRADE)
AND A PASSING STRANGER ASKED
IF SHE WAS HIS DAUGHTER.

ABILITY PARAMETERS
(5-POINT SCALE)

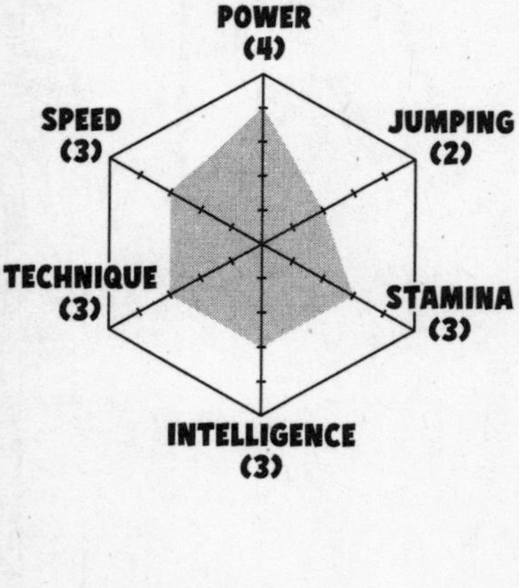
POWER
(4)
JUMPING
(2)
STAMINA
(3)
INTELLIGENCE
(3)
TECHNIQUE
(3)
SPEED
(3)

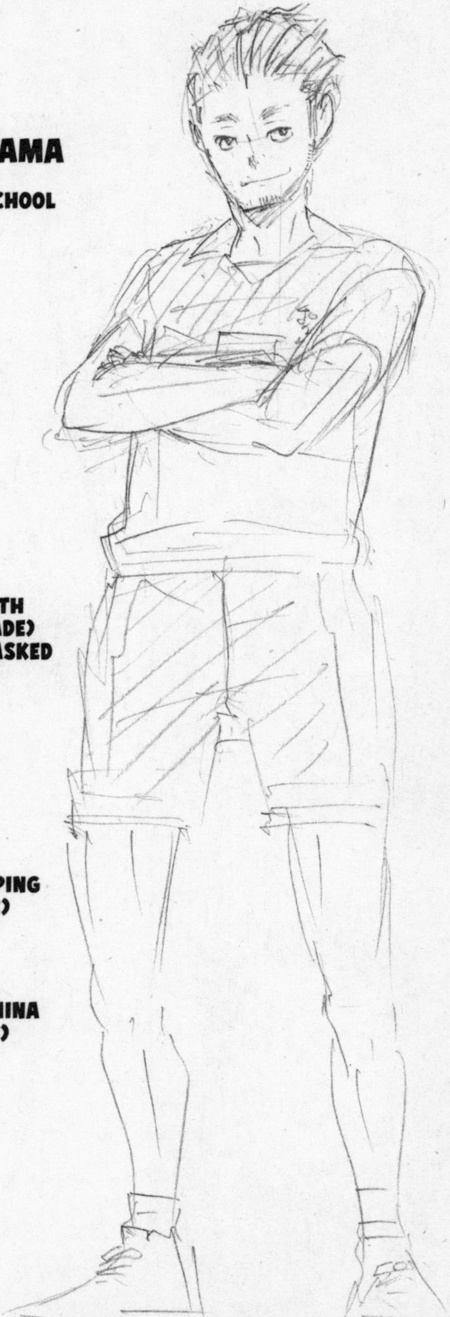

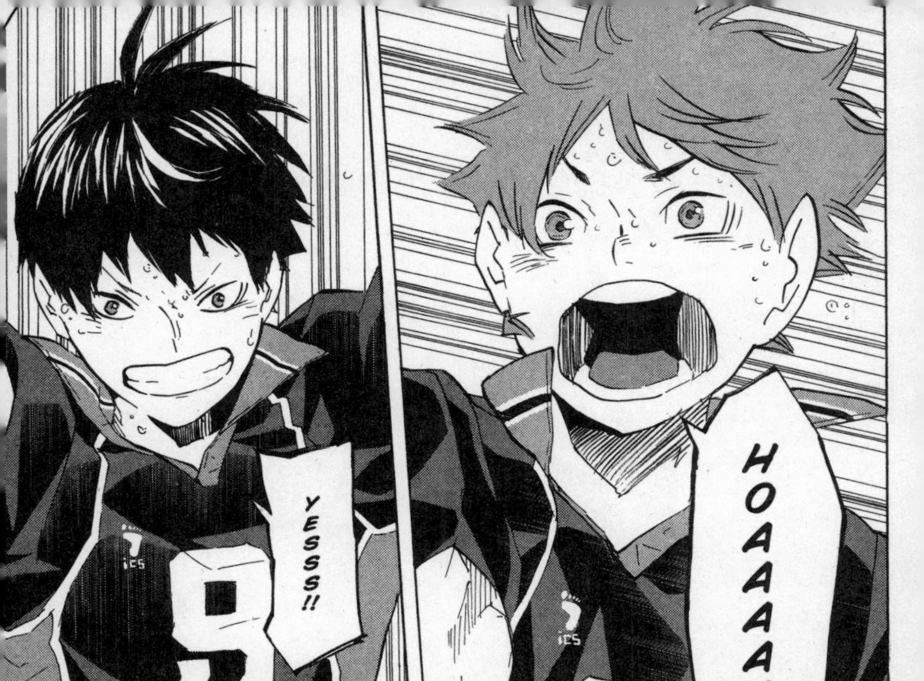
HOAAAAAA!!
YESSS!!

CHAPTER 122: Challenger

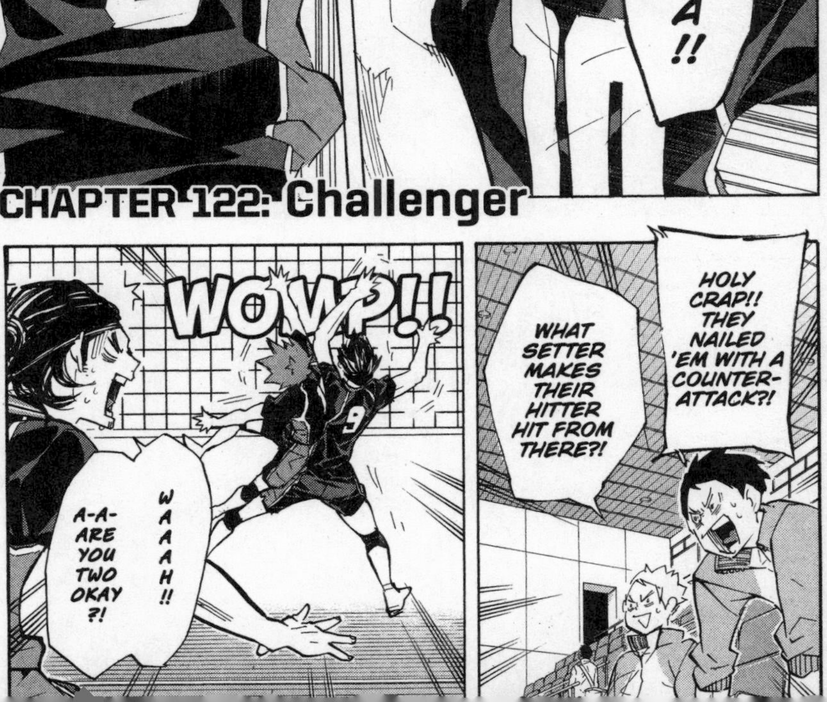
HOLY CRAP!! THEY NAILED 'EM WITH A COUNTER-ATTACK?!
WHAT SETTER MAKES THEIR HITTER HIT FROM THERE?!
WOMP!!
WAAAAH!!
A-A-ARE YOU TWO OKAY?!

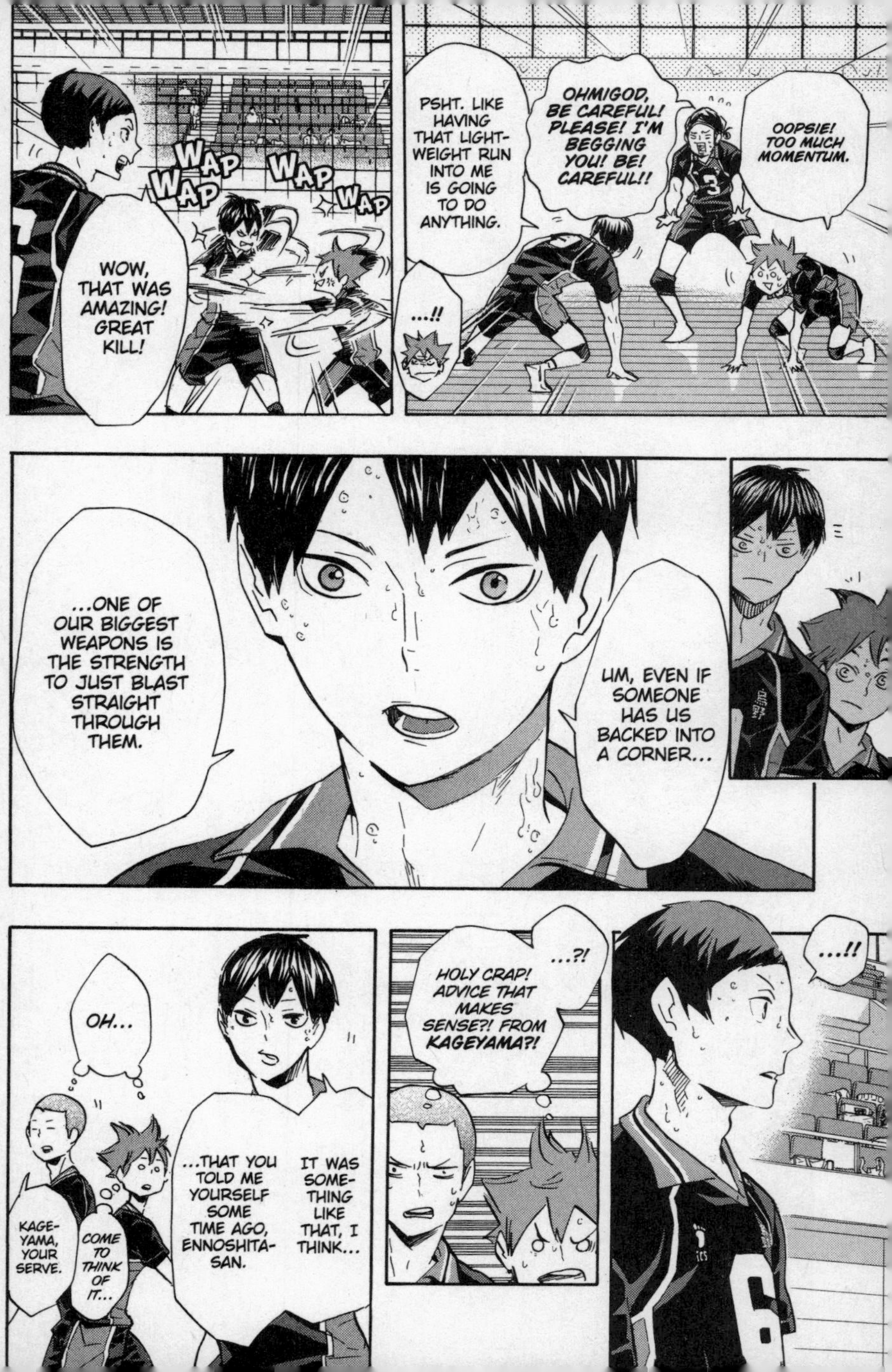

OOPSIE! TOO MUCH MOMENTUM.
OHMIGOD, BE CAREFUL! PLEASE! I'M BEGGING YOU! BE! CAREFUL!!
PSHT. LIKE HAVING THAT LIGHT-WEIGHT RUN INTO ME IS GOING TO DO ANYTHING.
...!!
WAP WAP WAP WAP
WOW, THAT WAS AMAZING! GREAT KILL!
UM, EVEN IF SOMEONE HAS US BACKED INTO A CORNER...
...ONE OF OUR BIGGEST WEAPONS IS THE STRENGTH TO JUST BLAST STRAIGHT THROUGH THEM.
...!!
...?!
HOLY CRAP! ADVICE THAT MAKES SENSE?! FROM KAGEYAMA?!
COME TO THINK OF IT...
IT WAS SOMETHING LIKE THAT, I THINK...
...THAT YOU TOLD ME YOURSELF SOME TIME AGO, ENNOSHITA-SAN.
OH...
KAGEYAMA, YOUR SERVE.

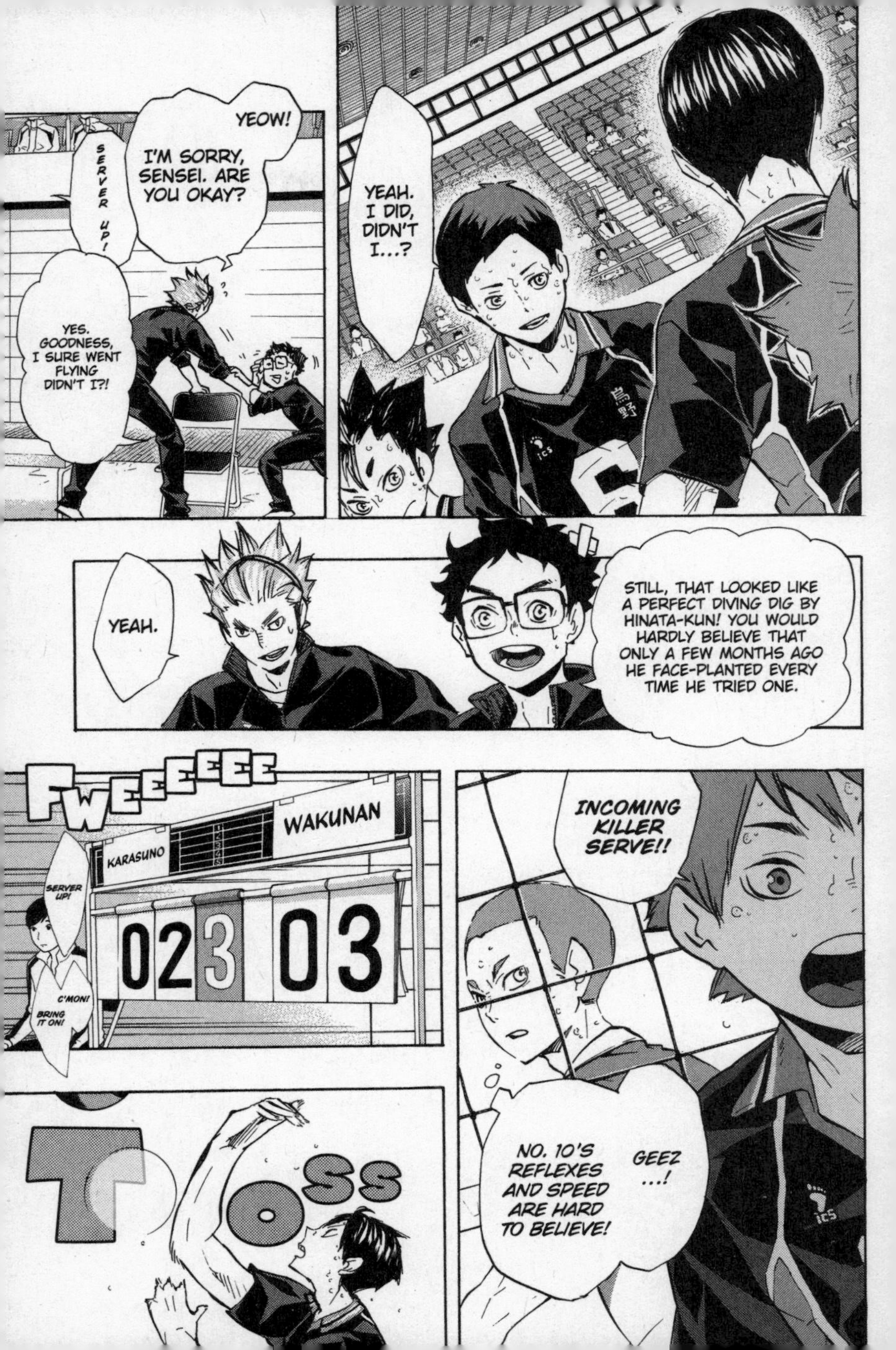

YEAH. I DID, DIDN'T I...?
YEOW!
I'M SORRY, SENSEI. ARE YOU OKAY?
SERVER UP!
YES. GOODNESS, I SURE WENT FLYING DIDN'T I?!
STILL, THAT LOOKED LIKE A PERFECT DIVING DIG BY HINATA-KUN! YOU WOULD HARDLY BELIEVE THAT ONLY A FEW MONTHS AGO HE FACE-PLANTED EVERY TIME HE TRIED ONE.
YEAH.
INCOMING KILLER SERVE!!
GEEZ ...!
NO. 10'S REFLEXES AND SPEED ARE HARD TO BELIEVE!
FWEEEEEE
WAKUNAN
KARASUNO
SERVER UP!
02 3 03
C'MON! BRING IT ON!
TOSS

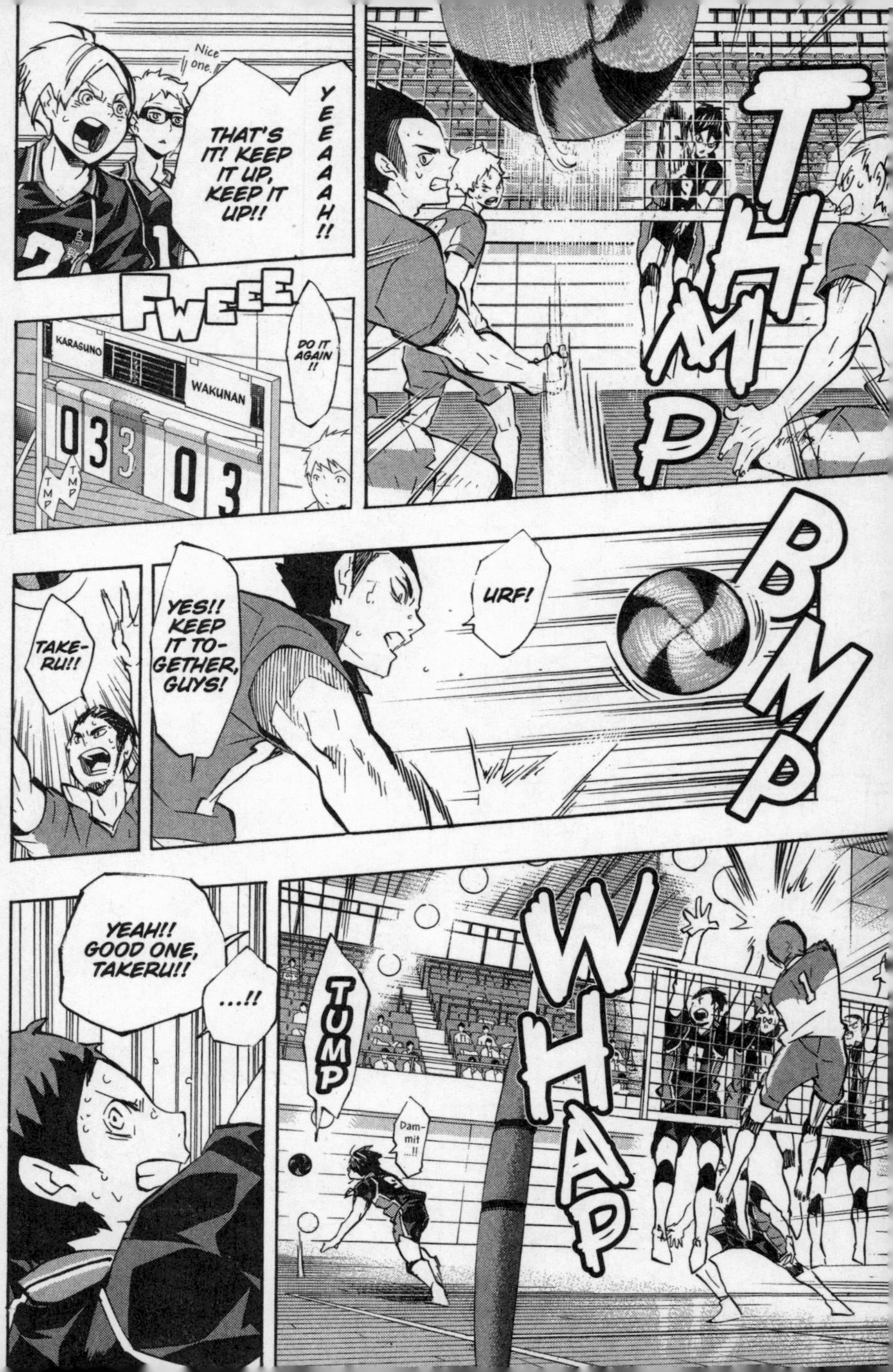
THUMP
YEEAAAAH!!
Nice one.
THAT'S IT! KEEP IT UP, KEEP IT UP!!
FWEEE
DO IT AGAIN!!
KARASUNO
WAKUNAN
03 3 03
TMP TMP
BOMP
URF!
YES!! KEEP IT TO-GETHER, GUYS!
TAKE-RU!!
WHAP
TUMP
Dam-mit...!!
...!!
YEAH!! GOOD ONE, TAKERU!!

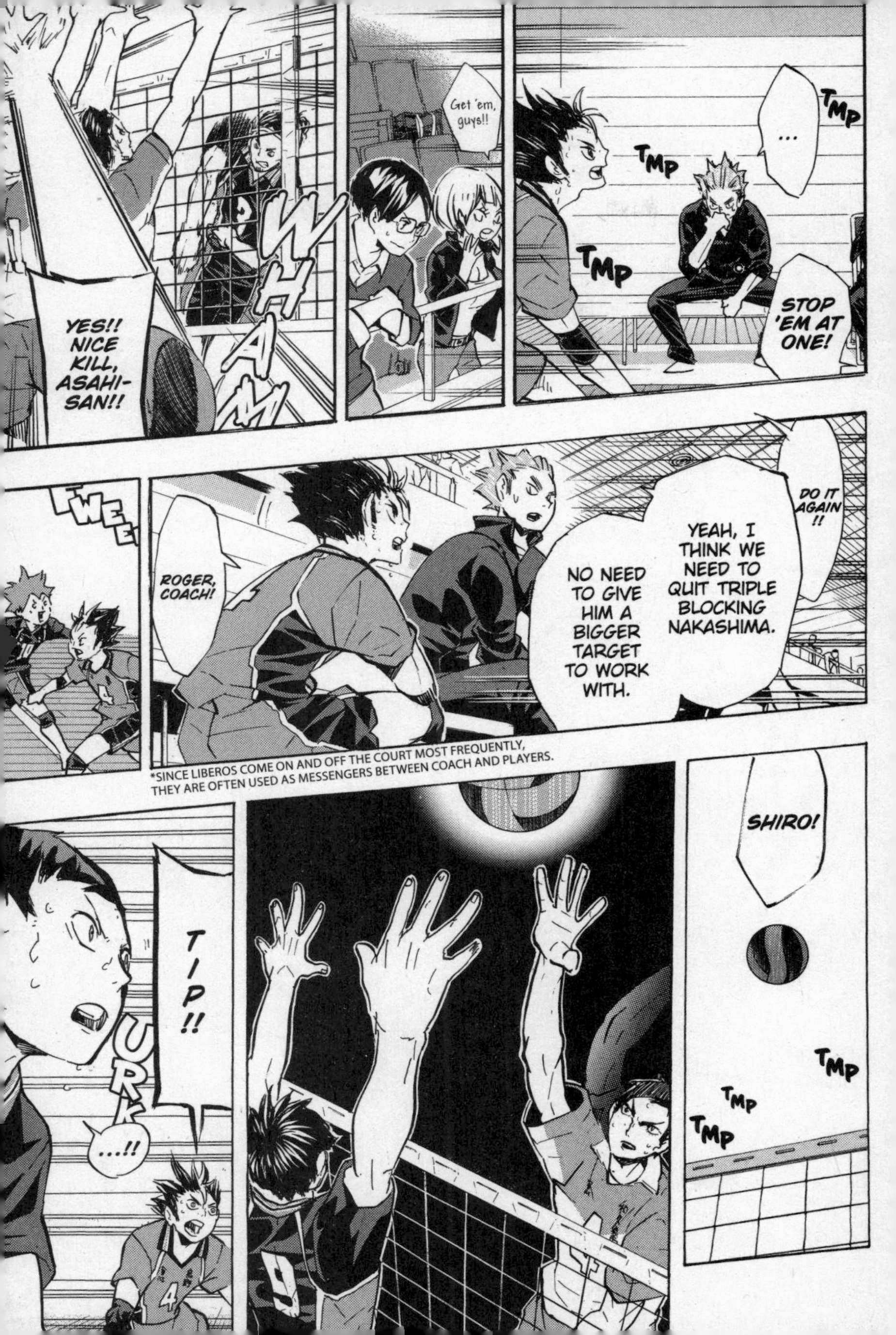
...
TMP
TMP
TMP
STOP 'EM AT ONE!
Get 'em, guys!!
YES!! NICE KILL, ASAHI-SAN!!
WHAM
DO IT AGAIN !!
YEAH, I THINK WE NEED TO QUIT TRIPLE BLOCKING NAKASHIMA.
NO NEED TO GIVE HIM A BIGGER TARGET TO WORK WITH.
ROGER, COACH!
FWEE
SHIRO!
TMP
TMP
TMP
TIP!!
URK
...!!

*SINCE LIBEROS COME ON AND OFF THE COURT MOST FREQUENTLY, THEY ARE OFTEN USED AS MESSENGERS BETWEEN COACH AND PLAYERS.

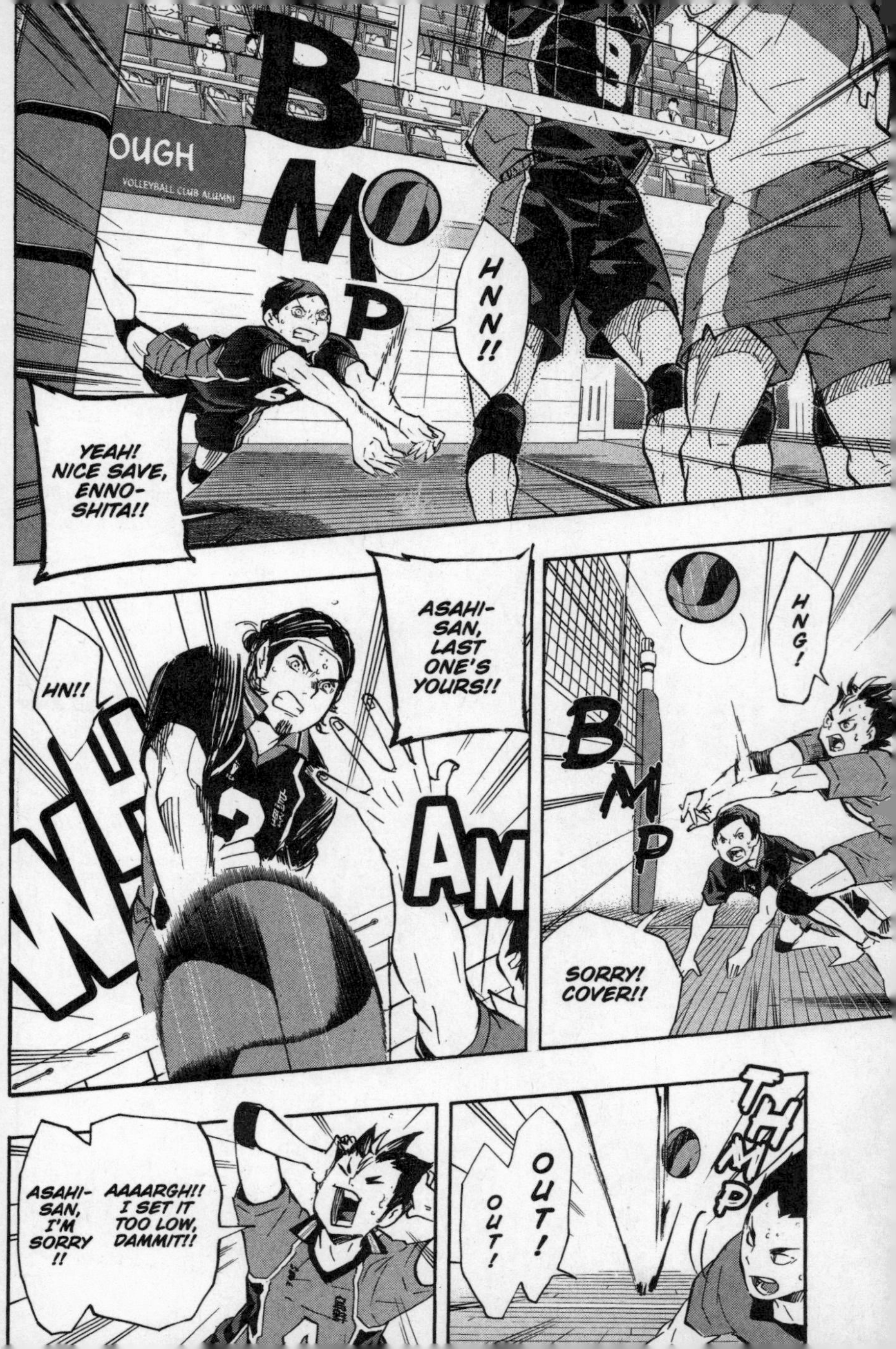
OUGH
VOLLEYBALL CLUB ALUMNI
BUMP
HNNN!!
YEAH! NICE SAVE, ENNO-SHITA!!
HNG!
BUMP
SORRY! COVER!!
ASAHI-SAN, LAST ONE'S YOURS!!
HN!!
AM
THUMP
OUT!
OUT!
AAAARGH!! I SET IT TOO LOW, DAMMIT!!
ASAHI-SAN, I'M SORRY!!

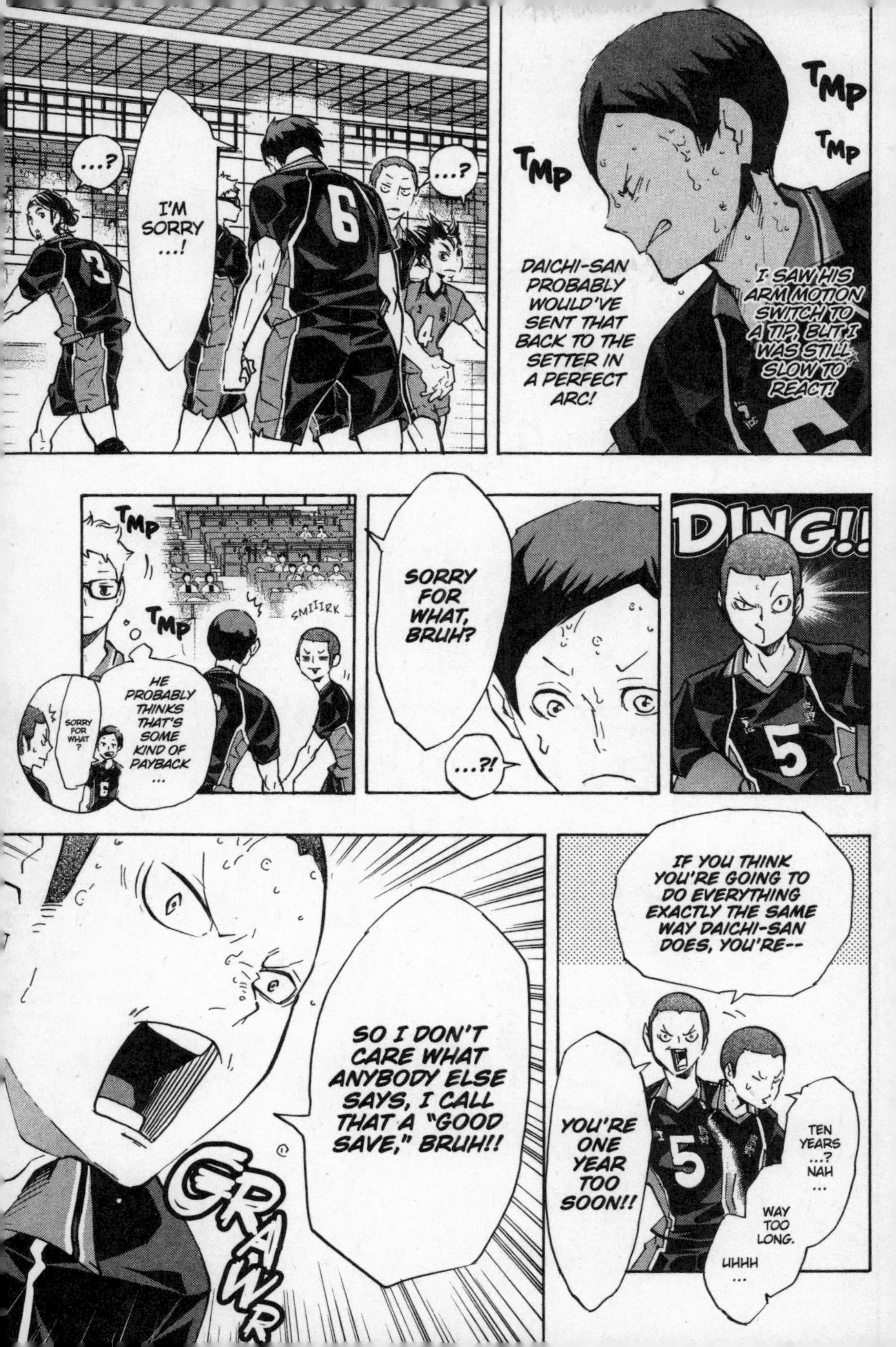
TMP
TMP
TMP
I SAW HIS ARM MOTION SWITCH TO A TIP, BUT I WAS STILL SLOW TO REACT!
DAICHI-SAN PROBABLY WOULD'VE SENT THAT BACK TO THE SETTER IN A PERFECT ARC!
...?
I'M SORRY ...!
...?
DING!!
SORRY FOR WHAT, BRUH?
...?!
TMP
TMP
SMIIIRK
HE PROBABLY THINKS THAT'S SOME KIND OF PAYBACK ...
SORRY FOR WHAT ?
IF YOU THINK YOU'RE GOING TO DO EVERYTHING EXACTLY THE SAME WAY DAICHI-SAN DOES, YOU'RE--
YOU'RE ONE YEAR TOO SOON!!
TEN YEARS ...? NAH ...
WAY TOO LONG.
UHHH ...
SO I DON'T CARE WHAT ANYBODY ELSE SAYS, I CALL THAT A "GOOD SAVE," BRUH!!
CRAWR

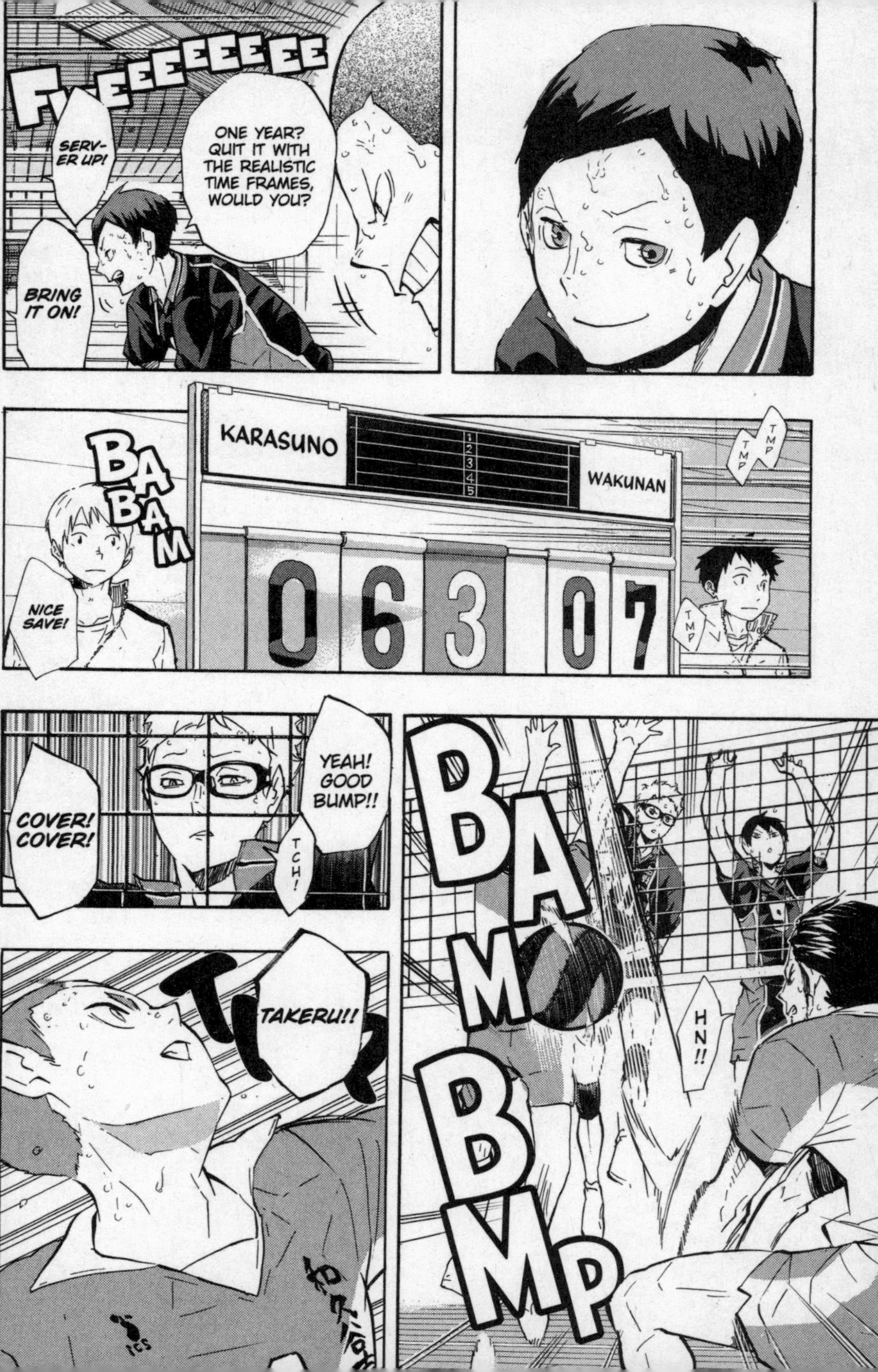

ONE YEAR? QUIT IT WITH THE REALISTIC TIME FRAMES, WOULD YOU?
EEEEEEEEE
SERV-ER UP!
BRING IT ON!
TMP TMP
WAKUNAN
KARASUNO
1 2 3 4 5
0 6 3 0 7
TMP
BABAM
NICE SAVE!
HN!!
BAM BUMP
YEAH! GOOD BUMP!!
TCH!
COVER! COVER!
TAKERU!!

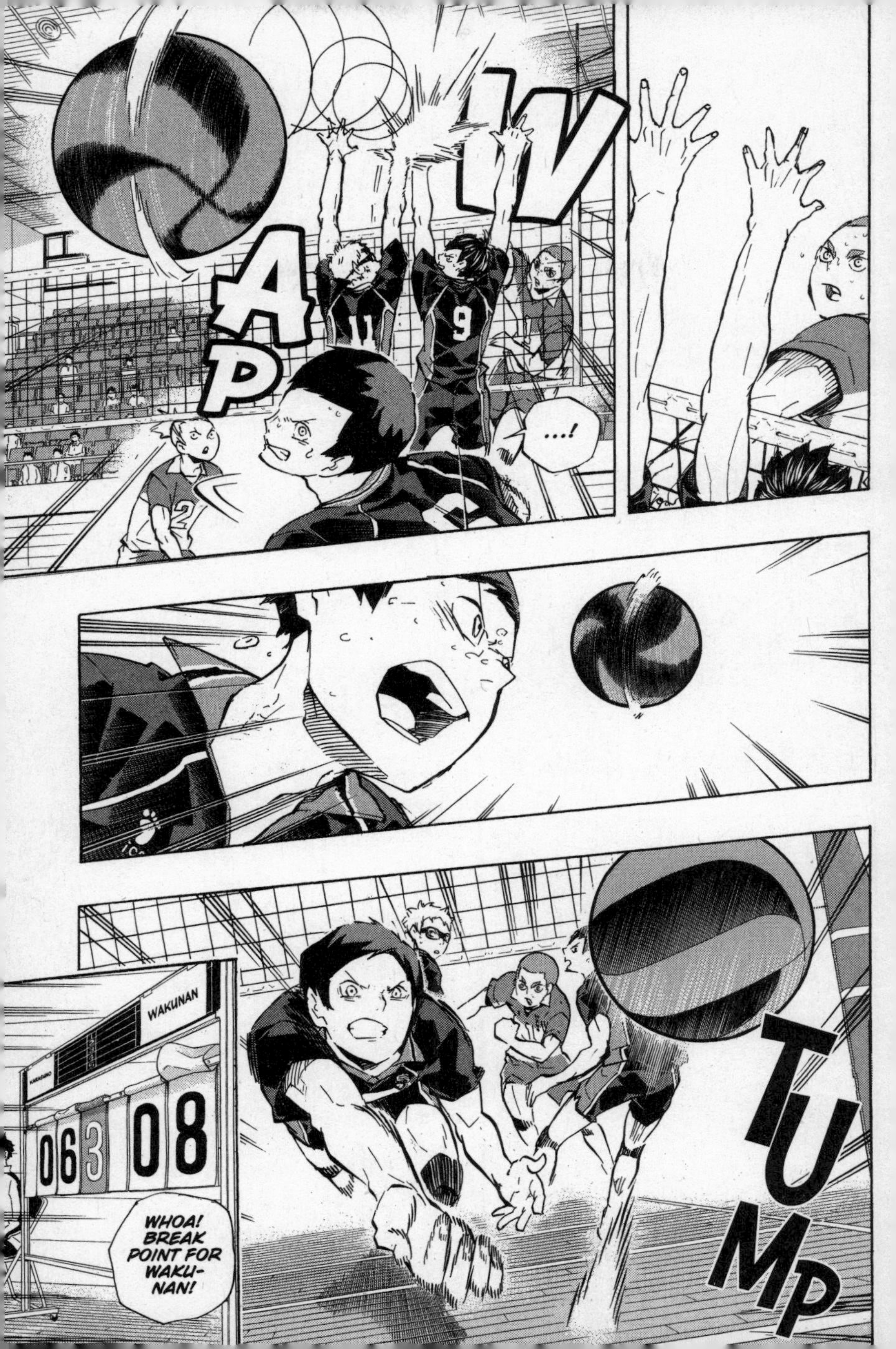

WAP
...!
TUMP
WAKUNAN
06 3 08
WHOA! BREAK POINT FOR WAKU-NAN!

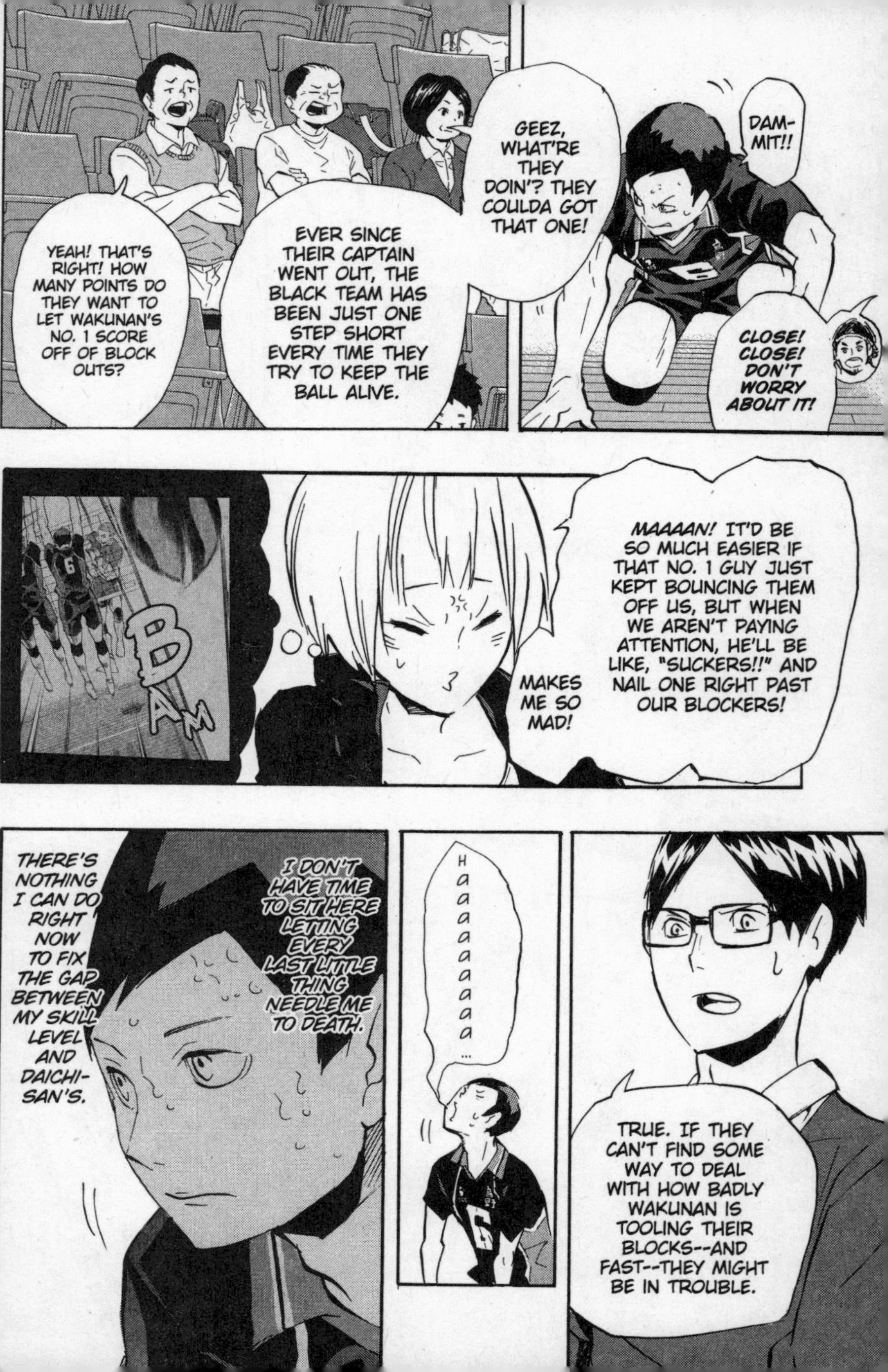
DAM-MIT!!
CLOSE! CLOSE! DON'T WORRY ABOUT IT!
GEEZ, WHAT'RE THEY DOIN'? THEY COULDA GOT THAT ONE!
EVER SINCE THEIR CAPTAIN WENT OUT, THE BLACK TEAM HAS BEEN JUST ONE STEP SHORT EVERY TIME THEY TRY TO KEEP THE BALL ALIVE.
YEAH! THAT'S RIGHT! HOW MANY POINTS DO THEY WANT TO LET WAKUNAN'S NO. 1 SCORE OFF OF BLOCK OUTS?
MAAAAN! IT'D BE SO MUCH EASIER IF THAT NO. 1 GUY JUST KEPT BOUNCING THEM OFF US, BUT WHEN WE AREN'T PAYING ATTENTION, HE'LL BE LIKE, "SUCKERS!!" AND NAIL ONE RIGHT PAST OUR BLOCKERS!
MAKES ME SO MAD!
BAM
TRUE. IF THEY CAN'T FIND SOME WAY TO DEAL WITH HOW BADLY WAKUNAN IS TOOLING THEIR BLOCKS--AND FAST--THEY MIGHT BE IN TROUBLE.
Haaaaaaaaaa...
I DON'T HAVE TIME TO SIT HERE LETTING EVERY LAST LITTLE THING NEEDLE ME TO DEATH.
THERE'S NOTHING I CAN DO RIGHT NOW TO FIX THE GAP BETWEEN MY SKILL LEVEL AND DAICHI-SAN'S.

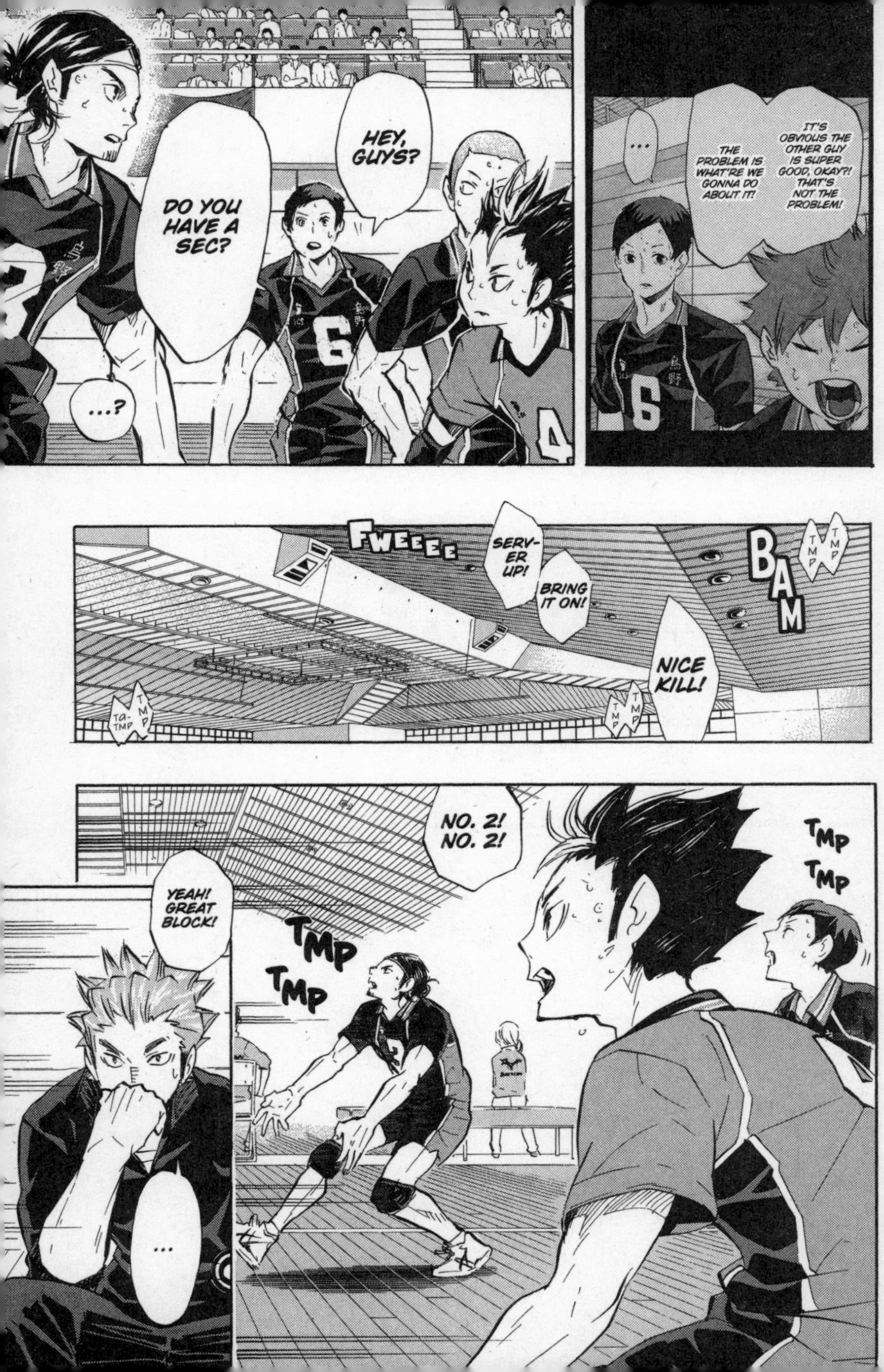
IT'S OBVIOUS THE OTHER GUY IS SUPER GOOD, OKAY?! THAT'S NOT THE PROBLEM!
THE PROBLEM IS WHAT'RE WE GONNA DO ABOUT IT!
...
HEY, GUYS?
DO YOU HAVE A SEC?
...?
TMP TMP
BAM
SERV-ER UP!
BRING IT ON!
FWEEEE
NICE KILL!
TMP TMP
TA-TMP TMP
TMP TMP
NO. 2! NO. 2!
TMP TMP
YEAH! GREAT BLOCK!
...

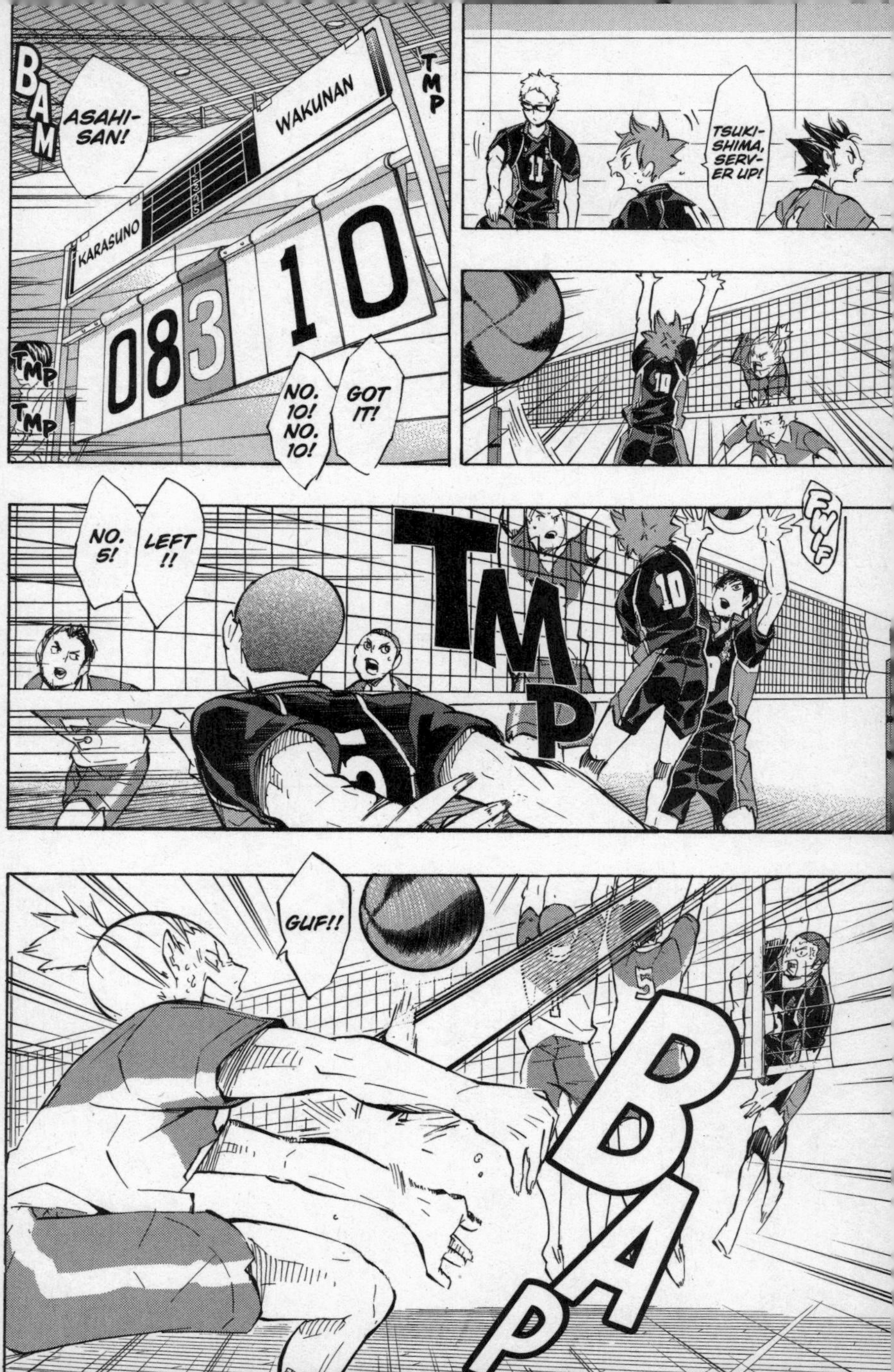

TSUKISHIMA, SERVER UP!
TMP
ASAHI-SAN!
BAM
WAKUNAN
KARASUNO
08
3
10
GOT IT!
NO. 10! NO. 10!
TMP
TMP
FWIF
TMP
LEFT!!
NO. 5!
GUF!!
BAP

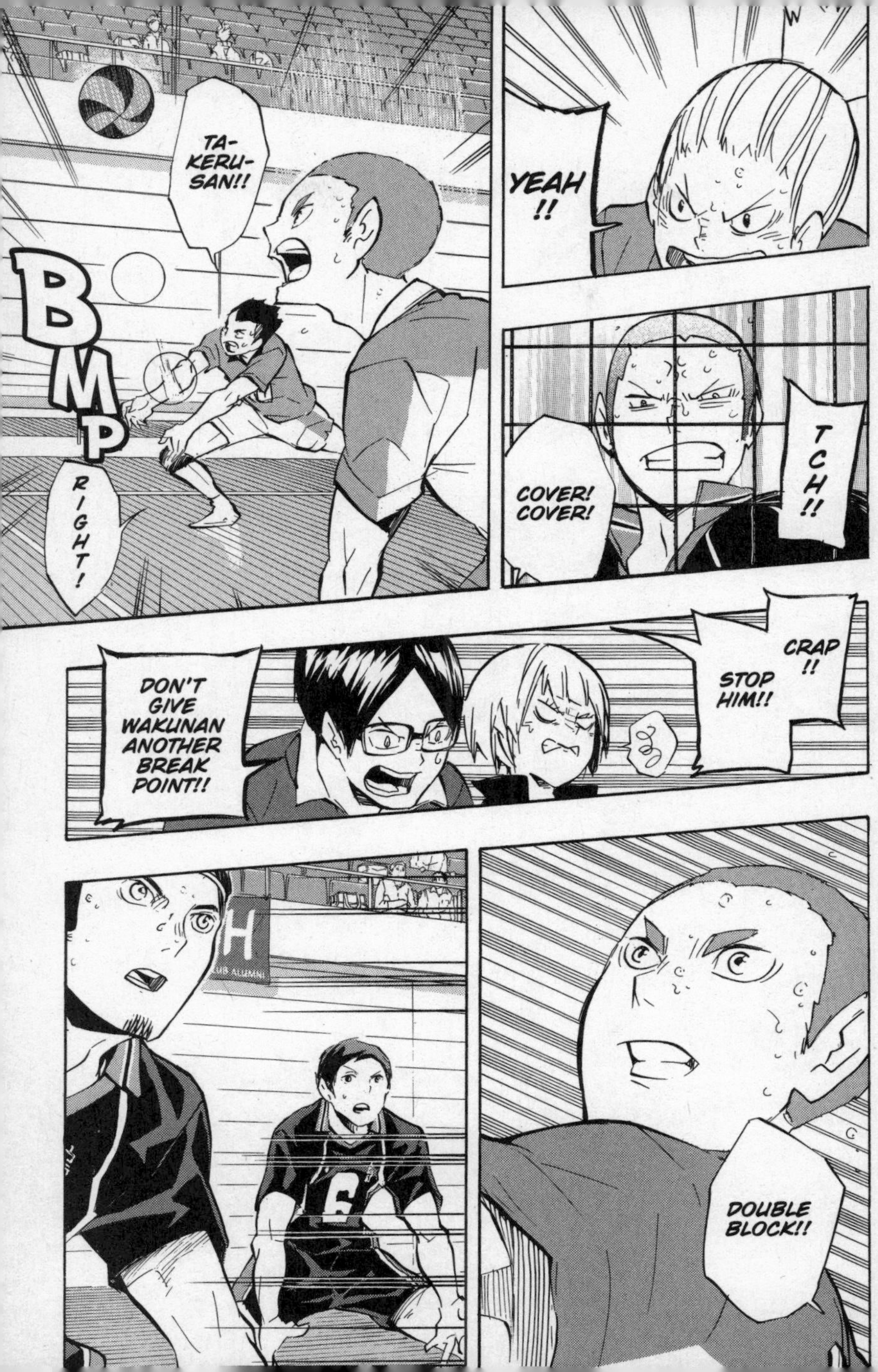
YEAH!!
TCH!!
COVER! COVER!
TA-KERU-SAN!!
BMP
RIGHT!
CRAP!!
STOP HIM!!
DON'T GIVE WAKUNAN ANOTHER BREAK POINT!!
DOUBLE BLOCK!!

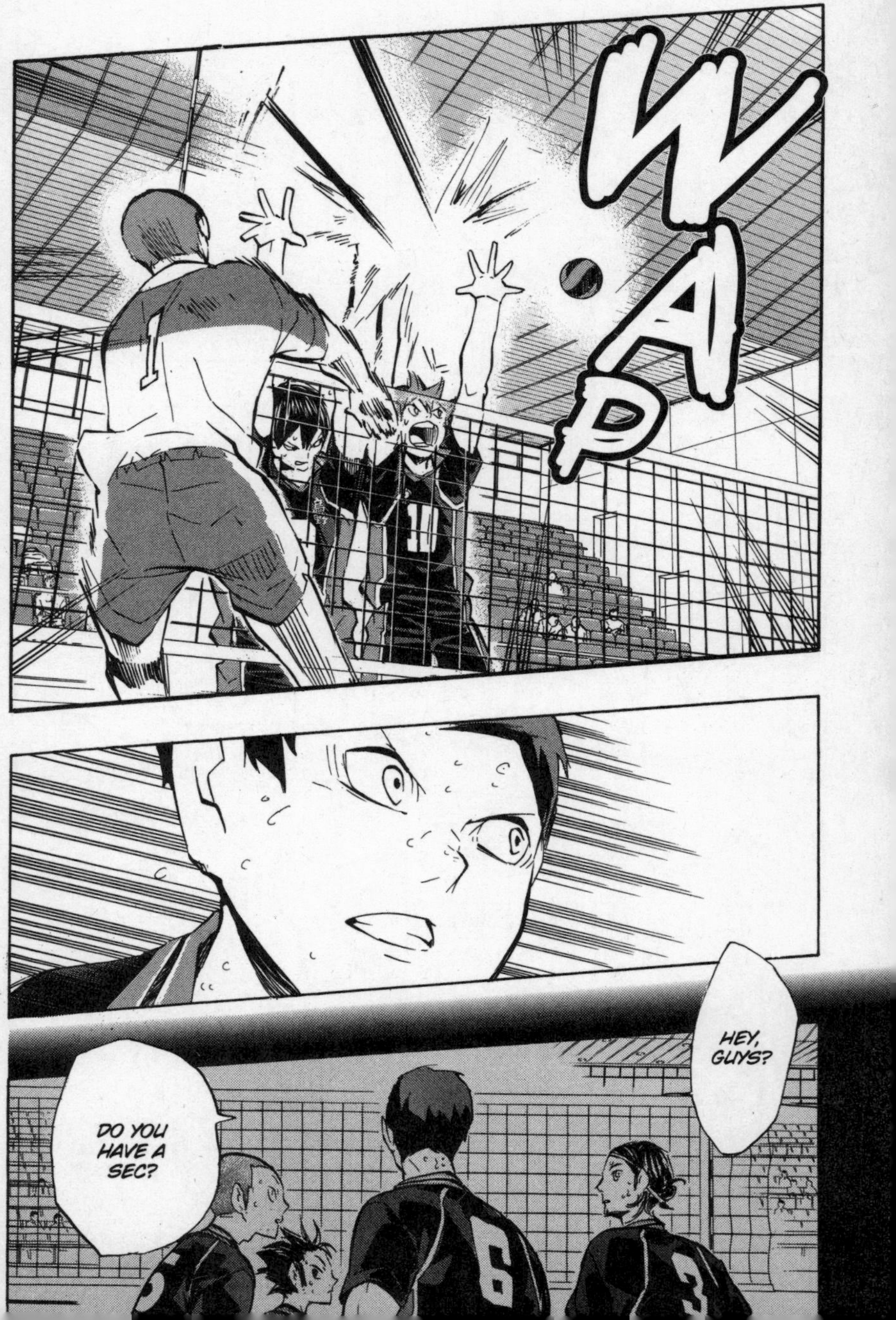
WAP
HEY, GUYS?
DO YOU HAVE A SEC?

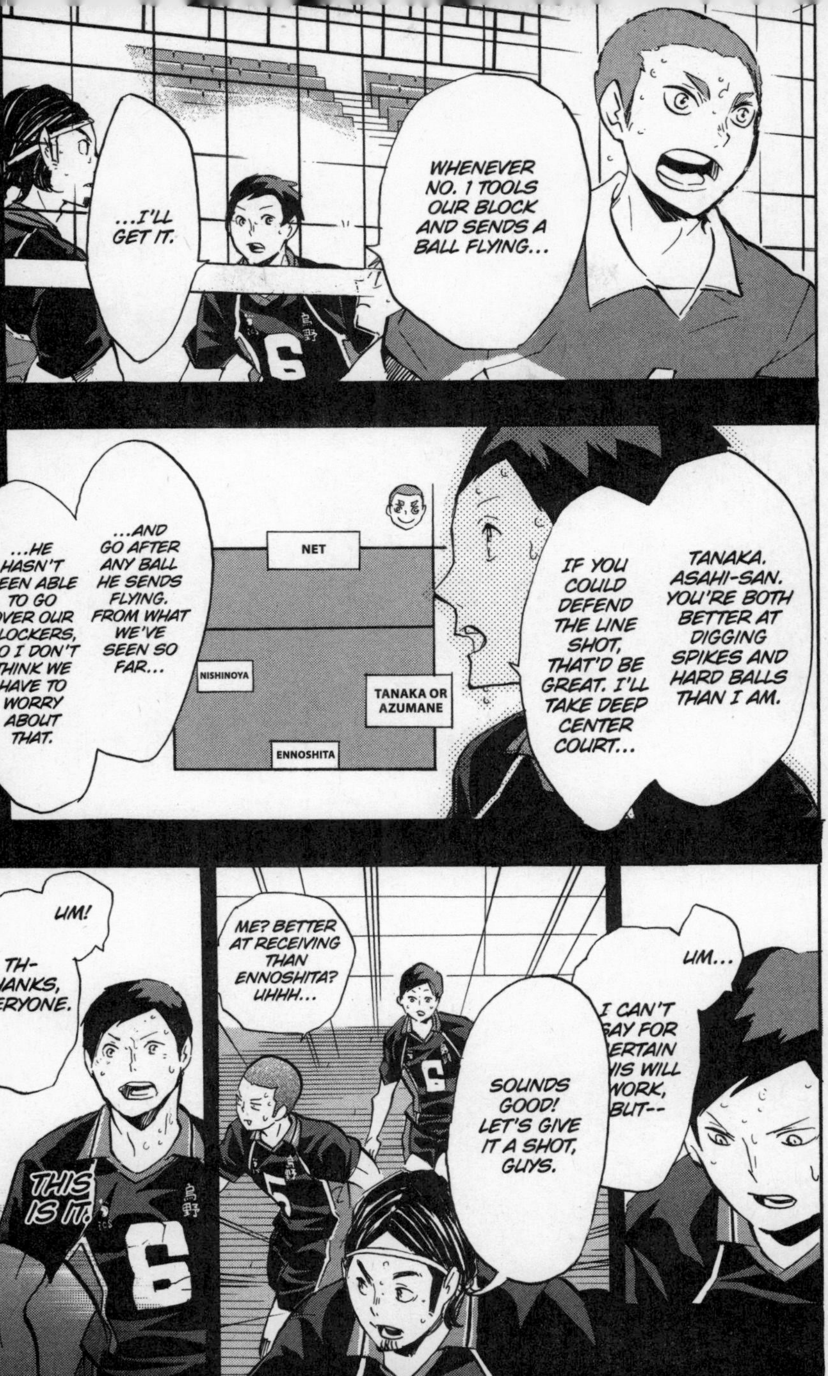
WHENEVER NO. 1 TOOLS OUR BLOCK AND SENDS A BALL FLYING...
...I'LL GET IT.
TANAKA. ASAHI-SAN. YOU'RE BOTH BETTER AT DIGGING SPIKES AND HARD BALLS THAN I AM.
IF YOU COULD DEFEND THE LINE SHOT, THAT'D BE GREAT. I'LL TAKE DEEP CENTER COURT...
NET
NISHINOYA
TANAKA OR AZUMANE
ENNOSHITA
...AND GO AFTER ANY BALL HE SENDS FLYING. FROM WHAT WE'VE SEEN SO FAR...
...HE HASN'T BEEN ABLE TO GO OVER OUR BLOCKERS, SO I DON'T THINK WE HAVE TO WORRY ABOUT THAT.
UM...
I CAN'T SAY FOR ERTAIN HIS WILL WORK, BUT--
SOUNDS GOOD! LET'S GIVE IT A SHOT, GUYS.
ME? BETTER AT RECEIVING THAN ENNOSHITA? UHHH...
UM!
TH- THANKS, EVERYONE.
THIS IS IT.

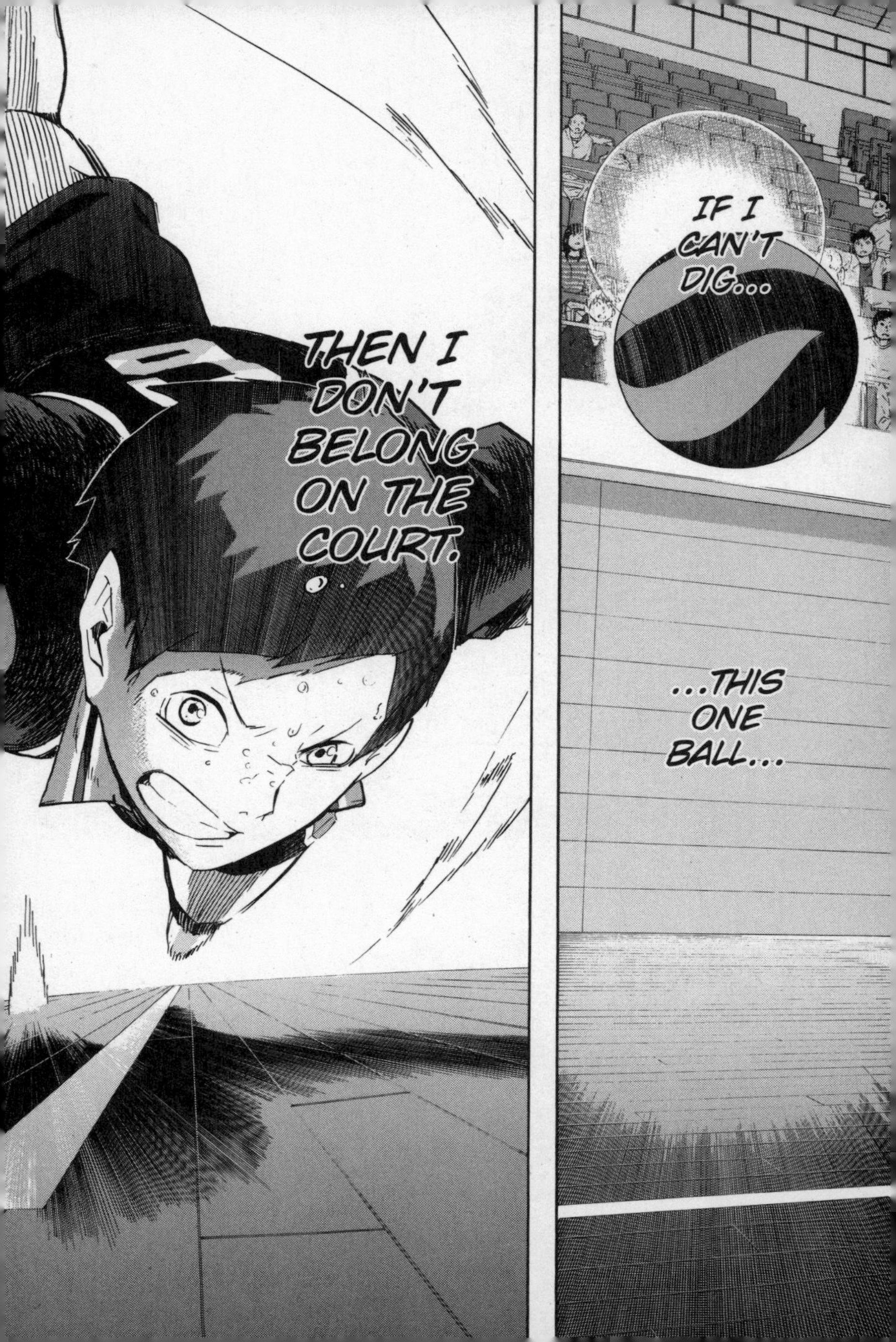
IF I CAN'T DIG...
...THIS ONE BALL...
THEN I DON'T BELONG ON THE COURT.

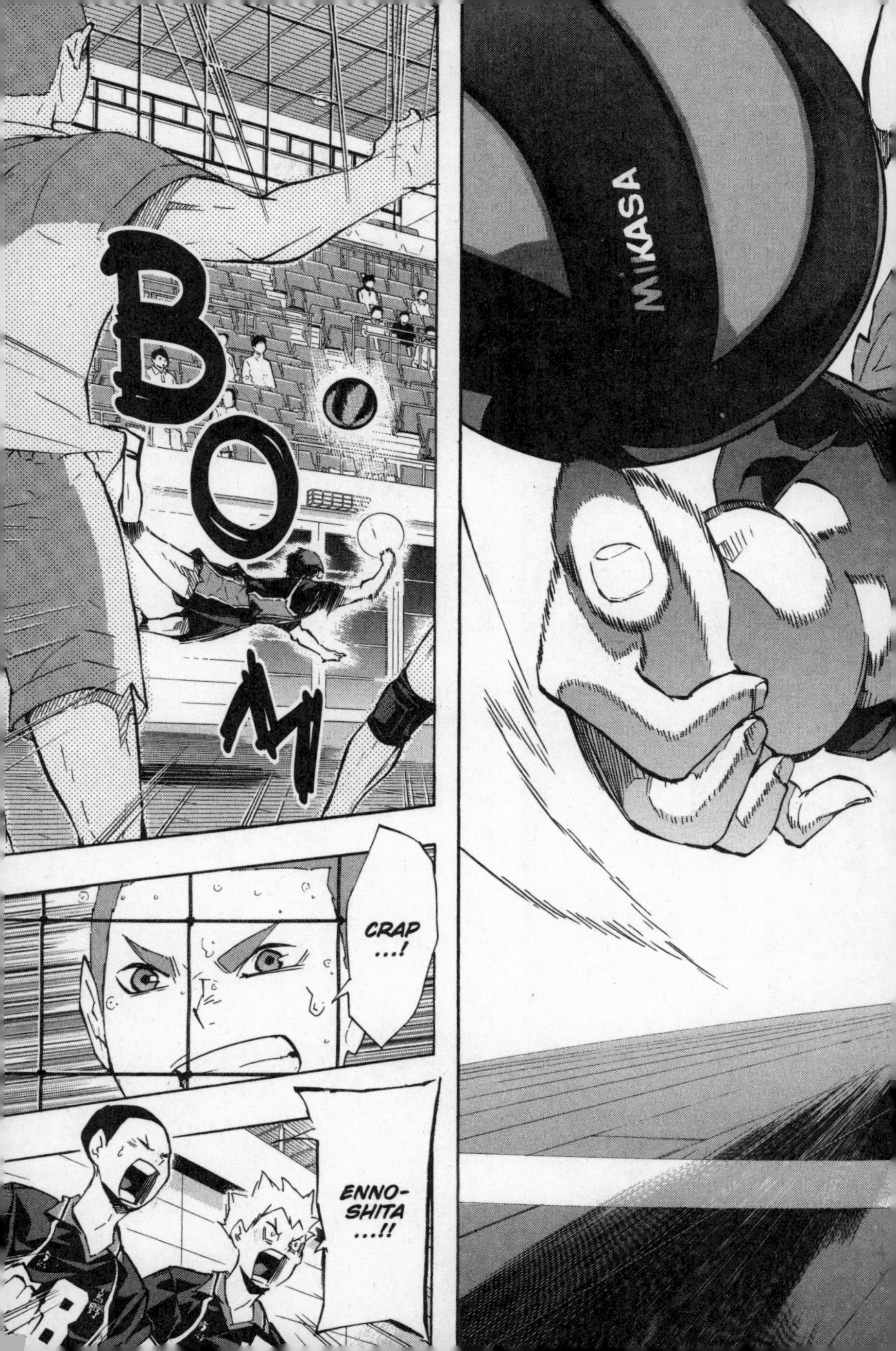
MIKASA
BOOM
CRAP ...!
ENNO-SHITA ...!!

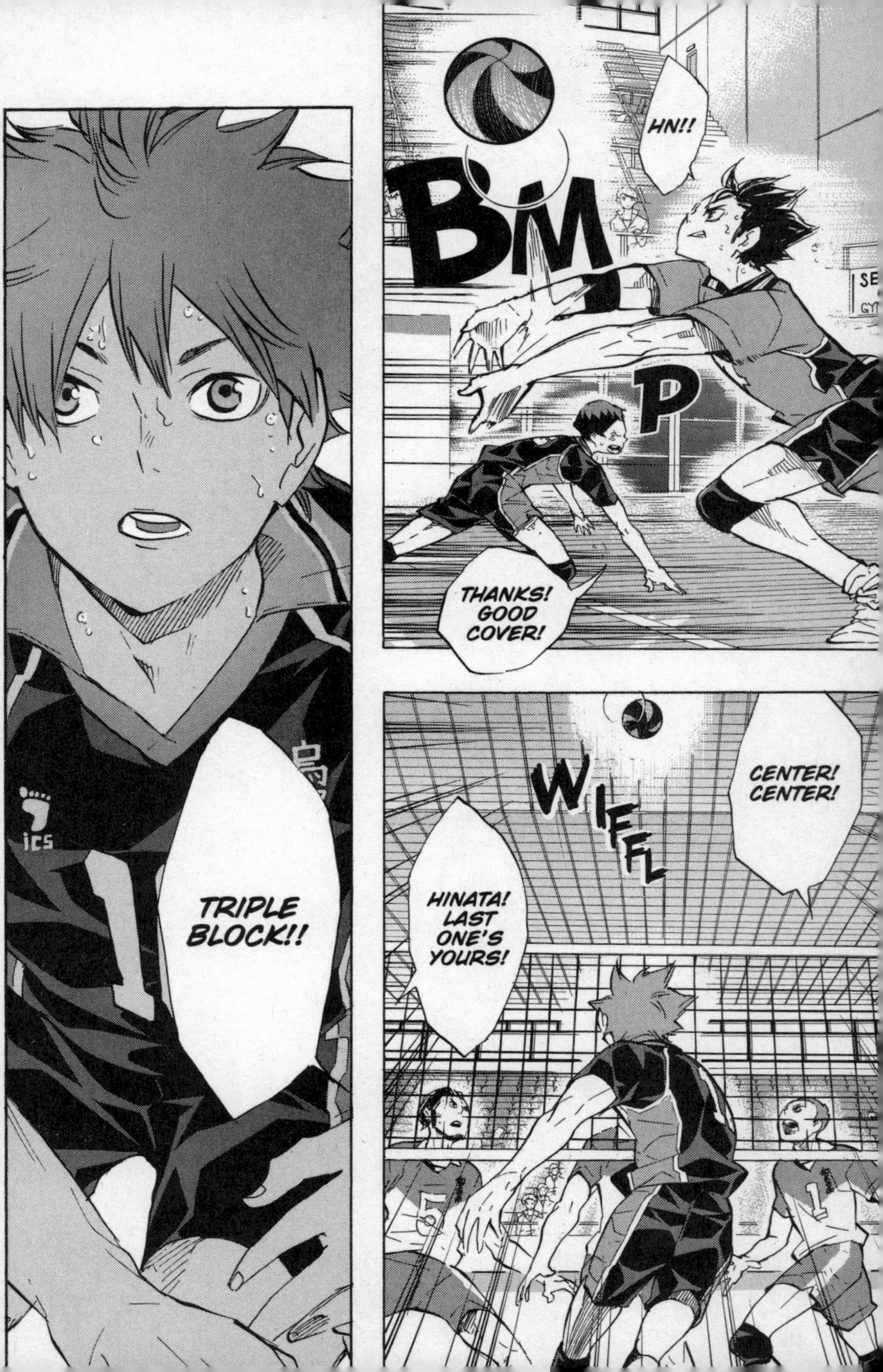
HN!!
BMP
THANKS! GOOD COVER!
CENTER! CENTER!
WIFFL
HINATA! LAST ONE'S YOURS!
TRIPLE BLOCK!!

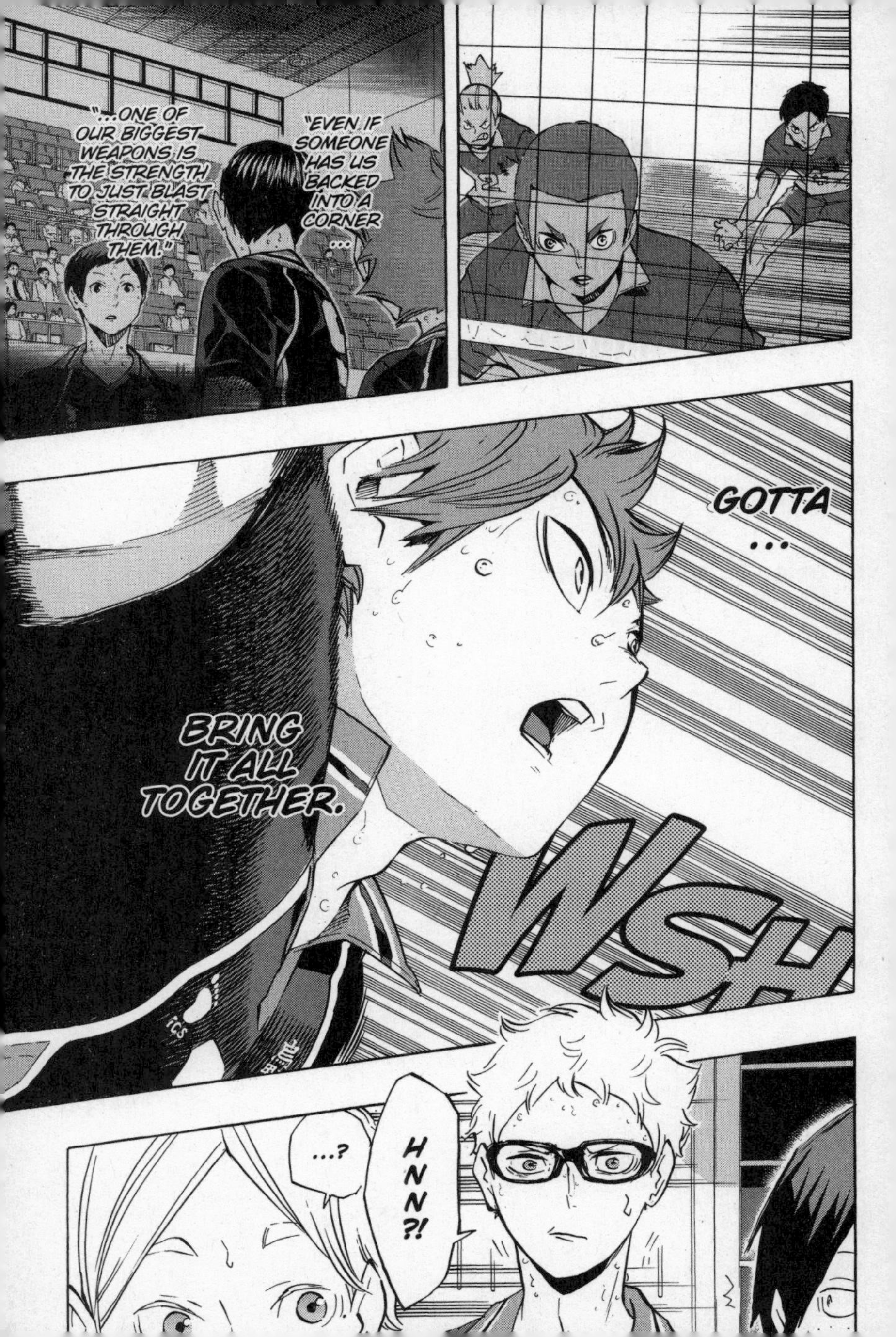
"EVEN IF SOMEONE HAS US BACKED INTO A CORNER...
"...ONE OF OUR BIGGEST WEAPONS IS THE STRENGTH TO JUST BLAST STRAIGHT THROUGH THEM."
GOTTA...
BRING IT ALL TOGETHER.
WSH
HNN?!
...?

YUKI SHIROISHI

WAKUTANI MINAMI HIGH SCHOOL
CLASS 3-3

POSITION:
WING SPIKER

HEIGHT: 5'10"

WEIGHT: 149 LBS.
(AS OF APRIL, 3RD YEAR OF HIGH SCHOOL)

ABILITY PARAMETERS
(5-POINT SCALE)

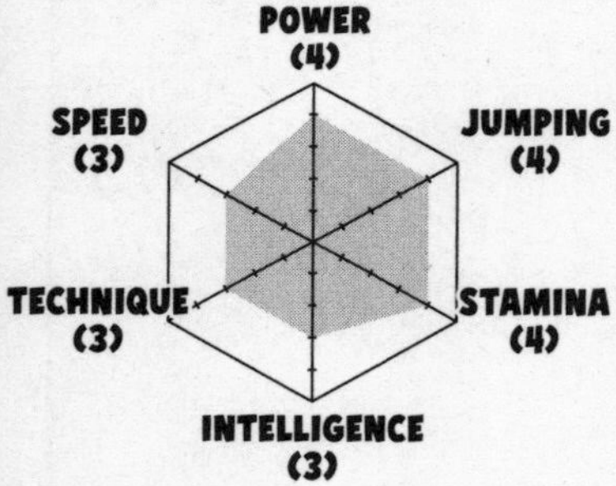
POWER (4)
JUMPING (4)
STAMINA (4)
INTELLIGENCE (3)
TECHNIQUE (3)
SPEED (3)

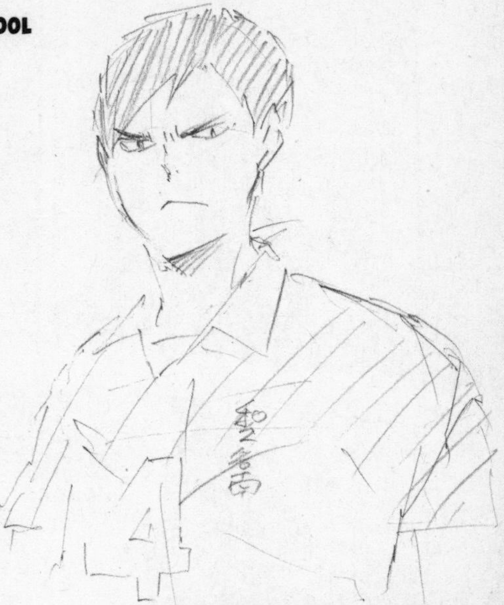

TEPPEI NARUKO

WAKUTANI MINAMI HIGH SCHOOL
CLASS 3-2

POSITION:
MIDDLE BLOCKER

HEIGHT: 6'0"

WEIGHT: 155 LBS.
(AS OF APRIL, 3RD YEAR OF HIGH SCHOOL)

ABILITY PARAMETERS
(5-POINT SCALE)

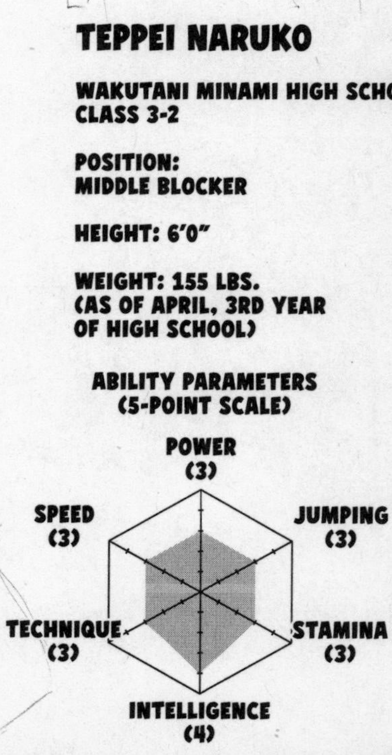
POWER (3)
JUMPING (3)
STAMINA (3)
INTELLIGENCE (4)
TECHNIQUE (3)
SPEED (3)

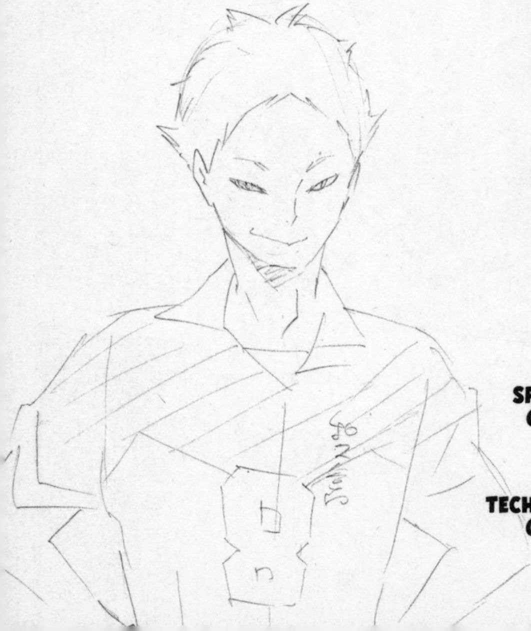

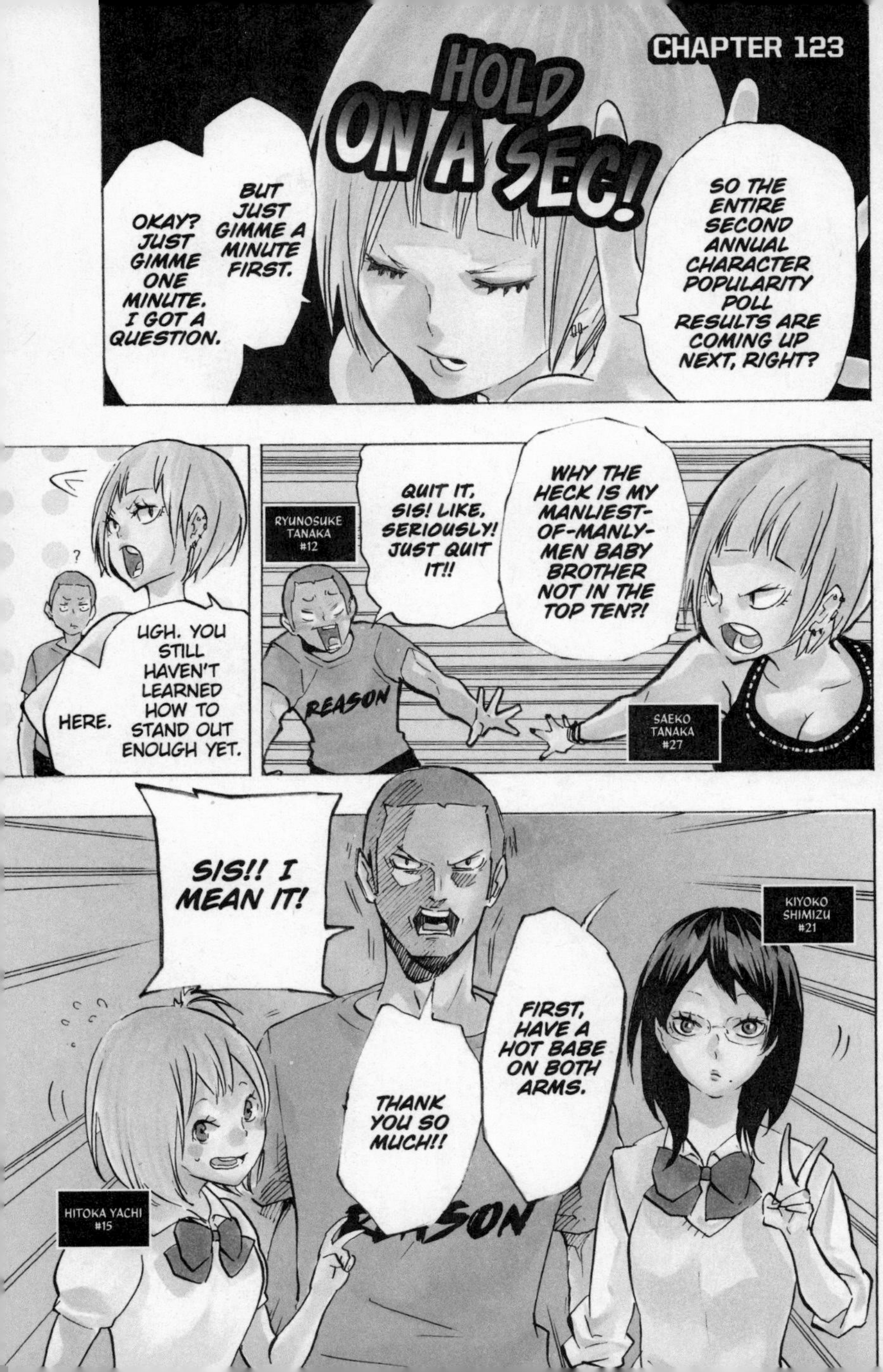
CHAPTER 123
HOLD ON A SEC!
SO THE ENTIRE SECOND ANNUAL CHARACTER POPULARITY POLL RESULTS ARE COMING UP NEXT, RIGHT?
BUT JUST GIMME A MINUTE FIRST.
OKAY? JUST GIMME ONE MINUTE. I GOT A QUESTION.
WHY THE HECK IS MY MANLIEST-OF-MANLY-MEN BABY BROTHER NOT IN THE TOP TEN?!
SAEKO TANAKA #27
QUIT IT, SIS! LIKE, SERIOUSLY! JUST QUIT IT!!
RYUNOSUKE TANAKA #12
REASON
?
UGH. YOU STILL HAVEN'T LEARNED HOW TO STAND OUT ENOUGH YET.
HERE.
KIYOKO SHIMIZU #21
FIRST, HAVE A HOT BABE ON BOTH ARMS.
SIS!! I MEAN IT!
THANK YOU SO MUCH!!
HITOKA YACHI #15

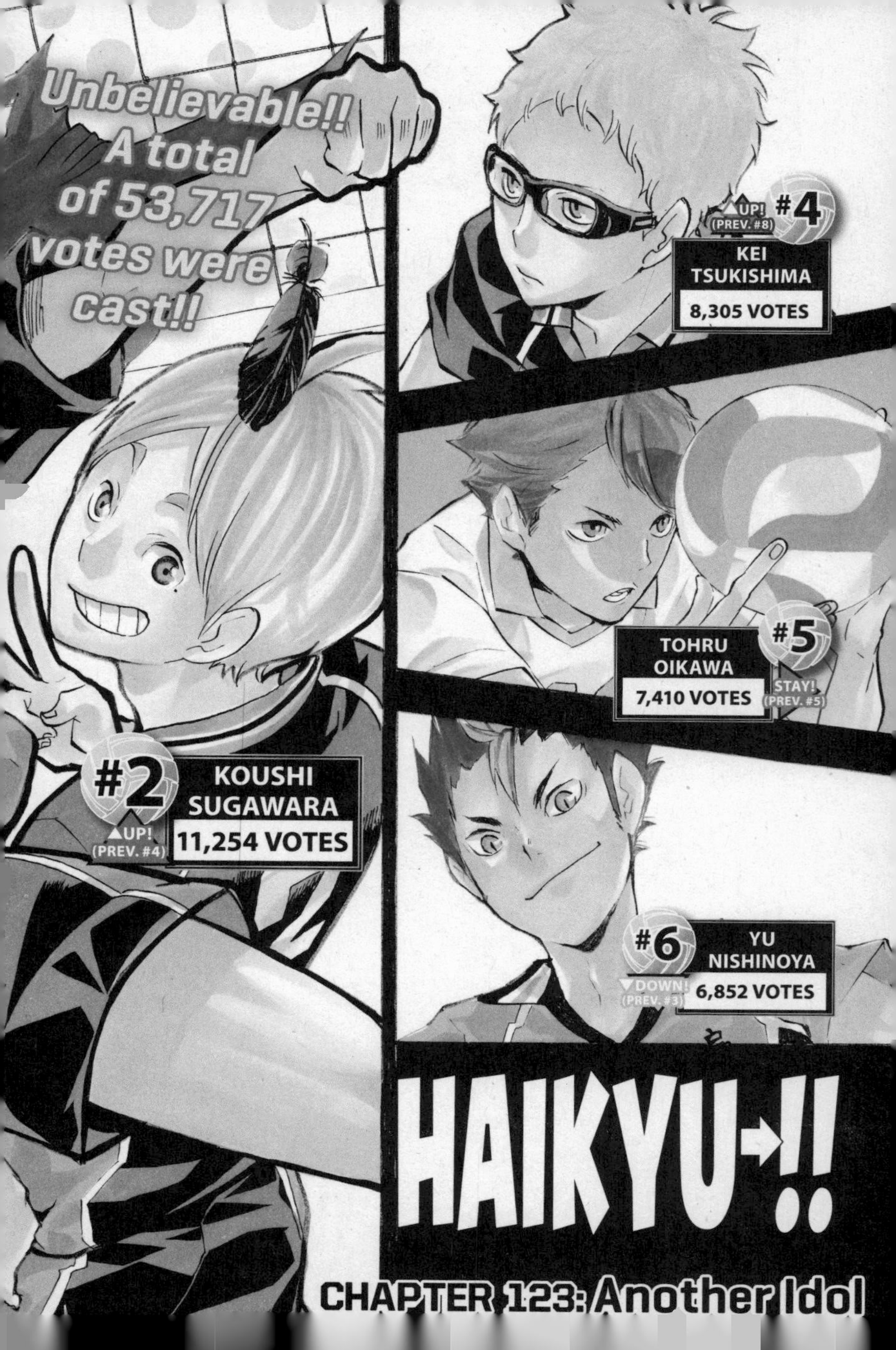
#4
UP! (PREV. #8)
KEI TSUKISHIMA
8,305 VOTES
#5
TOHRU OIKAWA
7,410 VOTES
STAY! (PREV. #5)
#6
YU NISHINOYA
DOWN! (PREV. #3)
6,852 VOTES
HAIKYU!!
CHAPTER 123: Another Idol
Unbelievable!! A total of 53,717 votes were cast!!
#2
KOUSHI SUGAWARA
UP! (PREV. #4)
11,254 VOTES

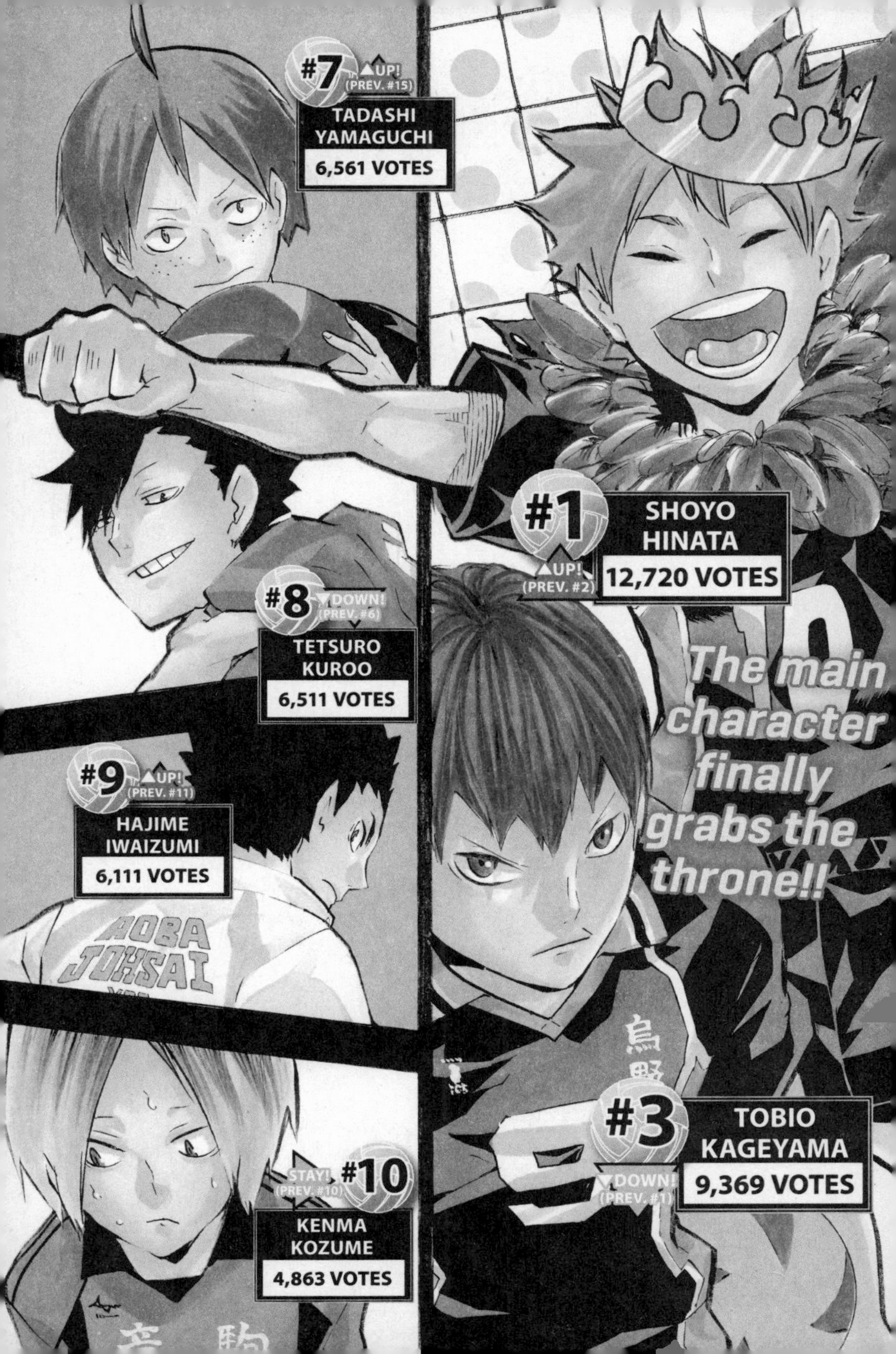
#1
▲UP! (PREV. #2)
SHOYO HINATA
12,720 VOTES
The main character finally grabs the throne!!
#3
▼DOWN! (PREV. #1)
TOBIO KAGEYAMA
9,369 VOTES
#7
▲UP! (PREV. #15)
TADASHI YAMAGUCHI
6,561 VOTES
#8
▼DOWN! (PREV. #6)
TETSURO KUROO
6,511 VOTES
#9
▲UP! (PREV. #11)
HAJIME IWAIZUMI
6,111 VOTES
AOBA JOHSAI
#10
STAY! (PREV. #10)
KENMA KOZUME
4,863 VOTES

WHO DID THOSE 53,717 VOTES GO TO?!

A FREE-FOR-ALL BATTLE DECIDED BY YOUR VOTES!!

HERE ARE THE RESULTS FOR #11 AND BEYOND!!

#11 DAICHI SAWAMURA
▲UP! (PREV. #12)
4,634 VOTES
THE PEOPLE'S CAPTAIN INCHES HIS WAY UP THE RANKS!

#12 RYUNOSUKE TANAKA
▼DOWN! (PREV. #9)
4,236 VOTES
THE PLAYER FOLLOWED BY THOSE IN THE KNOW!

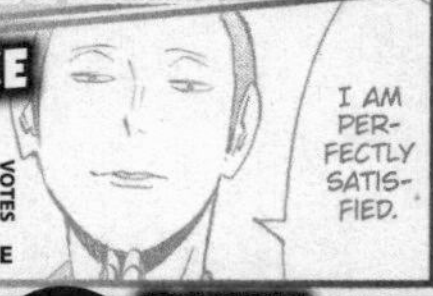
I AM PERFECTLY SATISFIED.

#13 ASAHI AZUMANE
▼DOWN! (PREV. #7)
4,003 VOTES
THE ACE YOU CAN TRUST IN A TIGHT SPOT!

#14 KEIJI AKAASHI
NEW!! (FIRST RANKING)
3,995 VOTES
AN AGENT FROM TOKYO SNEAKS HIS WAY ONTO THE CHARTS!

#15 HITOKA YACHI
NEW!! (FIRST RANKING)
3,987 VOTES
THE PESSIMISTIC CUTIE'S FAN CLUB IS GROWING!

#16 AKIRA KUNIMI
▲UP! (PREV. #24)
3,495 VOTES
THE PLAYER WHO COMES ON STRONG IN THE SECOND HALF STEPS UP HIS GAME!

#17 AKITERU TSUKISHIMA
NEW!! (FIRST RANKING)
3,258 VOTES
UNINTIMIDATED AFTER HIS TRAGIC STORY, HE CLIMBS INTO THE RANKINGS!

#18 KOTARO BOKUTO
NEW!! (FIRST RANKING)
3,084 VOTES
THE WHIMSICAL ACE IS CAUSING A RUCKUS IN THE RANKINGS TOO!

#19 MORISUKE YAKU
▼DOWN! (PREV. #14)
2,979 VOTES
NEKOMA'S "BIG BROTHER" FIGURE MAKES IT INTO THE TOP 20!

#20 LEV HAIBA
NEW!! (FIRST RANKING)
2,753 VOTES
THE "SLEEPING LION" OF NEKOMA MAKES HIS DEBUT!

▼FROM FAMILIAR FRIENDS TO UNEXPECTED ARRIVALS! RANKS #21~50▼

#21	KIYOKO SHIMIZU ▼ PREV. #13	2,640 VOTES
#22	MAKOTO SHIMADA ▼ PREV. #18	2,363 VOTES
#23	KENJI FUTAKUCHI ▼ PREV. #16	2,218 VOTES
#24	KEISHIN UKAI ▼ PREV. #17	2,084 VOTES
#25	WAKATOSHI USHIJIMA ▲ PREV. #38	1,848 VOTES
#26	TAKAHIRO HANAMAKI ▼ PREV. #25	1,723 VOTES
#27	SAEKO TANAKA ★ NEW ★	1,638 VOTES
#28	CHIKARA ENNOSHITA ▲ PREV. #33	1,602 VOTES
#29	YASUSHI KAMASAKI ▼ PREV. #13	1,420 VOTES
#30	TAKANOBU AONE ▼ PREV. #21	1,403 VOTES
#31	ISSEI MATSUKAWA ▲ PREV. UNRANKED	1,168 VOTES
#32	YUTARO KINDAICHI ▼ PREV. #29	975 VOTES
#33	KANAME MONIWA ▼ PREV. #28	901 VOTES
#34	AKINORI KONOHA ★ NEW ★	689 VOTES
#35	YUI MIYAMICHI ▼ PREV. #23	675 VOTES
#36	TAKEDA ITTETSU ▼ PREV. #27	664 VOTES
#37	SHOHEI FUKUNAGA ▼ PREV. #20	629 VOTES
#38	SOU INUOKA ▼ PREV. #32	621 VOTES
#39	HARUICHI FURUDATE ▼ PREV. #26	521 VOTES
#40	BABY CROW ▲ PREV. UNRANKED	517 VOTES
#41	HISASHI KINOSHITA ▼ PREV. #31	497 VOTES
#42	KAZUHITO NARITA ▼ PREV. #36	488 VOTES
#43	NATSU HINATA ★ NEW ★	470 VOTES
#44	SHIGERU YAHABA ▲ PREV. UNRANKED	459 VOTES
#45	KOSUKE SAKUNAMI ▲ PREV. UNRANKED	455 VOTES
#46	SHIMADA MART PIG ▼ PREV. #45	454 VOTES
#47	YUSUKE TAKINOUE ▼ PREV. #19	441 VOTES
#48	YUKITAKA IZUMI ▼ PREV. #37	439 VOTES
#49	YUZURU KOMAKI ★ NEW ★	395 VOTES
#50	HAYATO IKEJIRI ▼ PREV. #35	341 VOTES

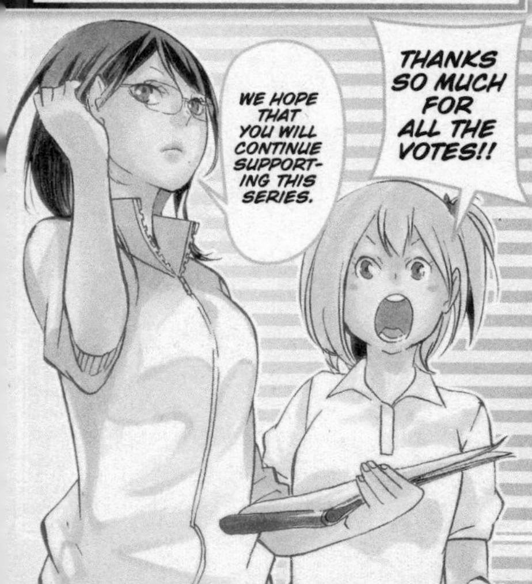
THANKS SO MUCH FOR ALL THE VOTES!!
WE HOPE THAT YOU WILL CONTINUE SUPPORTING THIS SERIES.

TRIPLE BLOCK!!

IF I HIT IT NOW...

THEY'LL STUFF ME.

HNN?!

...?

"RESET."

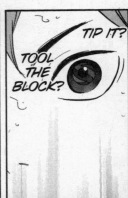

TIP IT?

TOOL THE BLOCK?

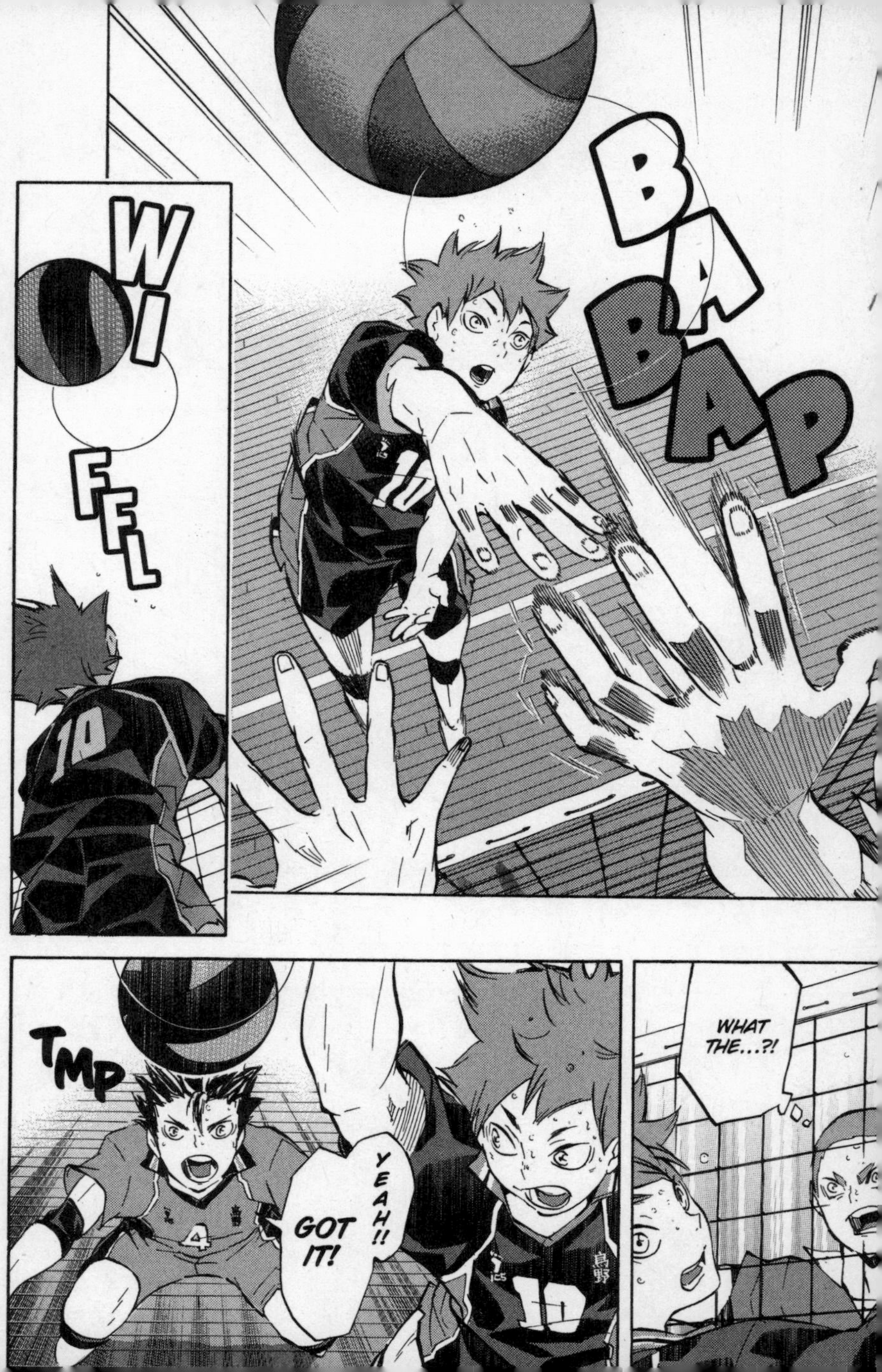
BA BAP
WIFFL
WHAT THE...?!
YEAH!!
TMP
GOT IT!

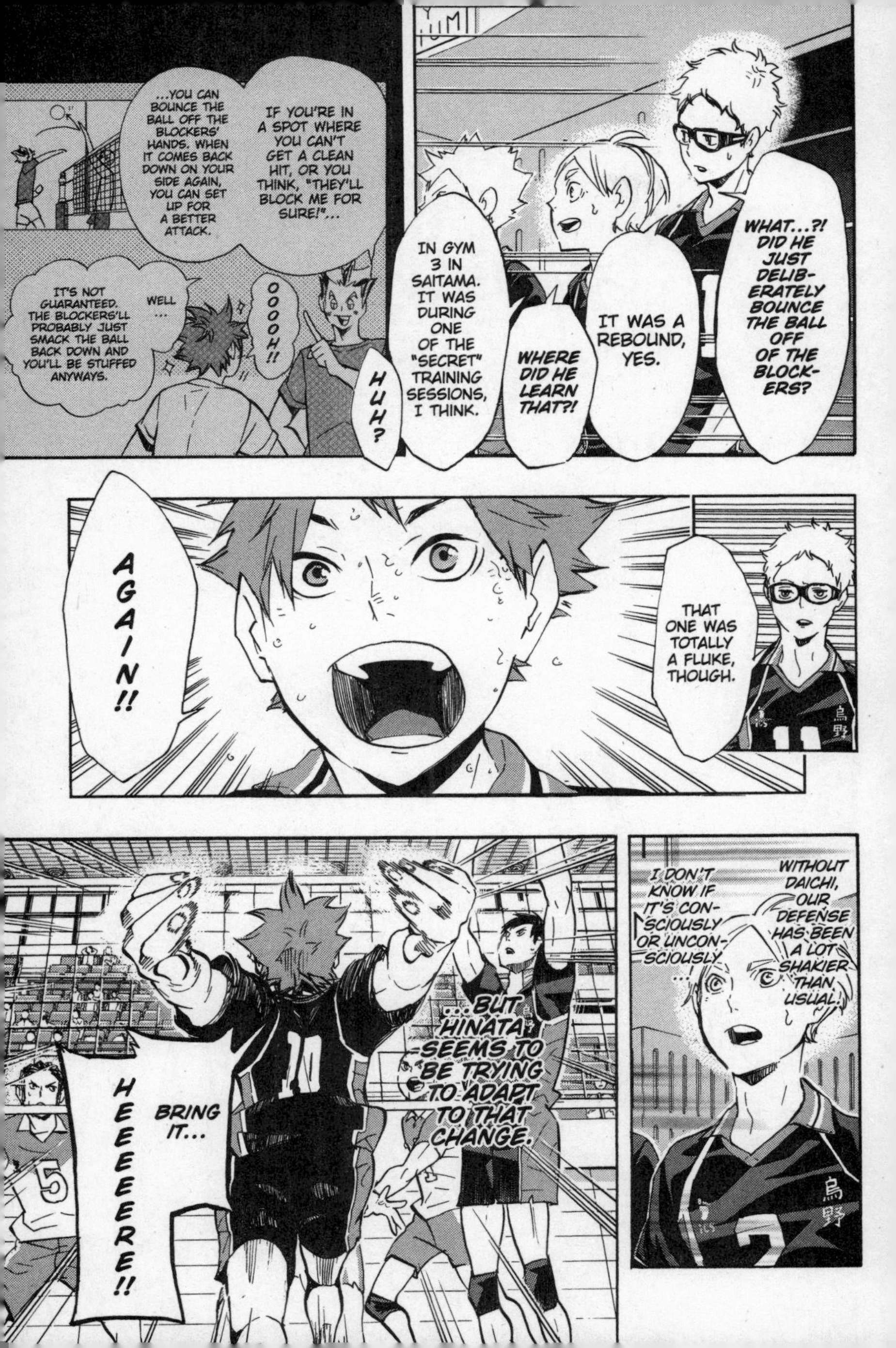
WHAT...?! DID HE JUST DELIBERATELY BOUNCE THE BALL OFF OF THE BLOCKERS?
IT WAS A REBOUND, YES.
WHERE DID HE LEARN THAT?!
IN GYM 3 IN SAITAMA. IT WAS DURING ONE OF THE "SECRET" TRAINING SESSIONS, I THINK.
HUH?
IF YOU'RE IN A SPOT WHERE YOU CAN'T GET A CLEAN HIT, OR YOU THINK, "THEY'LL BLOCK ME FOR SURE!"...
...YOU CAN BOUNCE THE BALL OFF THE BLOCKERS' HANDS. WHEN IT COMES BACK DOWN ON YOUR SIDE AGAIN, YOU CAN SET UP FOR A BETTER ATTACK.
OOOOH!!
WELL ...
IT'S NOT GUARANTEED. THE BLOCKERS'LL PROBABLY JUST SMACK THE BALL BACK DOWN AND YOU'LL BE STUFFED ANYWAYS.
THAT ONE WAS TOTALLY A FLUKE, THOUGH.
AGAIN!!
WITHOUT DAICHI, OUR DEFENSE HAS BEEN A LOT SHAKIER THAN USUAL.
I DON'T KNOW IF IT'S CONSCIOUSLY OR UNCONSCIOUSLY...
...BUT HINATA SEEMS TO BE TRYING TO ADAPT TO THAT CHANGE.
BRING IT...
HEEEEERE!!

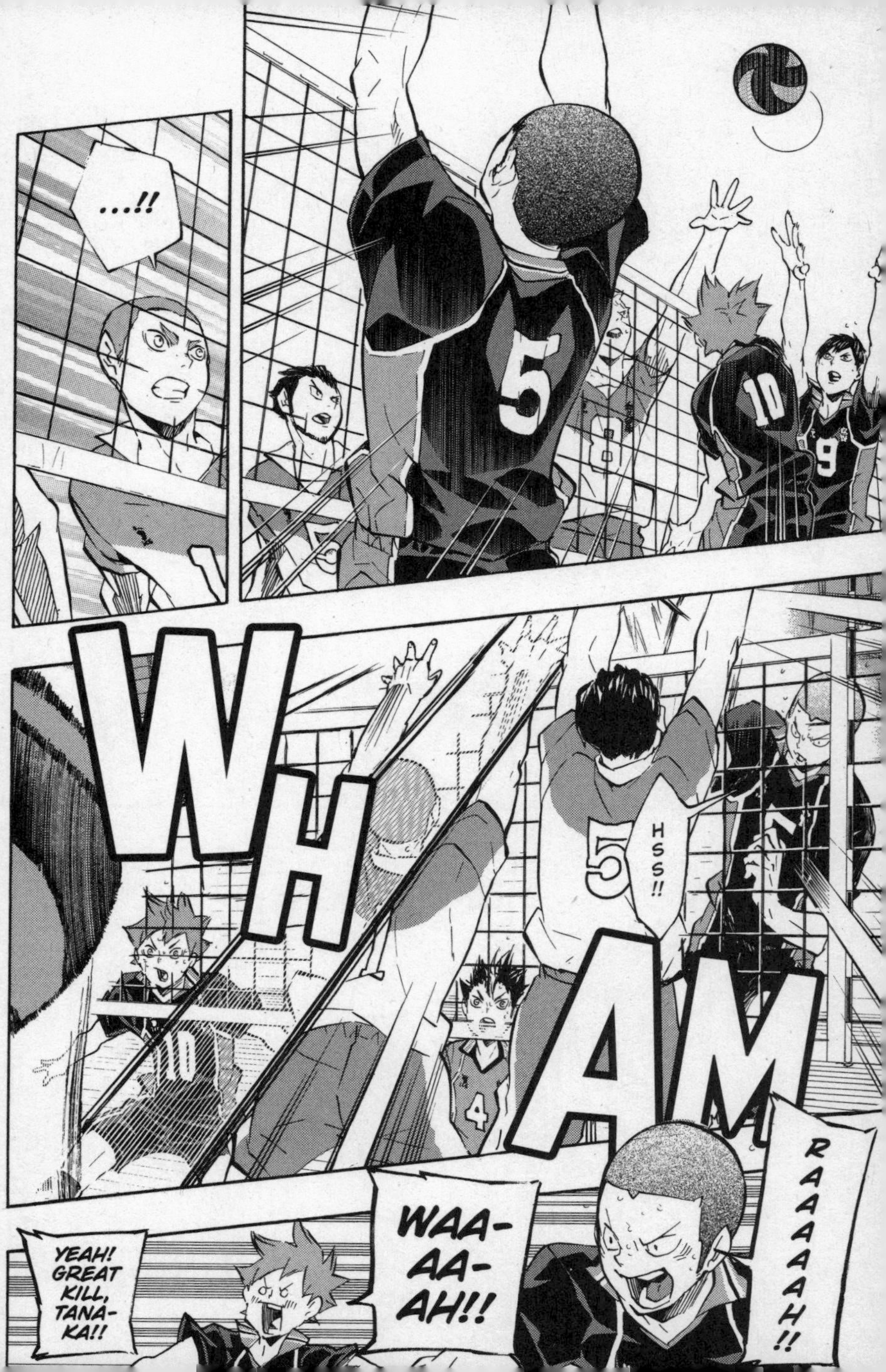
...!!
HSS!!
WHAM
RAAAAAH!!
WAA-AA-AH!!
YEAH! GREAT KILL, TANAKA!!

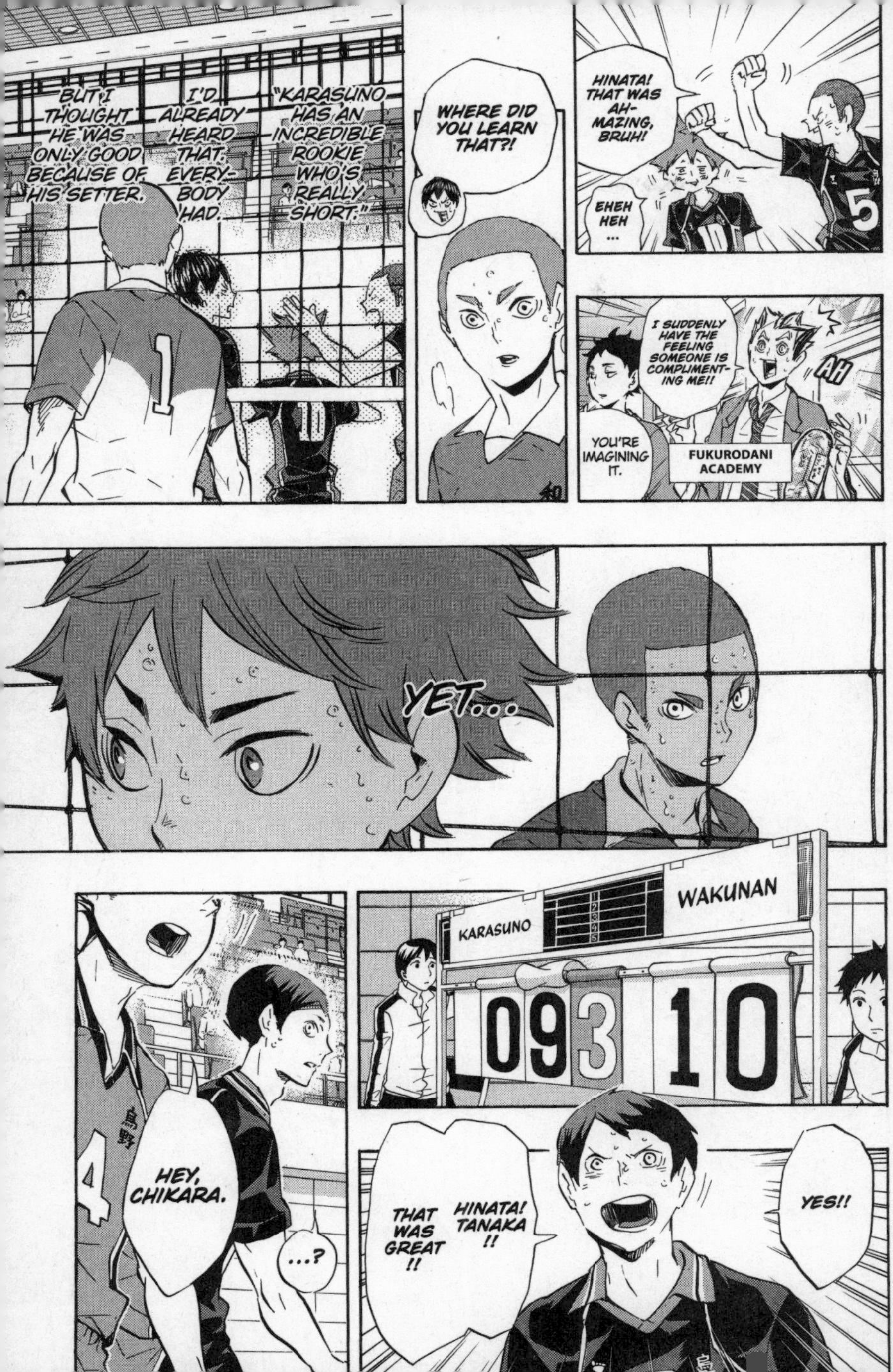
HINATA! THAT WAS AH-MAZING, BRUH!
EHEH HEH ...
I SUDDENLY HAVE THE FEELING SOMEONE IS COMPLIMENTING ME!!
AH
YOU'RE IMAGINING IT.
FUKURODANI ACADEMY
WHERE DID YOU LEARN THAT?!
"KARASUNO HAS AN INCREDIBLE ROOKIE WHO'S REALLY SHORT."
I'D ALREADY HEARD THAT. EVERYBODY HAD.
BUT I THOUGHT HE WAS ONLY GOOD BECAUSE OF HIS SETTER.
YET...
WAKUNAN
KARASUNO
093
10
YES!!
HINATA! TANAKA!!
THAT WAS GREAT!!
HEY, CHIKARA.
...?

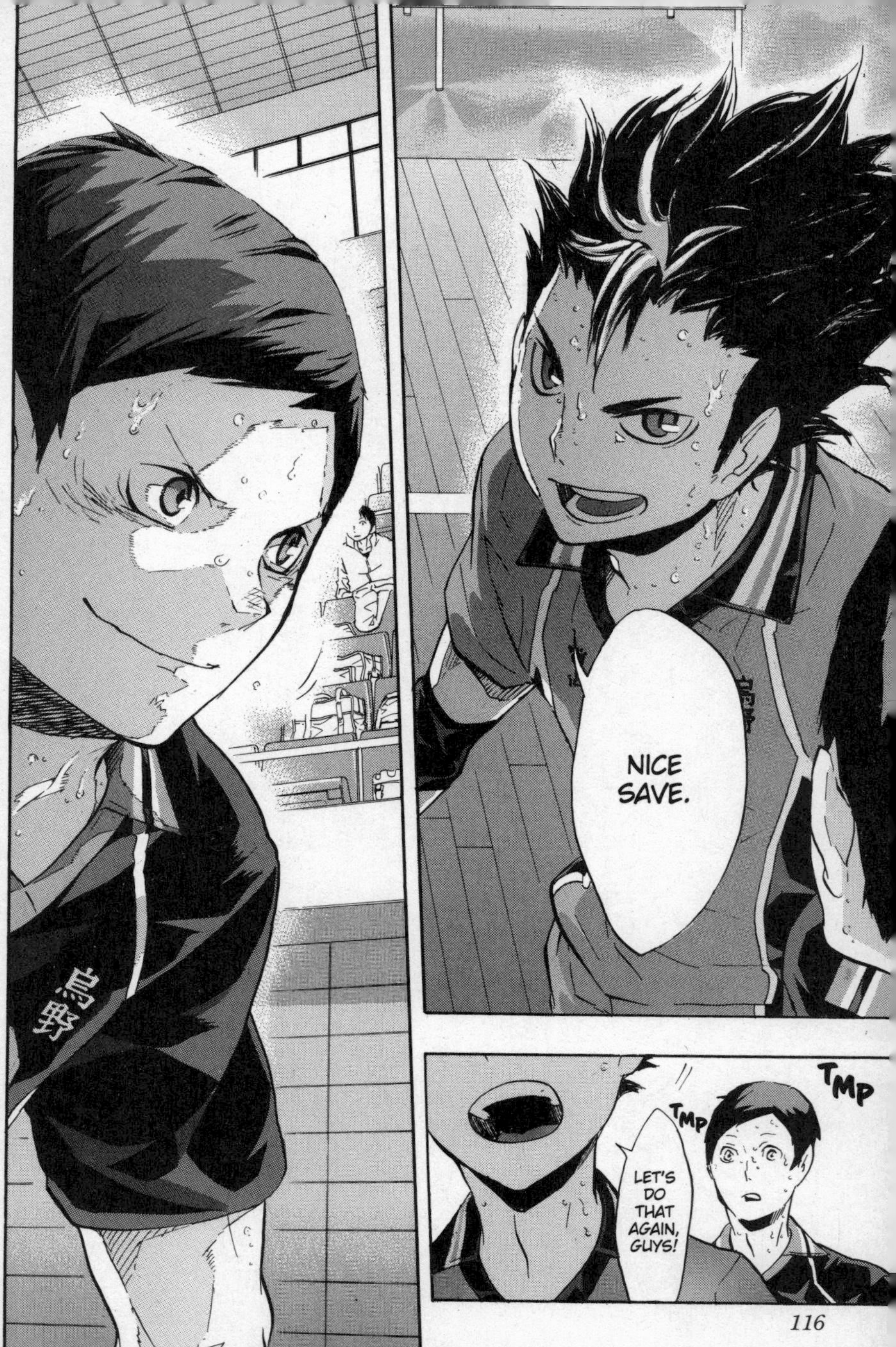
NICE SAVE.
TMP
TMP
LET'S DO THAT AGAIN, GUYS!

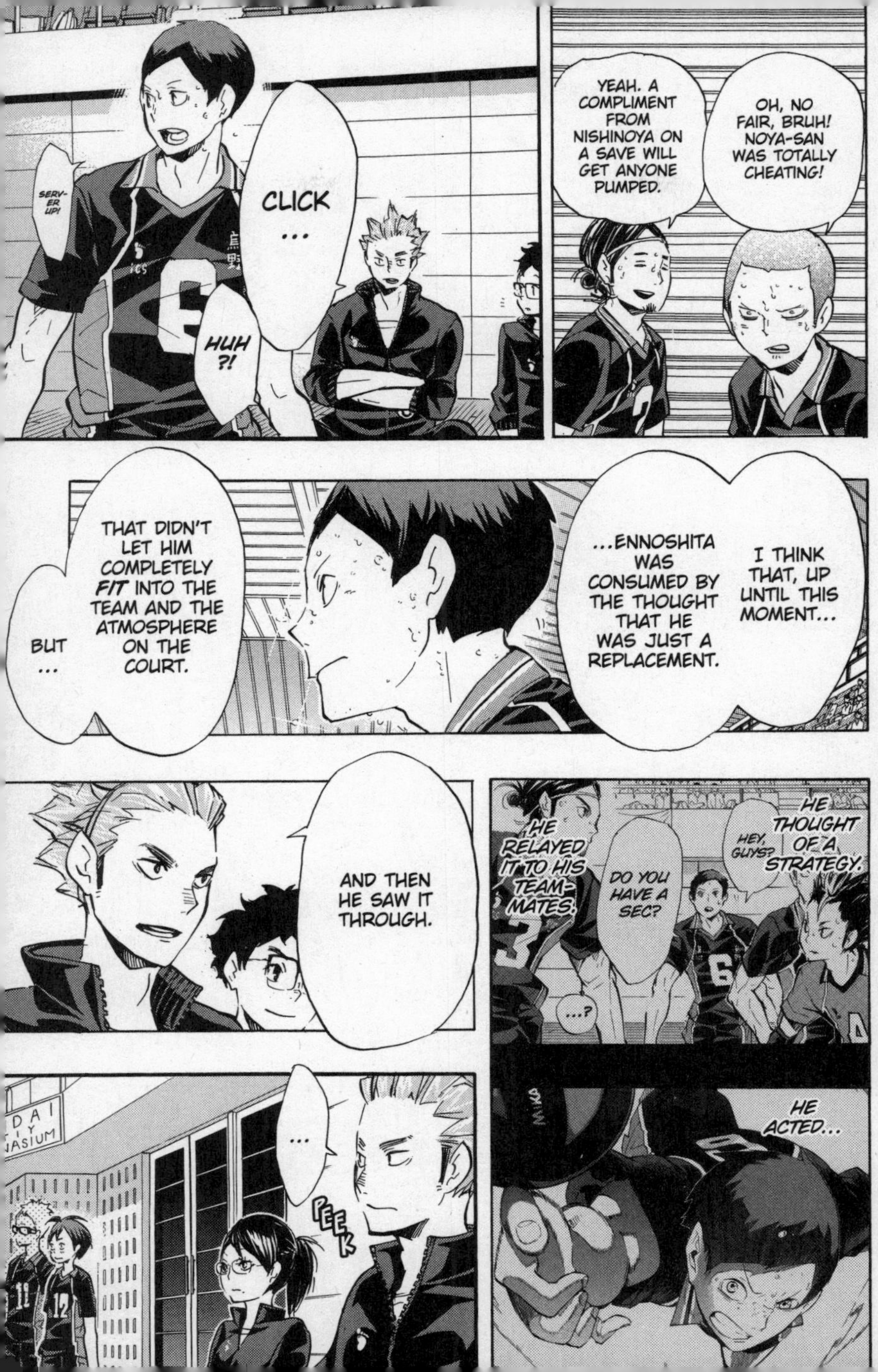
OH, NO FAIR, BRUH! NOYA-SAN WAS TOTALLY CHEATING!
YEAH. A COMPLIMENT FROM NISHINOYA ON A SAVE WILL GET ANYONE PUMPED.
CLICK ...
HUH ?!
SERV-ER UP!
I THINK THAT, UP UNTIL THIS MOMENT...
...ENNOSHITA WAS CONSUMED BY THE THOUGHT THAT HE WAS JUST A REPLACEMENT.
THAT DIDN'T LET HIM COMPLETELY FIT INTO THE TEAM AND THE ATMOSPHERE ON THE COURT.
BUT ...
HE THOUGHT OF A STRATEGY.
HEY, GUYS?
DO YOU HAVE A SEC?
HE RELAYED IT TO HIS TEAM-MATES.
...?
AND THEN HE SAW IT THROUGH.
HE ACTED...
...
PEEK
DAI
NASIUM

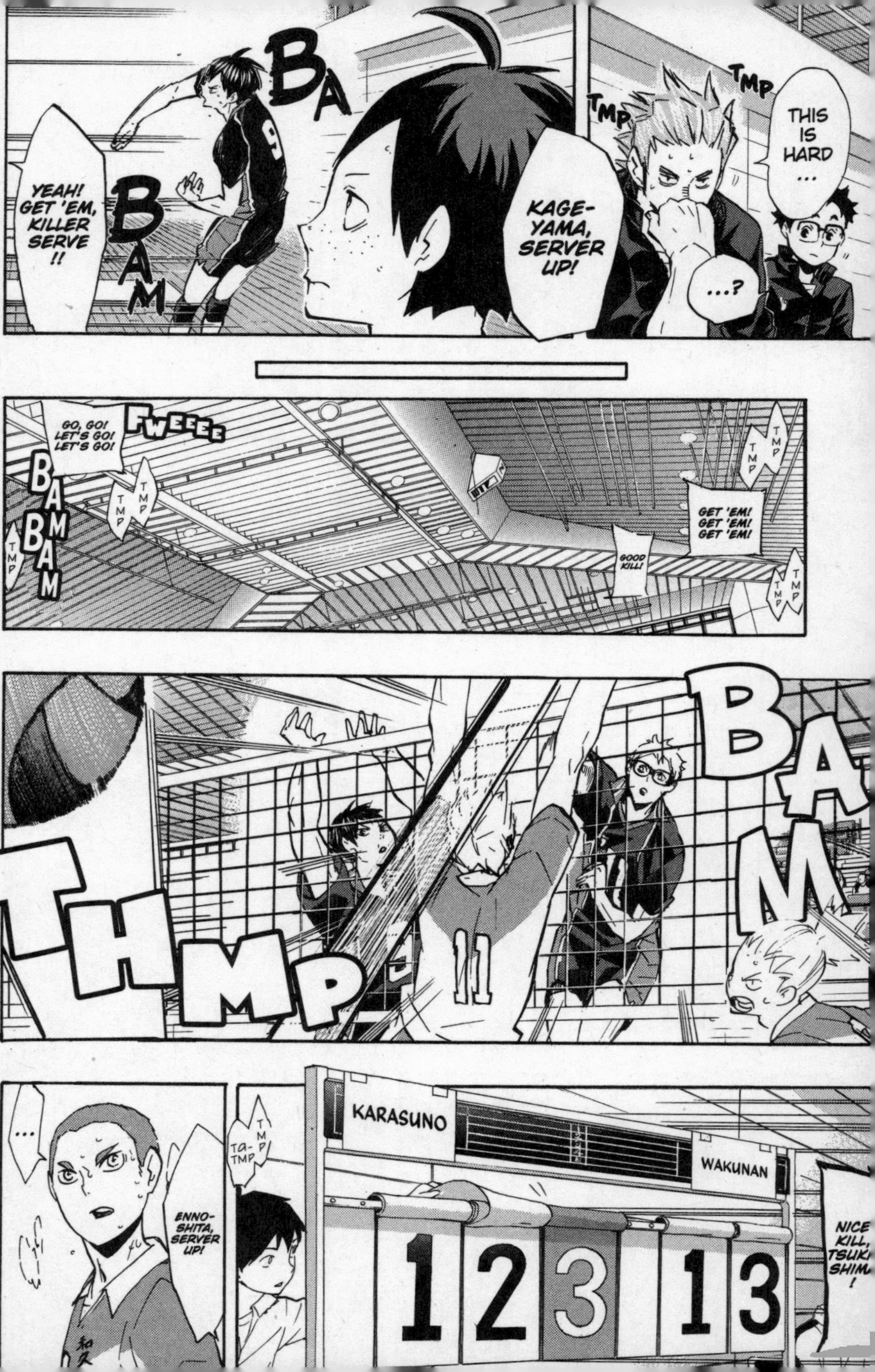
TMP
TMP
THIS IS HARD...
...?
KAGE-YAMA, SERVER UP!
BA
BAM
YEAH! GET 'EM, KILLER SERVE!!
TMP TMP
GET 'EM! GET 'EM! GET 'EM!
GOOD KILL!
TMP TMP
FWEEEE
GO, GO! LET'S GO! LET'S GO!
BABAM
TMP
BAM
THMP
NICE KILL, TSUKISHIM !
KARASUNO
WAKUNAN
12
3
13
TMP
Ta-TMP
ENNO-SHITA, SERVER UP!
...

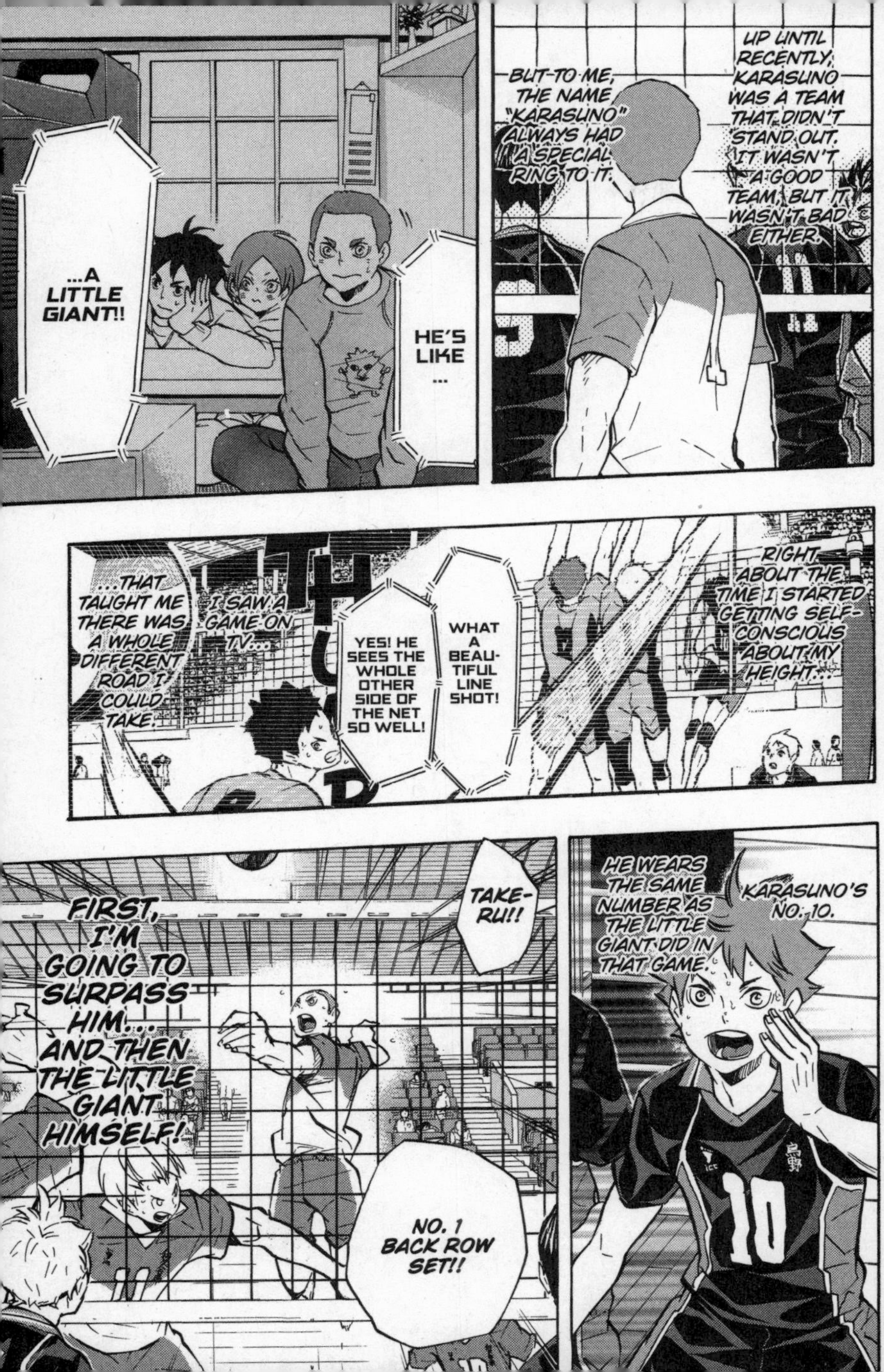
UP UNTIL RECENTLY, KARASUNO WAS A TEAM THAT DIDN'T STAND OUT. IT WASN'T A GOOD TEAM, BUT IT WASN'T BAD EITHER.
BUT TO ME, THE NAME "KARASUNO" ALWAYS HAD A SPECIAL RING TO IT.
HE'S LIKE...
...A LITTLE GIANT!!
RIGHT ABOUT THE TIME I STARTED GETTING SELF-CONSCIOUS ABOUT MY HEIGHT...
WHAT A BEAUTIFUL LINE SHOT!
YES! HE SEES THE WHOLE OTHER SIDE OF THE NET SO WELL!
THUD
I SAW A GAME ON TV...
...THAT TAUGHT ME THERE WAS A WHOLE DIFFERENT ROAD I COULD TAKE.
KARASUNO'S NO. 10.
HE WEARS THE SAME NUMBER AS THE LITTLE GIANT DID IN THAT GAME.
TAKERU!!
NO. 1 BACK ROW SET!!
FIRST, I'M GOING TO SURPASS HIM... AND THEN THE LITTLE GIANT HIMSELF!

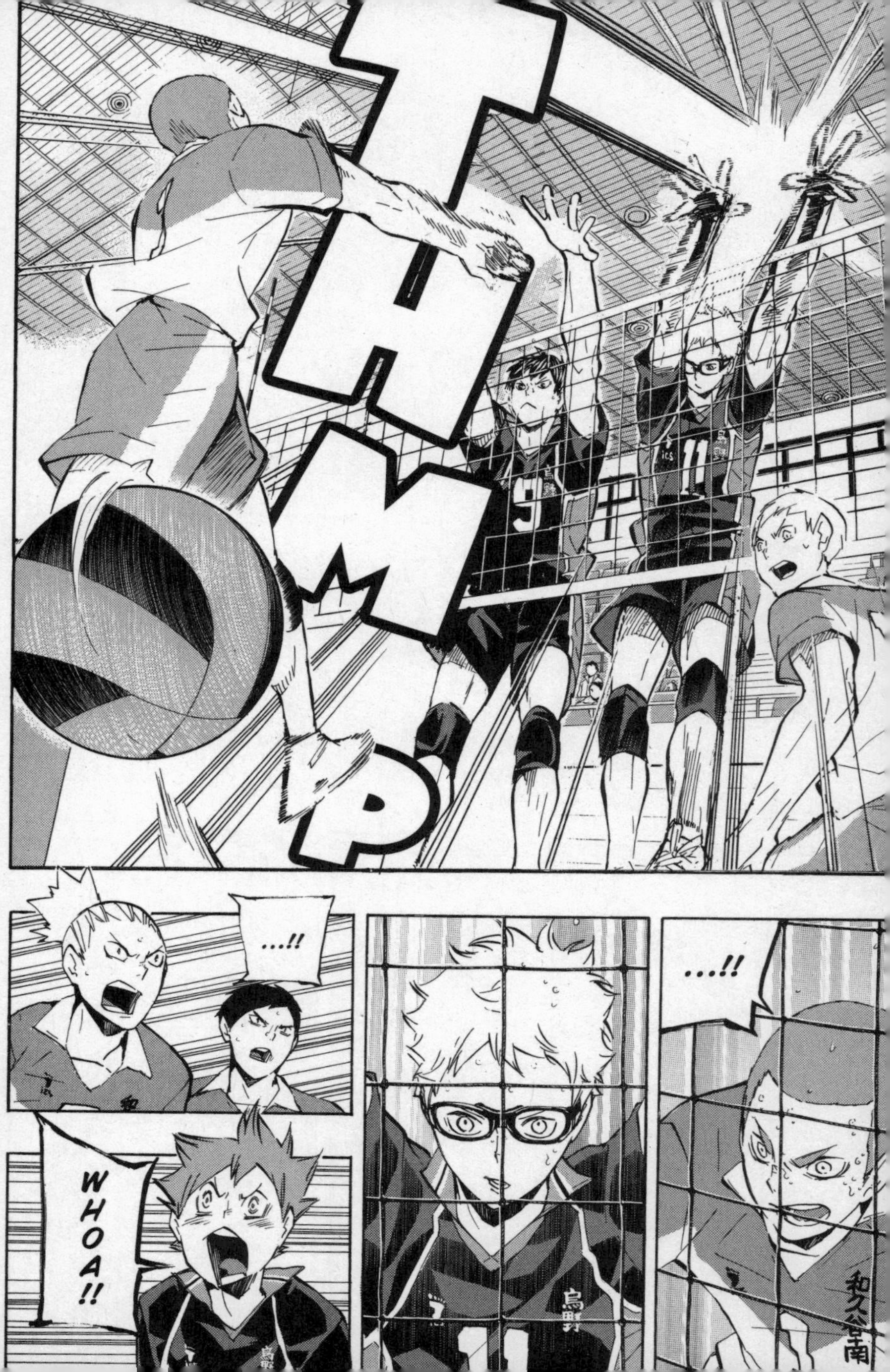

THUMP
...!!
和久谷南
...!!
WHOA!!

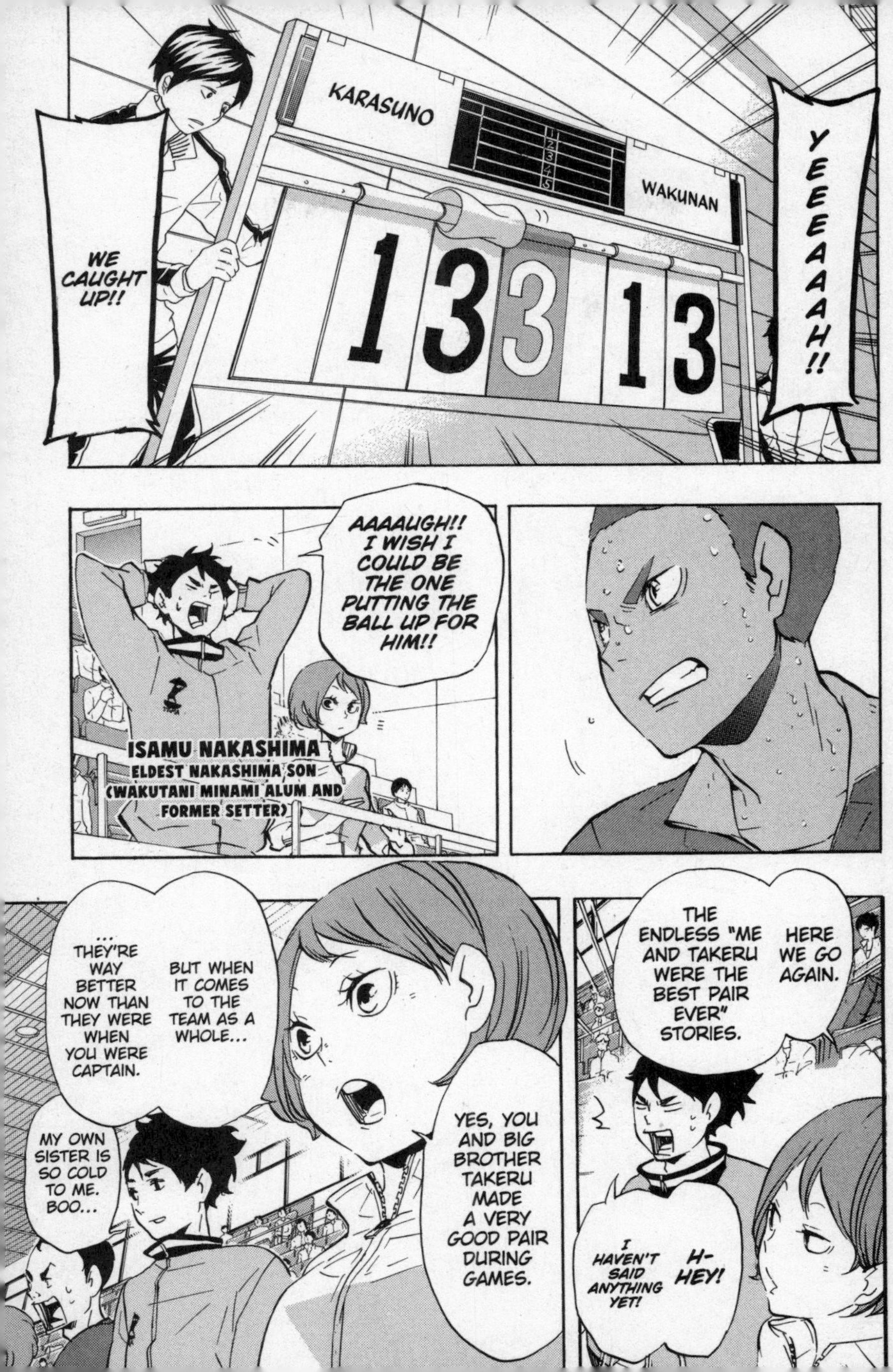
YEEEAAAAH!!
WAKUNAN
KARASUNO
13 3 13
WE CAUGHT UP!!
AAAAUGH!! I WISH I COULD BE THE ONE PUTTING THE BALL UP FOR HIM!!
ISAMU NAKASHIMA
ELDEST NAKASHIMA SON (WAKUTANI MINAMI ALUM AND FORMER SETTER)
HERE WE GO AGAIN.
THE ENDLESS "ME AND TAKERU WERE THE BEST PAIR EVER" STORIES.
H-HEY!
I HAVEN'T SAID ANYTHING YET!
YES, YOU AND BIG BROTHER TAKERU MADE A VERY GOOD PAIR DURING GAMES.
BUT WHEN IT COMES TO THE TEAM AS A WHOLE...
...THEY'RE WAY BETTER NOW THAN THEY WERE WHEN YOU WERE CAPTAIN.
MY OWN SISTER IS SO COLD TO ME. BOO...

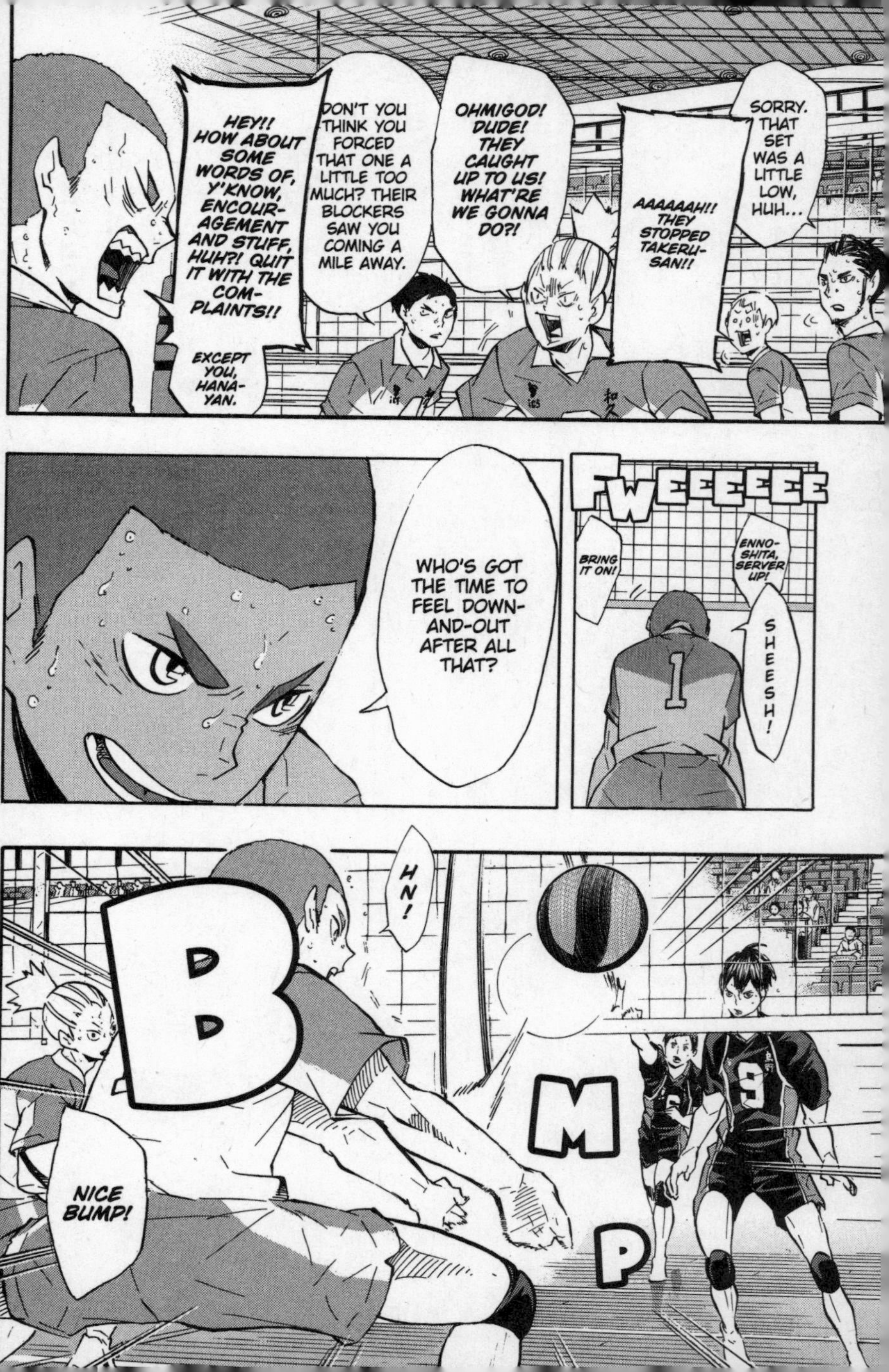
SORRY. THAT SET WAS A LITTLE LOW, HUH...
AAAAAAH!! THEY STOPPED TAKERU-SAN!!
OHMIGOD! DUDE! THEY CAUGHT UP TO US! WHAT'RE WE GONNA DO?!
DON'T YOU THINK YOU FORCED THAT ONE A LITTLE TOO MUCH? THEIR BLOCKERS SAW YOU COMING A MILE AWAY.
HEY!! HOW ABOUT SOME WORDS OF, Y'KNOW, ENCOURAGEMENT AND STUFF, HUH?! QUIT IT WITH THE COMPLAINTS!!
EXCEPT YOU, HANA-YAN.
FWEEEEEE
ENNOSHITA, SERVER UP!
BRING IT ON!
SHEESH!
WHO'S GOT THE TIME TO FEEL DOWN-AND-OUT AFTER ALL THAT?
HN!
BUMP
NICE BUMP!

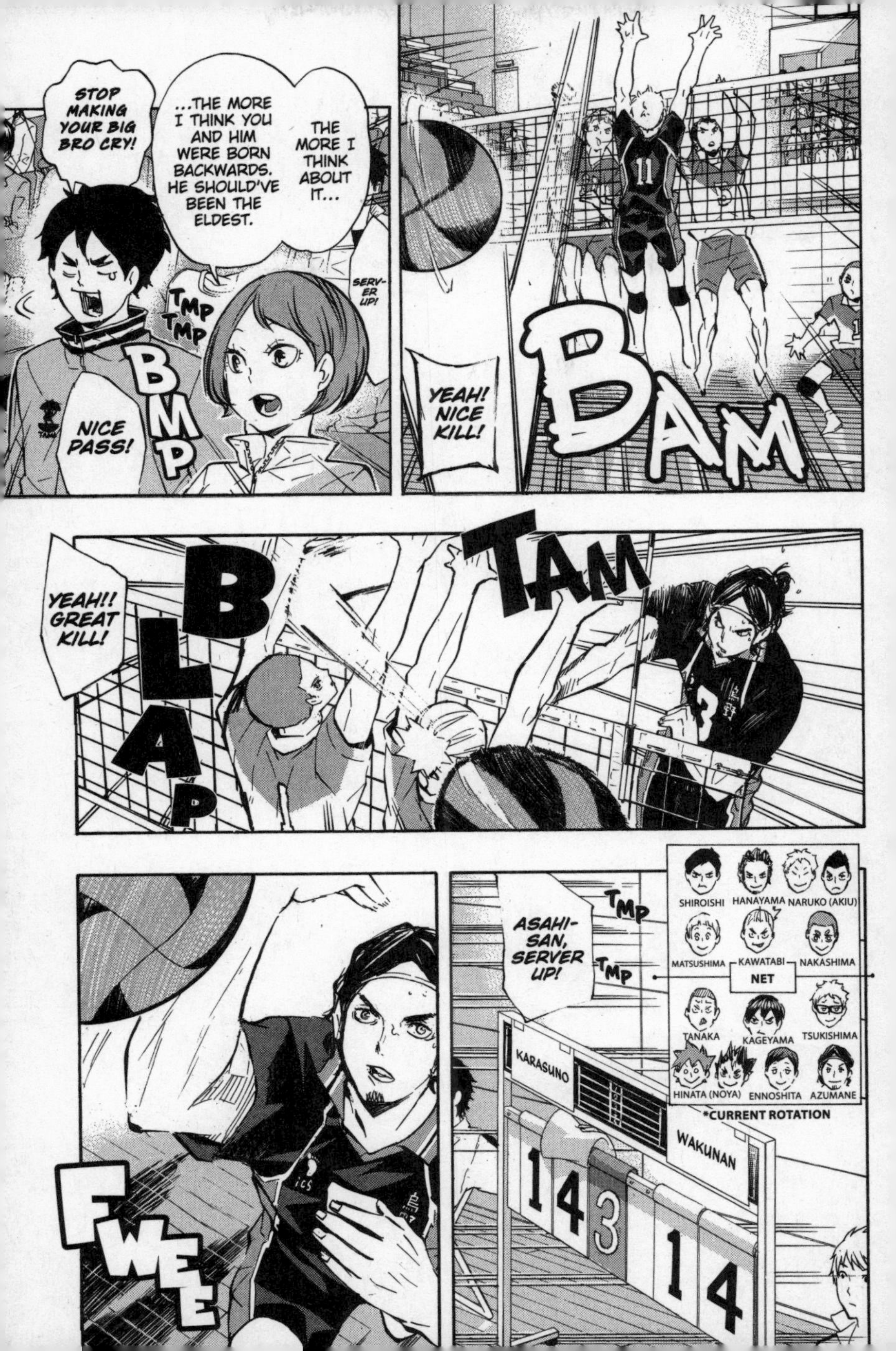
YEAH! NICE KILL!
BAM
SERVER-UP!
THE MORE I THINK ABOUT IT...
...THE MORE I THINK YOU AND HIM WERE BORN BACKWARDS. HE SHOULD'VE BEEN THE ELDEST.
STOP MAKING YOUR BIG BRO CRY!
TMP TMP
BMP
NICE PASS!
TAM
BLAP
YEAH!! GREAT KILL!
SHIROISHI
HANAYAMA
NARUKO (AKIU)
MATSUSHIMA
KAWATABI
NAKASHIMA
NET
TANAKA
KAGEYAMA
TSUKISHIMA
HINATA (NOYA)
ENNOSHITA
AZUMANE
*CURRENT ROTATION
TMP
TMP
ASAHI-SAN, SERVER UP!
KARASUNO
WAKUNAN
14
3
14
FWEEE

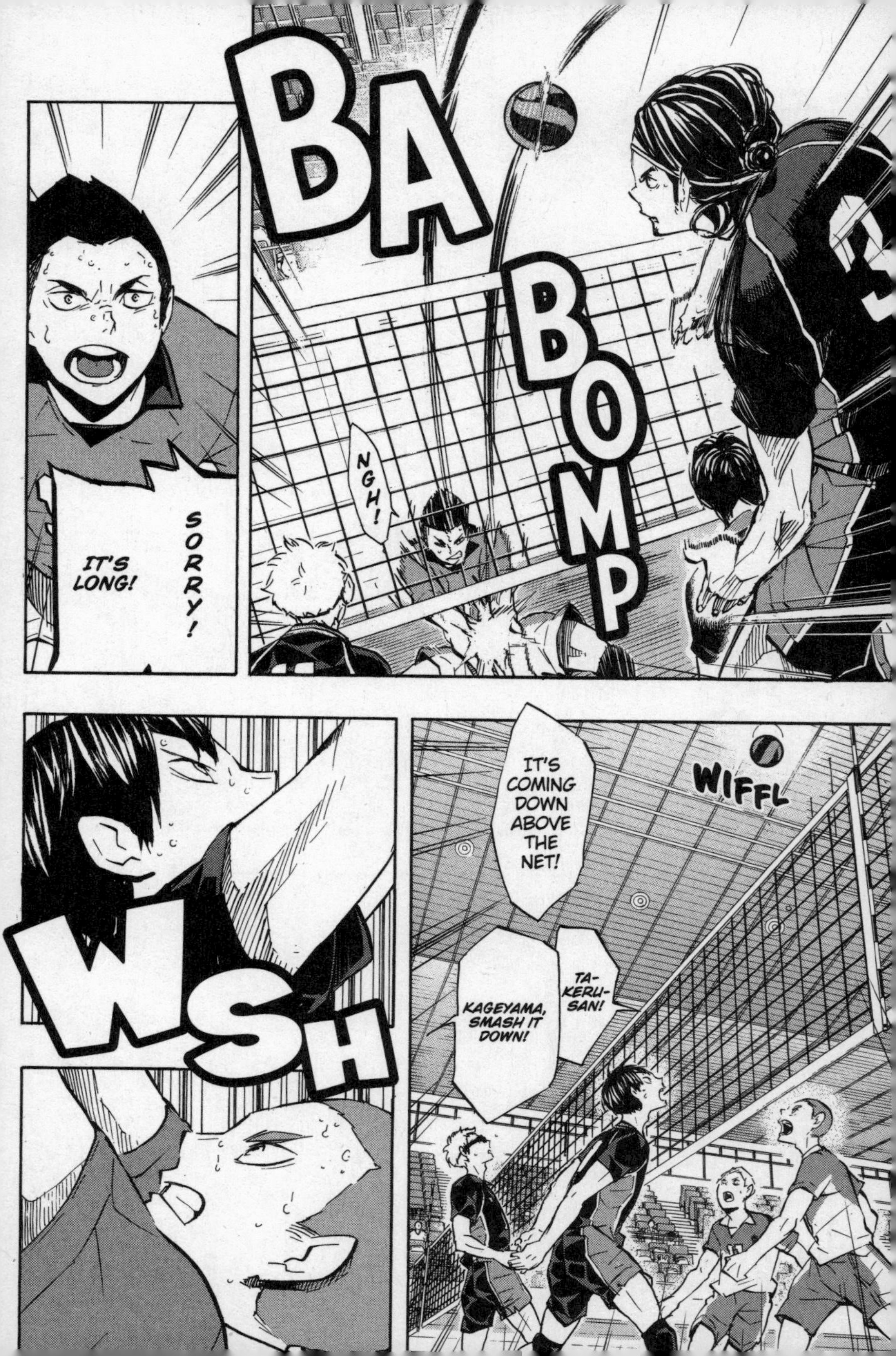
BA
BOMP
NGH!
SORRY!
IT'S LONG!
WIFFL
IT'S COMING DOWN ABOVE THE NET!
TA-KERU-SAN!
KAGEYAMA, SMASH IT DOWN!
WSH

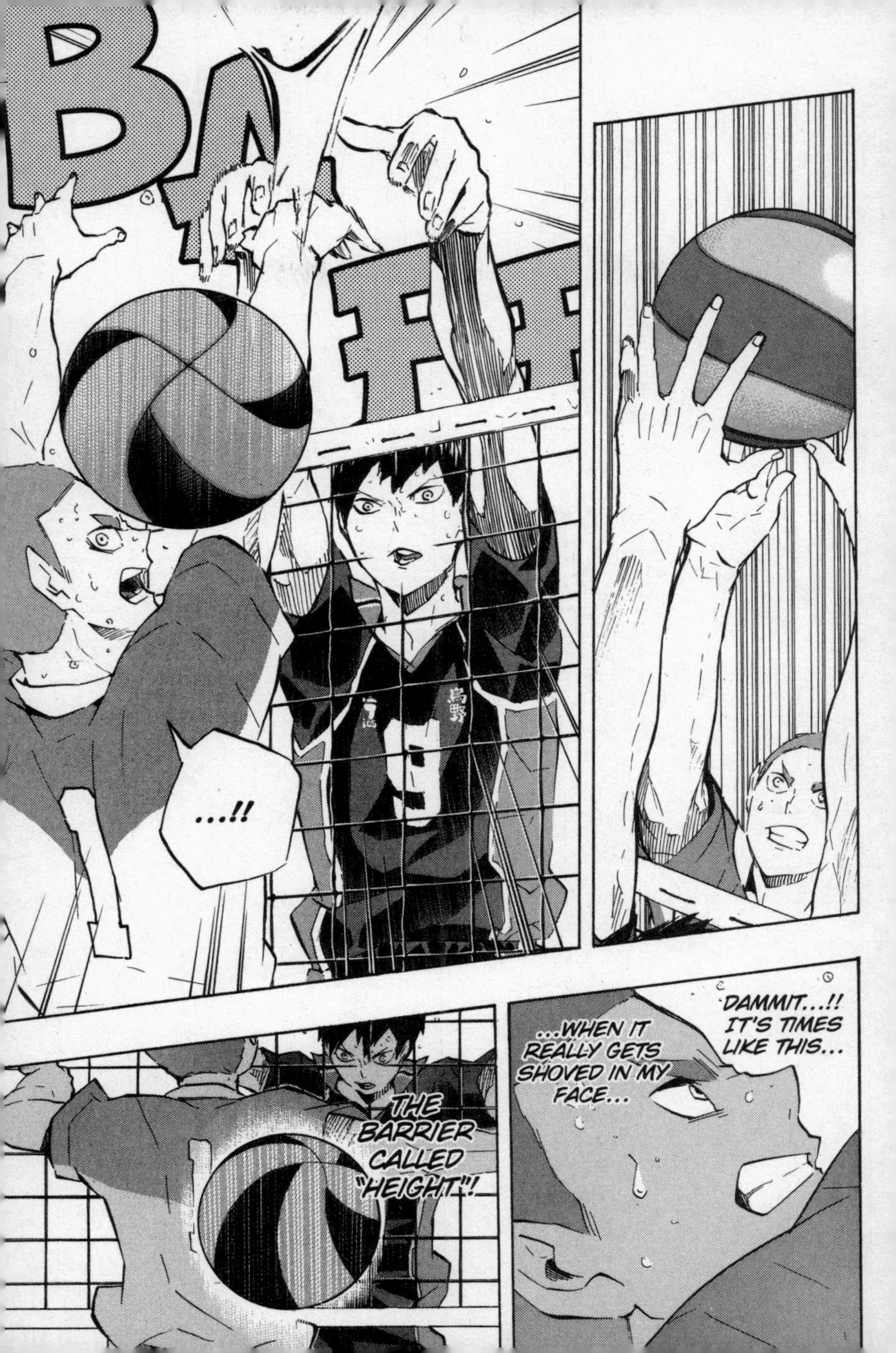
BAM
...!!
DAMMIT...!! IT'S TIMES LIKE THIS...
...WHEN IT REALLY GETS SHOVED IN MY FACE...
THE BARRIER CALLED "HEIGHT"!

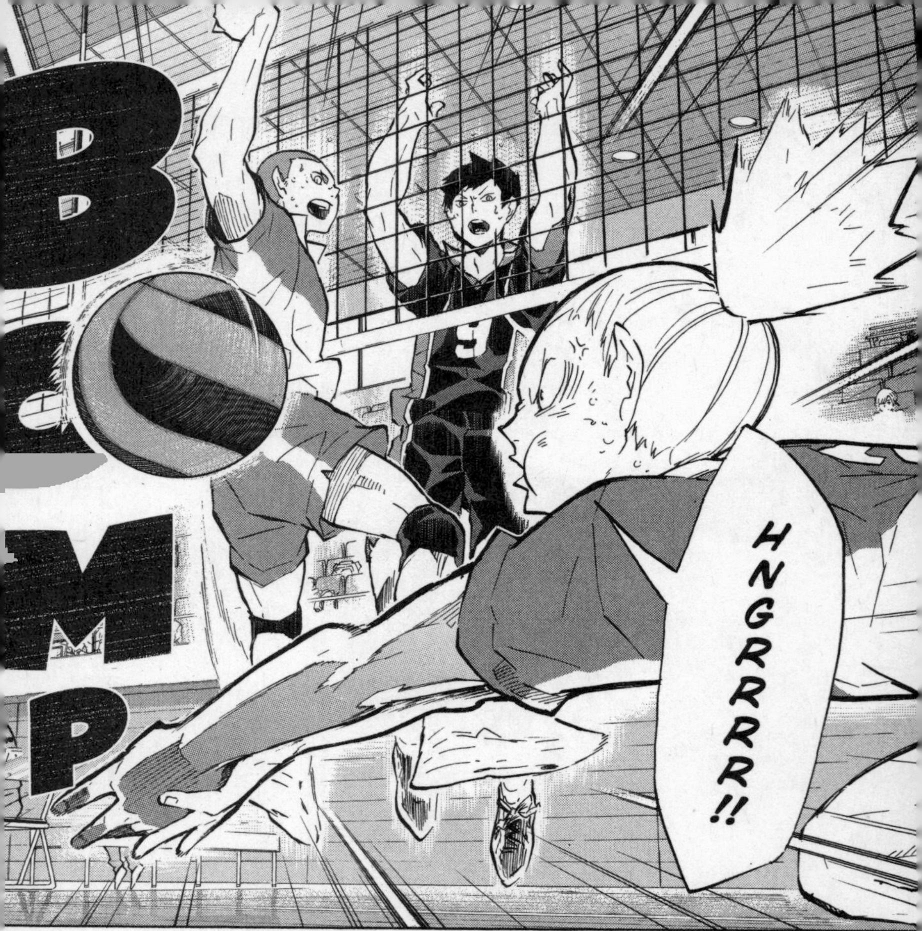
BOMP
HNGRRRR!!
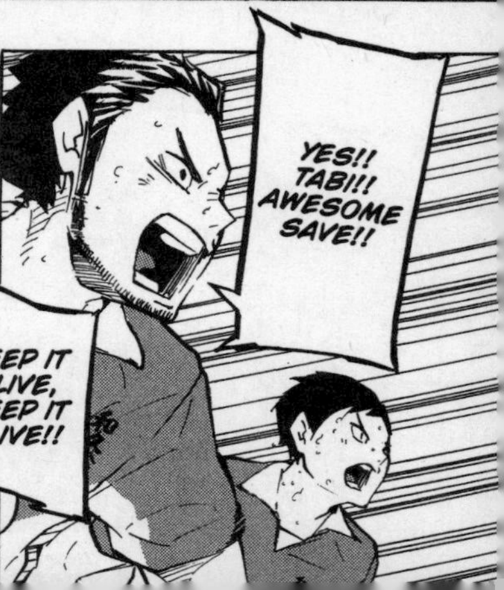
YES!! TABI!!! AWESOME SAVE!!
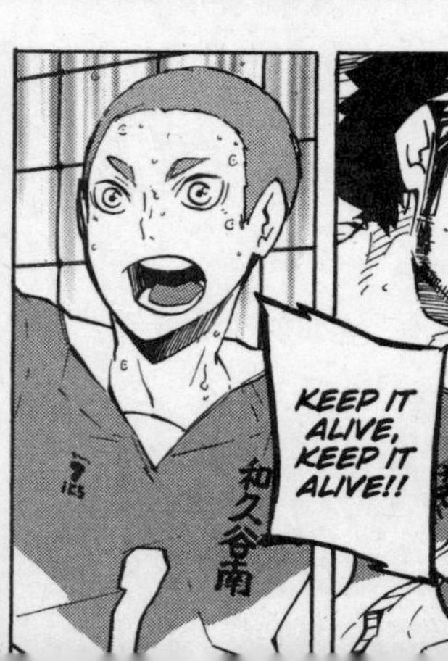
KEEP IT ALIVE, KEEP IT ALIVE!!
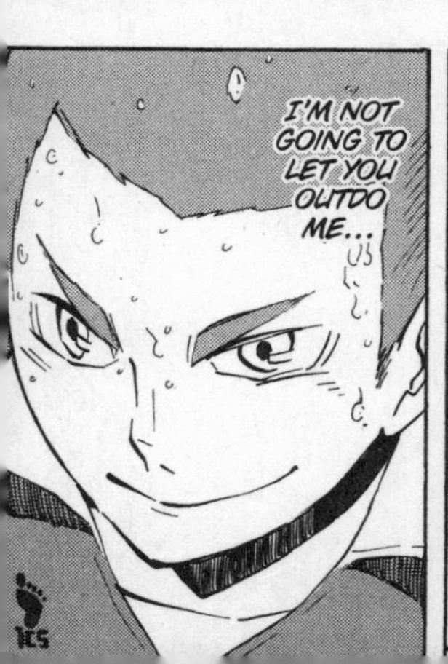
I'M NOT GOING TO LET YOU OUTDO ME...

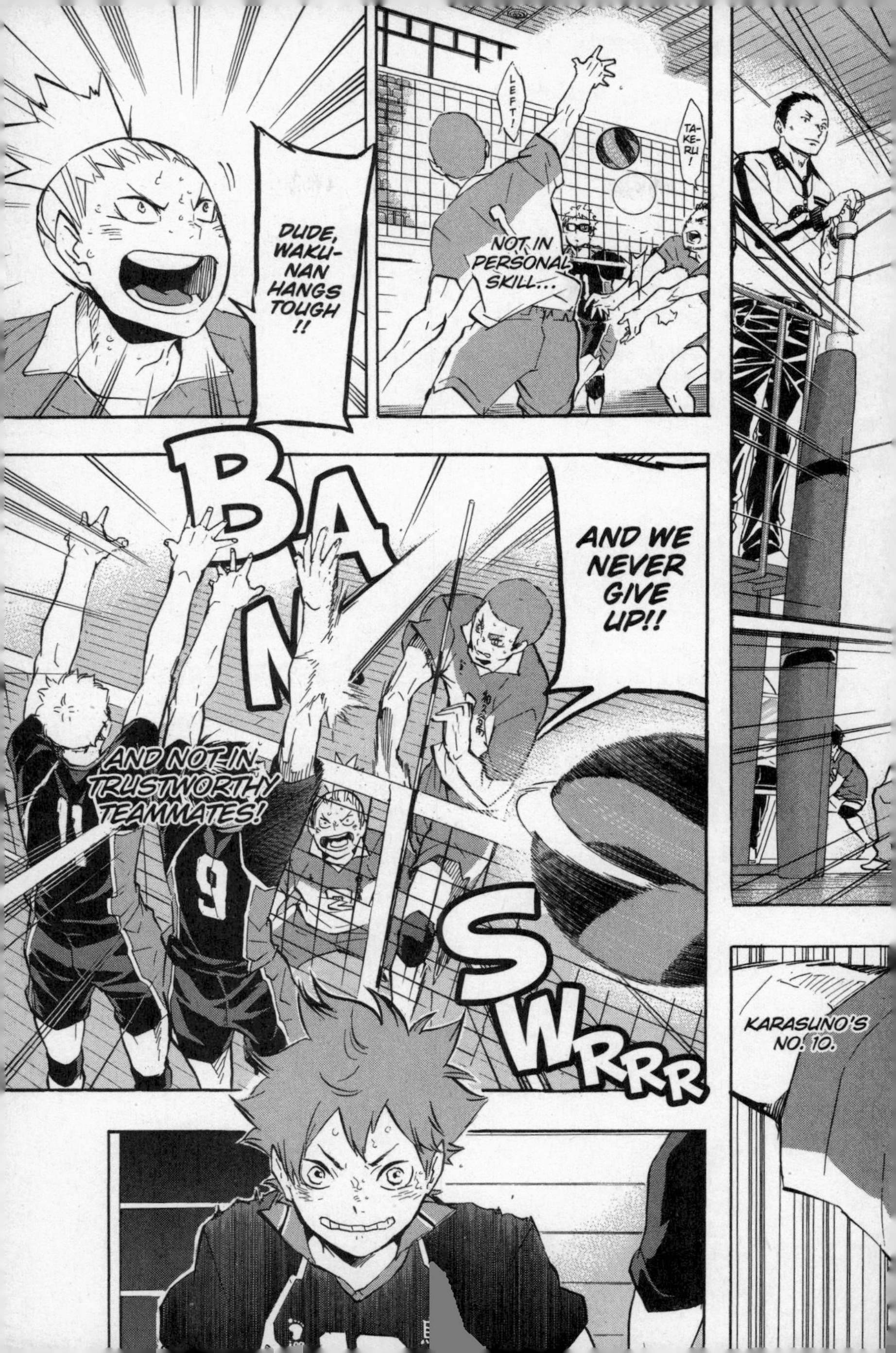

TAKERU!
LEFT!
NOT IN PERSONAL SKILL...
DUDE, WAKUNAN HANGS TOUGH!!
AND WE NEVER GIVE UP!!
BAM
AND NOT IN TRUSTWORTHY TEAMMATES!
SWRRR
KARASUNO'S NO. 10.

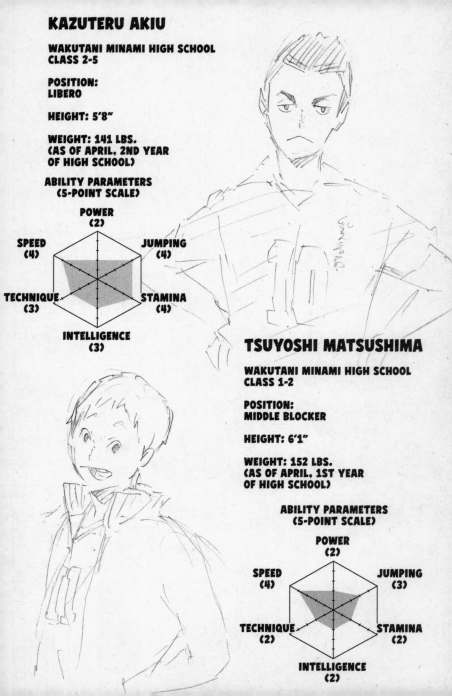

KAZUTERU AKIU

WAKUTANI MINAMI HIGH SCHOOL
CLASS 2-5

POSITION:
LIBERO

HEIGHT: 5'8"

WEIGHT: 141 LBS.
(AS OF APRIL, 2ND YEAR
OF HIGH SCHOOL)

ABILITY PARAMETERS
(5-POINT SCALE)

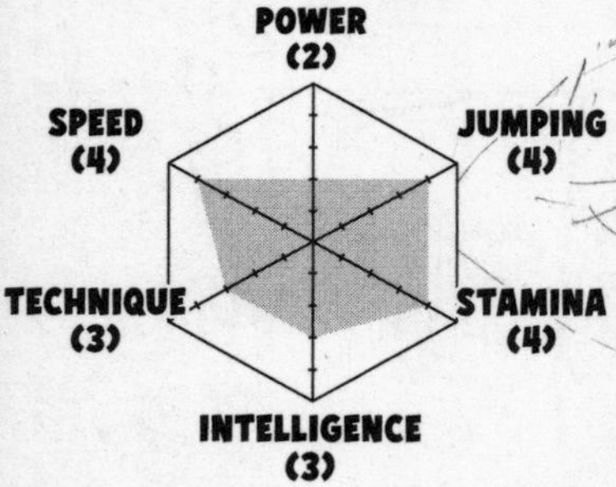
POWER (2)
JUMPING (4)
STAMINA (4)
INTELLIGENCE (3)
TECHNIQUE (3)
SPEED (4)

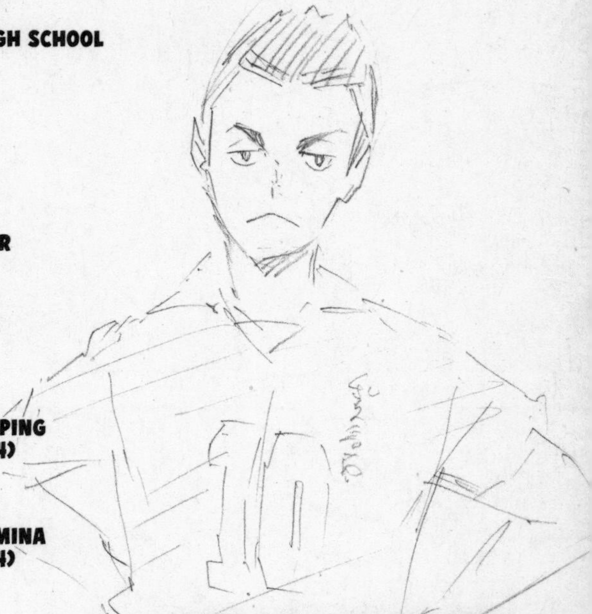

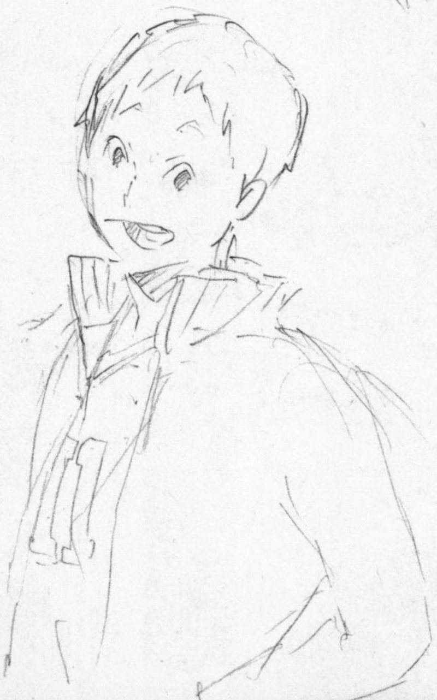

TSUYOSHI MATSUSHIMA

WAKUTANI MINAMI HIGH SCHOOL
CLASS 1-2

POSITION:
MIDDLE BLOCKER

HEIGHT: 6'1"

WEIGHT: 152 LBS.
(AS OF APRIL, 1ST YEAR
OF HIGH SCHOOL)

ABILITY PARAMETERS
(5-POINT SCALE)

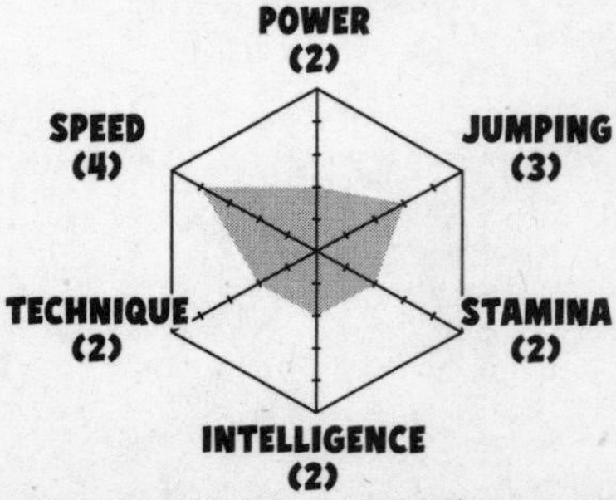
POWER (2)
JUMPING (3)
STAMINA (2)
INTELLIGENCE (2)
TECHNIQUE (2)
SPEED (4)

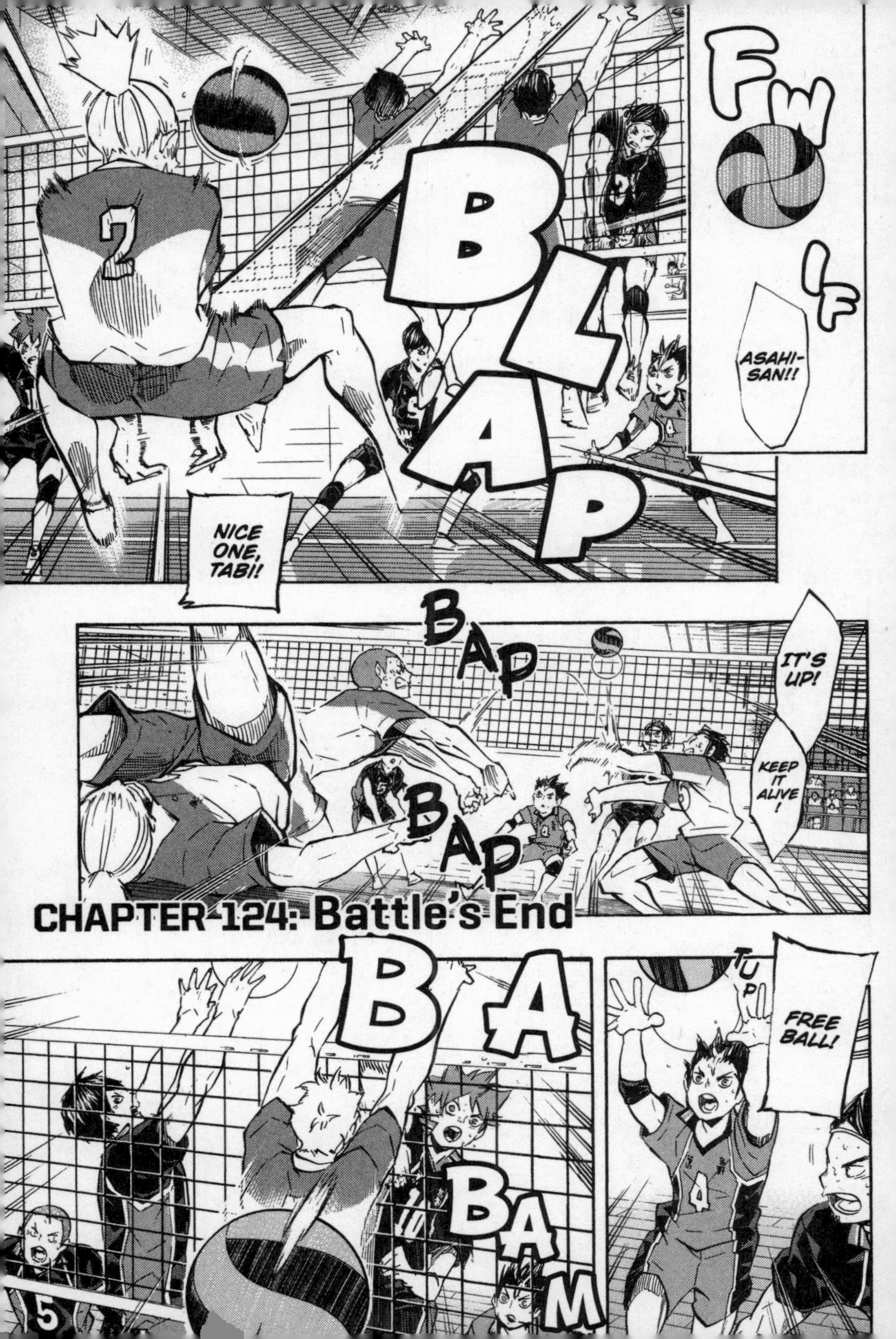
FWIF
ASAHI-SAN!!
BLAP
NICE ONE, TABI!
IT'S UP!
KEEP IT ALIVE!
BAP
BAP
CHAPTER 124: Battle's End
TUP
FREE BALL!
BA
BAM
5

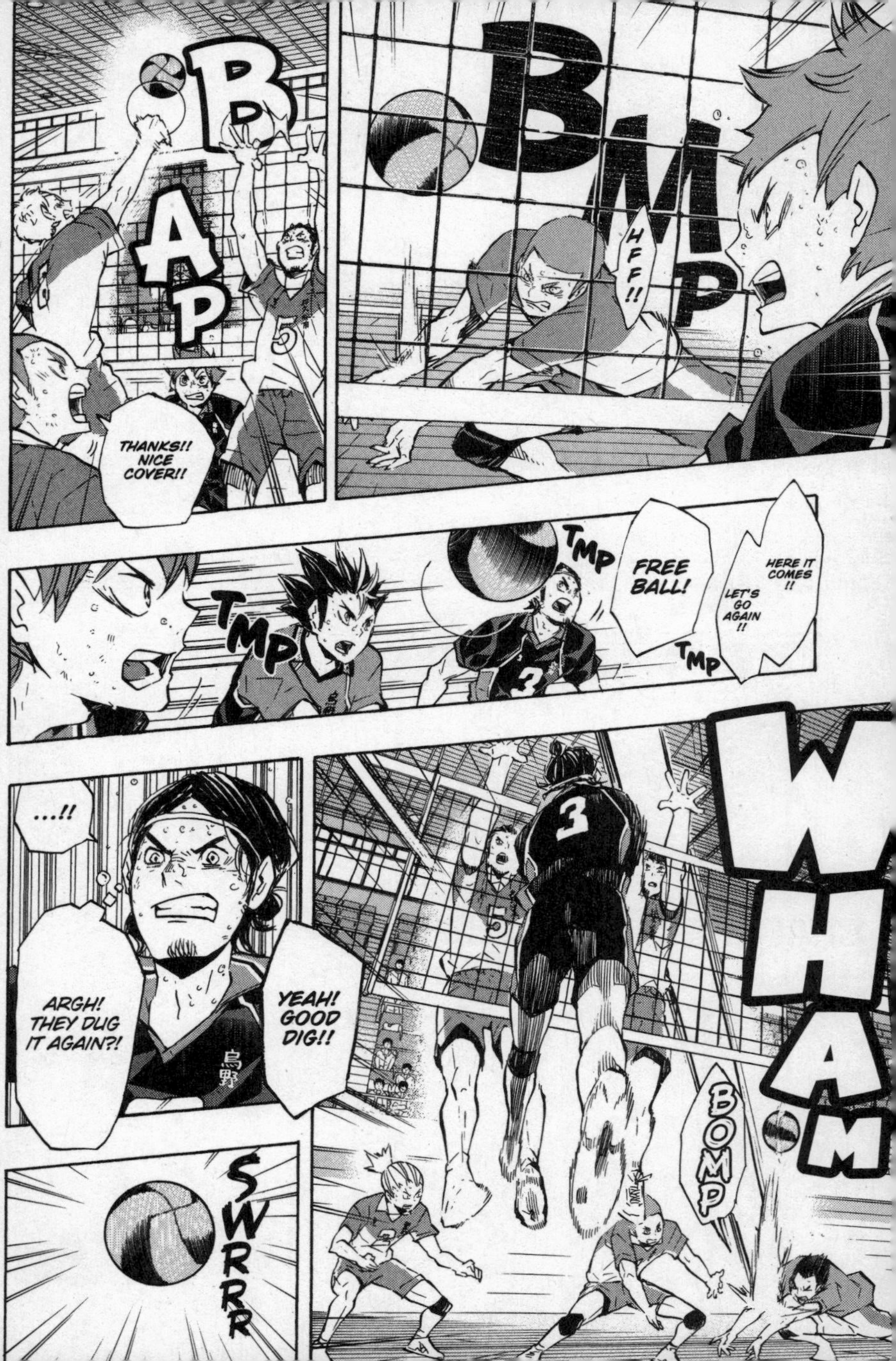
BMP
HFF!!
BAP
THANKS!! NICE COVER!!
HERE IT COMES!!
LET'S GO AGAIN!!
FREE BALL!
TMP
TMP
TMP
WHAM
BOMP
...!!
YEAH! GOOD DIG!!
ARGH! THEY DUG IT AGAIN?!
SWRRR

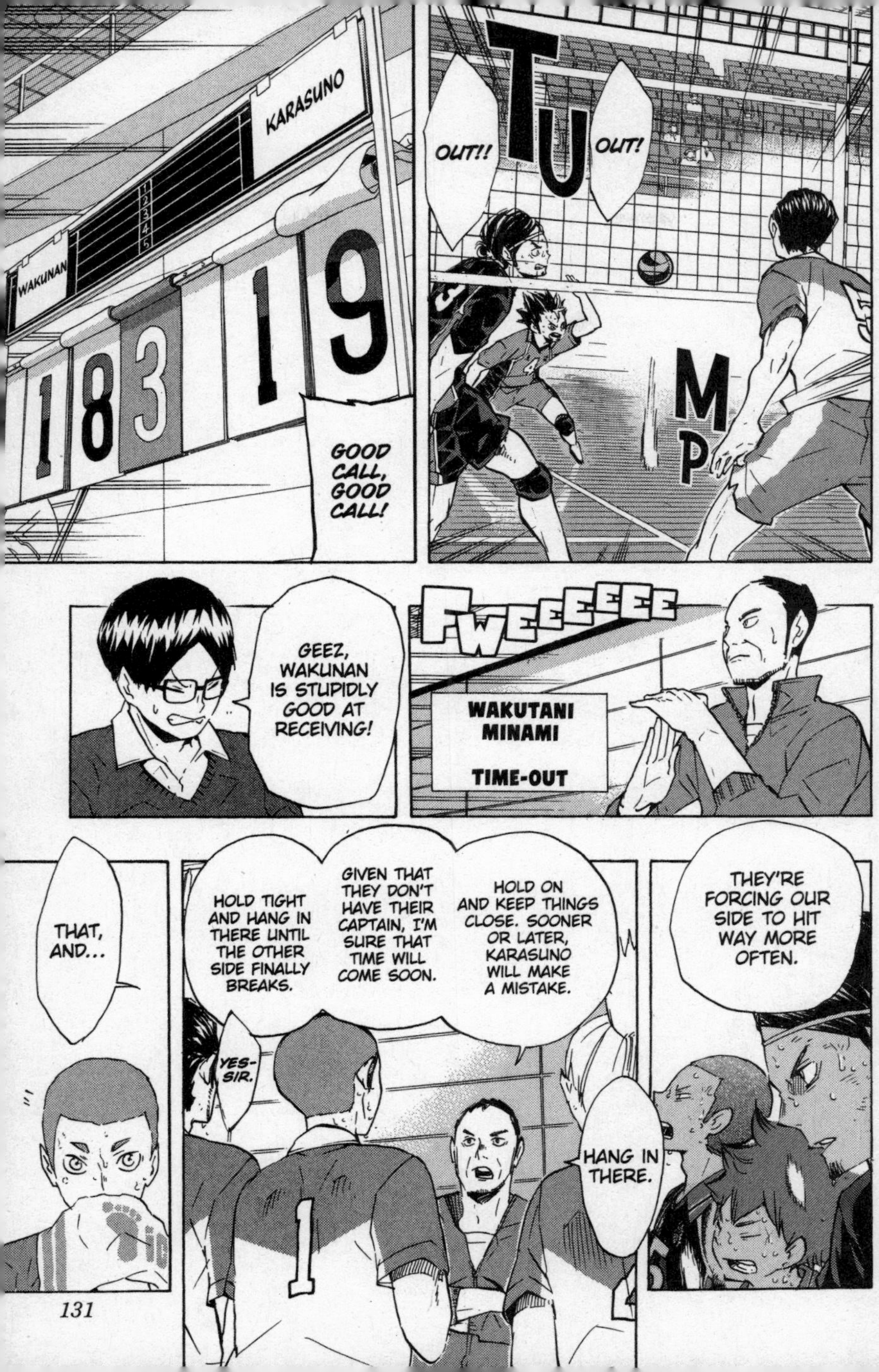
TU
OUT!
OUT!!
MP
KARASUNO
WAKUNAN
GOOD CALL, GOOD CALL!
FWEEEEEE
WAKUTANI MINAMI
TIME-OUT
GEEZ, WAKUNAN IS STUPIDLY GOOD AT RECEIVING!
THEY'RE FORCING OUR SIDE TO HIT WAY MORE OFTEN.
HOLD ON AND KEEP THINGS CLOSE. SOONER OR LATER, KARASUNO WILL MAKE A MISTAKE.
GIVEN THAT THEY DON'T HAVE THEIR CAPTAIN, I'M SURE THAT TIME WILL COME SOON.
HOLD TIGHT AND HANG IN THERE UNTIL THE OTHER SIDE FINALLY BREAKS.
HANG IN THERE.
YES-SIR.
THAT, AND...

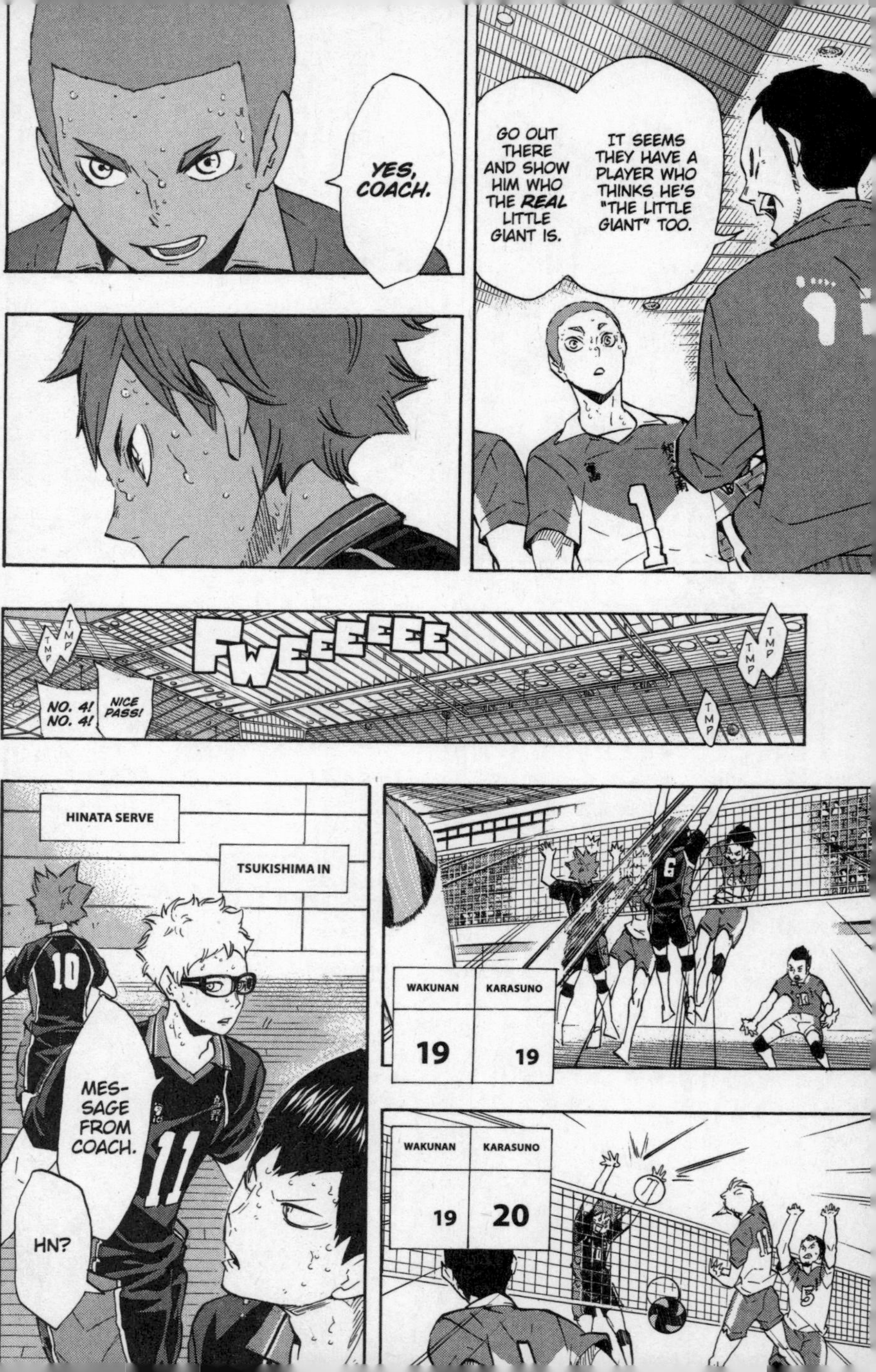
IT SEEMS THEY HAVE A PLAYER WHO THINKS HE'S "THE LITTLE GIANT" TOO.
GO OUT THERE AND SHOW HIM WHO THE REAL LITTLE GIANT IS.
YES, COACH.
TMP TMP TMP
FWEEEEEE
NICE PASS!
NO. 4! NO. 4!
TMP TMP
WAKUNAN 19 KARASUNO 19
WAKUNAN 19 KARASUNO 20
HINATA SERVE
TSUKISHIMA IN
MES-SAGE FROM COACH.
HN?

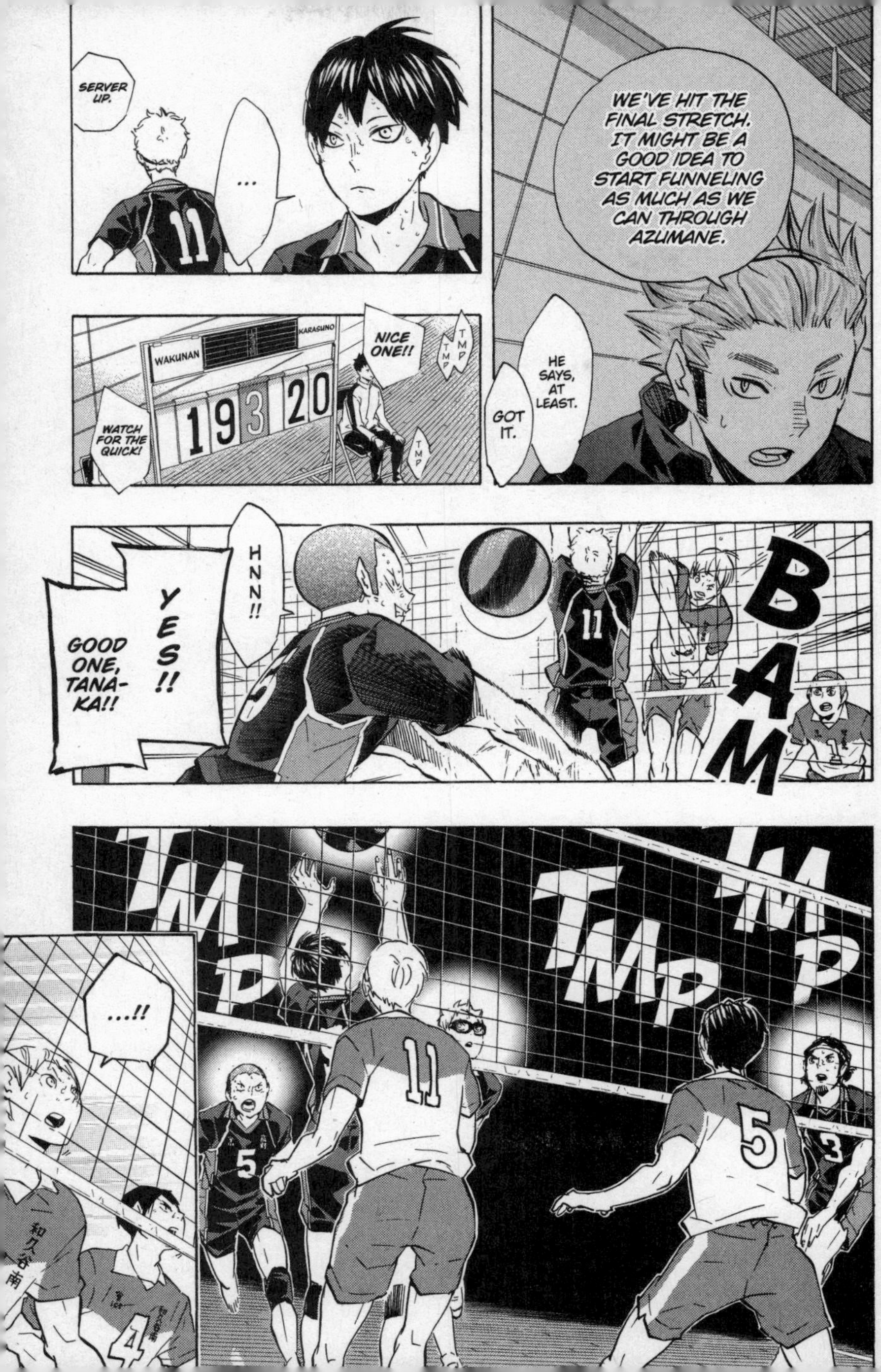
WE'VE HIT THE FINAL STRETCH. IT MIGHT BE A GOOD IDEA TO START FUNNELING AS MUCH AS WE CAN THROUGH AZUMANE.
HE SAYS, AT LEAST.
GOT IT.
SERVER UP.
...
NICE ONE!!
TMP TMP
KARASUNO
WAKUNAN
19 3 20
WATCH FOR THE QUICK!
TMP
BAM
HNN!!
YES!!
GOOD ONE, TANAKA!!
TMP
TMP
TMP
TMP
...!!
和久谷南

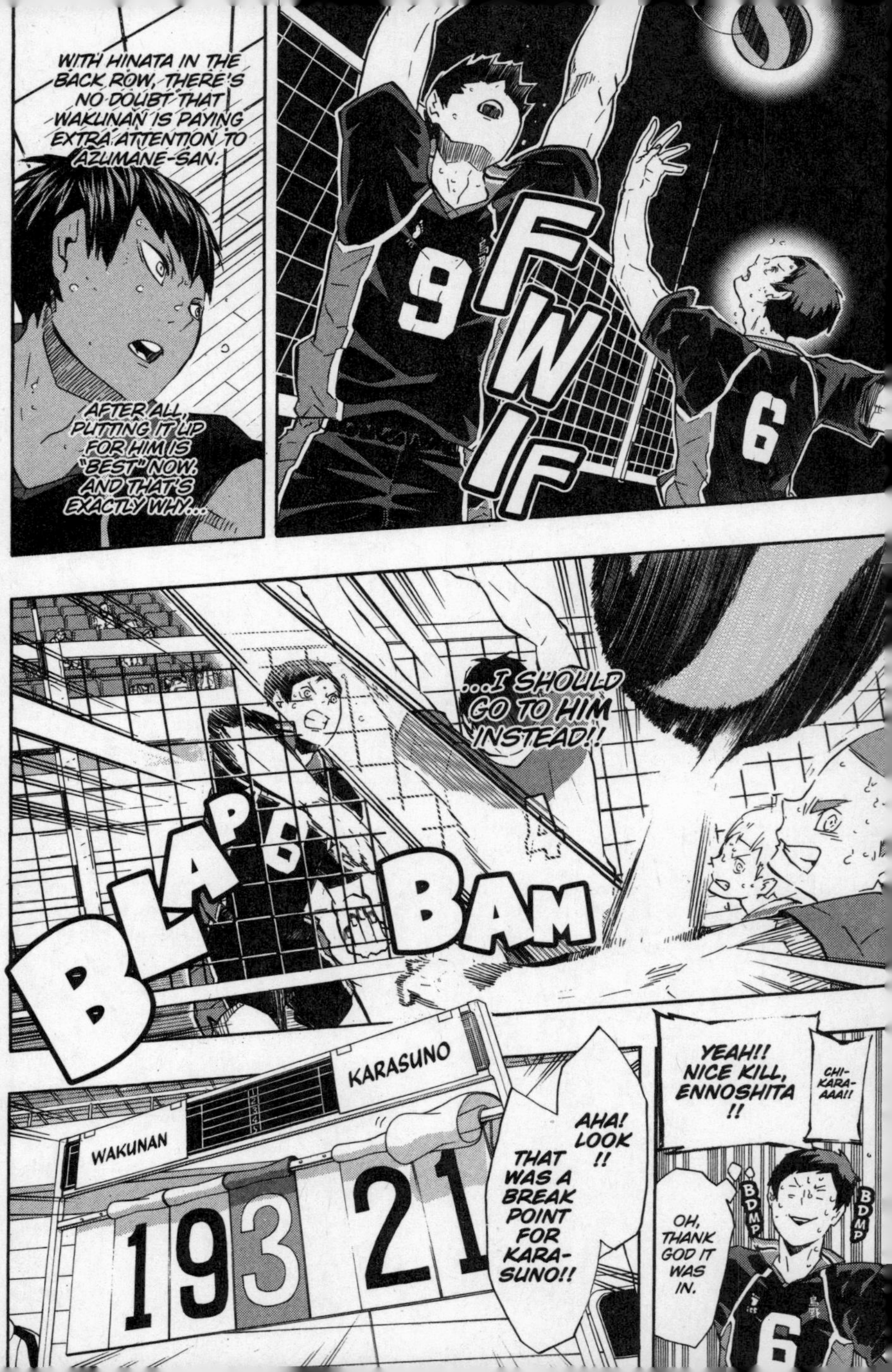
FWIF
WITH HINATA IN THE BACK ROW, THERE'S NO DOUBT THAT WAKUNAN IS PAYING EXTRA ATTENTION TO AZUMANE-SAN.
AFTER ALL, PUTTING IT UP FOR HIM IS "BEST" NOW. AND THAT'S EXACTLY WHY...
...I SHOULD GO TO HIM INSTEAD!!
BAM
BLAP
CHI-KARA-AAA!!
YEAH!! NICE KILL, ENNOSHITA!!
BDMP
BDMP
OH, THANK GOD IT WAS IN.
AHA! LOOK!!
THAT WAS A BREAK POINT FOR KARA-SUNO!!
KARASUNO
WAKUNAN
19
21

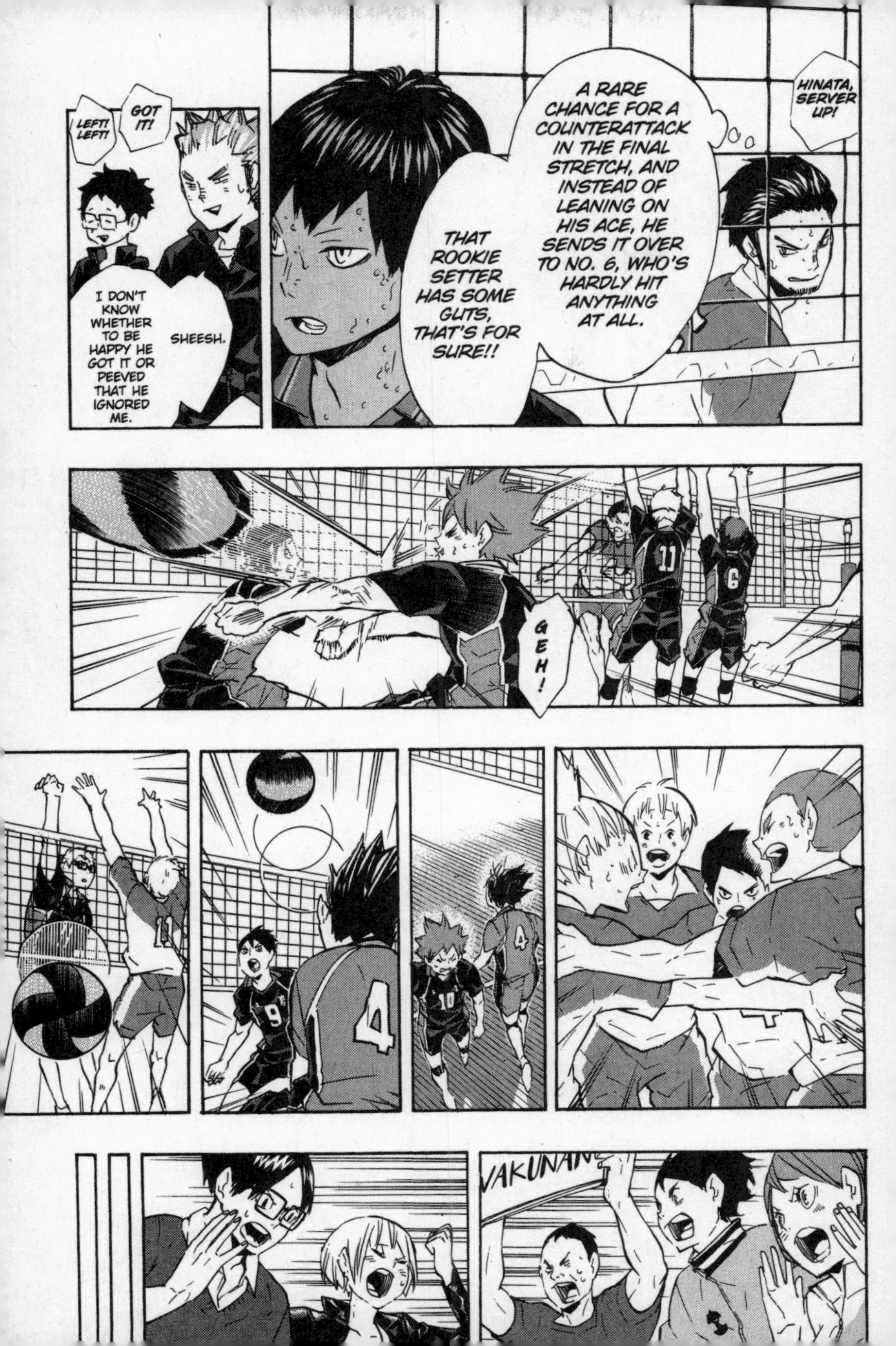
HINATA, SERVER UP!
A RARE CHANCE FOR A COUNTERATTACK IN THE FINAL STRETCH, AND INSTEAD OF LEANING ON HIS ACE, HE SENDS IT OVER TO NO. 6, WHO'S HARDLY HIT ANYTHING AT ALL.
THAT ROOKIE SETTER HAS SOME GUTS, THAT'S FOR SURE!!
GOT IT!
LEFT! LEFT!
SHEESH.
I DON'T KNOW WHETHER TO BE HAPPY HE GOT IT OR PEEVED THAT HE IGNORED ME.
GEH!

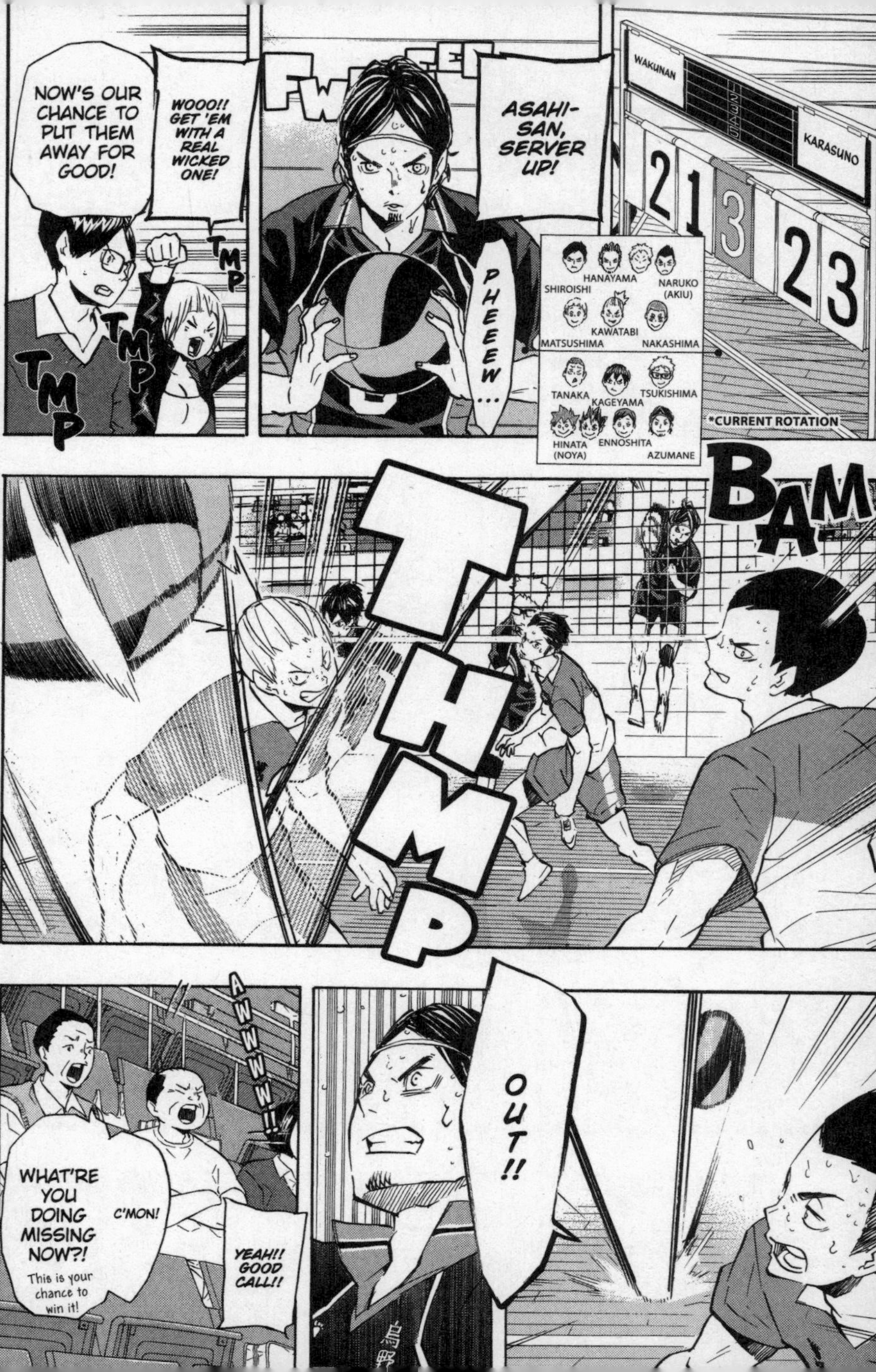
WAKUNAN
KARASUNO
21
3
23
SHIROISHI
HANAYAMA
NARUKO (AKIU)
MATSUSHIMA
KAWATABI
NAKASHIMA
TANAKA
KAGEYAMA
TSUKISHIMA
HINATA (NOYA)
ENNOSHITA
AZUMANE
*CURRENT ROTATION
ASAHI-SAN, SERVER UP!
PHEEEW...
FW
WOOO!! GET 'EM WITH A REAL WICKED ONE!
NOW'S OUR CHANCE TO PUT THEM AWAY FOR GOOD!
TMP
TMP
TMP
TMP
BAM
THMP
OUT!!
AWWWW!!
YEAH!! GOOD CALL!!
C'MON!
WHAT'RE YOU DOING MISSING NOW?!
This is your chance to win it!

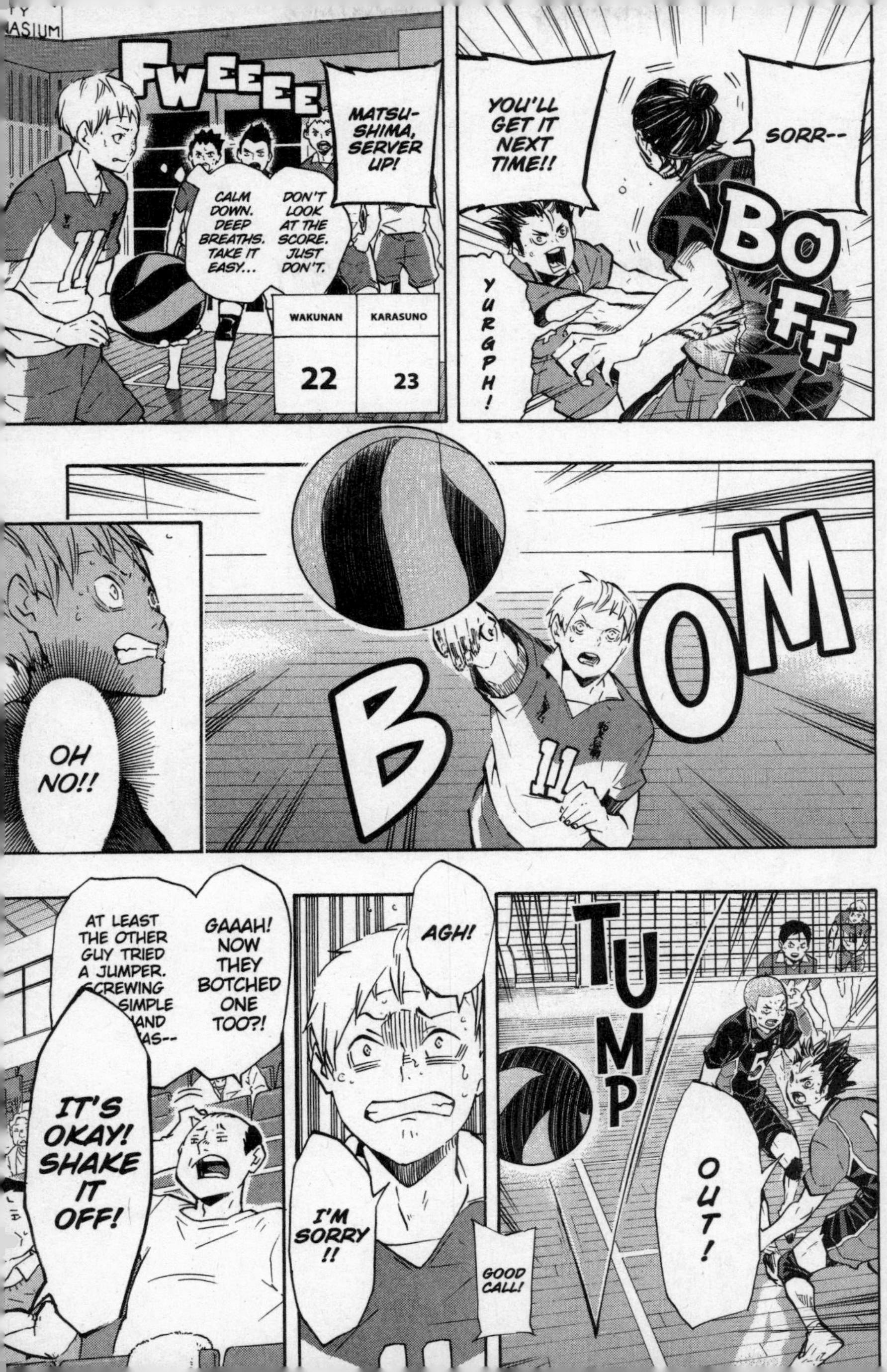
SORR--
YOU'LL GET IT NEXT TIME!!
BOFF
YURGPH!
MATSU-SHIMA, SERVER UP!
FWEEEE
DON'T LOOK AT THE SCORE. JUST DON'T.
CALM DOWN. DEEP BREATHS. TAKE IT EASY...
WAKUNAN 22
KARASUNO 23
BOOM
OH NO!!
TUMP
OUT!
AGH!
I'M SORRY!!
GOOD CALL!
GAAAH! NOW THEY BOTCHED ONE TOO?!
AT LEAST THE OTHER GUY TRIED A JUMPER.
IT'S OKAY! SHAKE IT OFF!

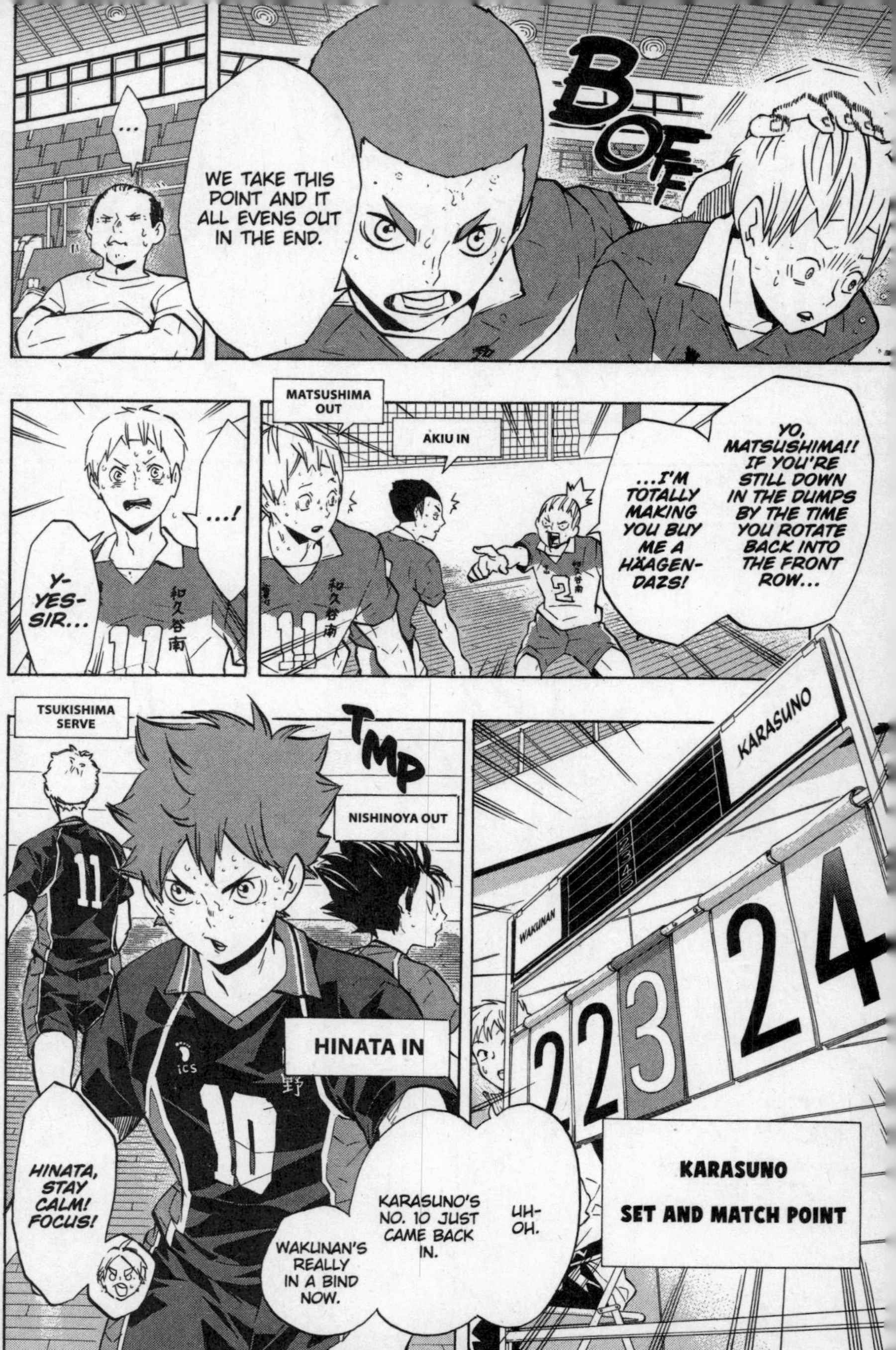
BOFF
WE TAKE THIS POINT AND IT ALL EVENS OUT IN THE END.
...
MATSUSHIMA OUT
AKIU IN
YO, MATSUSHIMA!! IF YOU'RE STILL DOWN IN THE DUMPS BY THE TIME YOU ROTATE BACK INTO THE FRONT ROW...
...I'M TOTALLY MAKING YOU BUY ME A HÄAGEN-DAZS!
...!
Y-YES-SIR...
KARASUNO
WAKUNAN
KARASUNO
SET AND MATCH POINT
TSUKISHIMA SERVE
TMP
NISHINOYA OUT
HINATA IN
UH-OH.
KARASUNO'S NO. 10 JUST CAME BACK IN.
WAKUNAN'S REALLY IN A BIND NOW.
HINATA, STAY CALM! FOCUS!

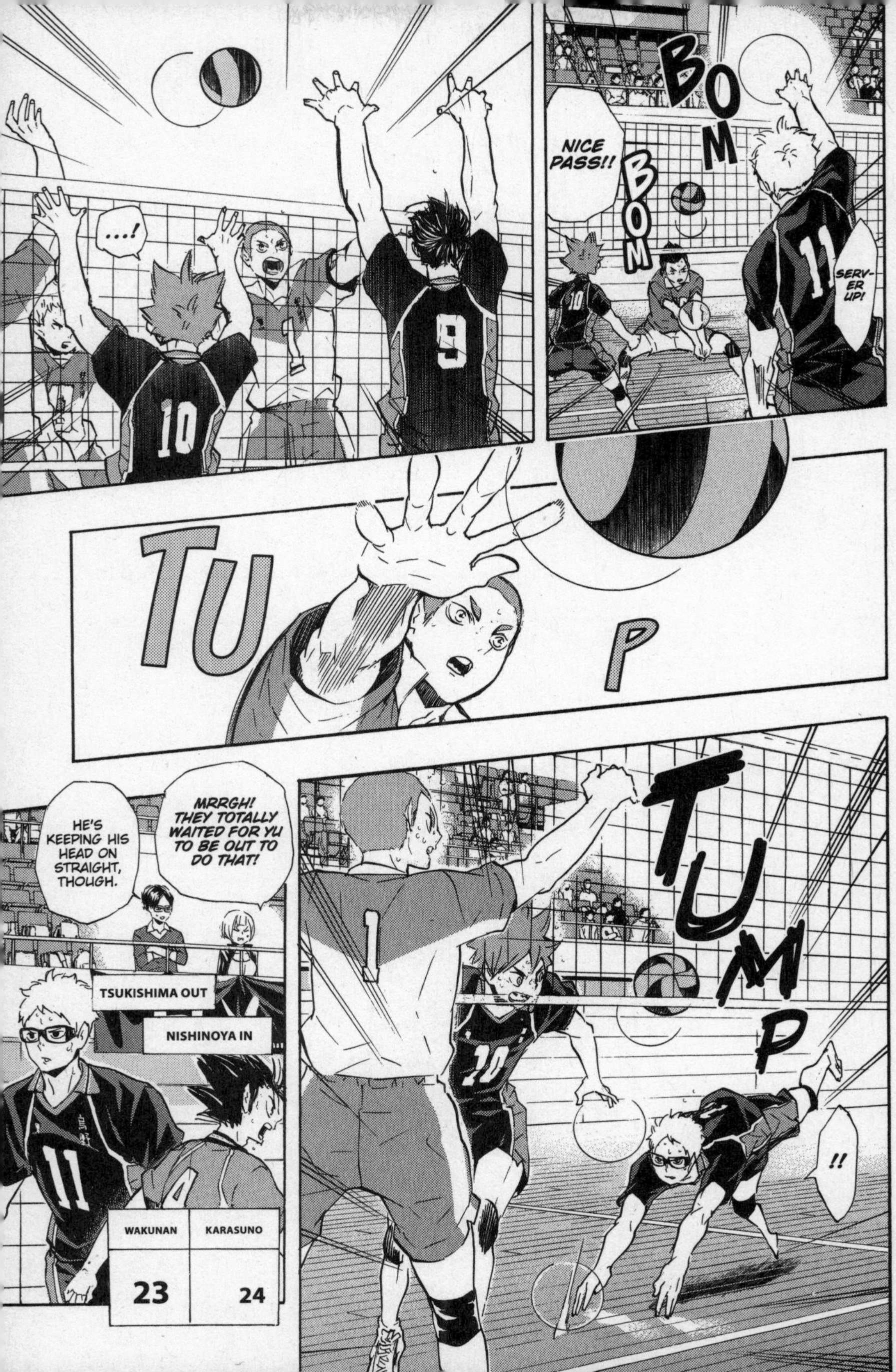
BOM
SERV-ER UP!
NICE PASS!!
BOM
BOM
...!
TU P
TUMP
!!
MRRGH! THEY TOTALLY WAITED FOR YU TO BE OUT TO DO THAT!
HE'S KEEPING HIS HEAD ON STRAIGHT, THOUGH.
TSUKISHIMA OUT
NISHINOYA IN
WAKUNAN
KARASUNO
23
24

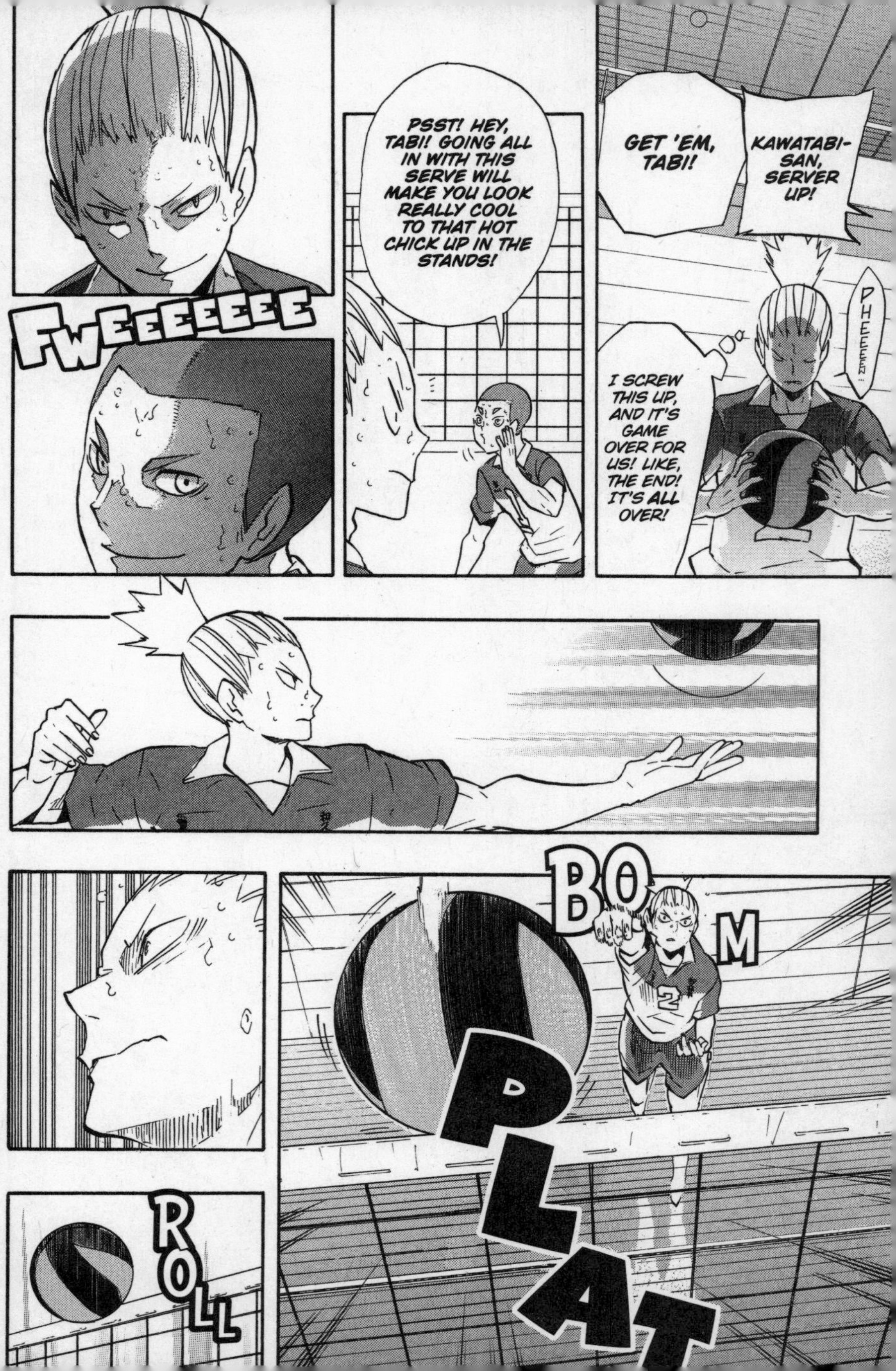
KAWATABI-SAN, SERVER UP!
GET 'EM, TABI!
PHEEEEEN...
I SCREW THIS UP, AND IT'S GAME OVER FOR US! LIKE, THE END! IT'S ALL OVER!
PSST! HEY, TABI! GOING ALL IN WITH THIS SERVE WILL MAKE YOU LOOK REALLY COOL TO THAT HOT CHICK UP IN THE STANDS!
FWEEEEEEE
BOOM
PLAT
ROLL

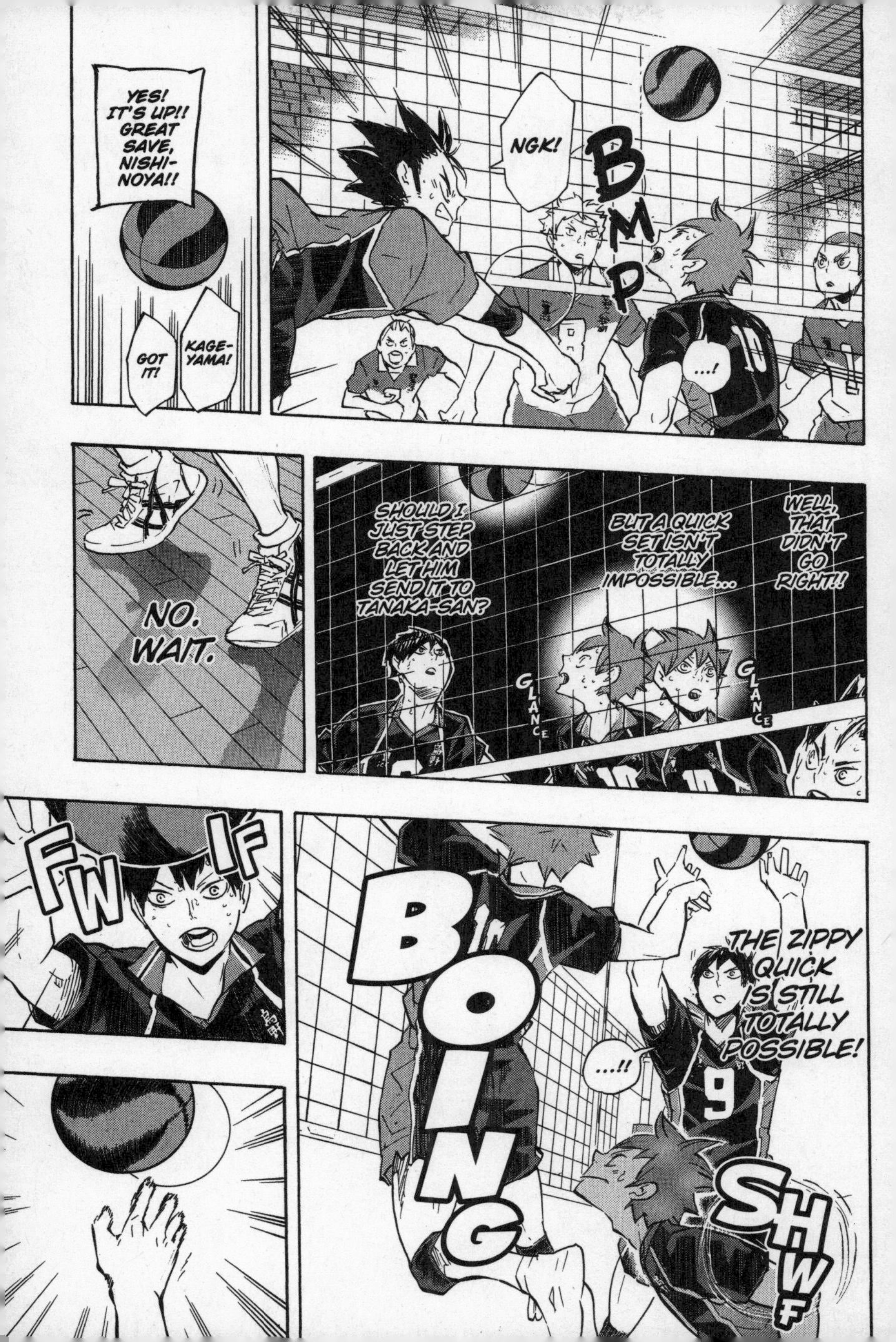
NGK!
BMP
...!
YES! IT'S UP!! GREAT SAVE, NISHI-NOYA!!
KAGE-YAMA!
GOT IT!
WELL, THAT DIDN'T GO RIGHT!!
BUT A QUICK SET ISN'T TOTALLY IMPOSSIBLE...
SHOULD I JUST STEP BACK AND LET HIM SEND IT TO TANAKA-SAN?
GLANCE
GLANCE
NO. WAIT.
BOING
THE ZIPPY QUICK IS STILL TOTALLY POSSIBLE!
...!!
SHWF
FWIF

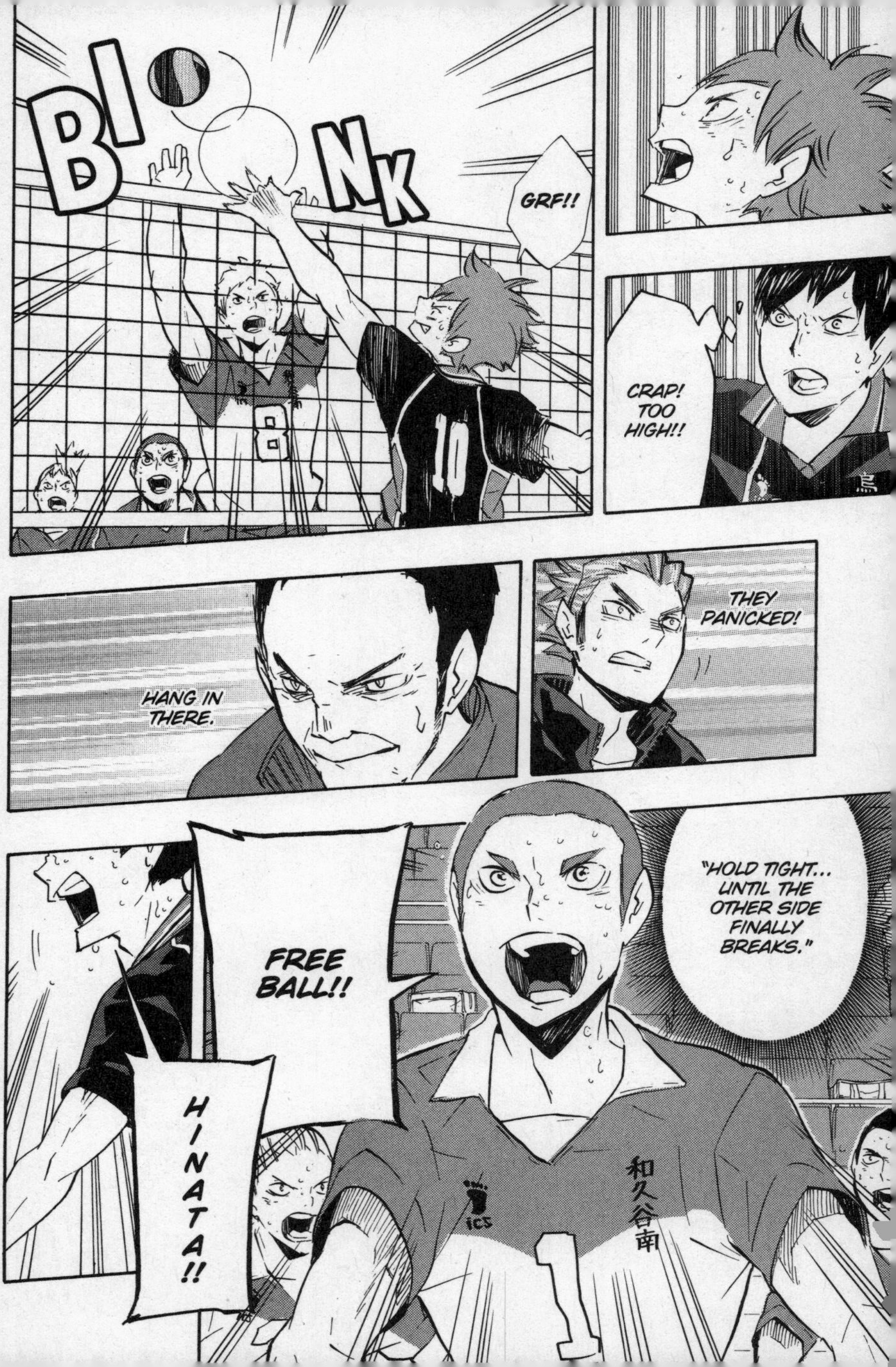
CRAP! TOO HIGH!!
BIONK
GRF!!
THEY PANICKED!
HANG IN THERE.
"HOLD TIGHT... UNTIL THE OTHER SIDE FINALLY BREAKS."
FREE BALL!!
HINATA!!

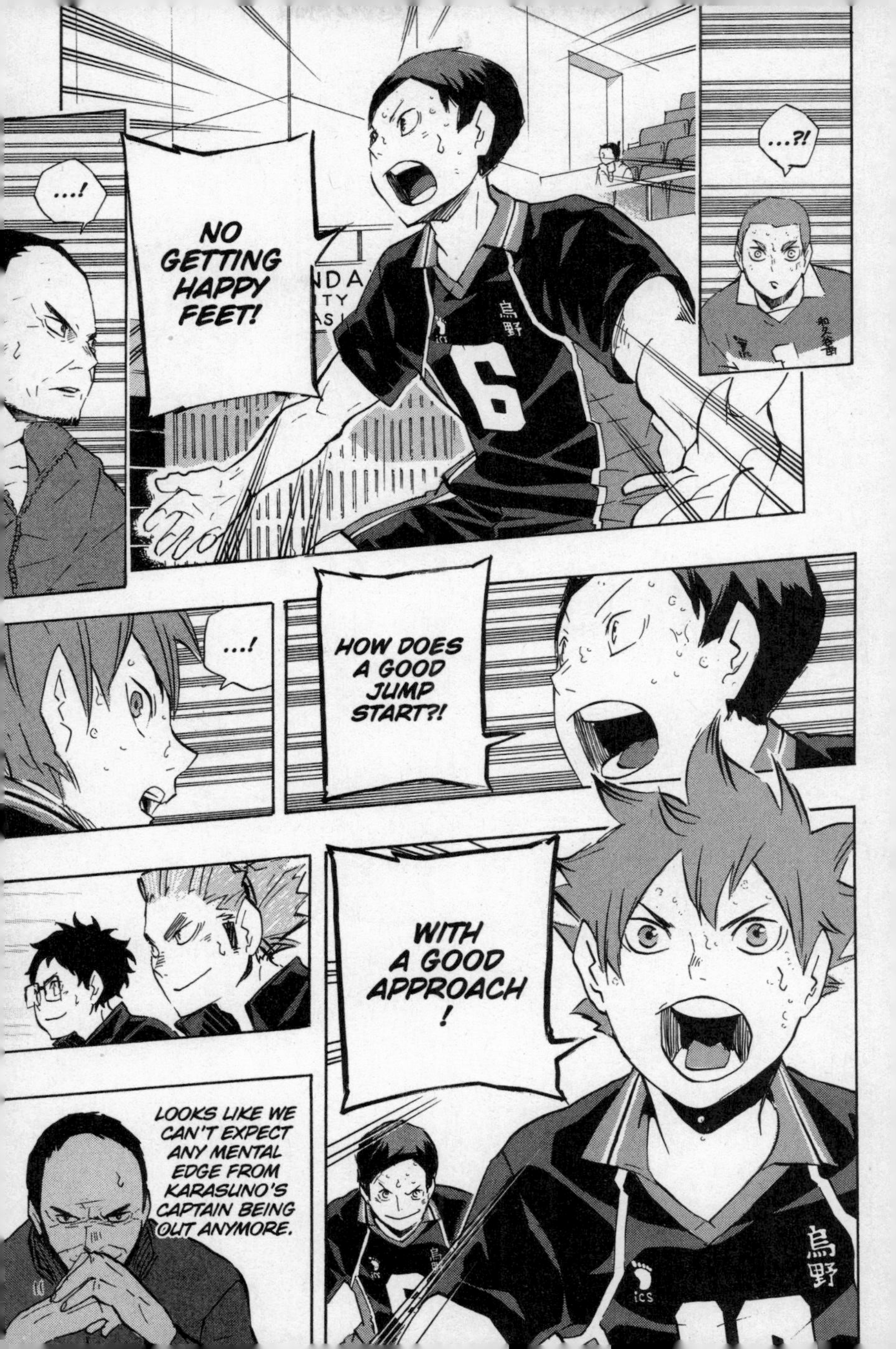
...?!
NO GETTING HAPPY FEET!
...!
HOW DOES A GOOD JUMP START?!
...!
WITH A GOOD APPROACH!
LOOKS LIKE WE CAN'T EXPECT ANY MENTAL EDGE FROM KARASUNO'S CAPTAIN BEING OUT ANYMORE.

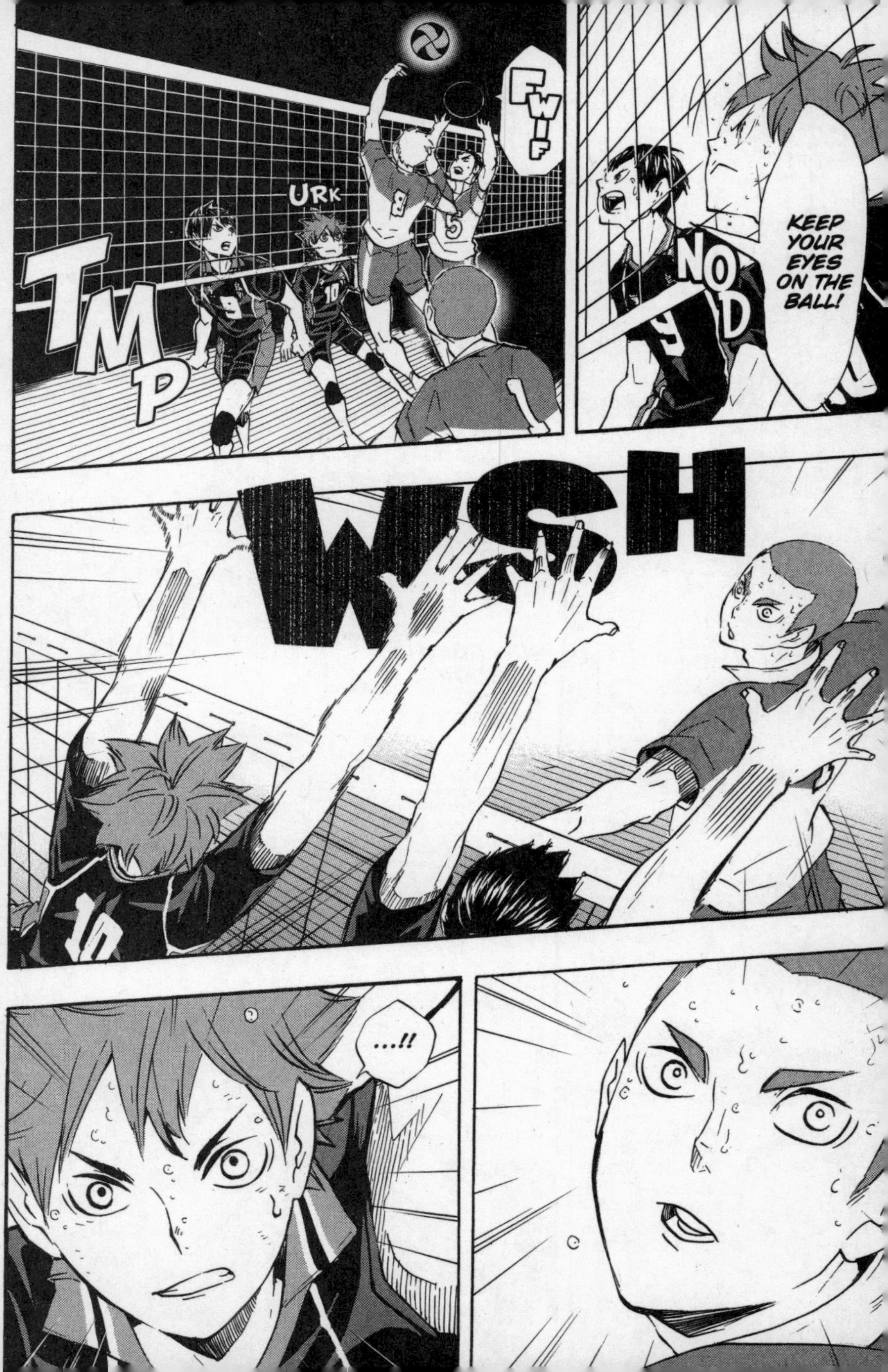
NOD
KEEP YOUR EYES ON THE BALL!
FWIF
URK
TMP
WSH
...!!

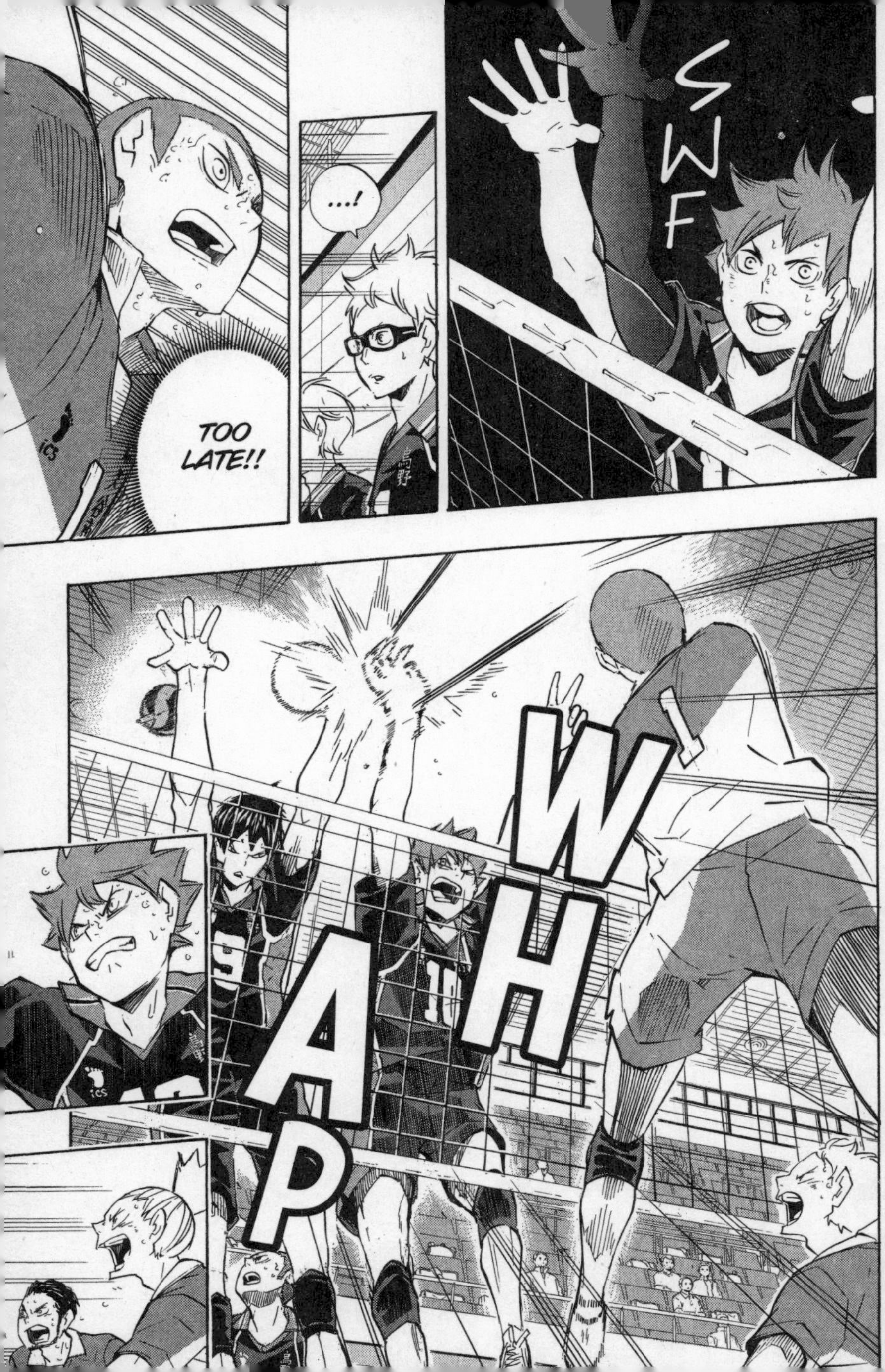
SWF
...!
TOO LATE!!
WHAP

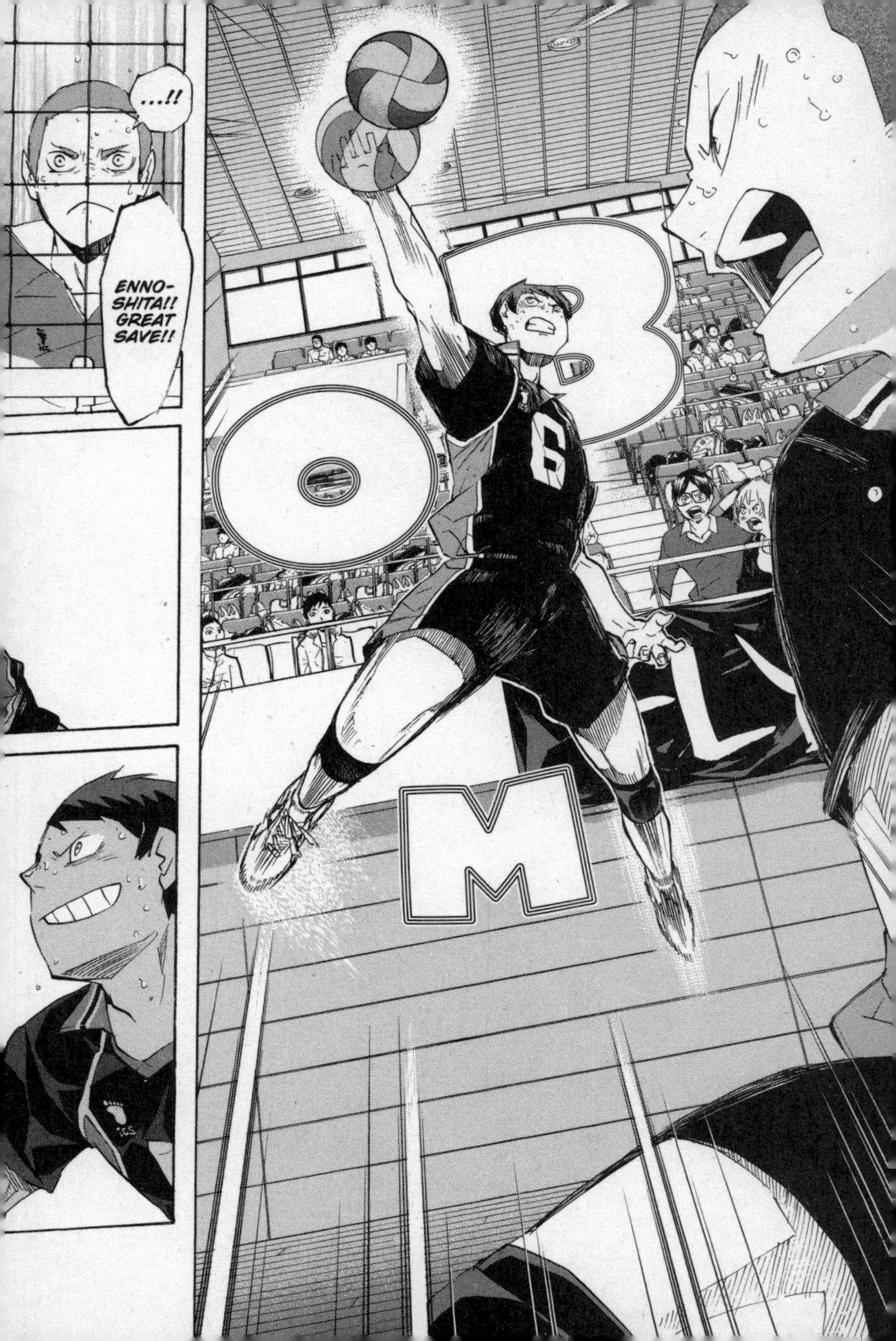
...!!
ENNO-SHITA!! GREAT SAVE!!

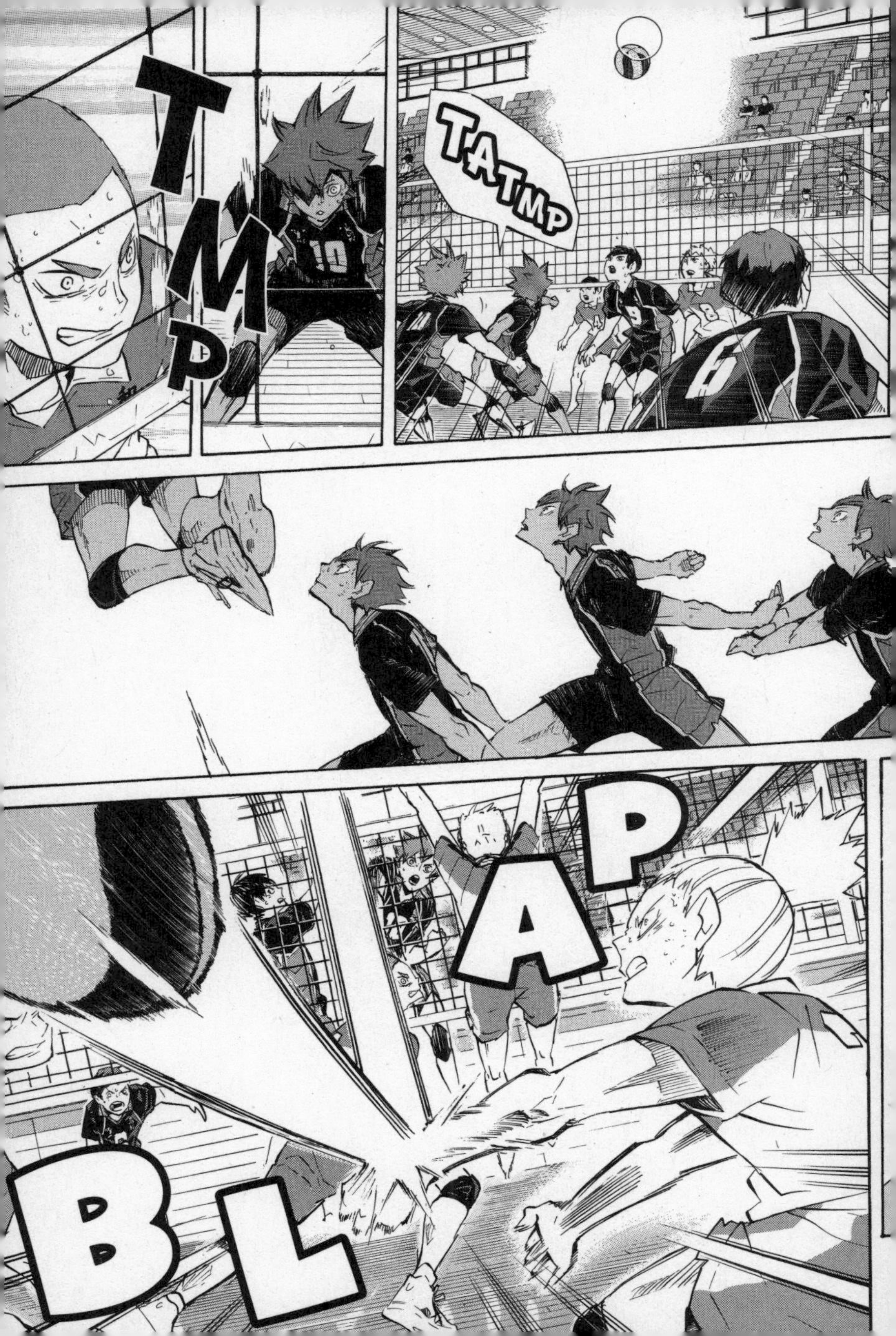
TATMP
TMP
BLAP

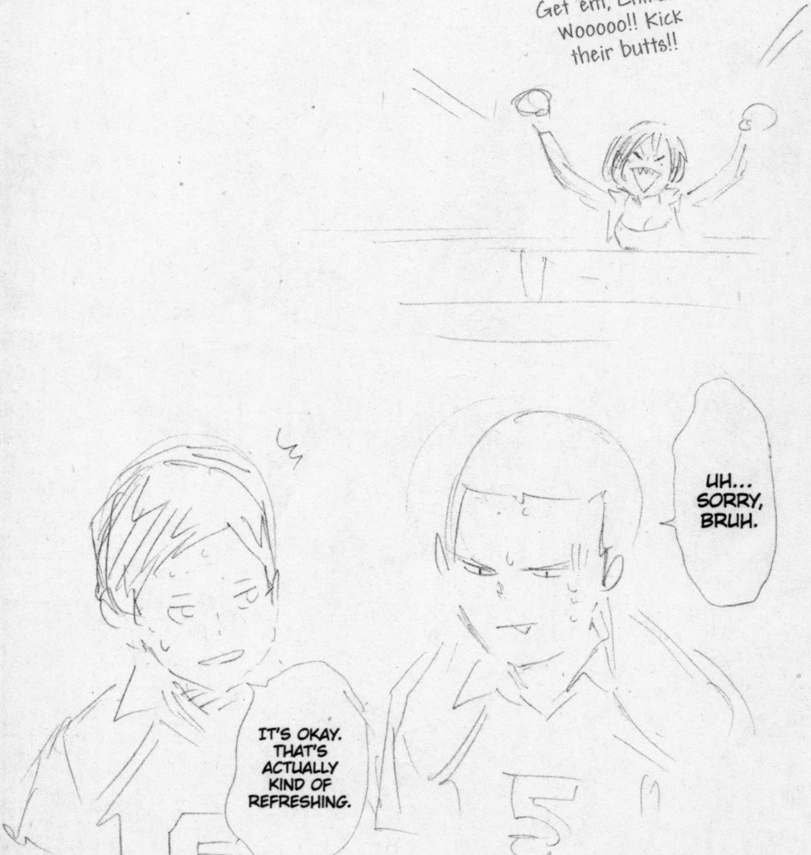
Get 'em, Chikara!! Wooooo!! Kick their butts!!
UH... SORRY, BRUH.
IT'S OKAY. THAT'S ACTUALLY KIND OF REFRESHING.

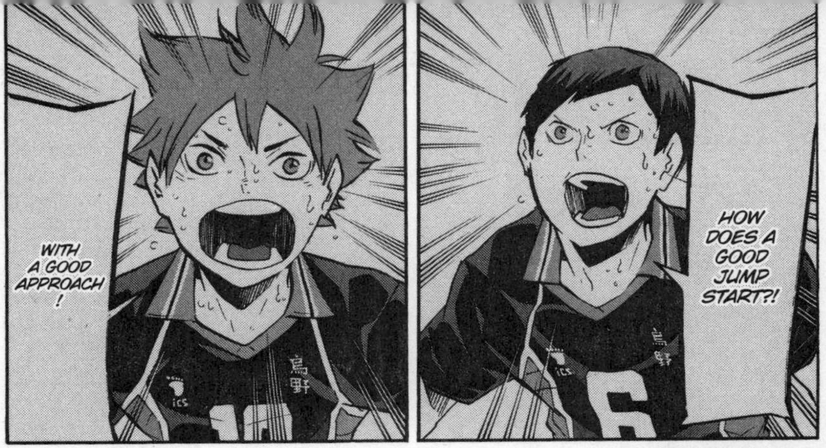
HOW DOES A GOOD JUMP START?!
WITH A GOOD APPROACH!

CHAPTER 125

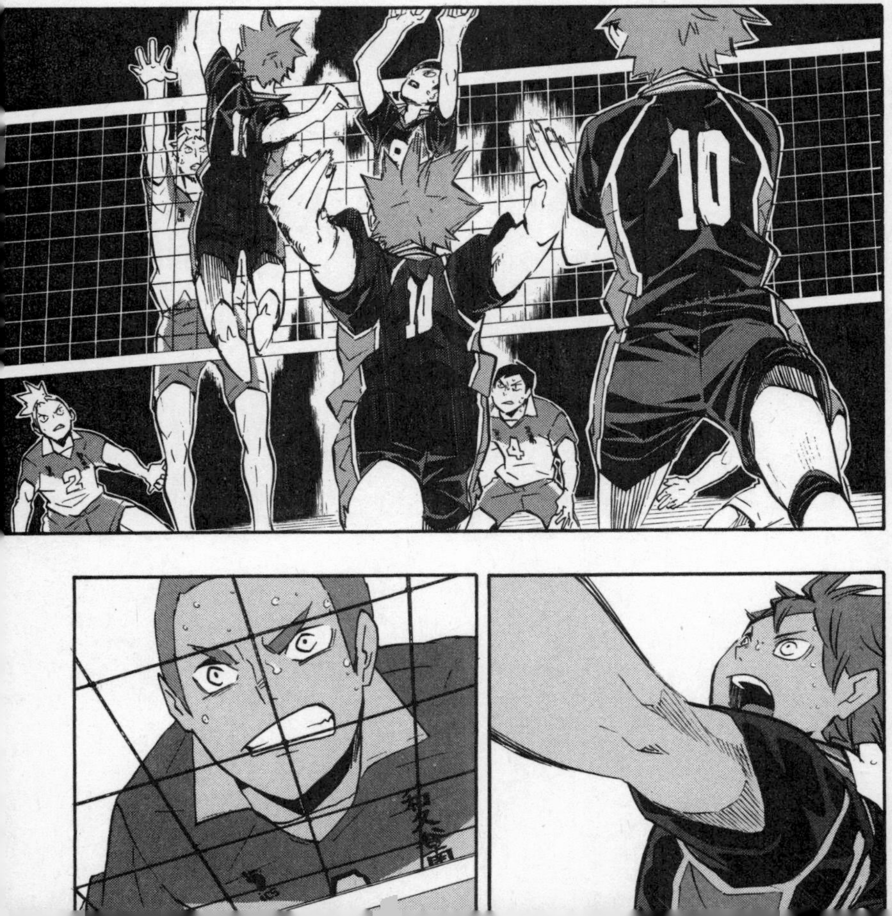

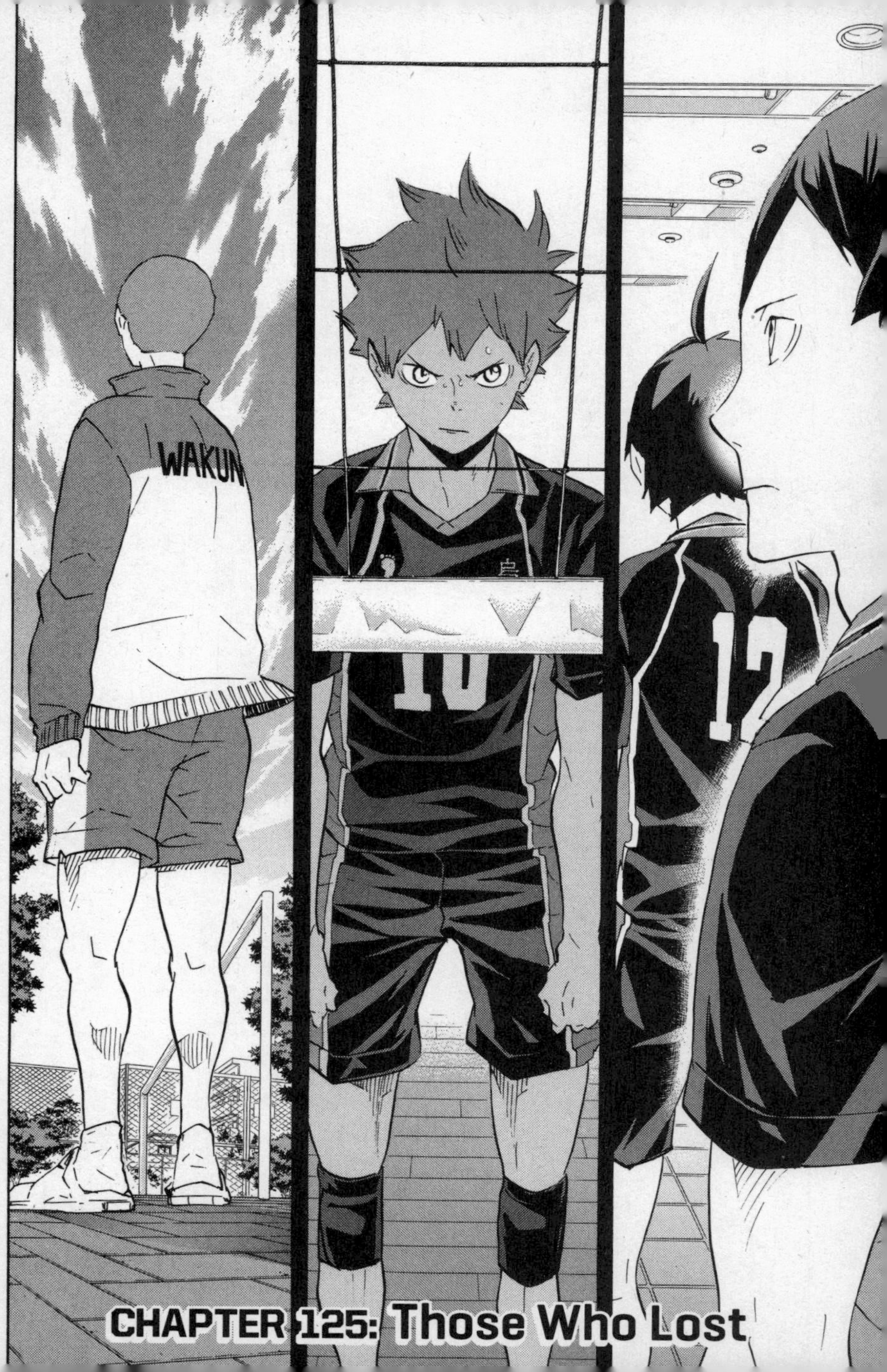
17
10
WAKUN

CHAPTER 125: Those Who Lost

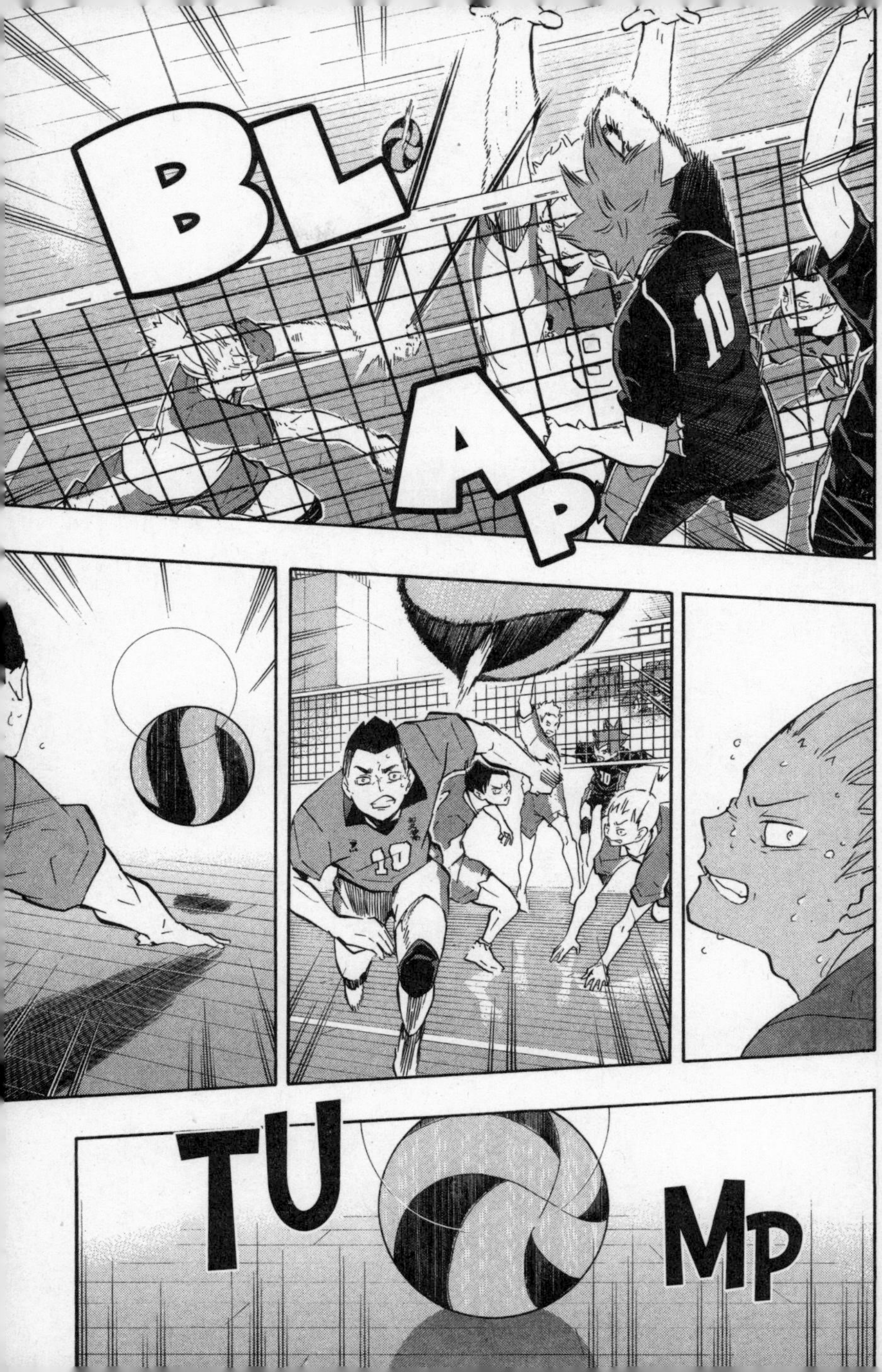
BLAP
TUMP

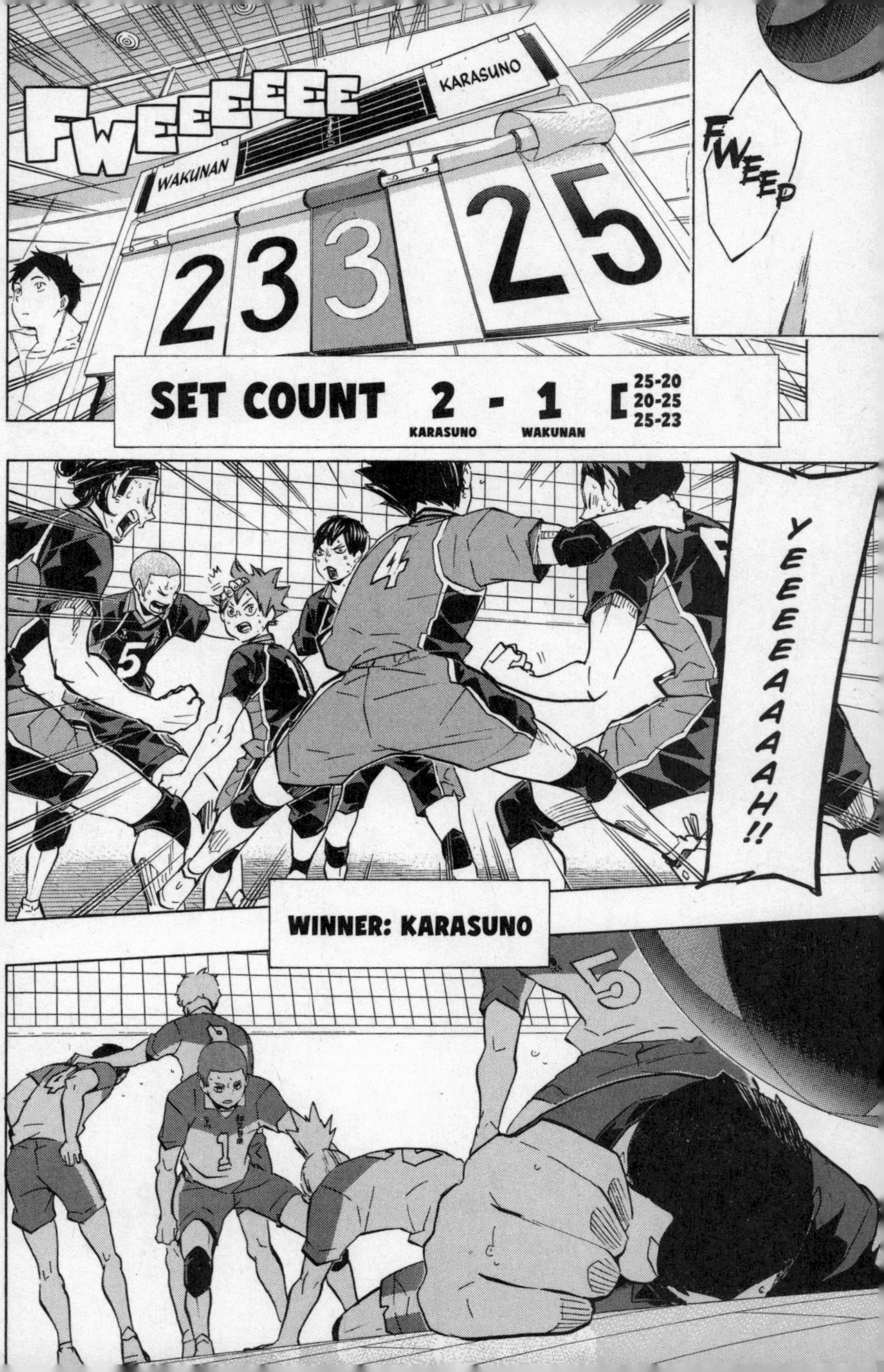
FWEEP
FWEEEEEE
KARASUNO
WAKUNAN
23
3
25
SET COUNT 2 - 1 [25-20 20-25 25-23
KARASUNO
WAKUNAN
YEEEEEAAAAAH!!
WINNER: KARASUNO

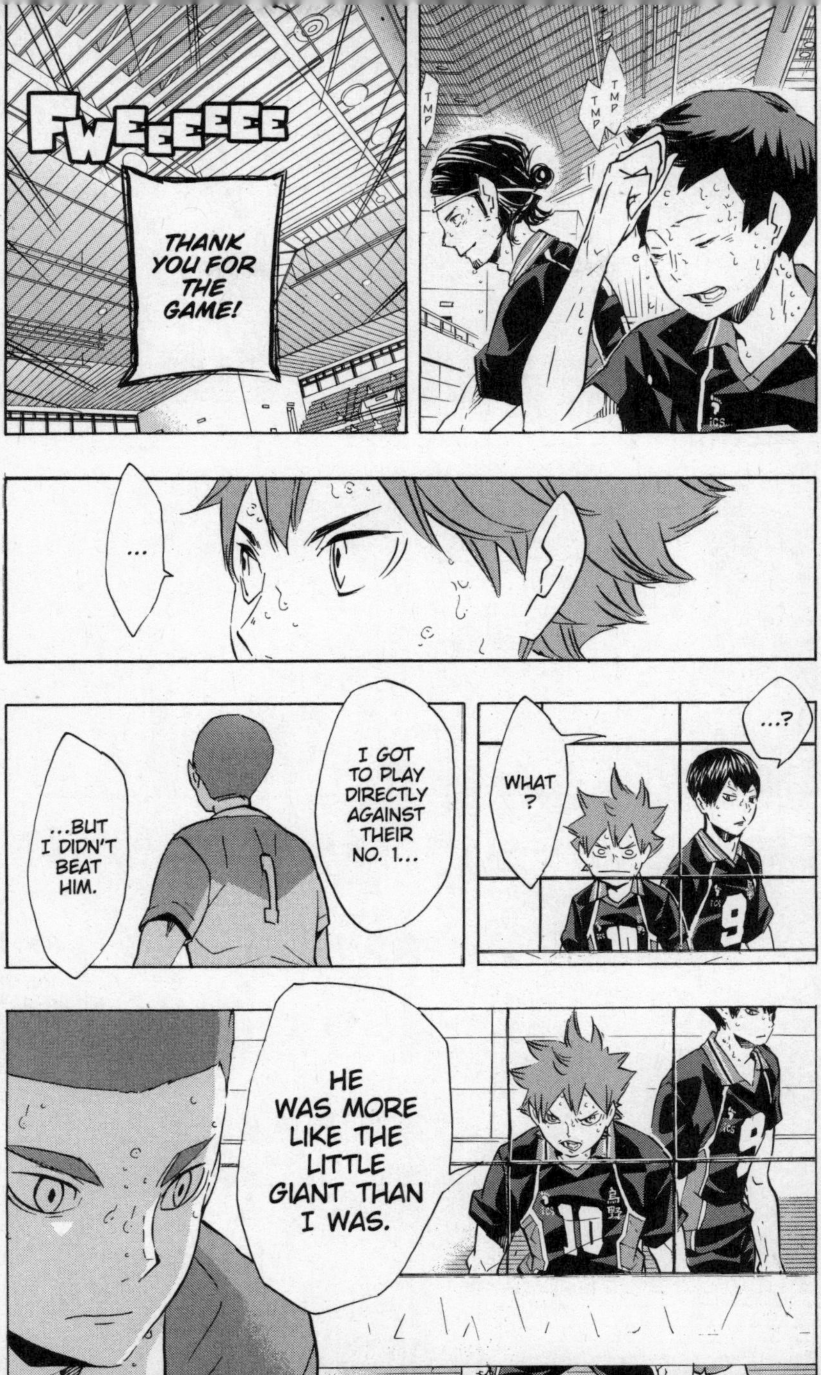
TMP TMP
TMP
FWEEEEEE
THANK YOU FOR THE GAME!
...
...?
WHAT ?
I GOT TO PLAY DIRECTLY AGAINST THEIR NO. 1...
...BUT I DIDN'T BEAT HIM.
HE WAS MORE LIKE THE LITTLE GIANT THAN I WAS.

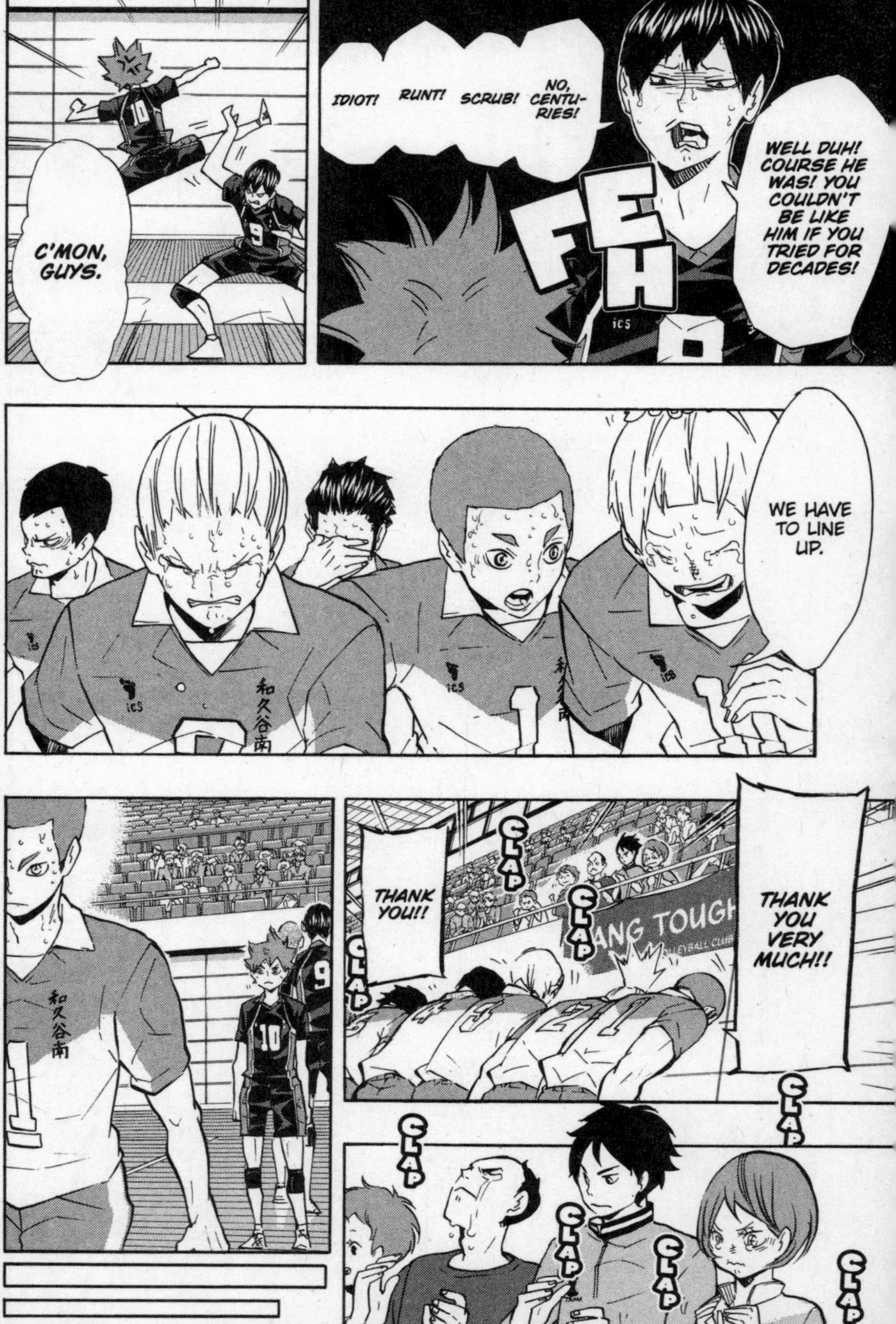

WELL DUH! COURSE HE WAS! YOU COULDN'T BE LIKE HIM IF YOU TRIED FOR DECADES!
FEH
NO, CENTURIES!
SCRUB!
RUNT!
IDIOT!
C'MON, GUYS.
WE HAVE TO LINE UP.
THANK YOU VERY MUCH!!
CLAP
CLAP
ANG TOUGH
THANK YOU!!
CLAP
CLAP
CLAP
CLAP
CLAP
CLAP
CLAP

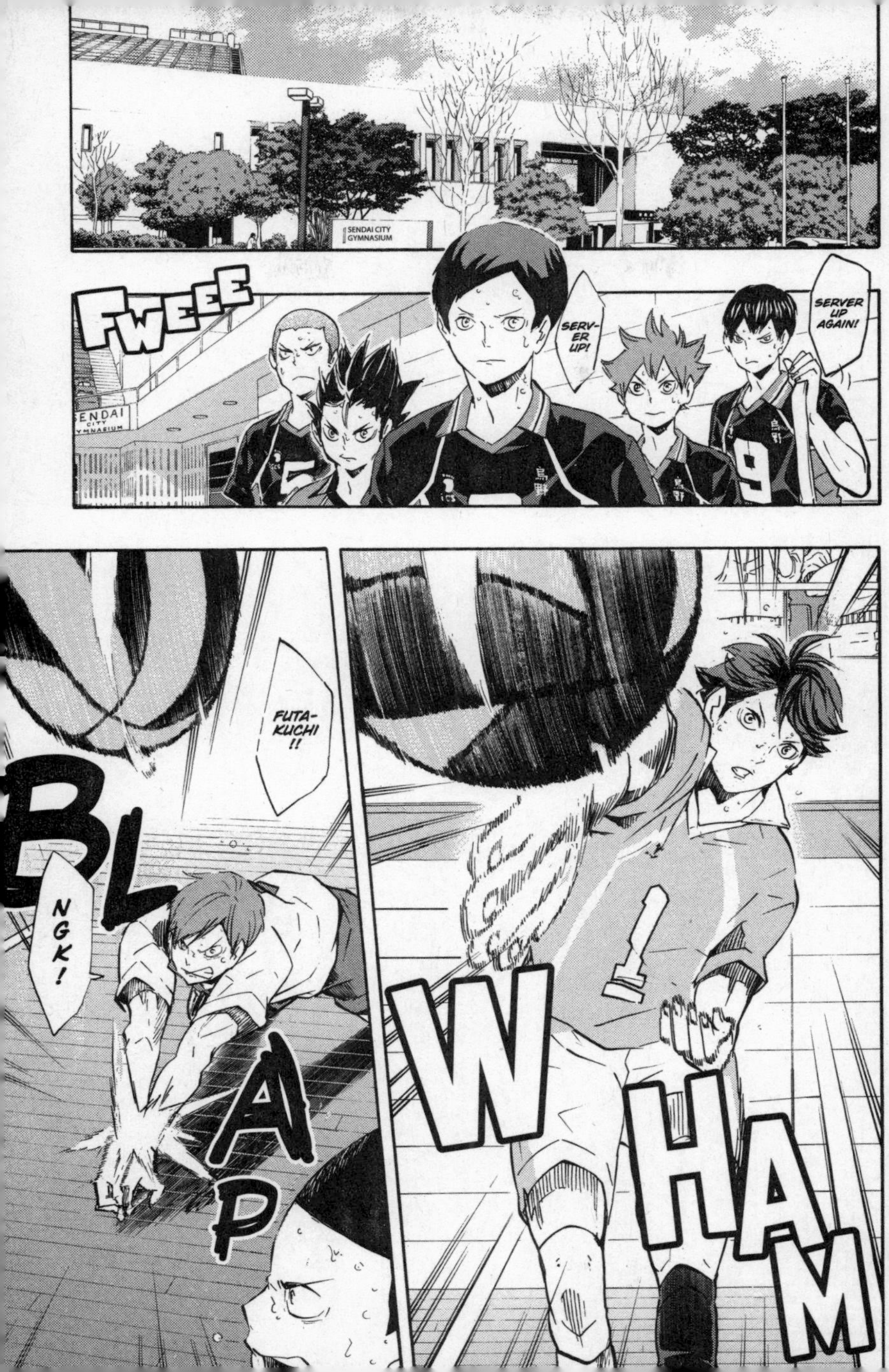
SENDAI CITY GYMNASIUM
SERVER UP AGAIN!
SERV-ER UP!
FWEEE
SENDAI CITY GYMNASIUM
WHAM
FUTA-KUCHI!!
BLAP
NGK!

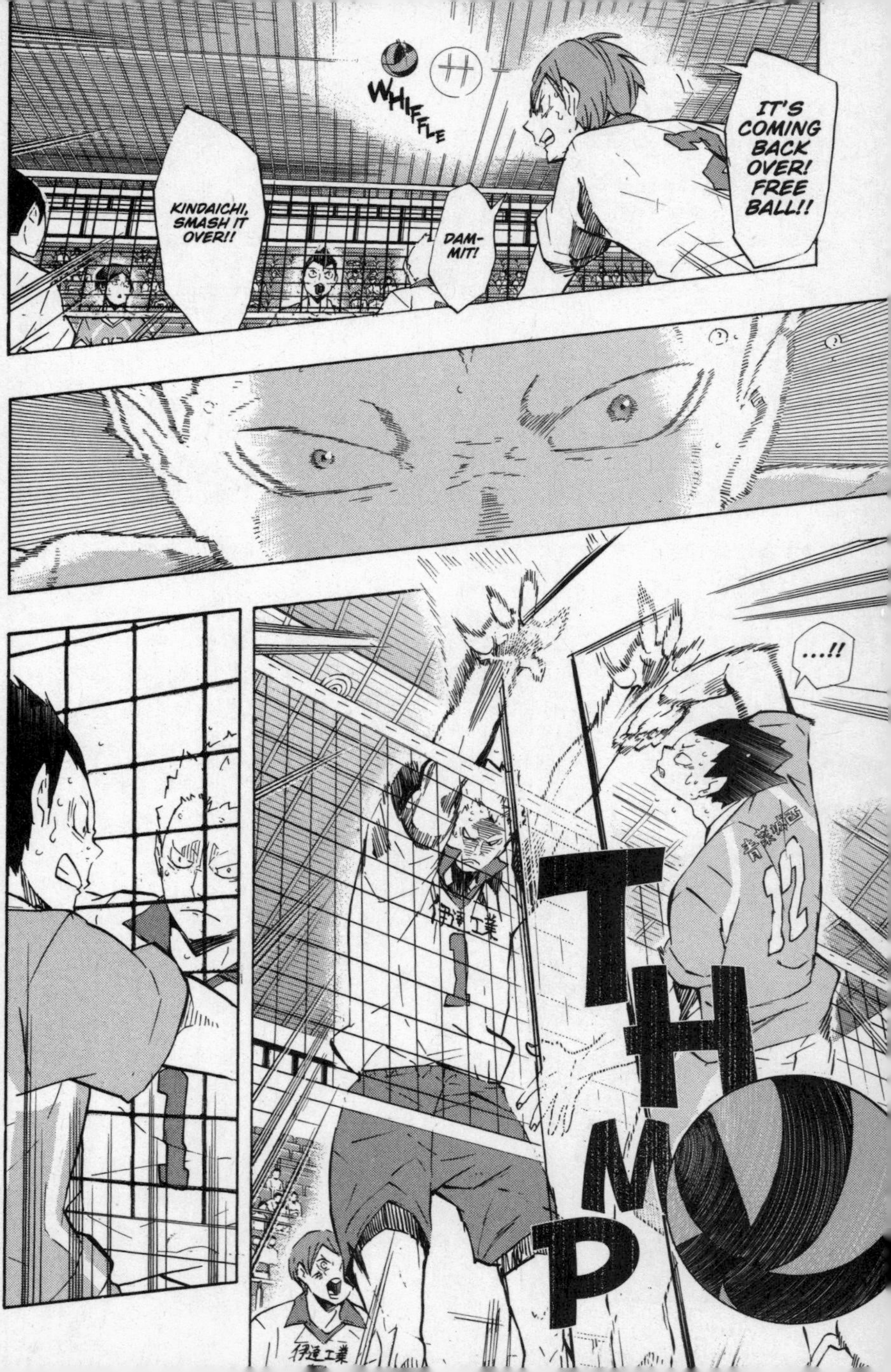
IT'S COMING BACK OVER! FREE BALL!!
WHIFFLE
DAM-MIT!
KINDAICHI, SMASH IT OVER!!
...!!
THMP

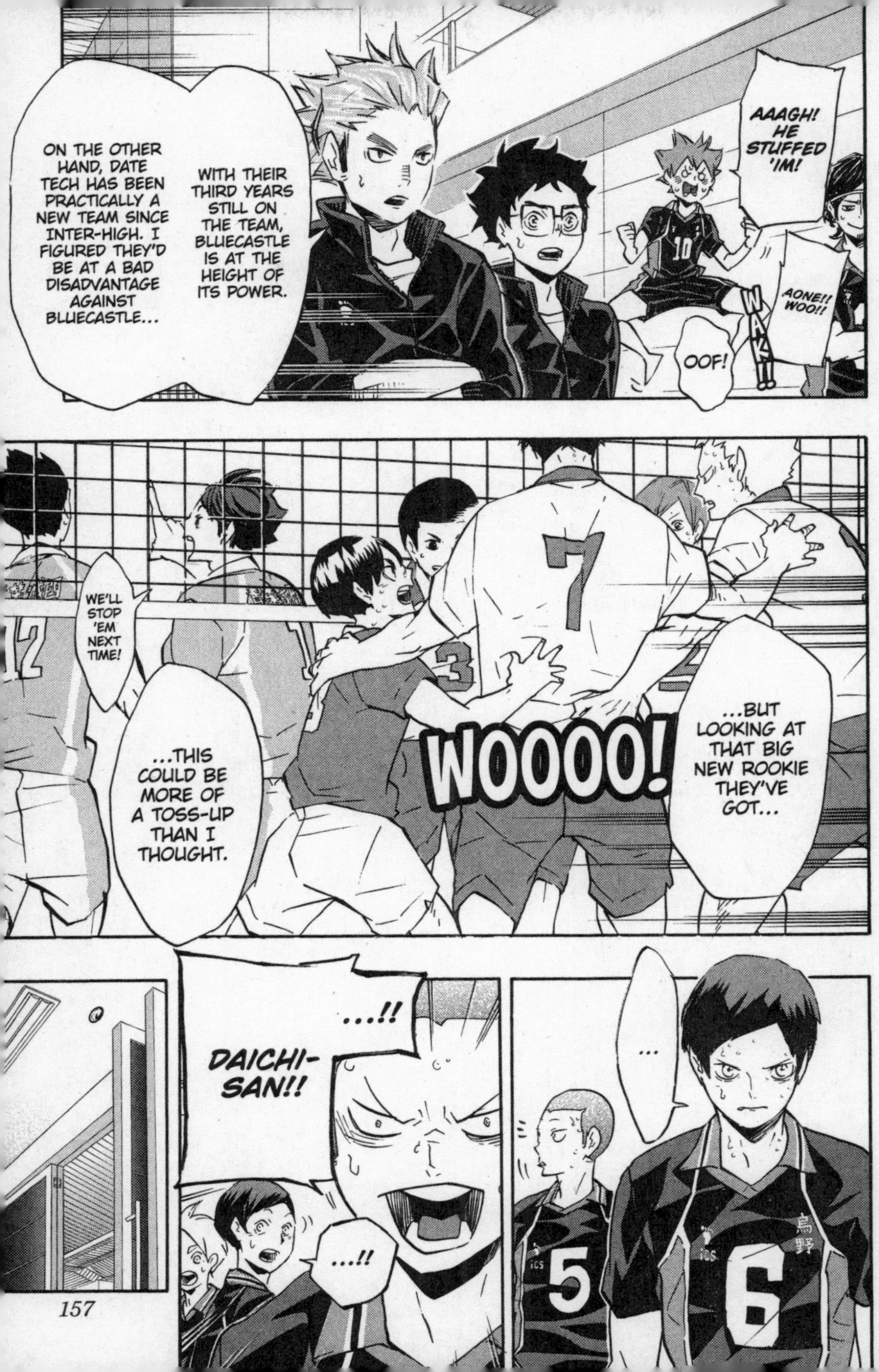
AAAGH! HE STUFFED 'IM!
AONE!! WOO!!
OOF!
WITH THEIR THIRD YEARS STILL ON THE TEAM, BLUECASTLE IS AT THE HEIGHT OF ITS POWER.
ON THE OTHER HAND, DATE TECH HAS BEEN PRACTICALLY A NEW TEAM SINCE INTER-HIGH. I FIGURED THEY'D BE AT A BAD DISADVANTAGE AGAINST BLUECASTLE...
...BUT LOOKING AT THAT BIG NEW ROOKIE THEY'VE GOT...
WOOOO!
WE'LL STOP 'EM NEXT TIME!
...THIS COULD BE MORE OF A TOSS-UP THAN I THOUGHT.
...
...!!
DAICHI-SAN!!
...!!

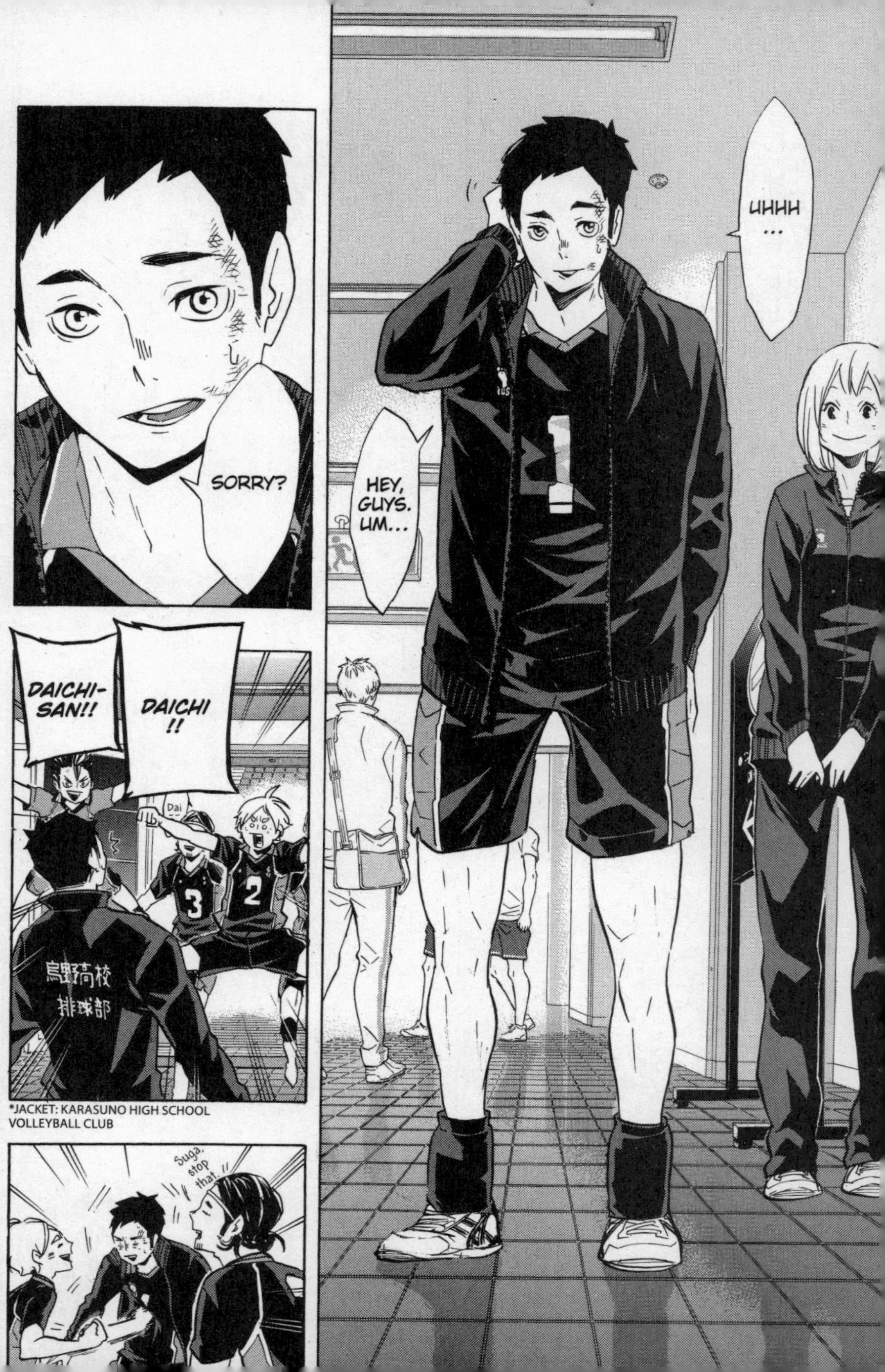
UHHH ...
HEY, GUYS. UM...
SORRY?
DAICHI !!
DAICHI-SAN!!
Dai
烏野高校
排球部
Suga, stop that.
*JACKET: KARASUNO HIGH SCHOOL VOLLEYBALL CLUB

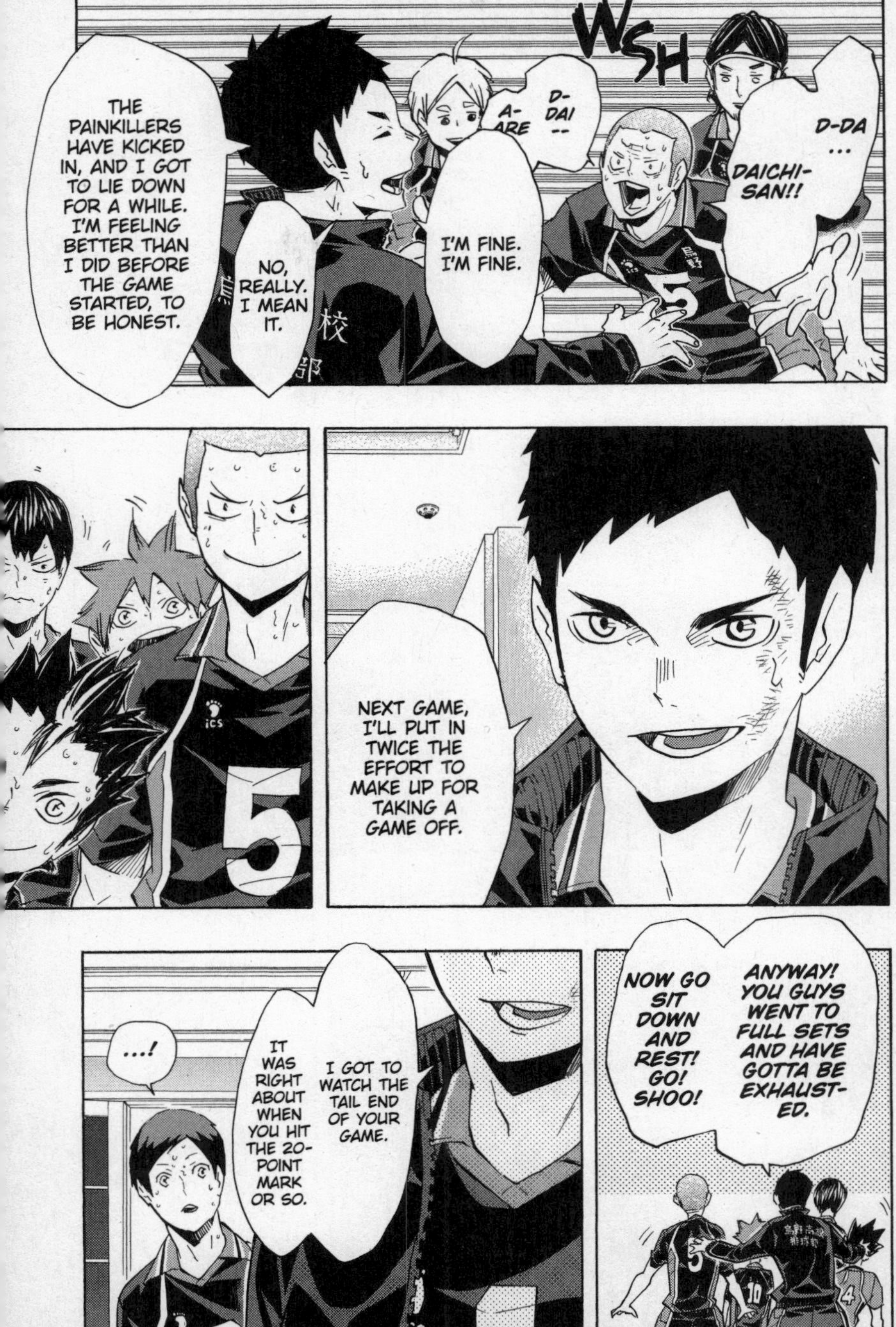
D-DA... DAICHI-SAN!!
WSH
D-DAI --
A-ARE
I'M FINE. I'M FINE.
NO, REALLY. I MEAN IT.
THE PAINKILLERS HAVE KICKED IN, AND I GOT TO LIE DOWN FOR A WHILE. I'M FEELING BETTER THAN I DID BEFORE THE GAME STARTED, TO BE HONEST.
NEXT GAME, I'LL PUT IN TWICE THE EFFORT TO MAKE UP FOR TAKING A GAME OFF.
ANYWAY! YOU GUYS WENT TO FULL SETS AND HAVE GOTTA BE EXHAUST-ED.
NOW GO SIT DOWN AND REST! GO! SHOO!
I GOT TO WATCH THE TAIL END OF YOUR GAME.
IT WAS RIGHT ABOUT WHEN YOU HIT THE 20-POINT MARK OR SO.
...!

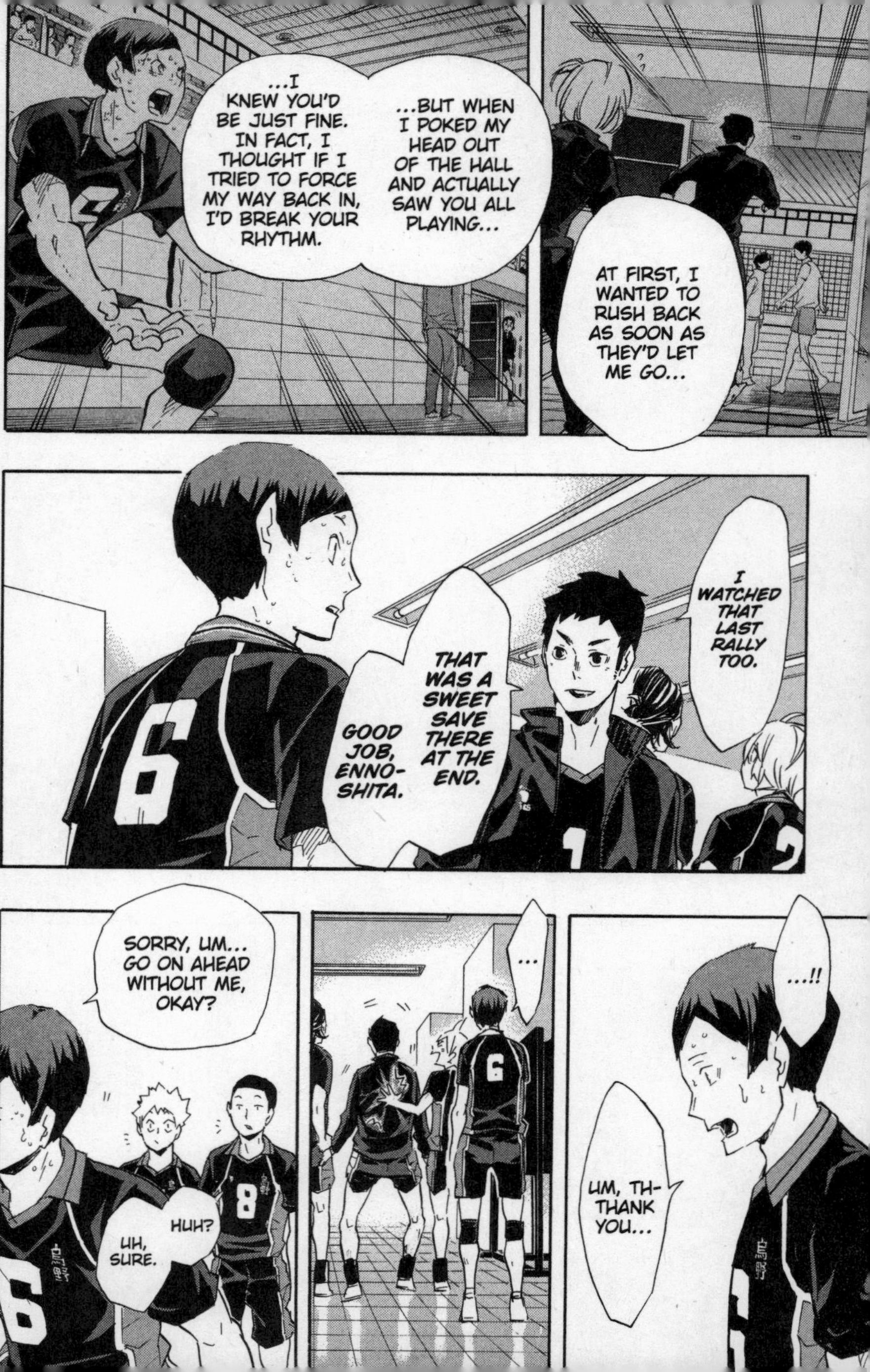
AT FIRST, I WANTED TO RUSH BACK AS SOON AS THEY'D LET ME GO...
...BUT WHEN I POKED MY HEAD OUT OF THE HALL AND ACTUALLY SAW YOU ALL PLAYING...
...I KNEW YOU'D BE JUST FINE. IN FACT, I THOUGHT IF I TRIED TO FORCE MY WAY BACK IN, I'D BREAK YOUR RHYTHM.
I WATCHED THAT LAST RALLY TOO.
THAT WAS A SWEET SAVE THERE AT THE END.
GOOD JOB, ENNO-SHITA.
...!!
UM, TH-THANK YOU...
...
SORRY, UM... GO ON AHEAD WITHOUT ME, OKAY?
HUH?
UH, SURE.

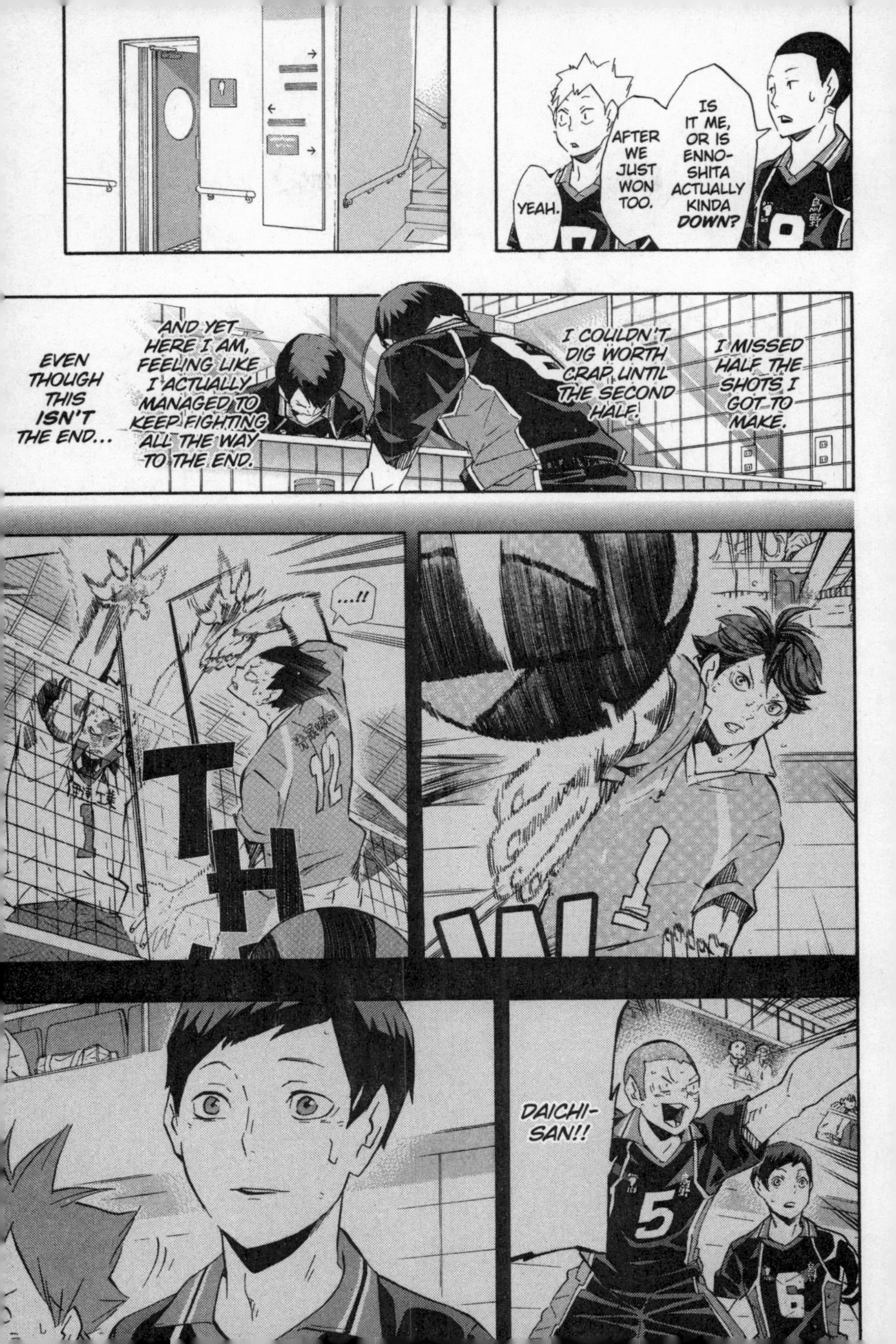
IS IT ME, OR IS ENNOSHITA ACTUALLY KINDA *DOWN?*
AFTER WE JUST WON TOO.
YEAH.
I MISSED HALF THE SHOTS I GOT TO MAKE.
I COULDN'T DIG WORTH CRAP UNTIL THE SECOND HALF.
AND YET HERE I AM, FEELING LIKE I ACTUALLY MANAGED TO KEEP FIGHTING ALL THE WAY TO THE END.
EVEN THOUGH THIS *ISN'T* THE END...
...!!
DAICHI-SAN!!

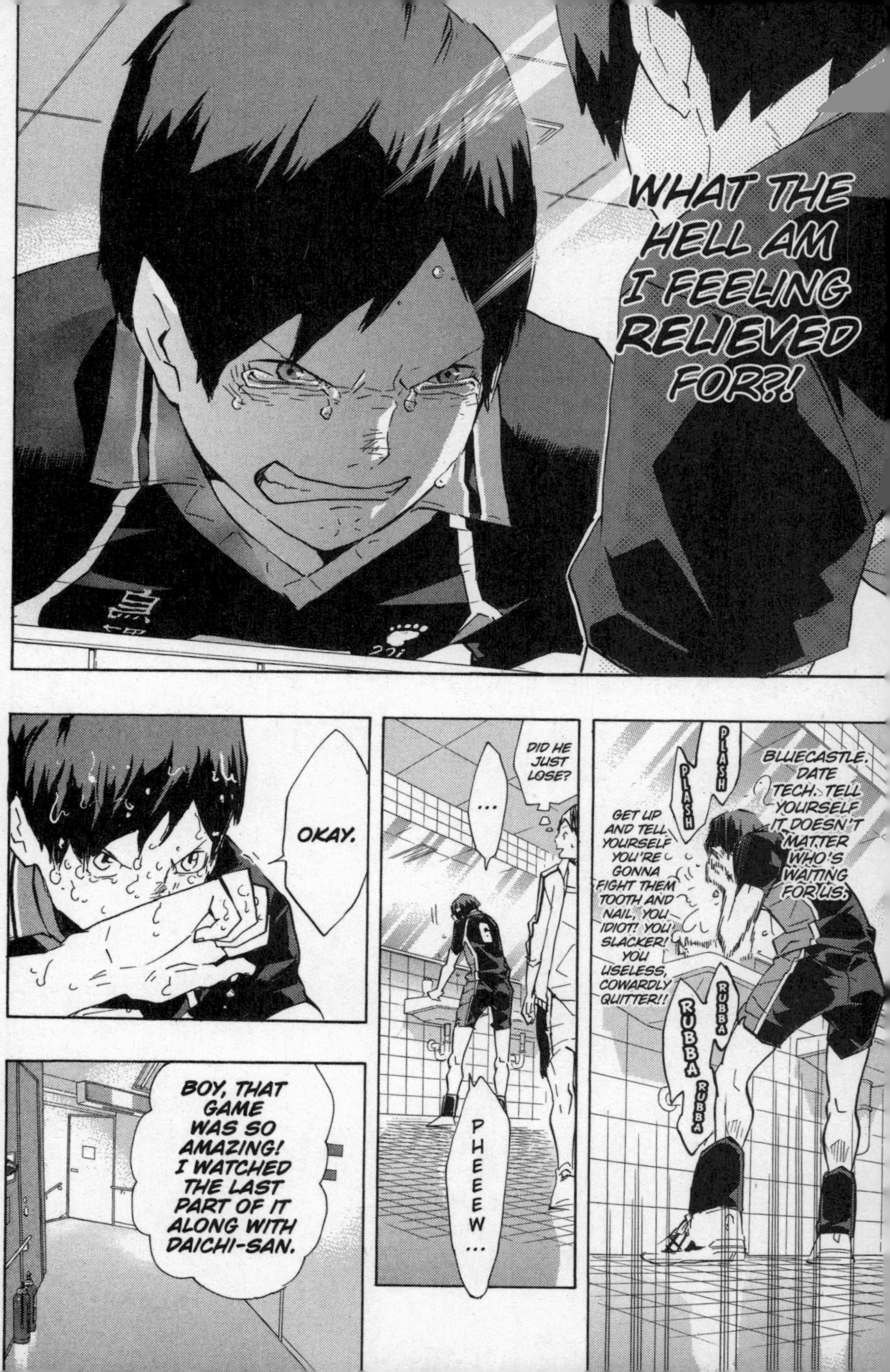
WHAT THE HELL AM I FEELING RELIEVED FOR?!
BLUECASTLE. DATE TECH. TELL YOURSELF IT DOESN'T MATTER WHO'S WAITING FOR US.
PLASH
PLASH
GET UP AND TELL YOURSELF YOU'RE GONNA FIGHT THEM TOOTH AND NAIL, YOU IDIOT! YOU SLACKER! YOU USELESS, COWARDLY QUITTER!!
RUBBA
RUBBA
RUBBA
RUBBA
DID HE JUST LOSE?
...
PHEEEW...
OKAY.
BOY, THAT GAME WAS SO AMAZING! I WATCHED THE LAST PART OF IT ALONG WITH DAICHI-SAN.

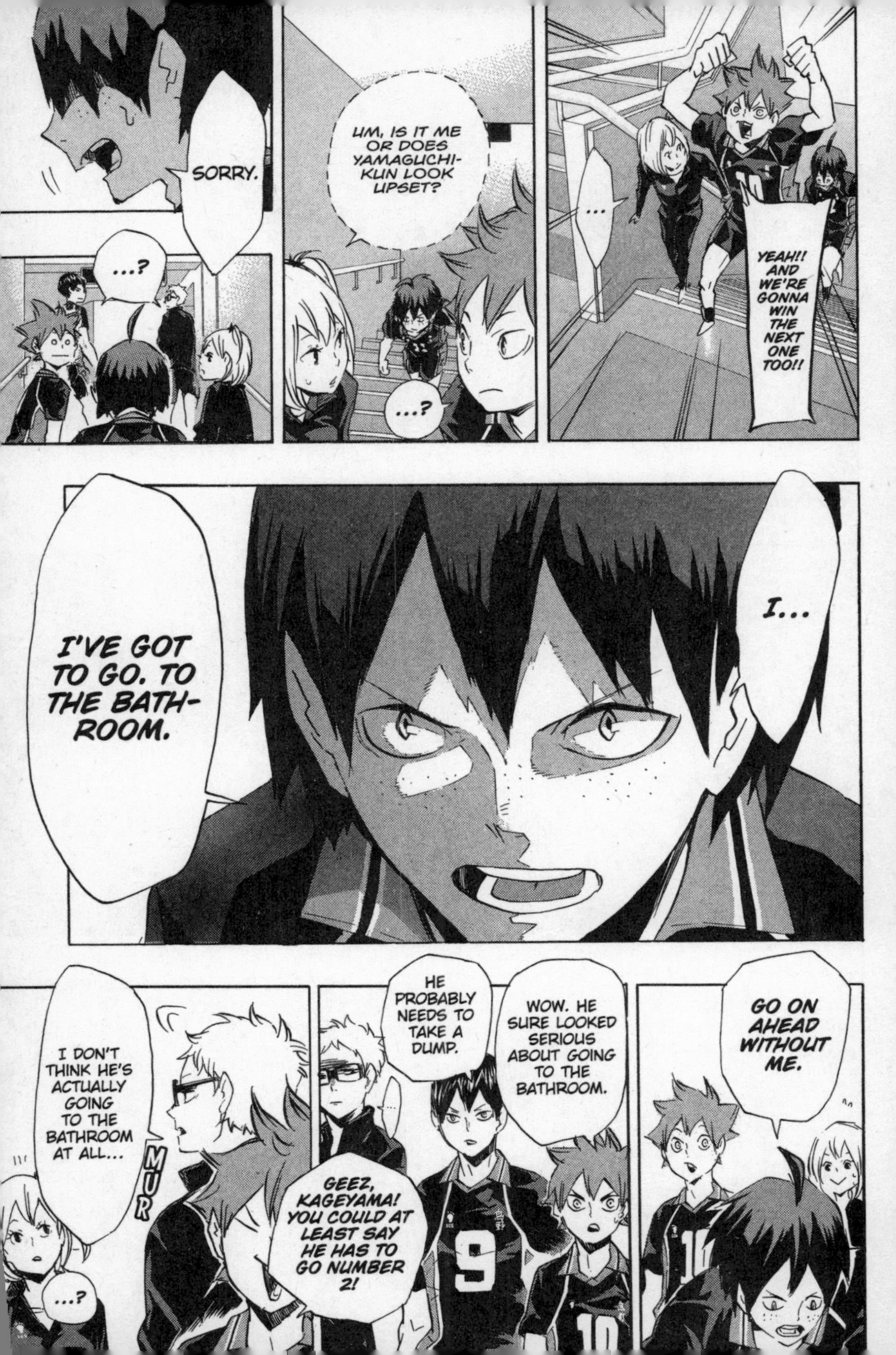
YEAH!! AND WE'RE GONNA WIN THE NEXT ONE TOO!!
...
UM, IS IT ME OR DOES YAMAGUCHI-KUN LOOK UPSET?
...?
SORRY.
...?
I...
I'VE GOT TO GO. TO THE BATH-ROOM.
GO ON AHEAD WITHOUT ME.
WOW. HE SURE LOOKED SERIOUS ABOUT GOING TO THE BATHROOM.
HE PROBABLY NEEDS TO TAKE A DUMP.
...
GEEZ, KAGEYAMA! YOU COULD AT LEAST SAY HE HAS TO GO NUMBER 2!
I DON'T THINK HE'S ACTUALLY GOING TO THE BATHROOM AT ALL...
MUR
...?

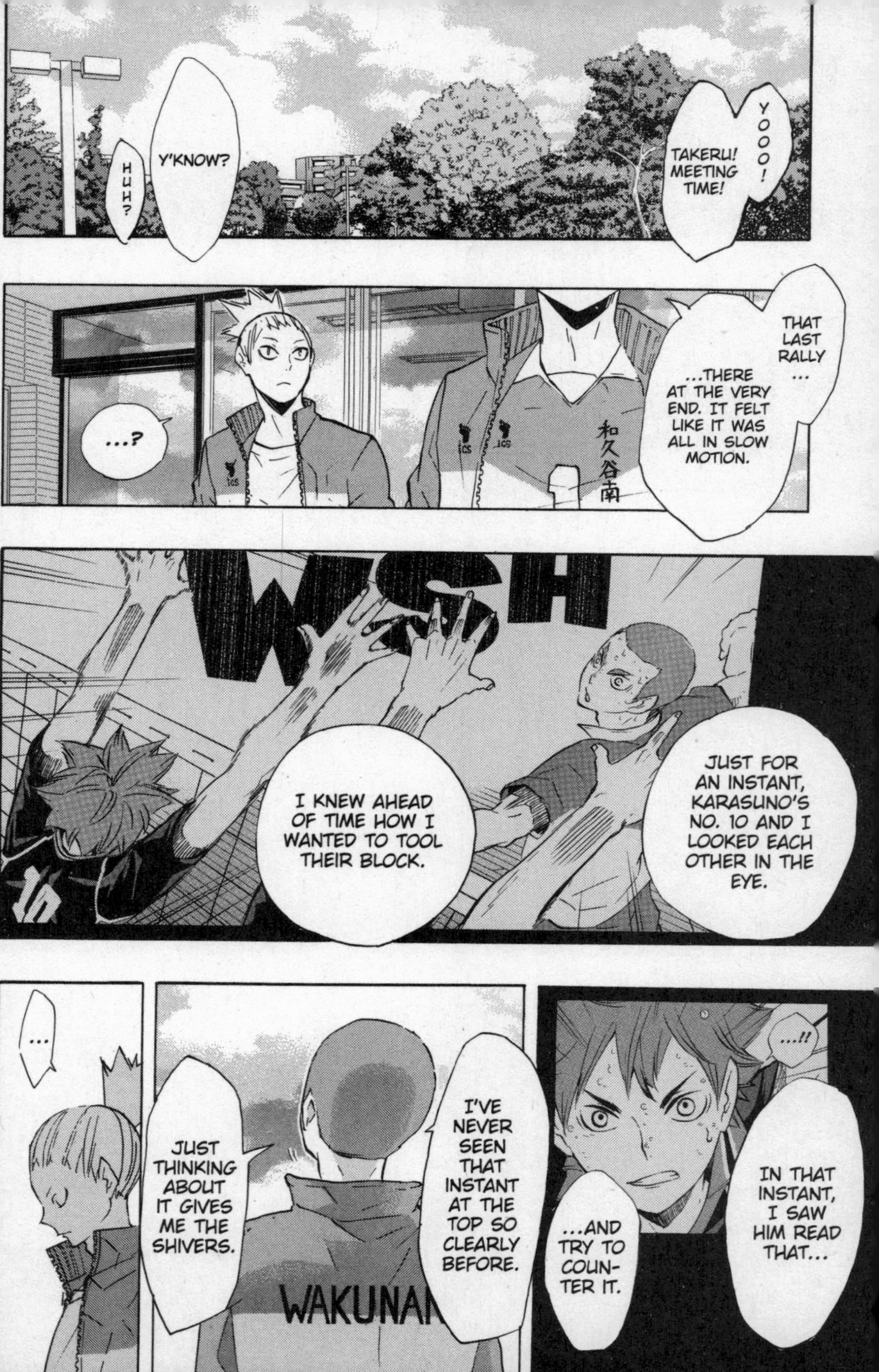
YOOO!
TAKERU! MEETING TIME!
Y'KNOW?
HUH?
THAT LAST RALLY...
...THERE AT THE VERY END. IT FELT LIKE IT WAS ALL IN SLOW MOTION.
和久谷南
...?
WSH
JUST FOR AN INSTANT, KARASUNO'S NO. 10 AND I LOOKED EACH OTHER IN THE EYE.
I KNEW AHEAD OF TIME HOW I WANTED TO TOOL THEIR BLOCK.
...!!
IN THAT INSTANT, I SAW HIM READ THAT...
...AND TRY TO COUNTER IT.
I'VE NEVER SEEN THAT INSTANT AT THE TOP SO CLEARLY BEFORE.
JUST THINKING ABOUT IT GIVES ME THE SHIVERS.
WAKUNAN
...

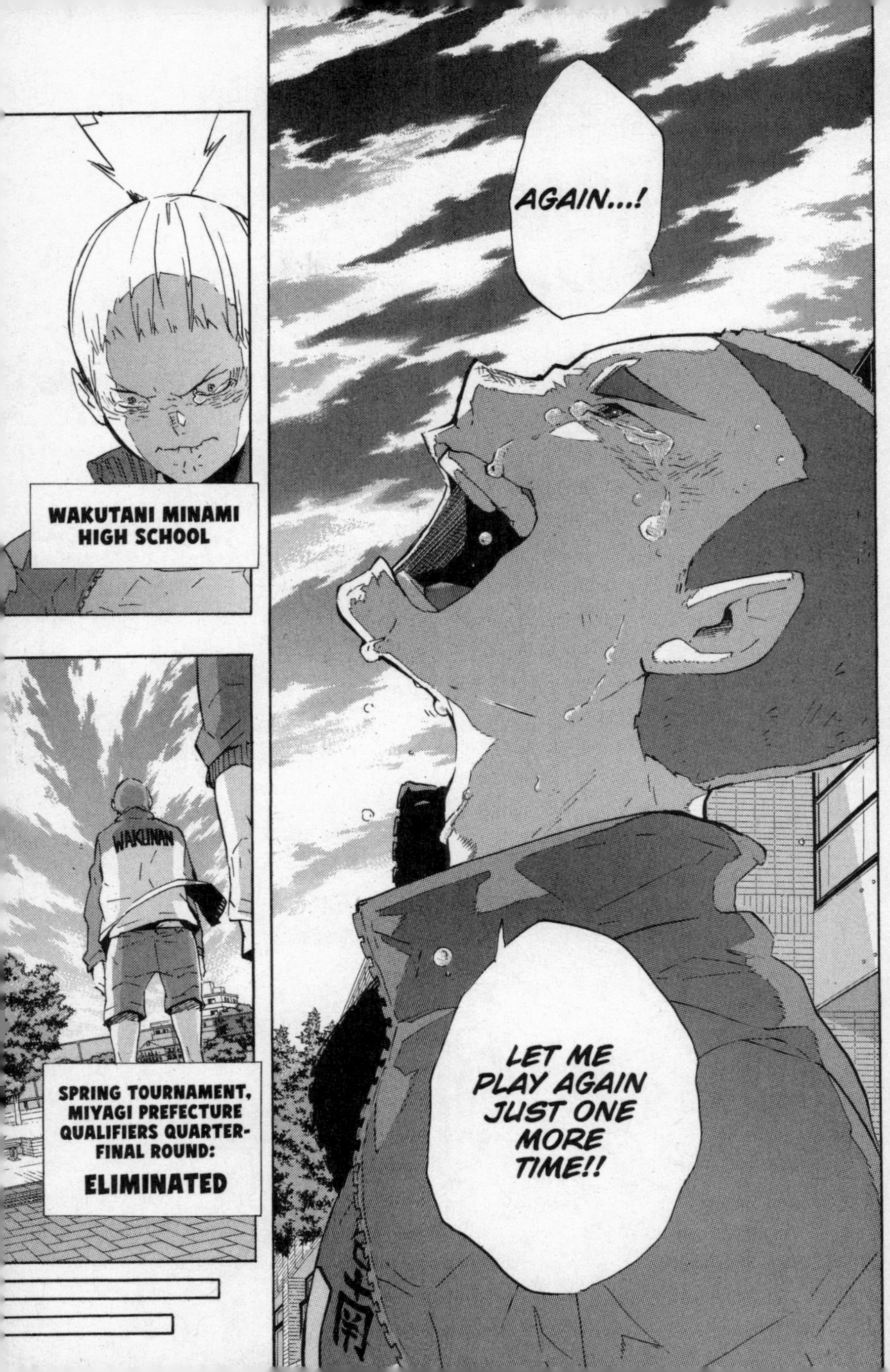
AGAIN...!
LET ME PLAY AGAIN JUST ONE MORE TIME!!
WAKUTANI MINAMI HIGH SCHOOL
WAKUNAN
SPRING TOURNAMENT, MIYAGI PREFECTURE QUALIFIERS QUARTER-FINAL ROUND:
ELIMINATED

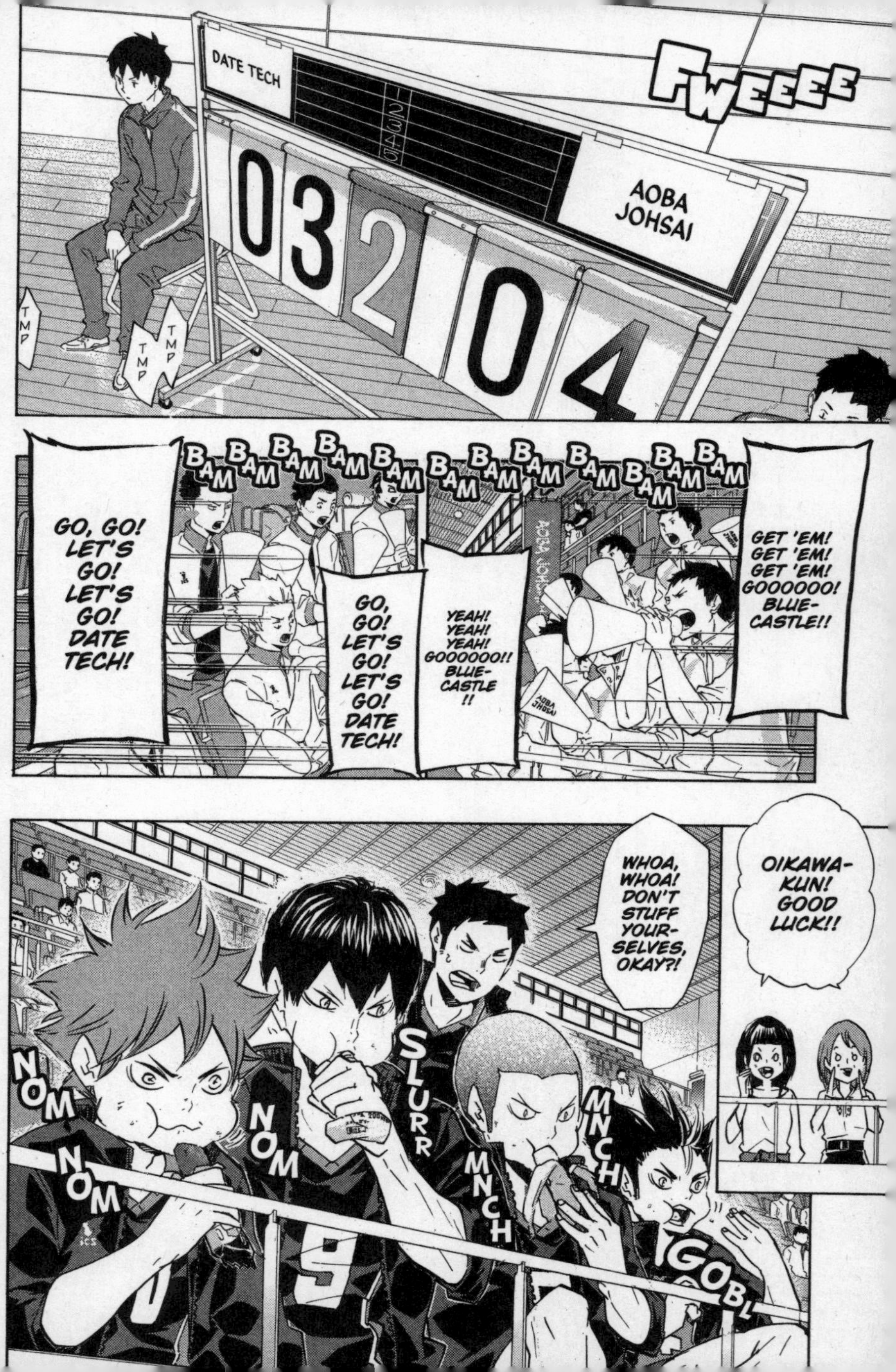
FWEEEE
DATE TECH
AOBA JOHSAI
03
2
04
TMP
TMP TMP
TMP
GET 'EM! GET 'EM! GET 'EM! GOOOOOO! BLUE-CASTLE!!
YEAH! YEAH! YEAH! GOOOOOO!! BLUE-CASTLE!!
GO, GO! LET'S GO! LET'S GO! DATE TECH!
GO, GO! LET'S GO! LET'S GO! DATE TECH!
BAM BAM BAM BAM BAM BAM BAM BAM BAM BAM BAM BAM
AOBA JOHSAI
OIKAWA-KUN! GOOD LUCK!!
WHOA, WHOA! DON'T STUFF YOURSELVES, OKAY?!
GOBL
MNCH MNCH
SLURR
NOM NOM
NOM NOM

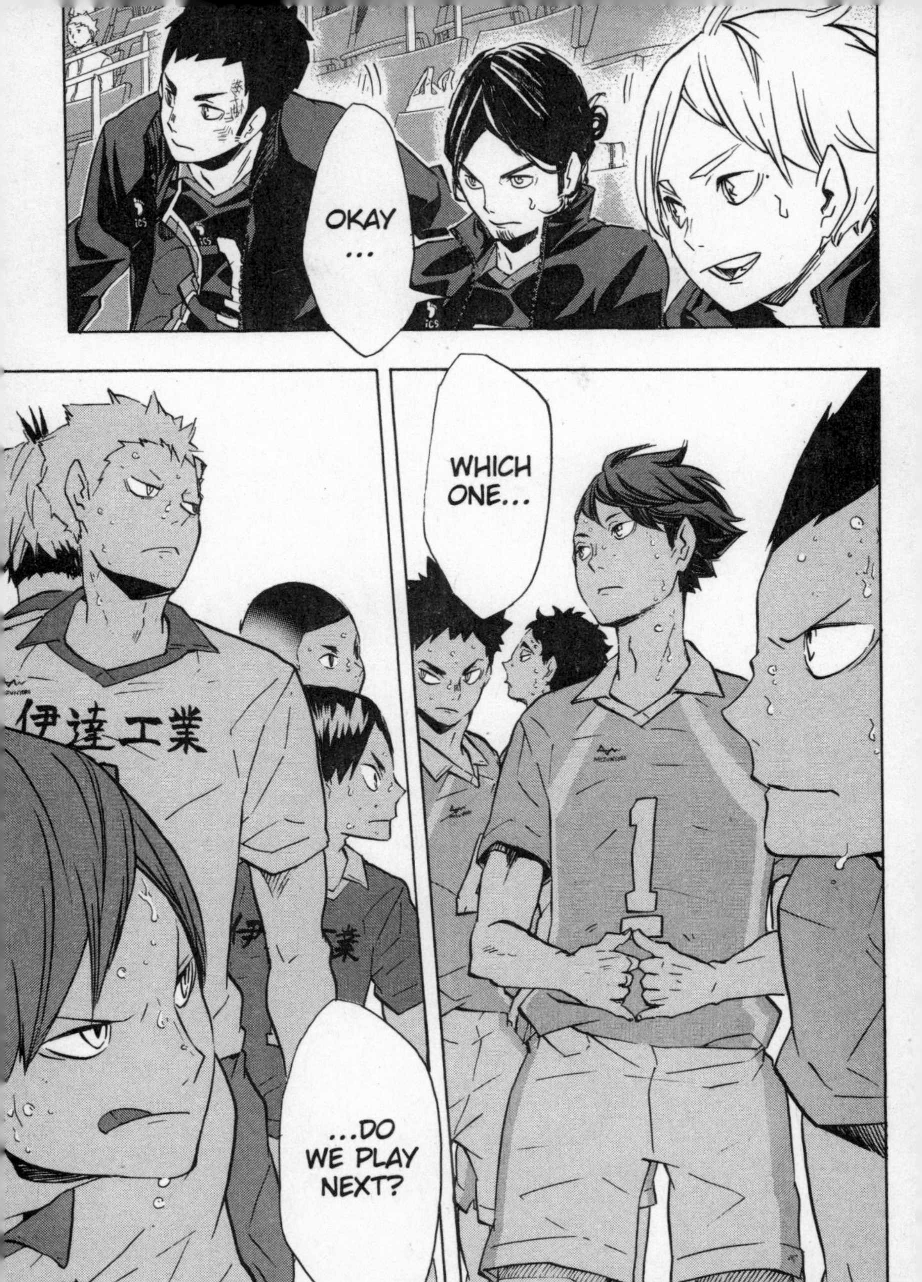
OKAY ...
WHICH ONE...
伊達工業
...DO WE PLAY NEXT?

HAIKYU!! VOL 14: QUITTER'S BATTLE (END)

NISEKYU→!!

NEXT IS A SHORT MANGA THAT *NISEKOI*
AUTHOR KOMI SENSEI AND I GOT TO
CREATE TOGETHER—"NISEKYU!!" I HOPE
YOU LIKE IT!

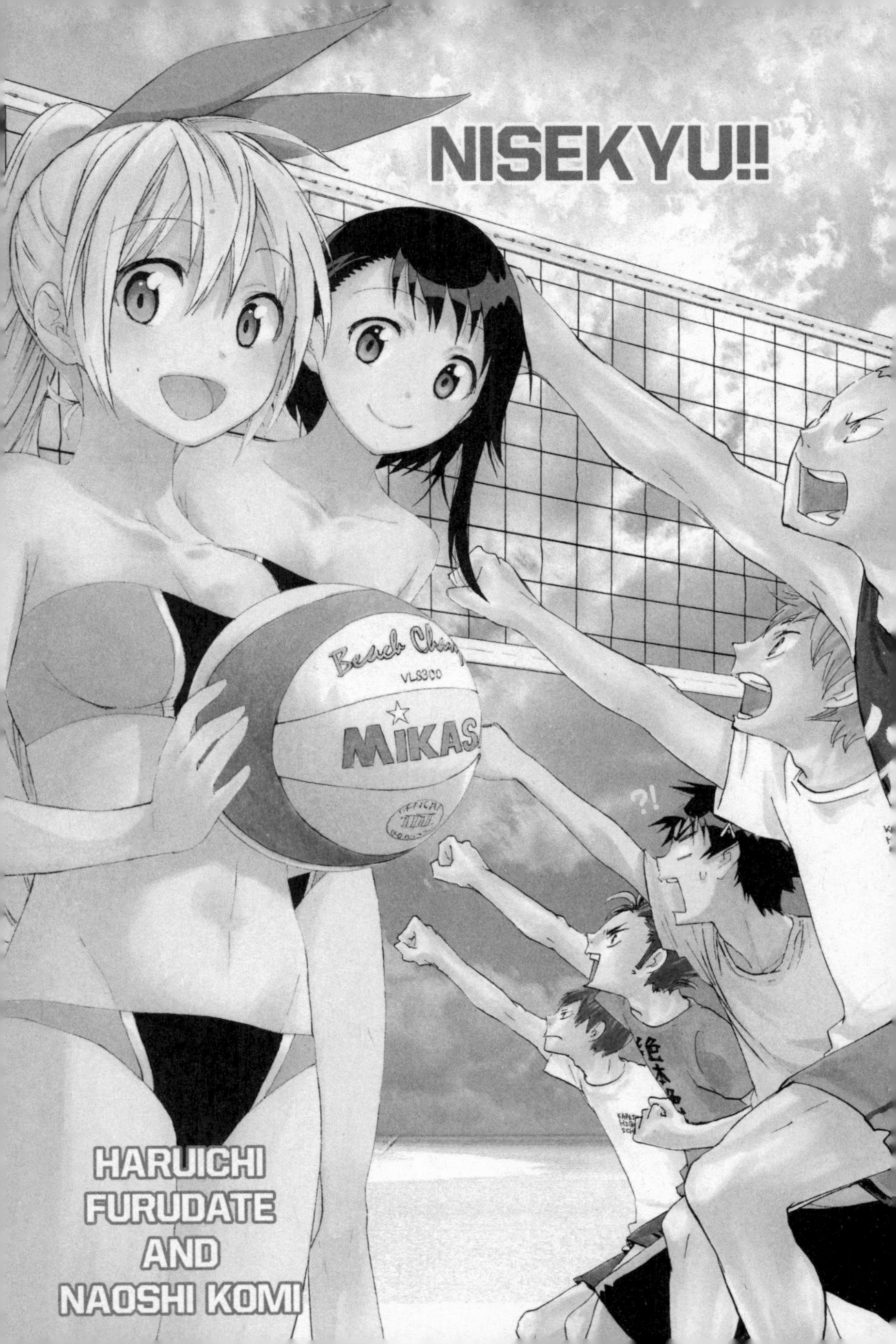
NISEKYU!!
VLS300
?!
HARUICHI
FURUDATE
AND
NAOSHI KOMI

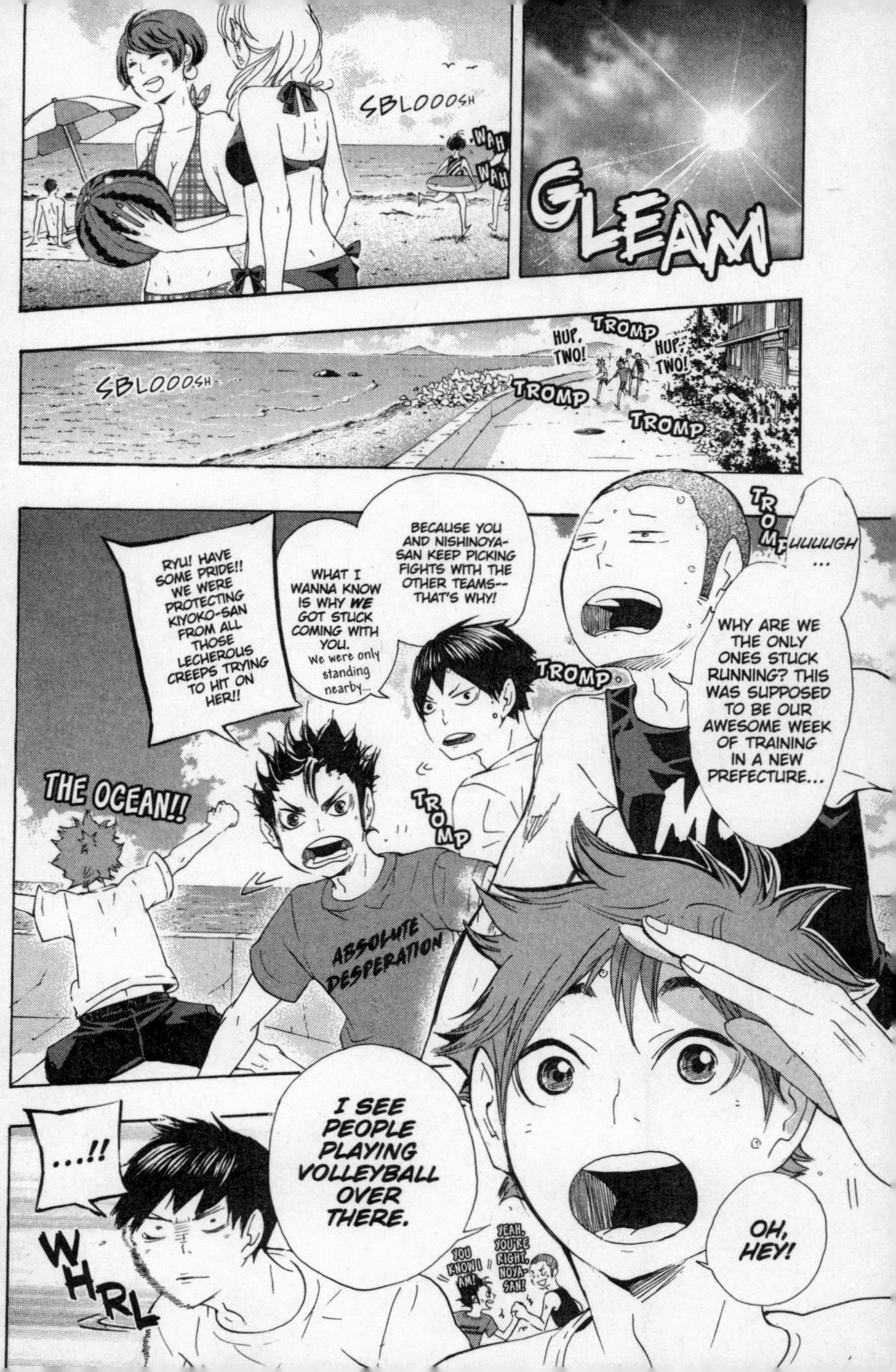
GLEAM
SBLOOOSH
WAH
WAH
TROMP
HUP, TWO!
HUP, TWO!
SBLOOOSH
TROMP
TROMP
TROMP
FUUUUUGH...
WHY ARE WE THE ONLY ONES STUCK RUNNING? THIS WAS SUPPOSED TO BE OUR AWESOME WEEK OF TRAINING IN A NEW PREFECTURE...
TROMP
BECAUSE YOU AND NISHINOYA-SAN KEEP PICKING FIGHTS WITH THE OTHER TEAMS--THAT'S WHY!
WHAT I WANNA KNOW IS WHY WE GOT STUCK COMING WITH YOU.
We were only standing nearby...
RYU! HAVE SOME PRIDE!! WE WERE PROTECTING KIYOKO-SAN FROM ALL THOSE LECHEROUS CREEPS TRYING TO HIT ON HER!!
TROMP
THE OCEAN!!
ABSOLUTE DESPERATION
OH, HEY!
I SEE PEOPLE PLAYING VOLLEYBALL OVER THERE.
YEAH, YOU'RE RIGHT, NOYA-SAN!
YOU KNOW I AM!
...!!
WHRL

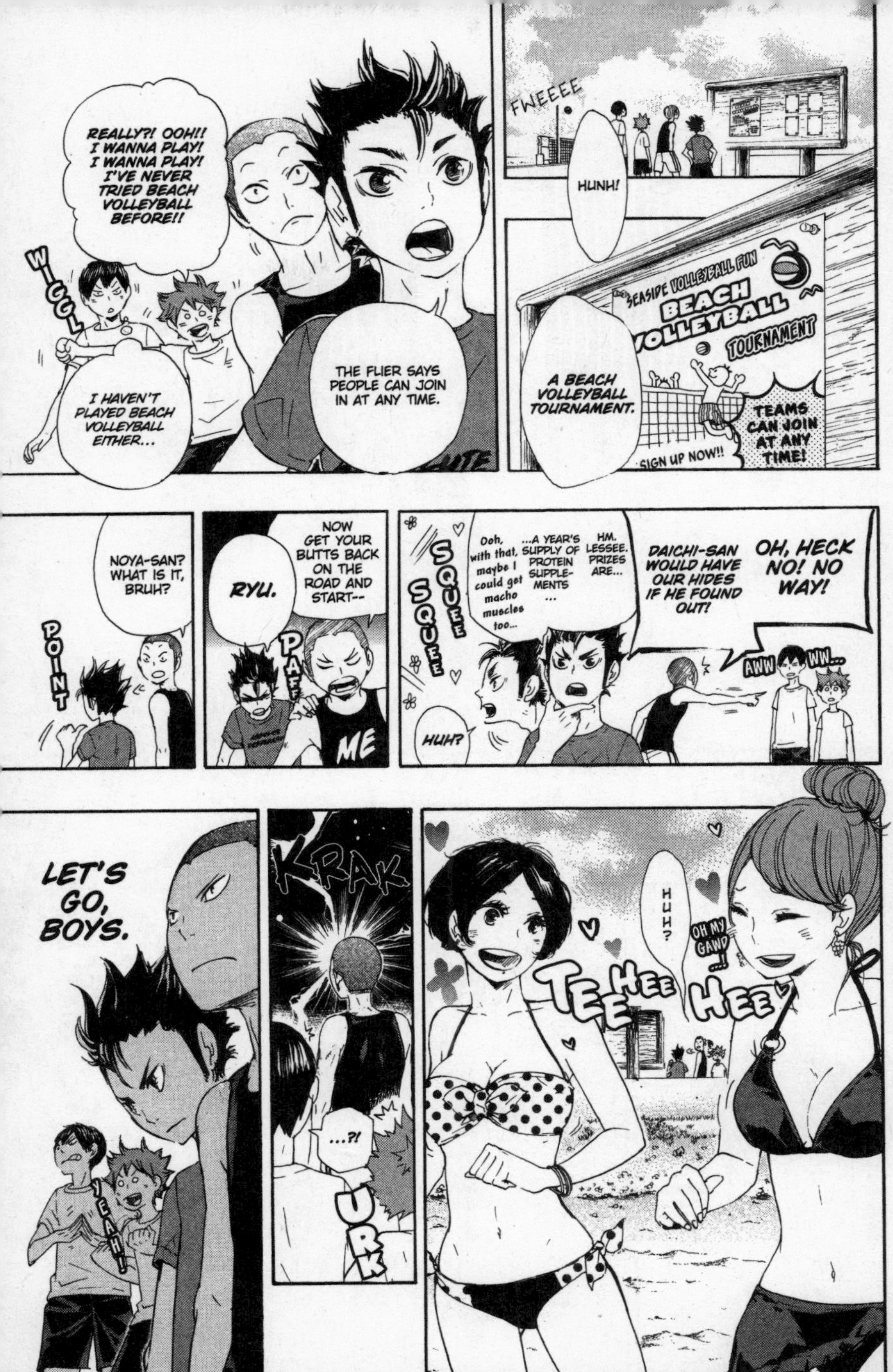
FWEEEE
HUNH!
SEASIDE VOLLEYBALL FUN
BEACH VOLLEYBALL TOURNAMENT
TEAMS CAN JOIN AT ANY TIME!
SIGN UP NOW!!
A BEACH VOLLEYBALL TOURNAMENT.
THE FLIER SAYS PEOPLE CAN JOIN IN AT ANY TIME.
REALLY?! OOH!! I WANNA PLAY! I WANNA PLAY! I'VE NEVER TRIED BEACH VOLLEYBALL BEFORE!!
WIGGL
I HAVEN'T PLAYED BEACH VOLLEYBALL EITHER...
OH, HECK NO! NO WAY!
DAICHI-SAN WOULD HAVE OUR HIDES IF HE FOUND OUT!
AWW WW...
HM. LESSEE. PRIZES ARE...
...A YEAR'S SUPPLY OF PROTEIN SUPPLE-MENTS ...
Ooh, with that, maybe I could get macho muscles too...
SQUEE
SQUEE
HUH?
NOW GET YOUR BUTTS BACK ON THE ROAD AND START--
RYU.
PAFF
NOYA-SAN? WHAT IS IT, BRUH?
POINT
HUH?
OH MY GAWD...!
TEE HEE HEE HEE
KRAK
...?!
URK
LET'S GO, BOYS.
YEAH!

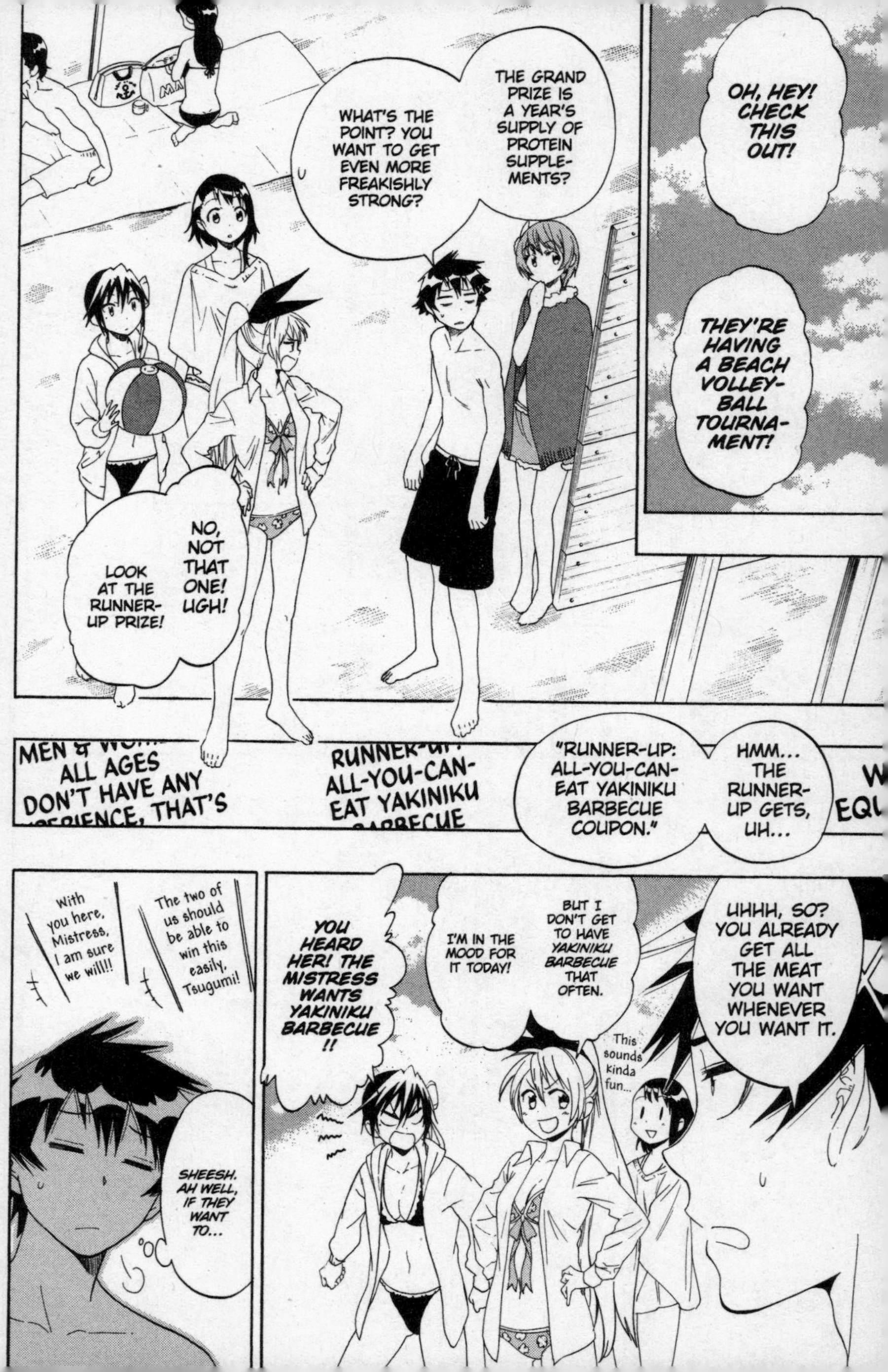
OH, HEY! CHECK THIS OUT!
THEY'RE HAVING A BEACH VOLLEY-BALL TOURNA-MENT!
THE GRAND PRIZE IS A YEAR'S SUPPLY OF PROTEIN SUPPLE-MENTS?
WHAT'S THE POINT? YOU WANT TO GET EVEN MORE FREAKISHLY STRONG?
NO, NOT THAT ONE! UGH!
LOOK AT THE RUNNER-UP PRIZE!
HMM... THE RUNNER-UP GETS, UH...
"RUNNER-UP: ALL-YOU-CAN-EAT YAKINIKU BARBECUE COUPON."
ALL-YOU-CAN-EAT YAKINIKU
ALL AGES DON'T HAVE ANY
THAT'S
UHHH, SO? YOU ALREADY GET ALL THE MEAT YOU WANT WHENEVER YOU WANT IT.
BUT I DON'T GET TO HAVE YAKINIKU BARBECUE THAT OFTEN.
I'M IN THE MOOD FOR IT TODAY!
YOU HEARD HER! THE MISTRESS WANTS YAKINIKU BARBECUE!!
This sounds kinda fun...
The two of us should be able to win this easily, Tsugumi!
With you here, Mistress, I am sure we will!!
SHEESH. AH WELL, IF THEY WANT TO...

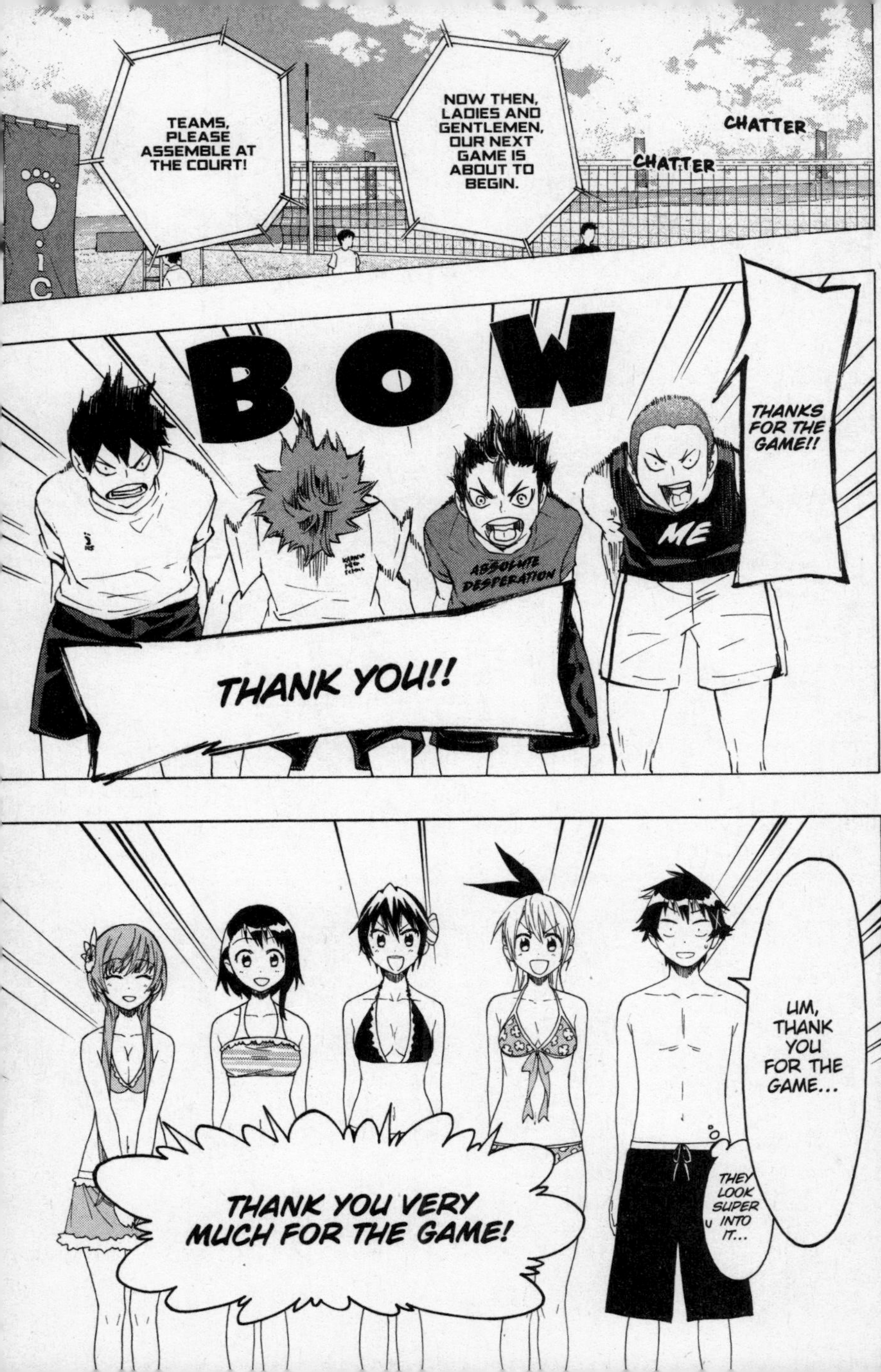
CHATTER
CHATTER
NOW THEN, LADIES AND GENTLEMEN, OUR NEXT GAME IS ABOUT TO BEGIN.
TEAMS, PLEASE ASSEMBLE AT THE COURT!
BOW
THANKS FOR THE GAME!!
ME
ABSOLUTE DESPERATION
THANK YOU!!
UM, THANK YOU FOR THE GAME...
THEY LOOK SUPER INTO IT...
THANK YOU VERY MUCH FOR THE GAME!

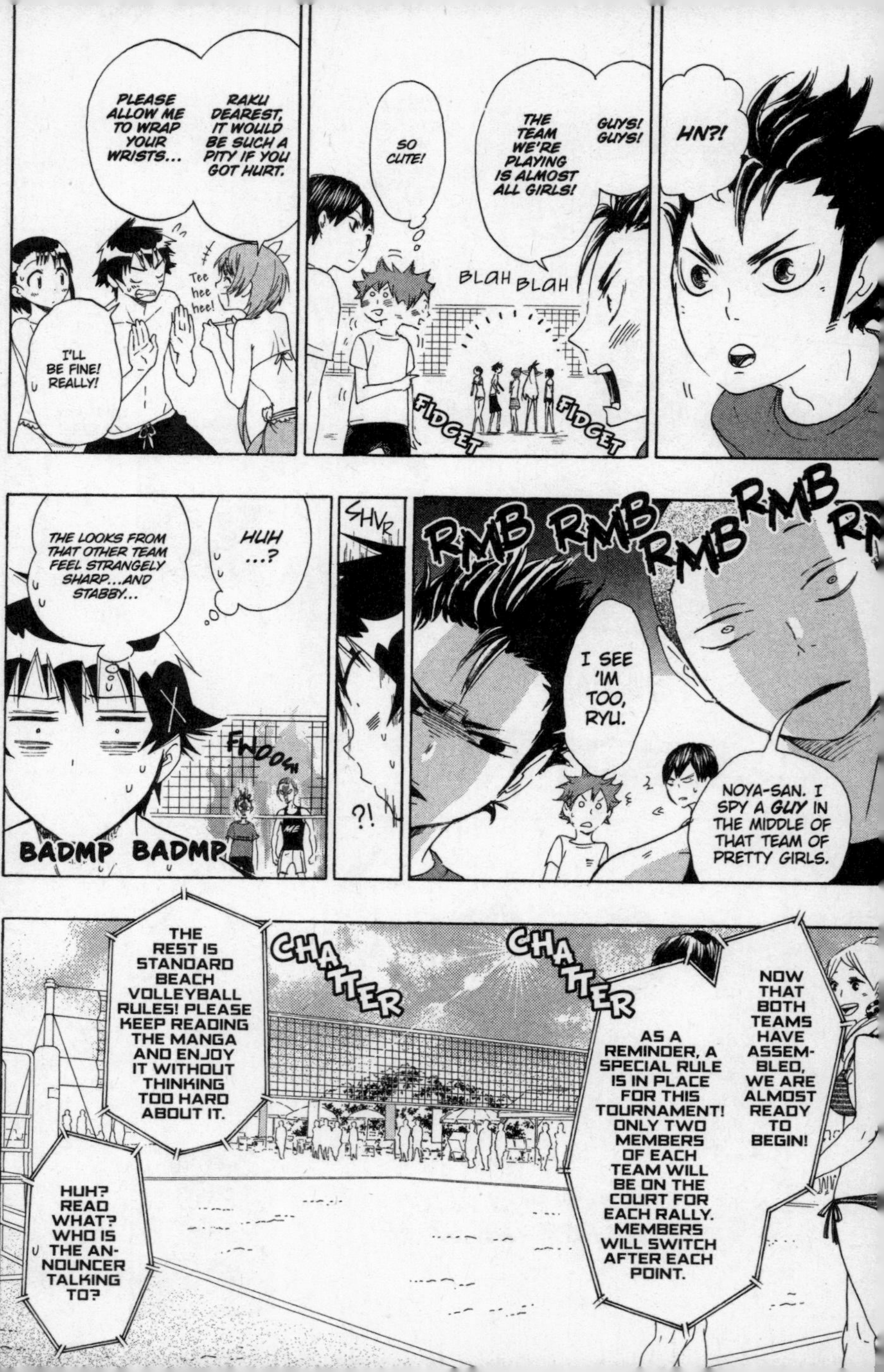
HN?!
GUYS! GUYS!
THE TEAM WE'RE PLAYING IS ALMOST ALL GIRLS!
SO CUTE!
BLAH BLAH
FIDGET FIDGET
RAKU DEAREST, IT WOULD BE SUCH A PITY IF YOU GOT HURT.
PLEASE ALLOW ME TO WRAP YOUR WRISTS...
Tee hee hee!
I'LL BE FINE! REALLY!
RMB RMB RMB RMB
NOYA-SAN. I SPY A GUY IN THE MIDDLE OF THAT TEAM OF PRETTY GIRLS.
I SEE 'IM TOO, RYU.
SHVR
?!
HUH ...?
THE LOOKS FROM THAT OTHER TEAM FEEL STRANGELY SHARP...AND STABBY...
FWOOSH
BADMP BADMP
NOW THAT BOTH TEAMS HAVE ASSEM-BLED, WE ARE ALMOST READY TO BEGIN!
AS A REMINDER, A SPECIAL RULE IS IN PLACE FOR THIS TOURNAMENT! ONLY TWO MEMBERS OF EACH TEAM WILL BE ON THE COURT FOR EACH RALLY. MEMBERS WILL SWITCH AFTER EACH POINT.
CHATTER CHATTER
THE REST IS STANDARD BEACH VOLLEYBALL RULES! PLEASE KEEP READING THE MANGA AND ENJOY IT WITHOUT THINKING TOO HARD ABOUT IT.
HUH? READ WHAT? WHO IS THE AN-NOUNCER TALKING TO?

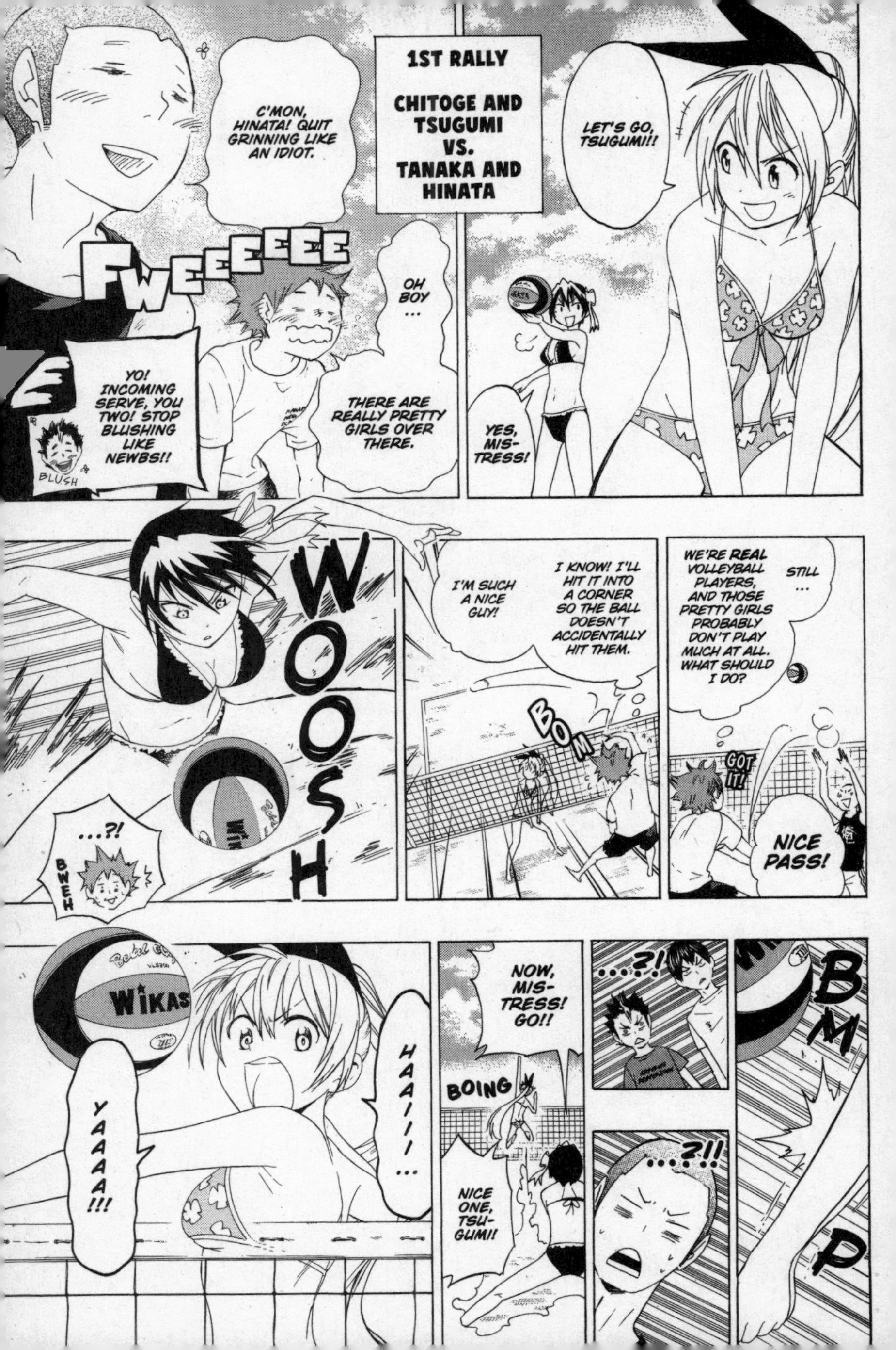
LET'S GO, TSUGUMI!!
YES, MIS-TRESS!
1ST RALLY
CHITOGE AND TSUGUMI VS. TANAKA AND HINATA
OH BOY ...
THERE ARE REALLY PRETTY GIRLS OVER THERE.
C'MON, HINATA! QUIT GRINNING LIKE AN IDIOT.
FWEEEEEE
YO! INCOMING SERVE, YOU TWO! STOP BLUSHING LIKE NEWBS!!
BLUSH
WE'RE REAL VOLLEYBALL PLAYERS, AND THOSE PRETTY GIRLS PROBABLY DON'T PLAY MUCH AT ALL. WHAT SHOULD I DO?
STILL ...
GOT IT!
NICE PASS!
I KNOW! I'LL HIT IT INTO A CORNER SO THE BALL DOESN'T ACCIDENTALLY HIT THEM.
I'M SUCH A NICE GUY!
BOM
WOOOSH
...?!
BWEH
BMP
...?!
...?!!
NOW, MIS-TRESS! GO!!
BOING
NICE ONE, TSU-GUMI!
HAAI!!...
YAAAAA!!!

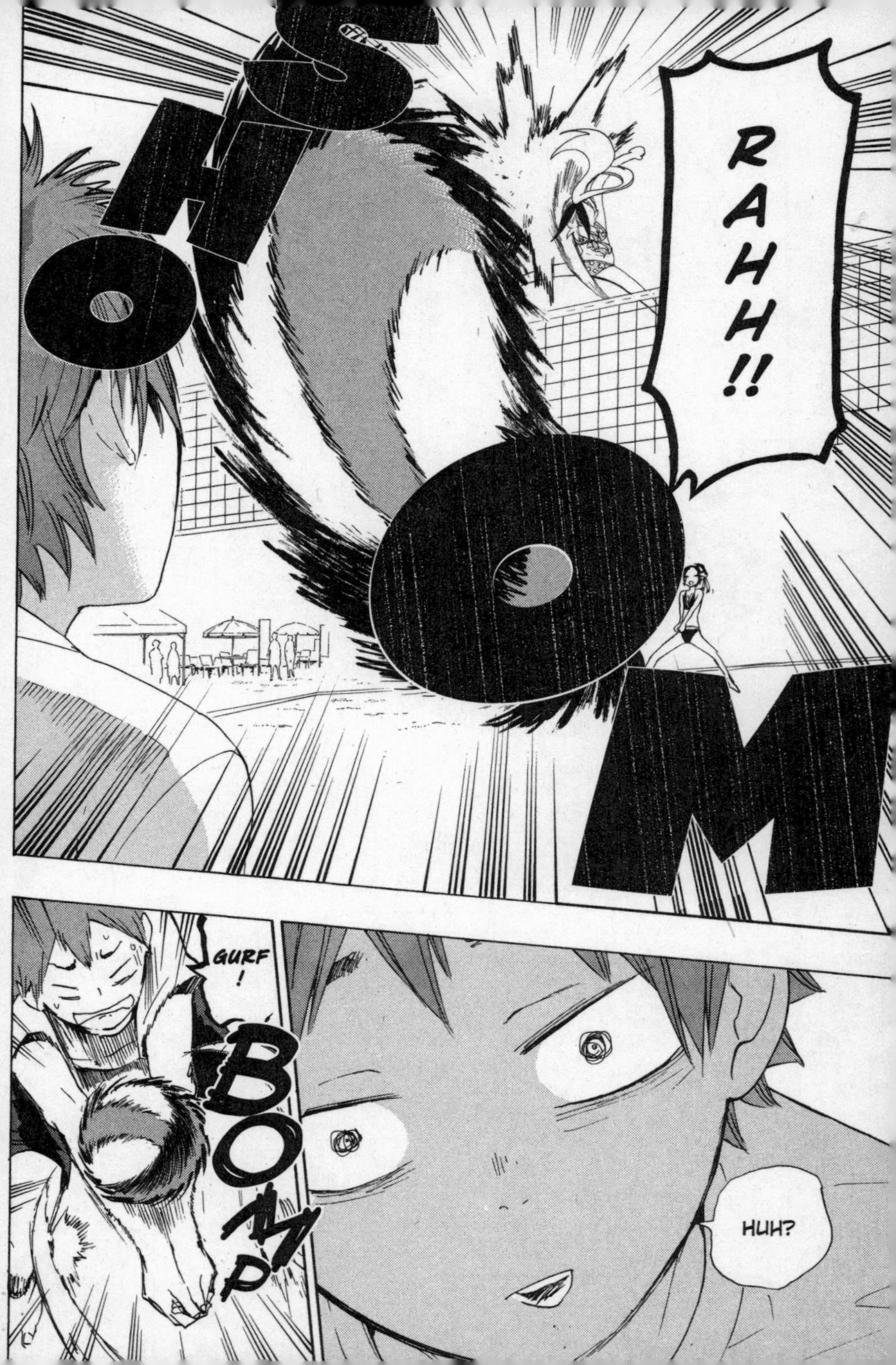
RAHHH!!
SHOOOM
HUH?
GURF!
BOMP

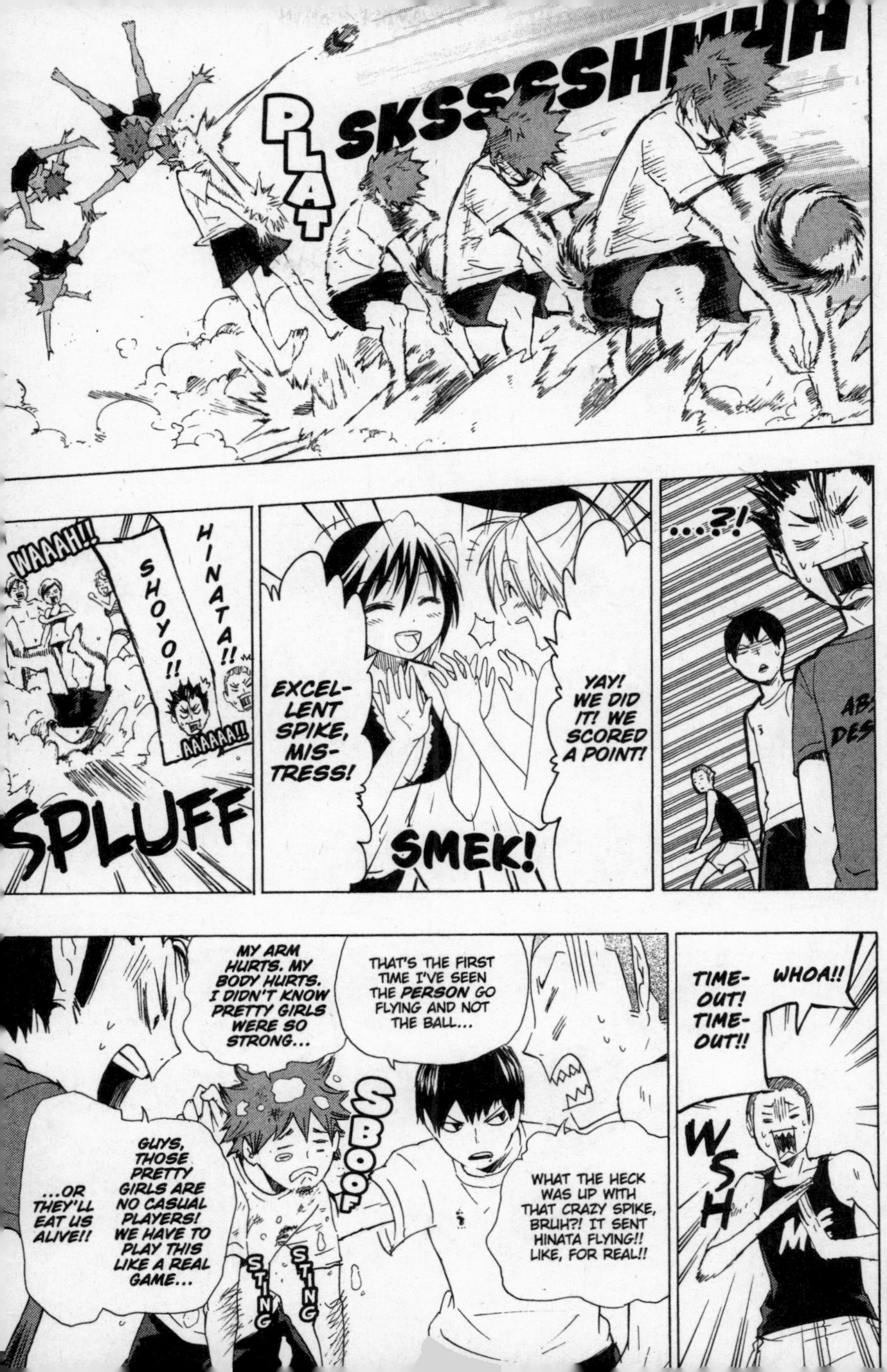
SKSSSSHHHUH
PLAT
...?!
YAY! WE DID IT! WE SCORED A POINT!
EXCEL-LENT SPIKE, MIS-TRESS!
SMEK!
HINATA!!
SHOYO!!
WAAAH!!
AAAAAA!!
SPLUFF
WHOA!!
TIME-OUT! TIME-OUT!!
WSH
THAT'S THE FIRST TIME I'VE SEEN THE *PERSON* GO FLYING AND NOT THE BALL...
MY ARM HURTS. MY BODY HURTS. I DIDN'T KNOW PRETTY GIRLS WERE SO STRONG...
WHAT THE HECK WAS UP WITH THAT CRAZY SPIKE, BRUH?! IT SENT HINATA FLYING!! LIKE, FOR REAL!!
SBOOF
GUYS, THOSE PRETTY GIRLS ARE NO CASUAL PLAYERS! WE HAVE TO PLAY THIS LIKE A REAL GAME...
...OR THEY'LL EAT US ALIVE!!
STING STING

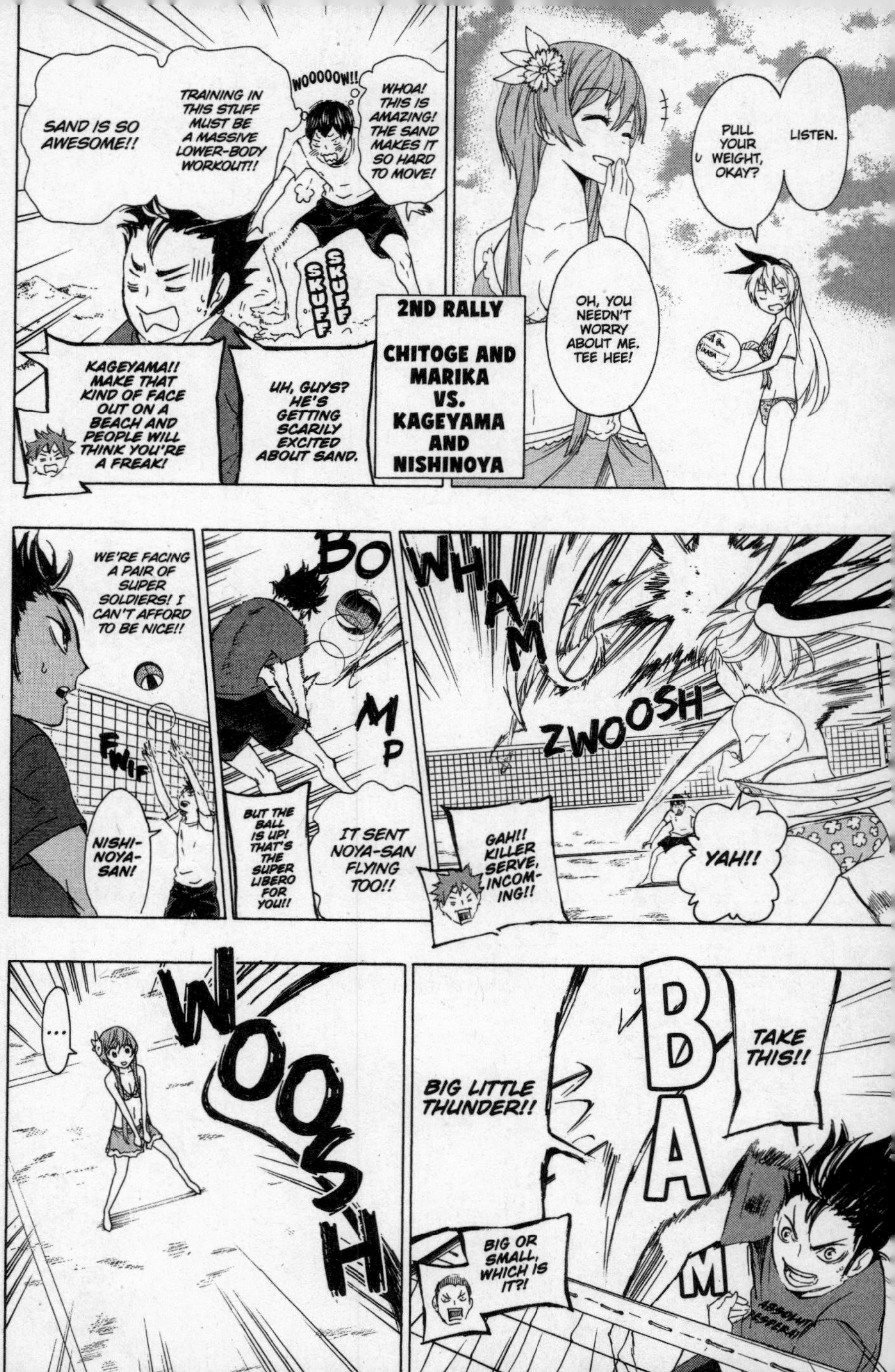

LISTEN.
PULL YOUR WEIGHT, OKAY?
OH, YOU NEEDN'T WORRY ABOUT ME. TEE HEE!
2ND RALLY
CHITOGE AND MARIKA VS. KAGEYAMA AND NISHINOYA
WHOA! THIS IS AMAZING! THE SAND MAKES IT SO HARD TO MOVE!
WOOOOOW!!
TRAINING IN THIS STUFF MUST BE A MASSIVE LOWER-BODY WORKOUT!!
SAND IS SO AWESOME!!
SKUFF SKUFF
UH, GUYS? HE'S GETTING SCARILY EXCITED ABOUT SAND.
KAGEYAMA!! MAKE THAT KIND OF FACE OUT ON A BEACH AND PEOPLE WILL THINK YOU'RE A FREAK!
YAH!!
WHAM
ZWOOSH
GAH!! KILLER SERVE, INCOMING!!
BOMP
IT SENT NOYA-SAN FLYING TOO!!
BUT THE BALL IS UP! THAT'S THE SUPER LIBERO FOR YOU!!
WE'RE FACING A PAIR OF SUPER SOLDIERS! I CAN'T AFFORD TO BE NICE!!
NISHI-NOYA-SAN!
TAKE THIS!!
BAM
BIG LITTLE THUNDER!!
BIG OR SMALL, WHICH IS IT?!
WOOOSH
...

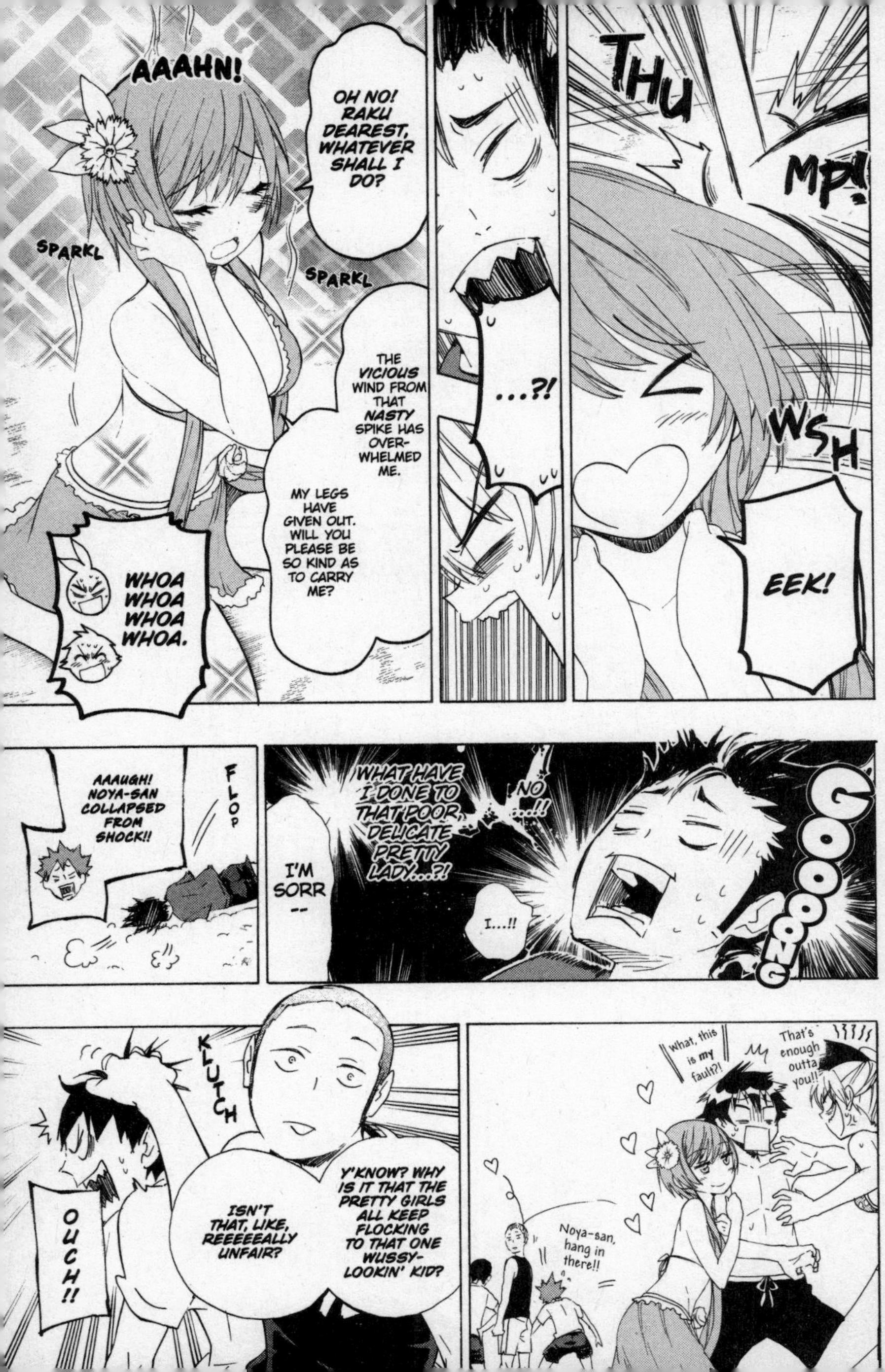
THUMP!
WSH
EEK!
...?!
AAAHN!
OH NO! RAKU DEAREST, WHATEVER SHALL I DO?
SPARKL
SPARKL
THE VICIOUS WIND FROM THAT NASTY SPIKE HAS OVERWHELMED ME.
MY LEGS HAVE GIVEN OUT. WILL YOU PLEASE BE SO KIND AS TO CARRY ME?
WHOA WHOA WHOA WHOA.
GOOOONG
WHAT HAVE I DONE TO THAT POOR, DELICATE PRETTY LADY...?!
NO...!!
I...!!
I'M SORR--
FLOP
AAAUGH! NOYA-SAN COLLAPSED FROM SHOCK!!
That's enough outta you!!
what, this is my fault?!
Noya-san, hang in there!!
KLUTCH
Y'KNOW? WHY IS IT THAT THE PRETTY GIRLS ALL KEEP FLOCKING TO THAT ONE WUSSY-LOOKIN' KID?
ISN'T THAT, LIKE, REEEEEALLY UNFAIR?
OUCH!!

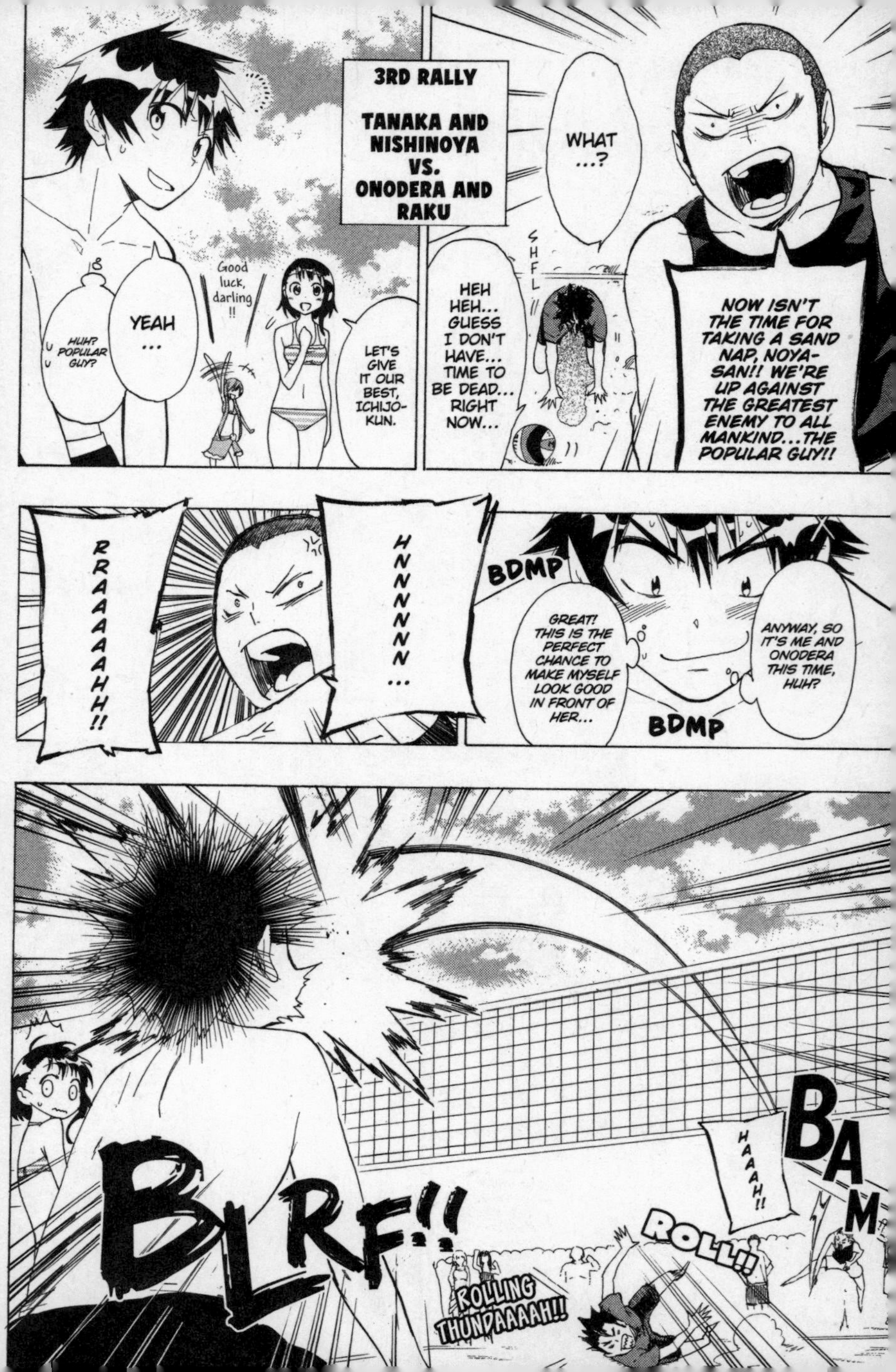
3RD RALLY
TANAKA AND NISHINOYA VS. ONODERA AND RAKU
WHAT ...?
NOW ISN'T THE TIME FOR TAKING A SAND NAP, NOYA-SAN!! WE'RE UP AGAINST THE GREATEST ENEMY TO ALL MANKIND...THE POPULAR GUY!!
SHFL
HEH HEH... GUESS I DON'T HAVE... TIME TO BE DEAD... RIGHT NOW...
LET'S GIVE IT OUR BEST, ICHIJO-KUN.
Good luck, darling!!
YEAH...
HUH? POPULAR GUY?
ANYWAY, SO IT'S ME AND ONODERA THIS TIME, HUH?
BDMP
GREAT! THIS IS THE PERFECT CHANCE TO MAKE MYSELF LOOK GOOD IN FRONT OF HER...
BDMP
HNNNNNN...
RRAAAAAAHH!!
BAM!
HAAAH!!
ROLL!!
ROLLING THUNDAAAAH!!
BLRF!!

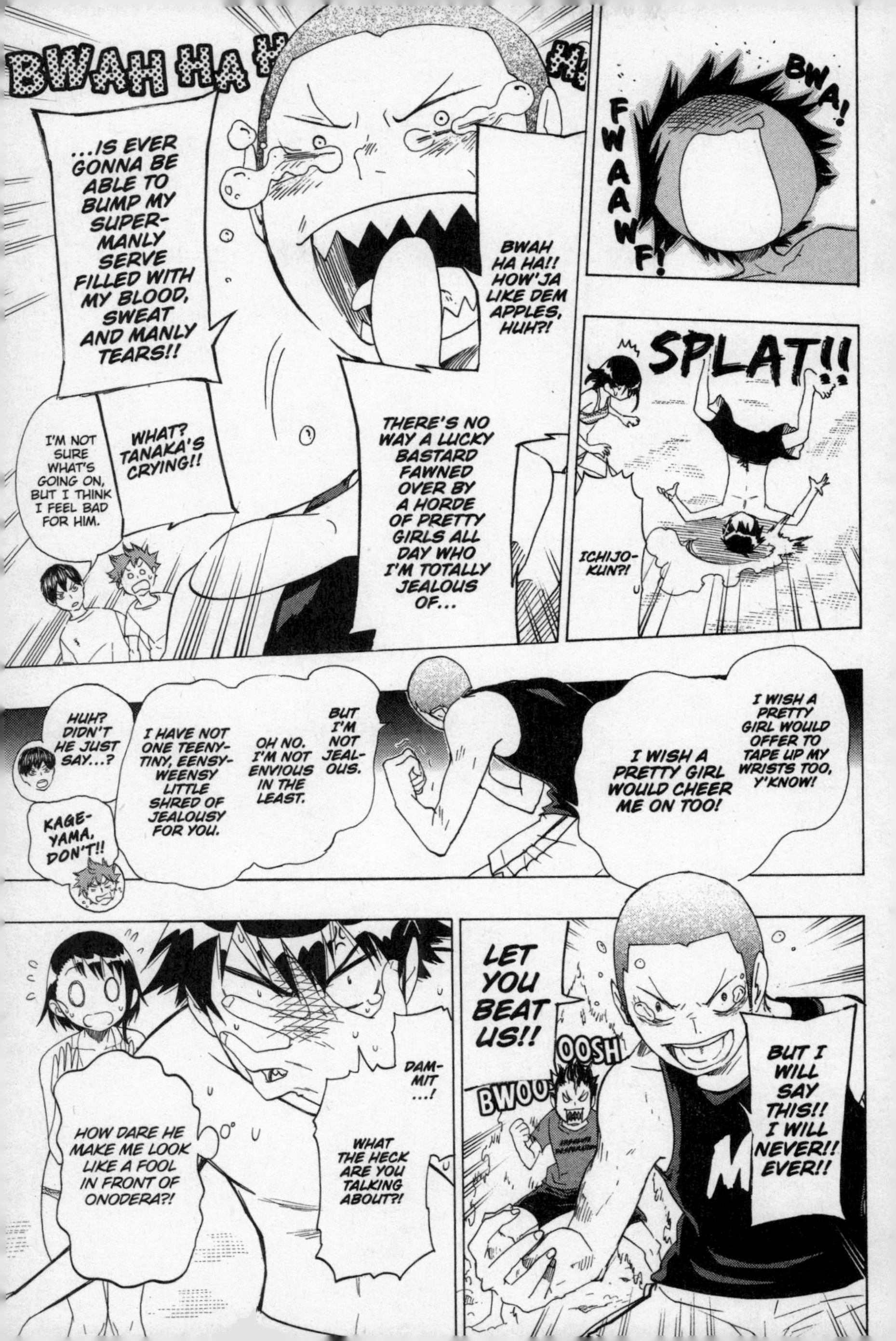
BWA!
FWAAAWF!
SPLAT!!
ICHIJO-KUN?!
BWAH HA
BWAH HA HA!! HOW'JA LIKE DEM APPLES, HUH?!
THERE'S NO WAY A LUCKY BASTARD FAWNED OVER BY A HORDE OF PRETTY GIRLS ALL DAY WHO I'M TOTALLY JEALOUS OF...
...IS EVER GONNA BE ABLE TO BUMP MY SUPER-MANLY SERVE FILLED WITH MY BLOOD, SWEAT AND MANLY TEARS!!
WHAT? TANAKA'S CRYING!!
I'M NOT SURE WHAT'S GOING ON, BUT I THINK I FEEL BAD FOR HIM.
I WISH A PRETTY GIRL WOULD OFFER TO TAPE UP MY WRISTS TOO, Y'KNOW!
I WISH A PRETTY GIRL WOULD CHEER ME ON TOO!
BUT I'M NOT JEAL-OUS.
OH NO. I'M NOT ENVIOUS IN THE LEAST.
I HAVE NOT ONE TEENY-TINY, EENSY-WEENSY LITTLE SHRED OF JEALOUSY FOR YOU.
HUH? DIDN'T HE JUST SAY...?
KAGE-YAMA, DON'T!!
BUT I WILL SAY THIS!! I WILL NEVER!! EVER!!
LET YOU BEAT US!!
BWOO-OOSH
DAM-MIT ...!
WHAT THE HECK ARE YOU TALKING ABOUT?!
HOW DARE HE MAKE ME LOOK LIKE A FOOL IN FRONT OF ONODERA?!

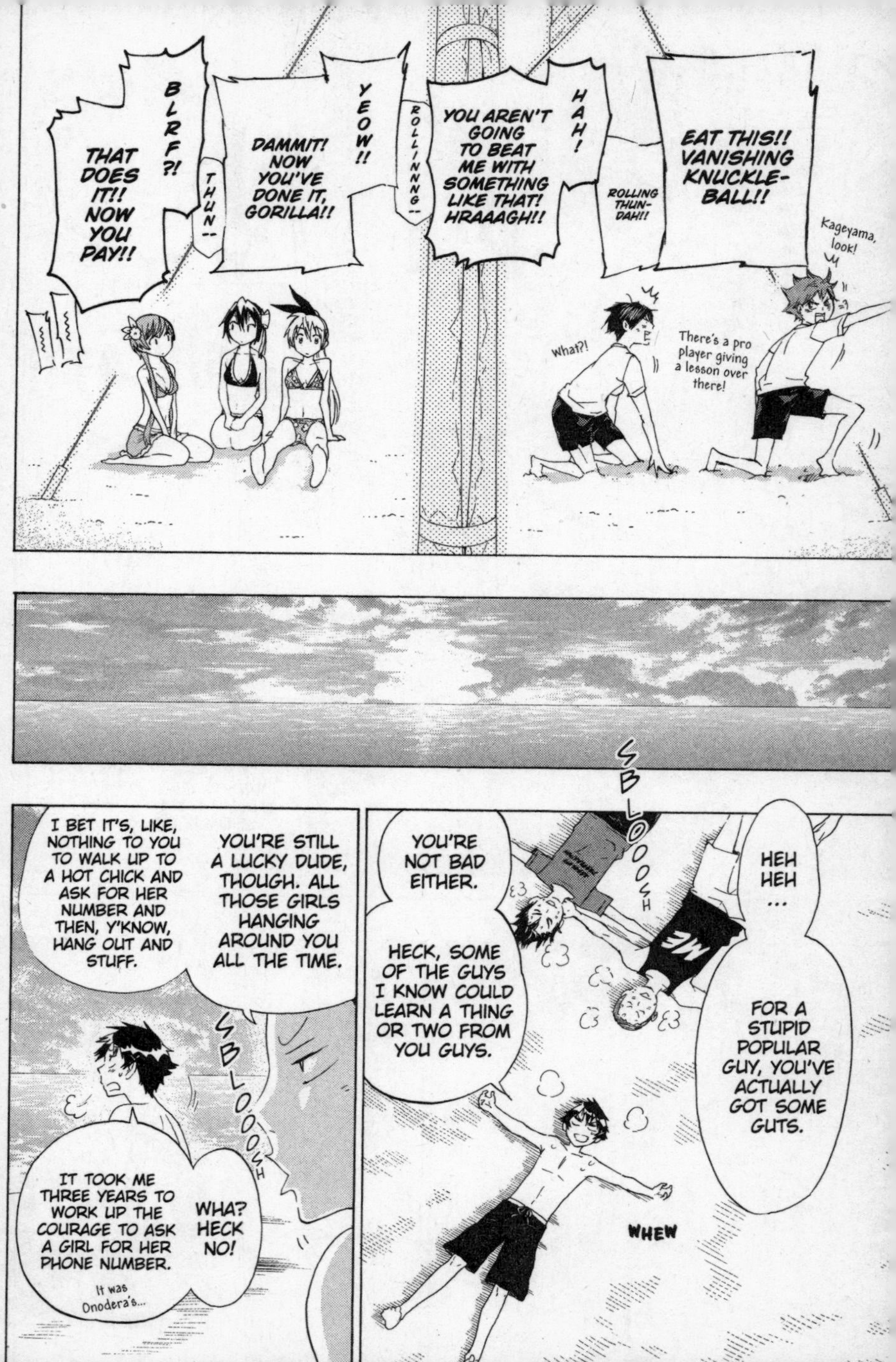
EAT THIS!! VANISHING KNUCKLE-BALL!!
ROLLING THUN-DAH!!
Kageyama, look!
HAH!
YOU AREN'T GOING TO BEAT ME WITH SOMETHING LIKE THAT! HRAAAGH!!
ROLLINNNG--
YEOW!!
DAMMIT! NOW YOU'VE DONE IT, GORILLA!!
THUN--
BLRF?!
THAT DOES IT!! NOW YOU PAY!!
There's a pro player giving a lesson over there!
What?!
SBLOOOOSH
HEH HEH...
FOR A STUPID POPULAR GUY, YOU'VE ACTUALLY GOT SOME GUTS.
YOU'RE NOT BAD EITHER.
HECK, SOME OF THE GUYS I KNOW COULD LEARN A THING OR TWO FROM YOU GUYS.
WHEW
YOU'RE STILL A LUCKY DUDE, THOUGH. ALL THOSE GIRLS HANGING AROUND YOU ALL THE TIME.
I BET IT'S, LIKE, NOTHING TO YOU TO WALK UP TO A HOT CHICK AND ASK FOR HER NUMBER AND THEN, Y'KNOW, HANG OUT AND STUFF.
SBLOOOOSH
WHA? HECK NO!
IT TOOK ME THREE YEARS TO WORK UP THE COURAGE TO ASK A GIRL FOR HER PHONE NUMBER.
It was Onodera's...

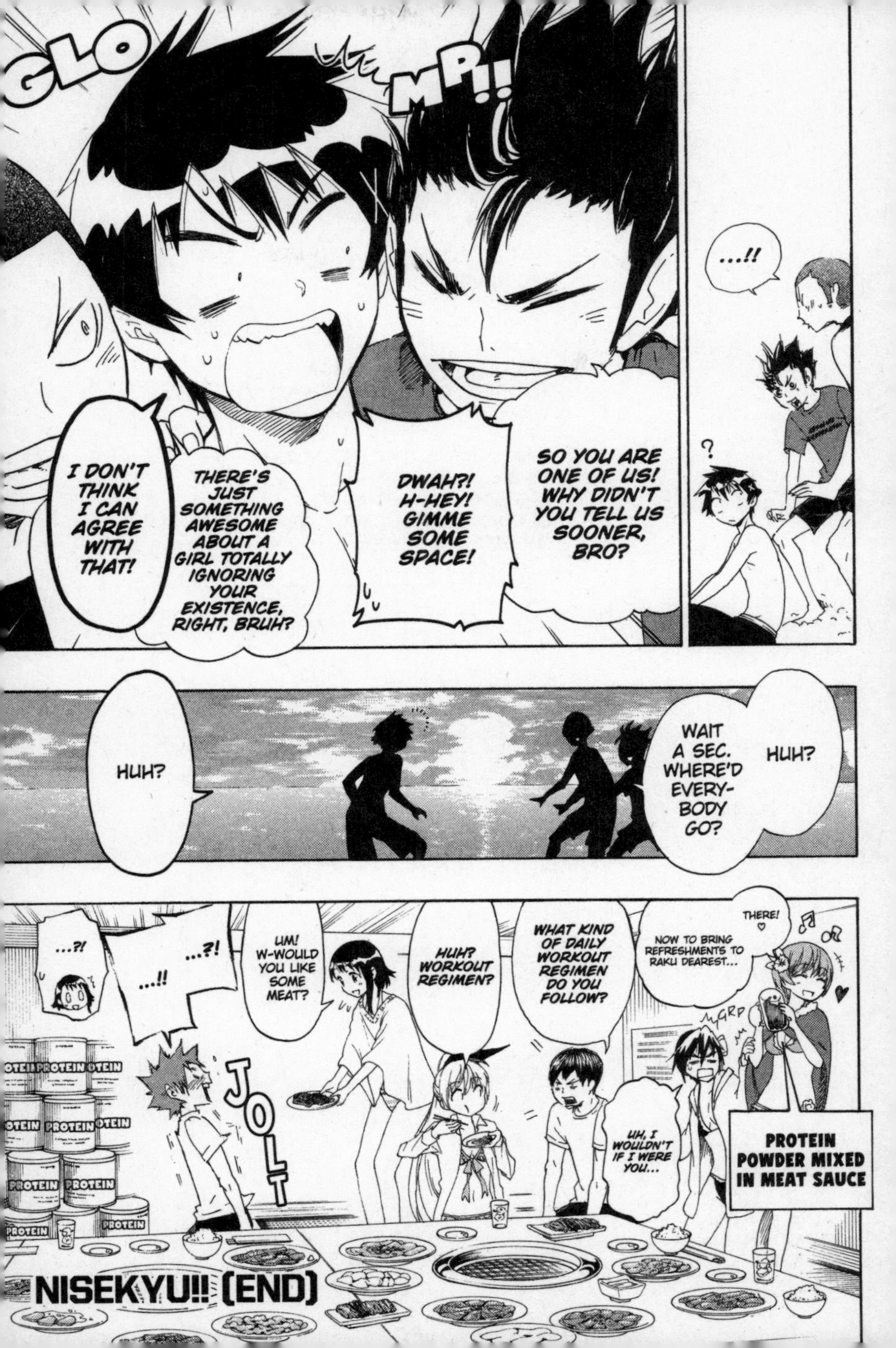
...!!
?
GLO
MP!!
SO YOU ARE ONE OF US! WHY DIDN'T YOU TELL US SOONER, BRO?
DWAH?! H-HEY! GIMME SOME SPACE!
THERE'S JUST SOMETHING AWESOME ABOUT A GIRL TOTALLY IGNORING YOUR EXISTENCE, RIGHT, BRUH?
I DON'T THINK I CAN AGREE WITH THAT!
HUH?
WAIT A SEC. WHERE'D EVERY-BODY GO?
HUH?
THERE!
NOW TO BRING REFRESHMENTS TO RAKU DEAREST...
GRP
PROTEIN POWDER MIXED IN MEAT SAUCE
WHAT KIND OF DAILY WORKOUT REGIMEN DO YOU FOLLOW?
UH, I WOULDN'T IF I WERE YOU...
HUH? WORKOUT REGIMEN?
UM! W-WOULD YOU LIKE SOME MEAT?
...?!
...!!
JOLT
...?!
PROTEIN
NISEKYU!! (END)

NEXT IS THE SHORT MANGA I GOT
TO DRAW FOR *SAIKYO JUMP* FOR
V-BALL CARDS.

V-BALL CARDS IS A CARD GAME
THAT COMES SURPRISINGLY
CLOSE TO APPROXIMATING A
REAL VOLLEYBALL GAME. I REALLY
SUGGEST YOU TRY IT!

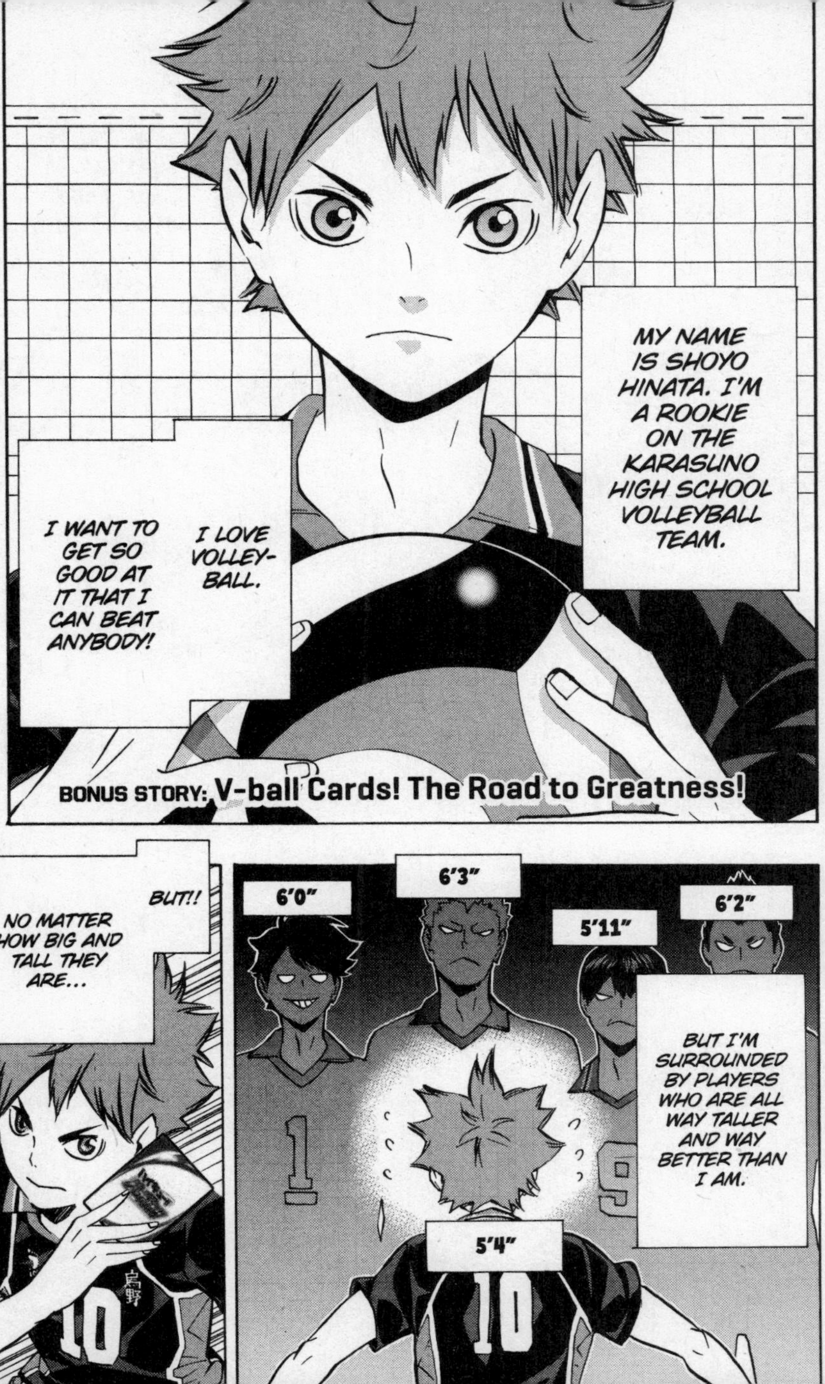
MY NAME IS SHOYO HINATA. I'M A ROOKIE ON THE KARASUNO HIGH SCHOOL VOLLEYBALL TEAM.
I LOVE VOLLEY-BALL.
I WANT TO GET SO GOOD AT IT THAT I CAN BEAT ANYBODY!
BONUS STORY: V-ball Cards! The Road to Greatness!
6'2"
6'3"
5'11"
6'0"
BUT I'M SURROUNDED BY PLAYERS WHO ARE ALL WAY TALLER AND WAY BETTER THAN I AM.
5'4"
BUT!!
NO MATTER HOW BIG AND TALL THEY ARE...

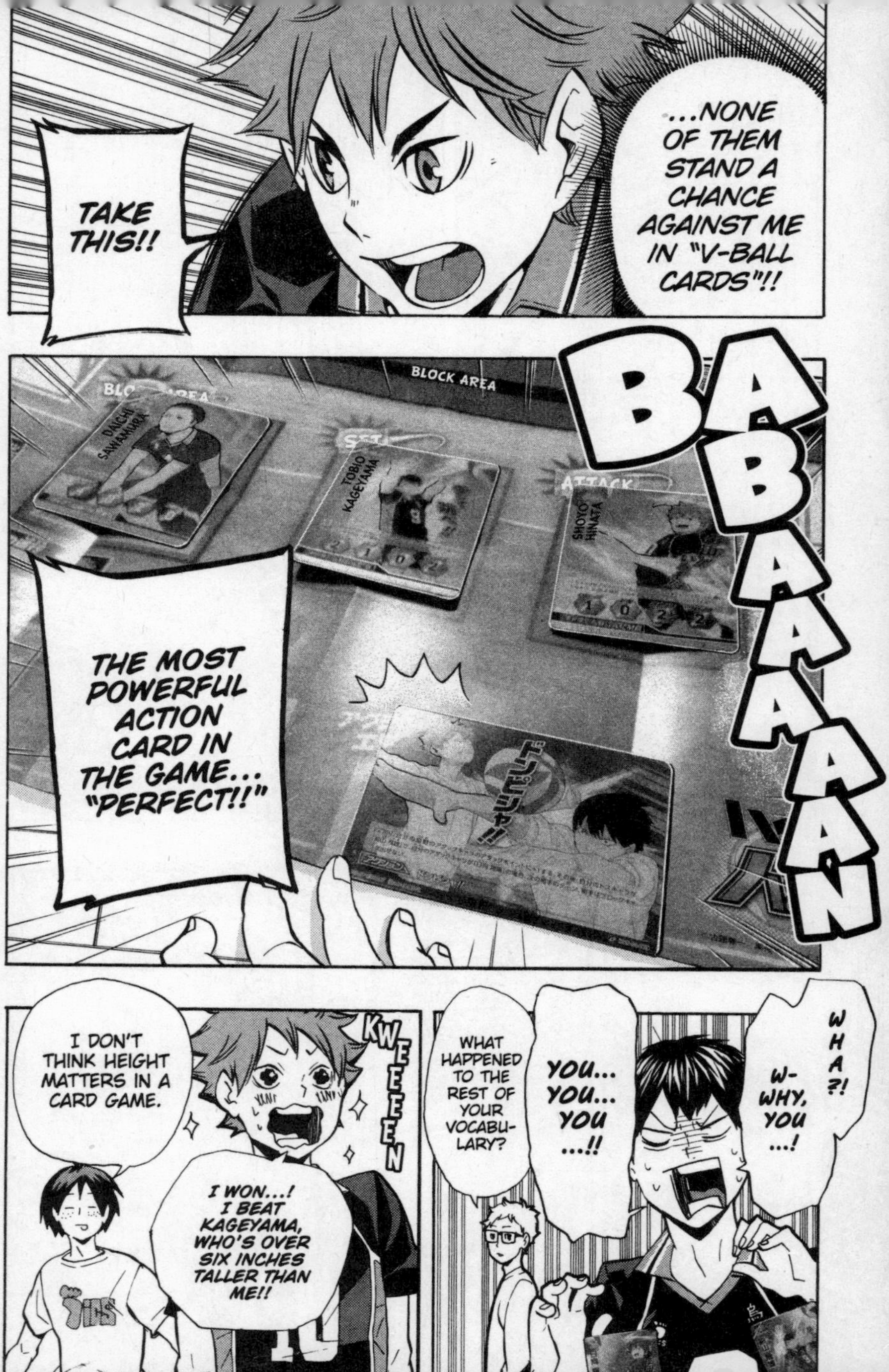
...NONE OF THEM STAND A CHANCE AGAINST ME IN "V-BALL CARDS"!!
TAKE THIS!!
BABAAAAAN
BLOCK AREA
DAICHI SAWAMURA
TOBIO KAGEYAMA
SHOYO HINATA
THE MOST POWERFUL ACTION CARD IN THE GAME... "PERFECT!!"
WHA?!
W-WHY, YOU...!
YOU... YOU... YOU...!!
WHAT HAPPENED TO THE REST OF YOUR VOCABU-LARY?
KWEEEEN
I WON...! I BEAT KAGEYAMA, WHO'S OVER SIX INCHES TALLER THAN ME!!
I DON'T THINK HEIGHT MATTERS IN A CARD GAME.

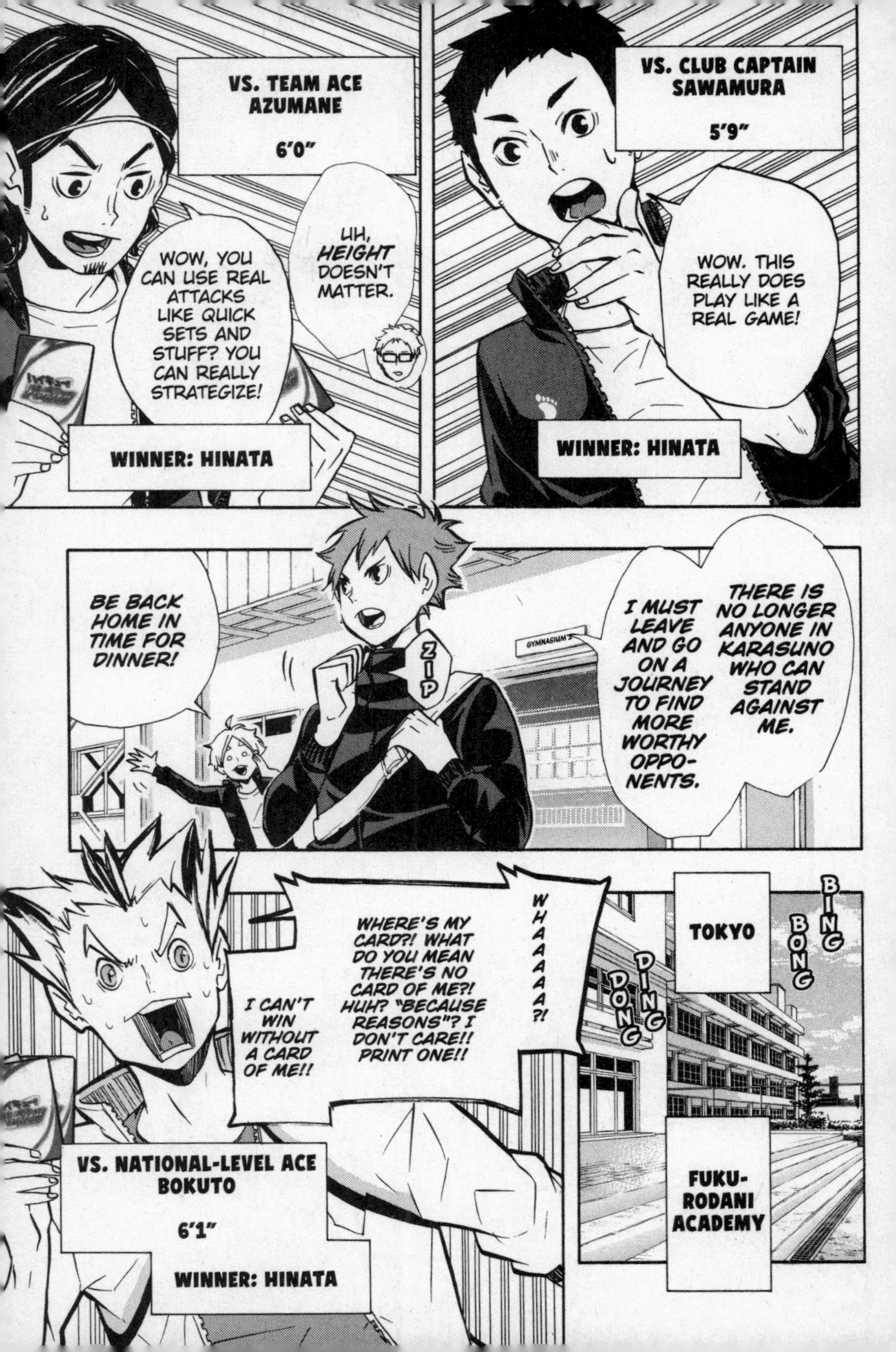
VS. CLUB CAPTAIN SAWAMURA
5'9"
WOW. THIS REALLY DOES PLAY LIKE A REAL GAME!
WINNER: HINATA
VS. TEAM ACE AZUMANE
6'0"
UH, HEIGHT DOESN'T MATTER.
WOW, YOU CAN USE REAL ATTACKS LIKE QUICK SETS AND STUFF? YOU CAN REALLY STRATEGIZE!
WINNER: HINATA
THERE IS NO LONGER ANYONE IN KARASUNO WHO CAN STAND AGAINST ME.
I MUST LEAVE AND GO ON A JOURNEY TO FIND MORE WORTHY OPPO-NENTS.
ZIP
GYMNASIUM 2
BE BACK HOME IN TIME FOR DINNER!
BING
BONG
TOKYO
DING
DONG
FUKU-RODANI ACADEMY
WHAAAAAA?!
WHERE'S MY CARD?! WHAT DO YOU MEAN THERE'S NO CARD OF ME?! HUH? "BECAUSE REASONS"? I DON'T CARE!! PRINT ONE!!
I CAN'T WIN WITHOUT A CARD OF ME!!
VS. NATIONAL-LEVEL ACE BOKUTO
6'1"
WINNER: HINATA

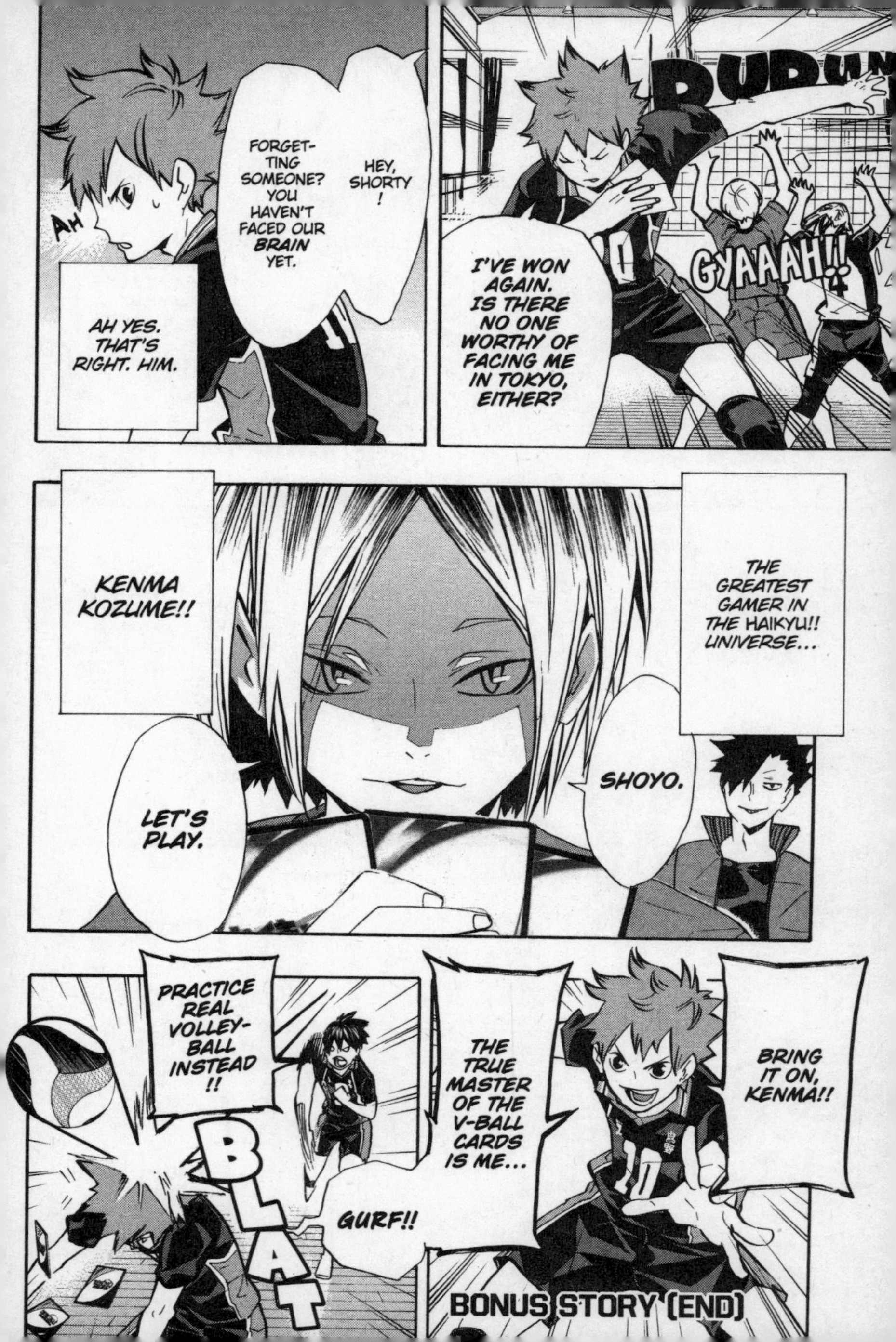

DUDUN
GYAAAH!!
I'VE WON AGAIN. IS THERE NO ONE WORTHY OF FACING ME IN TOKYO, EITHER?
HEY, SHORTY!
FORGETTING SOMEONE? YOU HAVEN'T FACED OUR BRAIN YET.
AH
AH YES. THAT'S RIGHT. HIM.
THE GREATEST GAMER IN THE HAIKYU!! UNIVERSE...
SHOYO.
KENMA KOZUME!!
LET'S PLAY.
BRING IT ON, KENMA!!
THE TRUE MASTER OF THE V-BALL CARDS IS ME...
BONUS STORY (END)
PRACTICE REAL VOLLEY-BALL INSTEAD!!
GURF!!
BLAT

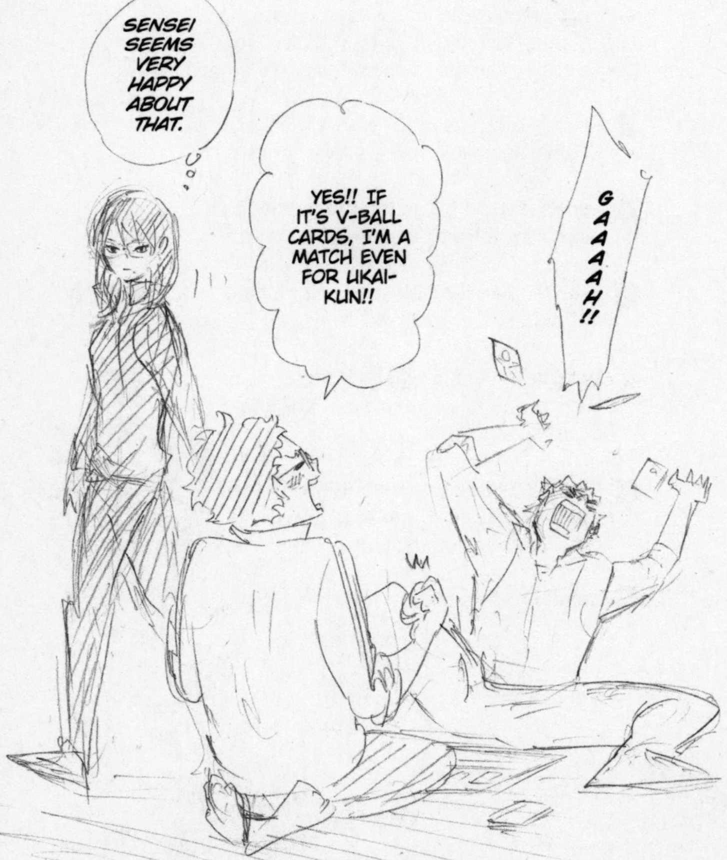
GAAAAAH!!
YES!! IF IT'S V-BALL CARDS, I'M A MATCH EVEN FOR UKAI-KUN!!
SENSEI SEEMS VERY HAPPY ABOUT THAT.

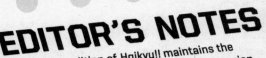

EDITOR'S NOTES

The English edition of Haikyu!! maintains the honorifics used in the original Japanese version. For those of you who are new to these terms, here's a brief explanation to help with your reading experience!

When saying someone's name in Japanese, a suffix is often attached to indicate how familiar the speaker is with the person. Some are more polite and respectful, while others are endearing.

1 **-kun** is often used for young men or boys, usually someone you are familiar with.

2 **-chan** is used for young children and can be used as a term of endearment.

3 **-san** is used for someone you respect or are not close to, or to be polite.

4 **Senpai** is used for someone who is older than you or in a higher position or grade in school.

5 **Kohai** is used for someone who is younger than you or in a lower position or grade in school.

6 **Sensei** means teacher.

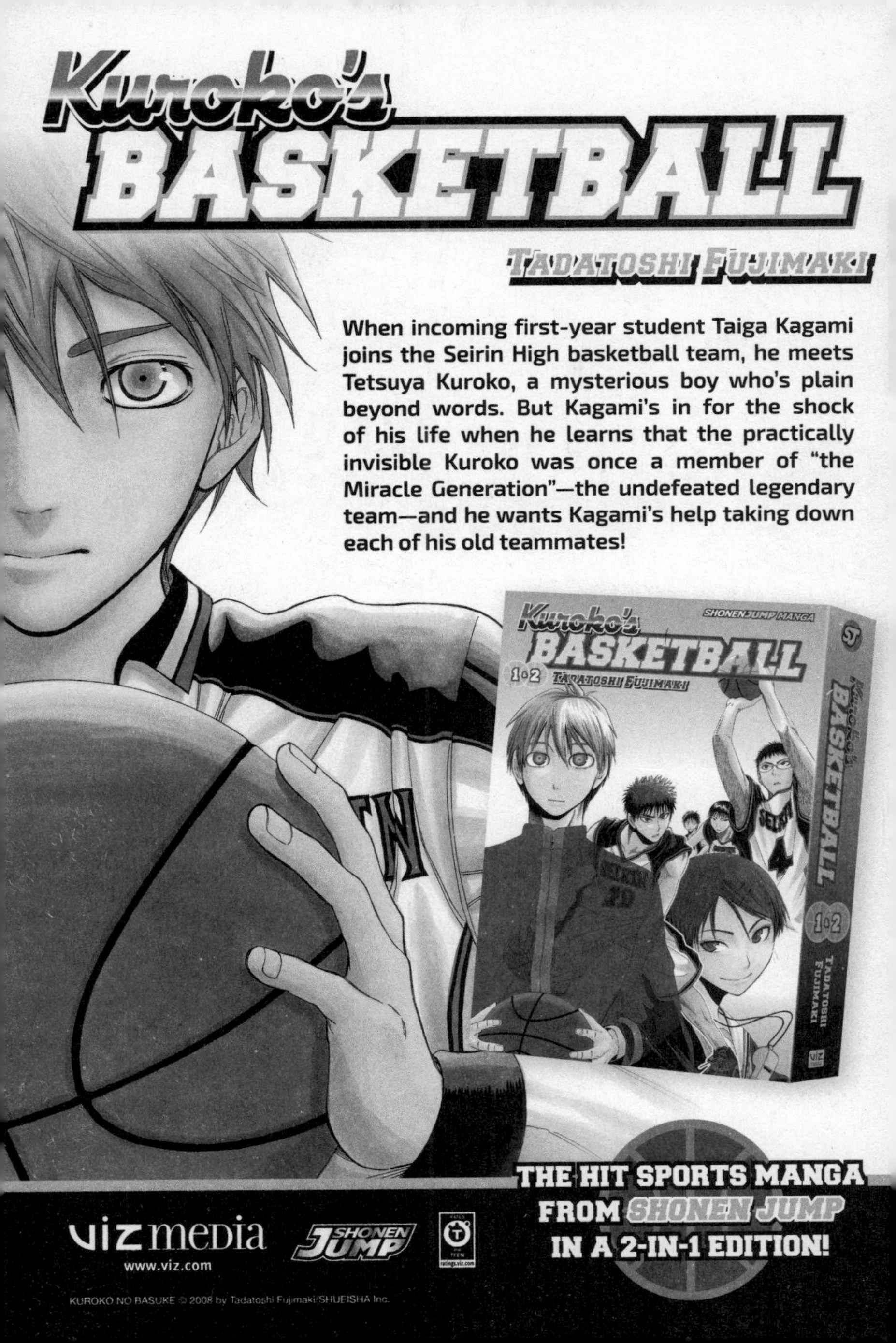
Kuroko's
BASKETBALL
TADATOSHI FUJIMAKI
When incoming first-year student Taiga Kagami joins the Seirin High basketball team, he meets Tetsuya Kuroko, a mysterious boy who's plain beyond words. But Kagami's in for the shock of his life when he learns that the practically invisible Kuroko was once a member of "the Miracle Generation"—the undefeated legendary team—and he wants Kagami's help taking down each of his old teammates!
SHONEN JUMP MANGA
Kuroko's
BASKETBALL
1•2
TADATOSHI FUJIMAKI
THE HIT SPORTS MANGA
FROM SHONEN JUMP
IN A 2-IN-1 EDITION!
viz media
www.viz.com
SHONEN JUMP
T
TEEN
ratings.viz.com
KUROKO NO BASUKE © 2008 by Tadatoshi Fujimaki/SHUEISHA Inc.

G'morning!

You're Reading the WRONG WAY!

HAIKYU!! reads from right to left, starting in the upper-right corner. Japanese is read from right to left, meaning that action, sound effects and word-balloon order are completely reversed from English order.

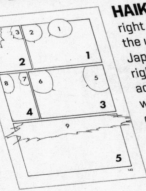